A Dictionary of Literary Symbols

This is the first dictionary of symbols to be based on literature, rather than "universal" psychological archetypes or myths. It explains and illustrates the literary symbols that we all frequently encounter (such as swan, rose, moon, gold), and gives hundreds of cross-references and quotations. The dictionary concentrates on English literature, but its entries range widely from the Bible and classical authors to the twentieth century, taking in American and European literatures. For this new edition, Michael Ferber has included over twenty completely new entries (including bear, holly, sunflower, and tower), and has added to many of the existing entries. Enlarged and enriched from the first edition, its informed style and rich references make this book an essential tool not only for literary and classical scholars, but for all students of literature.

MICHAEL FERBER is Professor of English and Humanities at the University of New Hampshire. His books include *The Poetry of William Blake* (1991), *The Poetry of Shelley* (1993), and *A Companion to European Romanticism* (2005).

A Dictionary of Literary Symbols

Second edition

Michael Ferber

CAMBRIDGE
UNIVERSITY PRESS

CAMBRIDGE UNIVERSITY PRESS
Cambridge, New York, Melbourne, Madrid, Cape Town, Singapore, São Paulo

Cambridge University Press
The Edinburgh Building, Cambridge CB2 8RU, UK

Published in the United States of America by Cambridge University Press, New York

www.cambridge.org
Information on this title: www.cambridge.org/9780521690546

First published 1999
Second edition 2007

Printed in the United Kingdom at the University Press, Cambridge

A catalogue record for this publication is available from the British Library

ISBN 978-0-521-87042-9 hardback
ISBN 978-0-521-69054-6 paperback

For Lucy

Contents

Acknowledgments

I must first thank my colleague Douglas Lanier for helping me think through this dictionary from the outset, for encouragement during early frustrations, and for a great deal of detailed advice. E. J. Kenney of Peterhouse, Cambridge, saved me from a number of mistakes in Latin and offered countless suggestions about not only classical but English literature; his notes would make a useful and delightful little book by themselves. David Norton made many helpful suggestions regarding biblical passages. Two graduate students at the University of New Hampshire gave valuable assistance, Heather Wood at an early phase by collecting data from books not close at hand and William Stroup by going over by every entry with a keen eye to readability and cuts. My wife Susan Arnold also cheerfully read every entry and offered many helpful ideas.

I am grateful to Maria Pantelia for providing me with the *Thesaurus Linguae Graecae* on CD-ROM and advice on how to use it. Cynthia Pawlek of Baker Library, Dartmouth, initiated me into the English Poetry Data-Base, also on disk, Robin Lent, Deborah Watson, and Peter Crosby of Dimond Library at UNH patiently handled my many requests and, during the reconstruction of the library, even set up a little room just large enough for the Leob classical series and me. I also made good use of the library of Gonville and Caius College, Cambridge, and I thank Gordon Hunt for his good offices there.

The Humanities Center of UNH gave me a grant for a semester's leave and an office in which to store unwieldy concordances and work in peace; its director Burt Feintuch and administrator Joanne Sacco could not have been more hospitable.

For contributing ideas, quotations, references, and encouragement I also thank Ann and Warner Berthoff, Barbara Cooper, Michael DePorte, Patricia Emison, John Ernest, Elizabeth Hageman, Peter Holland, Edward Larkin, Ronald LeBlanc, Laurence Marschall, Susan Schibanoff, and Charles Simic. My editor at Cambridge University Press, Josie Dixon, not only solicited Professors Kenney and Norton to go over my entries but made many helpful suggestions herself while shepherding the book through its complex editing process. For the errors and weaknesses that remain despite all this expert help I am of course responsible.

Abbreviations

Bible

AV	Authorized Version (King James Version) of the Bible (1611). All quotations are from this version unless otherwise stated.
NT	New Testament. Quotations from the NT that are paralleled in more than one Gospel are cited from the first in which they appear (usually Matthew).
OT	Old Testament
NEB	New English Bible (1961)

Pindar

Olymp.	*Olympian*
Pyth.	*Pythian*
Isth.	*Isthmian*
Nem.	*Nemean*

Horace

Quotations from Horace are from the "Odes" or *Carmina* unless otherwise stated.

Ovid

Met.	*Metamorphoses*

Apuleius

Met.	*Metamorphoses* (or *The Golden Ass*)

Chaucer

CT	*Canterbury Tales* (Gen. Pro. = General Prologue, Pro. = Prologue)
PF	*Parliament of Fowls*
TC	*Troilus and Criseyde*

Spenser

FQ	*Faerie Queene* (Pro. = Prologue)
SC	*Shepheardes Calendar*

Shakespeare

1H4, 2H4	*King Henry the Fourth, Part One, Part Two*
1H6, 2H6, 3H6	*King Henry the Sixth, Part One, Part Two, Part Three*
2GV	*Two Gentlemen of Verona*
12N	*Twelfth Night*
AC	*Antony and Cleopatra*
AWEW	*All's Well that Ends Well*

AYLI	*As You Like it*
CE	*The Comedy of Errors*
Cor	*Coriolanus*
Cym	*Cymbeline*
H5	*King Henry the Fifth*
H8	*King Henry the Eighth*
JC	*Julius Caesar*
KJ	*King John*
Lear	*King Lear*
LLL	*Love's Labour's Lost*
MAAN	*Much Ado about Nothing*
MM	*Measure for Measure*
MND	*A Midsummer Night's Dream*
MV	*The Merchant of Venice*
MWW	*The merry Wives of Windsor*
Per	*Pericles*
R2	*King Richard the Second*
R3	*King Richard the Third*
RJ	*Romeo and Juliot*
TC	*Troilus and Cressida*
Timon	*Timon of Athens*
Titus	*Titus Andronicus*
TS	*The Taming of the Shrew* (Ind. = Induction)
WT	*The Winter's Tale*

Line numbers for Shakespeare are keyed to the Riverside edition; they will not vary by much from any modern edition.

Milton

PL	*Paradise Lost*

Shelley

PU	*Prometheus Unbound*

Introduction

The idea for this dictionary came to me while I was reading a student essay on Byron's "Stanzas Written on the Road between Florence and Pisa," which sets the true glory of youthful love against the false glory of an old man's literary renown. After a promising start the student came to a halt before these lines: "the myrtle and ivy of sweet two-and-twenty | Are worth all your laurels, though ever so plenty." His copy lacked footnotes, and he lacked experience of poetry before the Romantics. With disarming candor he confessed that he had no idea what these three plants were doing in the poem, and then desperately suggested that Byron might have seen them on the road somewhere between Florence and Pisa and been inspired to put them in his poem the way you might put plants in your office. I wrote in the margin that these were symbolic plants and he had to look them up. But where, exactly, do you send a student to find out the symbolic meaning of myrtle? The *Oxford English Dictionary* was all I could come up with, but I felt certain there must be a handier source, designed for readers of literature, with a good set of quotations from ancient times to modern. But there is no such book.

A dozen times since then I have asked colleagues and librarians if they knew of one. They were all sure they did, or thought "there must be one," but they could never find it. Several of them came up with Cirlot's *Dictionary of Symbols*, but that work, whatever its uses, is the last thing I would recommend to a student. It has no entry at all for myrtle. Under ivy it mentions the Phrygian god Attis and its eunuch-priests and then says, "It is a feminine symbol denoting a force in need of protection." One can hardly imagine the interpretations of Byron that would arise from those claims. Under laurel it names Apollo and mentions poets, but has nothing about fame, and it goes on about "inner victories over the negative and dissipative influence of the base forces."

Only slightly better are two recent ones: Hans Biedermann's *Dictionary of Symbolism: Cultural Icons and the Meanings Behind Them*, translated from the German, and Jean Chevalier and Alain Gheerbrant's *Penguin Dictionary of Symbols*, translated from the French. Both range widely but unsystematically over the cultures of the world, packing Mayan and Chinese meanings next to those from medieval alchemy. The latter book, much the larger, lacks an entry for myrtle; under ivy it discusses Dionysus, which is on the right track, but it says nothing about its uses in Roman poetry that lie behind Byron. Neither book quotes widely from poetry or prose fiction.

If no adequate dictionary exists, but everyone thinks it does (because it must), that seemed a good reason to write one. It was also a reason not to write one, for if even the Germans have not produced one, as it seemed, it might be beyond mortal powers. After all, anything can be a symbol, and a comprehensive dictionary might require thousands of entries. After some hesitation, however, I decided the thing can be done, and the present book is the result.

Its title is somewhat misleading. It would be more correct, if ungainly, to call it *A Selective Dictionary of Traditional Western Literary Symbols and Conventions, Mainly in Poetry*, and I shall follow the terms in that hypothetical title as I describe the book's features.

It was only by drastically limiting the range of possible symbols, of course, that I could proceed with it. Yet it is more comprehensive than one might think. This dictionary covers only traditional symbols, those that have been used over many years by many authors. Most entries begin with the Bible or the classics and trace examples through to fairly recent writers, with an emphasis on British literature, and especially on Chaucer, Spenser, Shakespeare, Milton, and the Romantics; they also typically include a few examples from Italian, French, Spanish, German, or Russian literature (especially from Dante and Goethe). The tradition is more stable than I had first guessed, at least until the twentieth century; nightingales and cypresses carry with them their ancient associations, and even where they are invoked in new ways those connotations may still be in play. There is no need, moreover, to take up the significance of the lathe in Flaubert's *Madame Bovary*, the pistols in Ibsen's *Hedda Gabler*, the mysterious sound in Act 2 of Chekhov's *Cherry Orchard*, the madeleine in Proust, or the leaden circles of sound from Big Ben that permeate Woolf's *Mrs Dalloway*. These must be worked out by the reader in each case, and no dictionary on a reasonable scale could help much. What readers need to know, in any case, are the traditional symbols, the routine furniture of literature over thousands of years, which often appear without explanation, and which gradually gain in connotation as the tradition lengthens and alludes to itself. Whether it informs the meaning of an individual work is often a subtle question – does it matter that the bird that seeks "your cradle narrow / Near my Bosom" in Blake's "The Blossom" is a sparrow, with its associations of lust? Or that the tree that Akhmatova especially liked but is now a stump was a willow, with its suggestion of maidenhood or fruitlessness? ("The Willow") – but the question cannot even be entertained without a knowledge of the tradition. I do not know how many of these traditional symbols there are, but the number cannot be very large, and I am hoping that a book with 175 of the most important ones, along with cross-references, will be complete enough to constitute a useful reference work.

I have tried to be copious with quotations and citations in each entry, risking redundancy, in order to give a sense of the history of a symbol and the range of its contexts. Simply to give definitions of symbols would have made for a short book but a misleading one, for often only a listing of examples can convey what a symbol has meant. I have aimed, too, to interest the scholar or experienced reader as well as to help the beginning student. There are doubtless important omissions within many of the entries – indeed until the moment I yielded the manuscript to the typesetter I was continually turning up material that I wondered how I had missed – but I have done my best within strict word limits to include interesting variations as well as the most typical senses.

That all the references are to western literature, counting the Bible as one of its prime sources, would not seem to require a defense, but more than one colleague has questioned my "western-centric bias" and urged that I undertake a truly multi-cultural dictionary of the all the world's literary symbols. It sounded like a wonderful project, but not for me, or for any one mortal. Two days reading through Chinese and Japanese poetry in translation gave me a glimpse into what it might entail. The swallow, I learned, is seen as a harbinger of spring, just as it is in western poetry: the thirteenth-century poet Chiang K'uei ponders the time "When swallows come to ask where spring is." But another common image for spring, plum blossoms, is not common in western poetry. Since plum blossoms often appear amid late-winter snow, they are tokens of hardiness and courage as well as forerunners of spring (somewhat, but not quite, like the almond blossom in the west); one commentator suggests that they represent the promise of the perfect beauty of the cherry blossoms that come later. In England, however, if we may trust Ben Jonson, it is "The early cherry, with the later plum," that mark the usual order ("To Penshurst" 41). The cuckoo, or rather the bird translated as "cuckoo" in English, seems not to be the same species as the European bird, which is known for laying its eggs in other birds' nests. The oriental "cuckoo" is known for its beautiful song and its straight flight. In the call of the cuckoo the Chinese heard *kui k'u*, "go home"; in Japanese, its charming name *hototogisu* may be written in characters that mean "bird of time"; in both cultures the bird suggests homesickness. It is also associated with the moon. All of this is quite the opposite of the harsh song of cuckoldry! And so it goes. There are close similarities to western usage, not surprising since we all live in the same world, and there are sharp differences, not surprising either since fauna and flora, not to mention human culture, vary from place to place. The task of working out the details in a comparison of just two traditions would be daunting. It would be difficult even to decide whether to enter the two "cuckoos" under one name or two. I hope nevertheless that scholars expert in other languages will undertake to produce dictionaries like this one for each tradition, if they do not exist already, so we might look forward to a systematic study of "comparative metaphorics."

This is a dictionary of symbols in literature, not myth, painting, folklore, dreams, alchemy, astrology, the Tarot pack, the Kabbalah, or the Jungian collective unconscious. Myths come into it, of course, insofar as they take literary form, but no proper names have entries. The reader who misses them can easily find several excellent dictionaries of classical mythology. That there are also excellent books about iconography in European painting allows me to omit citations from that tradition, both the Christian symbolism seen in countless paintings of the Annunciation, the Crucifixion, the martyrdom of saints, and the like, and the emblem books of the Renaissance. By "literature" I mean for the most part the "high" literature of the standard western canon. To modern eyes this tradition may seem an elite affair, in contrast not only to proverbs and ballads but to fairy tales, popular plays and songs, seasonal rituals, and other kinds of folklore, from all of which this dictionary might have drawn more than the few examples it has. The limits of space (and time) must be the main plea against having done so, but one should remember that a great deal of Greek literature was "popular" in its day, as were Shakespeare and many other writers, and many bits of folklore live on in them that have died out among the folk. I have also tried to include a few references to less well-known writers. Those with a particular interest in women, African-American, Latin-American, or "post-colonial" writers may find them underrepresented, but this dictionary does not seem the right place to argue for a new canon. It is my sense, too, that at least through the nineteenth century, women, blacks, and other "others" did not use symbols in ways notably different from the dominant tradition. As for alchemy and the other mystical traditions, they have certainly found a place here and there in literature, but except for a few references I have had to leave out the often difficult and lengthy explanations they would require.

This dictionary depends on no particular definition of "symbol." I have chosen to err on the side of generosity rather than exclude something one might want to know, and many instances come closer to metaphor, allusion, or even motif than to symbol strictly defined. I also include some conventions, commonplaces, or "topoi," the standard ways a thing has been represented. So I include dawn, death, dream, nature, and certain other subjects not so much for what they have stood for as for what other things have stood for them.

For several reasons the great majority of examples is taken from poetry. Nearly all the oldest western literature is in verse, and until the modern era the poetic genres were the most prestigious and most frequently published. Poetry tends, too, to be denser in symbolism than novels or stories, though there is plenty of symbolic prose fiction. It is much easier, too, to scan poetry for key words or ideas than to scan prose, as there are concordances for most poets (in book or electronic form) but very few for novelists. I have been able to find fifty occurrences of a symbol in a dozen poets in a few minutes, but for novelists I can mainly rack my memory or that of colleagues. I have nevertheless included quite a few prose examples, helped at times by scholarly studies of one symbol, yet in the end I don't think it would make much difference to the range of entries and meanings within entries if there were no prose examples at all.

Sometimes the entries are rather long. Readers may find more about the nightingale than they strictly need for understanding a passage by Shakespeare or Keats. Most annotated student editions of classic works, either from limits of space or the wish not to seem intimidating, give only minimal information in the notes, and so they fail to convey the richness of the tradition and suggest instead that there is a code or algebra of literature. I also think it is interesting in itself to see many threads of nightingale meanings woven together in a long entry, and it lets one take a bearing on the whole history of western poetry.

This is not to say that whenever a nightingale appears in a poem it must mean all the things it ever meant, or that it must allude to all the previous appearances of nightingales. What Freud said about cigars is sometimes true of literary symbols: sometimes a nightingale is just a nightingale, or little more than a way of saying that night has come. On the other hand, most poets have absorbed the traditional language of poetry and assume their readers or listeners have done so too. The implied reader of most poetry is an expert on nightingales, even if that reader has never heard or seen one. If it is possible for a nightingale to make an "innocent" appearance after 2,800 years in western literature it must be under special literary conditions that somehow both invoke and erase the associations the nightingale has acquired, as perhaps Coleridge does in "The Nightingale" as early as 1798, or Wallace Stevens much more recently in "The Man on the Dump," where the nightingale is included in the great garbage pile of worn-out poetic images. To repeat an earlier point, the ideal is to know the tradition and then decide in each case to what extent it is still in play.

Note on sources

There is one advantage, perhaps, in the incompleteness of this dictionary, and that is that readers, if they enjoy the existing entries but miss a particular symbol, can have the pleasure of researching it themselves. The best place to begin, in fact, is the *Oxford English Dictionary*, which will at least give a few quotations. There are comparable dictionaries in French and Italian; the German one, begun by the Grimm Brothers, is wonderful but its citations are from editions now very old and rare. If you read a little German, you can make use of the great *Real-Encyklopädie der classischen Altertumswissenschaft*, edited by Pauly, Wissowa, and Kroll, in many volumes, which is an astounding work of scholarship, a kind of super-concordance to Greek and Latin literature. Even without Greek and Latin you can get something out of the two large Oxford dictionaries, which are generous with quotations; you will need to learn the Greek alphabet, but then you can track the citations in facing-page translations in the Loeb series published by Harvard University Press. A good university library will have concordances to the major poets; when you have found lines, say, from Shakespeare, go to one of the scholarly editions of the individual plays (Cambridge, Oxford, or Arden) and check the footnotes to the lines with your symbol: they may well give sources going back to the Romans. The great scholarly editions of Greek and Latin classics are usually bursting with references to sources and parallels. Also helpful are dictionaries of proverbs, especially Stevenson's *Home Book of Proverbs, Maxims and Familiar Phrases*, and indexes to titles, first lines, and last lines of poetry. I have listed several more works in the "General" section of the bibliography.

After many quotations from languages other than English I have given the last name of the translator. Except for a few historically important translations (e.g., Chapman, Dryden, Pope), I have used readily available modern ones; classical texts other than Homer and Virgil are generally from the Loeb, Penguin, or Oxford World's Classics versions. The brief unattributed translations are "my own," that is, they are usually so simple and inevitable as to be common property.

An asterisk before a word indicates that it is a hypothetical or unattested form.

Introduction to the second edition

For the second edition I have written twenty new entries, expanded nearly thirty existing entries, and added a dozen works to the bibliography.

I have also corrected a few errors, mostly citations, in the first edition. For pointing them out I am grateful to Yatsuo Uematsu, who translated the first edition into Japanese, and to Laimantas Jonušys, who translated it into Lithuanian. I also thank Laura Smith for some useful tips.

A Dictionary of Literary Symbols

A

Absinthe   *see* **Wormwood**

Adder   *see* **Serpent**

Aeolian harp   The aeolian harp (or lyre) or wind harp was invented by the German Jesuit Athanasius Kircher and described by him in 1650. It is a long, narrow wooden box with a thin belly and with eight to twelve strings stretched over two bridges and tuned in unison; it is to be placed in a window (or a grotto) where the wind will draw out a harmonious sound. (Aeolus is the Greek king in charge of the winds; he first appears in Homer's *Odyssey* 10.) In the next century James Oswald, a Scots composer and cellist, made one, and it soon became well known.

It just as soon became an irresistible poetic symbol, first in English, then in French and German. James Thomson described the harp in *The Castle of Indolence*: "A certain Musick, never known before, | Here sooth'd the pensive melancholy Mind; | Full easily obtain'd. Behoves no more, | But sidelong, to the gently-waving Wind, | To lay the well-tun'd Instrument reclin'd; | From which, with airy flying Fingers light, | Beyond each mortal Touch the most refin'd, | The God of Winds drew Sounds of deep Delight: | Whence, with just Cause, *The Harp of Aeolus* it hight" (1.352–60). Thomson also wrote an "Ode on Aeolus's Harp." It was already so well known by the 1750s that the opening line of Gray's "Progress of Poetry" – "Awake, Aeolian lyre, awake" – was misconstrued; Gray added a note quoting Pindar's "Aeolian song" and "Aeolian strings" to make clear that he was referring to a mode of Greek music, not the wind harp. (To the ancients, however, "Aeolian lyre" might refer to Sappho and Alcaeus, whose lyrics were in the Aeolian dialect of Greek.)

In poetry any harp can become an aeolian harp if suspended in the open air. Alluding to Psalm 137, where the exiled Jews "hanged our harps upon the willows" by the rivers of Babylon, William Cowper ends his long poem "Expostulation" by calling on his muse to "hang this harp upon yon aged beech, | Still murm'ring with the solemn truths I teach" (718–19).

Among the English Romantics the wind harp became a favorite image, capable of many extensions. In "The Eolian Harp," perhaps the most extended poetic treatment of the subject, Coleridge is prompted by the harp's "soft floating witchery of sound" (20) to consider "the one Life within us and abroad, | Which meets all motion and becomes its soul" (26–27), and then speculates: "And what if all of animated nature | Be but organic Harps diversely fram'd, | That tremble into thought, as o'er them sweeps | Plastic and vast, one intellectual breeze, | At once the Soul of each, and God of all?" (44–48). Coleridge may have been influenced by the associationist psychology of David Hartley, according to whom sensation depends on "vibrations" carried by the nerves to the brain, where new but fainter vibrations are created. Diderot, in *D'Alembert's Dream*, has a similar but more explicitly musical model of sensation and memory, as does Herder, in *Kalligone*.

Both Wordsworth and Coleridge used the metaphor of the internal breeze or breath responding to the inspiration of a natural wind. So Wordsworth begins the 1805 *Prelude*, "Oh there is blessing in this gentle breeze," where the breeze serves as a kind of epic muse; a little later he reflects, "For I, methought, while the sweet breath of Heaven / Was blowing on my body, felt within / A corresponding mild creative breeze, / A vital breeze..." (41–44) and then likens himself to an aeolian harp (103–07). In "Dejection," Coleridge compares himself to an "AEolian lute, / Which better far were mute" (7–8).

Shelley has frequent recourse to the image (e.g., *Queen Mab* 1.52–53, *Alastor* 42–45, 667–68) and extends it in interesting ways. It is quietly implicit in *Queen Mab* 8.19–20: "The dulcet music swelled / Concordant with the life-strings of the soul." He develops an idea in Coleridge's "Dejection," where the raving wind is told that a crag or tree or grove would make fitter instruments than the lute, by imagining that the winds come to the pines to hear the harmony of their swinging ("Mont Blanc" 20–24); in his "Ode to the West Wind" he implores the wind to "Make me thy lyre, even as the forest is" (57). In his "Defence of Poetry," Shelley explicitly likens man to an aeolian lyre, but adds "there is a principle within the human being...which acts otherwise than in the lyre, and produces not melody, alone, but harmony, by an internal adjustment of the sounds or motions thus excited to the impressions which excite them."

The aeolian harp enters French poetry with André Chénier's *Elégies* (no. 22): "I am the absolute owner of my memory; / I lend it a voice, powerful magician, / Like an aeolian harp in the evening breezes, / And each of my senses resounds to this voice." It appears as similes in the influential romantic novels *Les Natchez* by Chateaubriand and *Corinne* by Germaine de Staël.

In Germany, Hölderlin in "Die Wanderung" ("The Migration") makes the link Shelley makes: "and the forests / All rustled, every lyre / In unison / At heaven's gentle touch" (trans. Sieburth). Goethe stages a brief "Conversation" between two Aeolian harps, male and female, and Schiller alludes to the harp in "The Dignity of Women." The song of Ariel that opens Goethe's *Faust, Part II* is accompanied by aeolian harps. Half a century later Mörike writes "To an Aeolian Harp," where the wind blows from the green tomb of "the youth I loved so much": "As the wind gusts more briskly, / A lovely cry of the harp / Repeats, to my sweet dismay, / The sudden emotion of my soul." The Russian poet Tyutchev hears a harp at midnight grieving like a fallen angel; for a moment we feel faith and joy, "as if the sky flowed through our veins," but it cannot last, and we sink back into "wearisome dreams" ("The Gleam", trans. Bidney).

In America, Emerson praises the one sure musician whose wisdom will not fail, the Aeolian harp, which "trembles to the cosmic breath" and which alone of all poets can utter "These syllables that Nature spoke" ("The Harp"). Thoreau wrote "Rumors from an Aeolian Harp," a song *from* a harp, not about one, and in *Walden* he employs the metaphor several times. As a theme or allusion, the harp seems to have lingered longer in America than elsewhere, appearing as late as 1888 in a poem by Melville, "The Aeolian Harp at the Surf Inn."

Kircher noted that several sounds may be produced by one string, suggesting that the string is to the wind as a prism to light, breaking up a unified motion or essence into its component parts. William Jones developed the theory that "the Eolian harp may be considered as an air-prism." That idea may account for the connection between the aeolian harp and the "Harp of Memnon," which was thought to be concealed within a colossal statue of an Egyptian pharoah and would sound when the first ray of sunlight struck it each morning. "For as old Memnon's image," Akenside writes, "long renown'd / By fabling Nilus, to the quivering touch / Of Titan's ray, with each repulsive string / Consenting, sounded through the warbling air / Unbidden strains; even so did Nature's hand / To certain species of external things, / Attune the finer organs of the mind" (*Pleasures of Imagination* 109–15). Amelia Opie mentions Memnon's harp in her "Stanzas Written under Aeolus' Harp." Byron lightly alludes to Memnon, "the Ethiop king / Whose statue turns a harper once a day" (*Deformed Transformed* 1.531–32).

At least two composers have written music "for" an aeolian harp: the Romantics Berlioz, in his *Lélio* (opus 14b), and Chopin, in his Etude opus 25, no. 1.

Air   *see* **Breath, Wind**

Albatross   The albatross, of which there are several species, is a large web-footed bird with a hooked beak and narrow wings, found mainly in the southern oceans. The white Wandering Albatross, with a wing span of thirteen feet, is the best known; when it follows a ship it is a striking sight, and sailors have long considered it a bird of good omen.

The first half of the name seems to derive from Latin *albus*, "white," but the b was inserted into "alcatras," from Portuguese *alcatraz*, used of the albatross, cormorant, frigate bird, or pelican, from Arabic *al-ghattas*, the white-tailed sea-eagle.

As early as the sixth century there are records of the bird following ships. The most famous albatross in literature is the one in Coleridge's *Rime of the Ancient Mariner*; since then "albatross" has come to mean a burden of guilt or sin. Melville, in *Moby-Dick*, chapter 42, has a memorable description of an albatross. It was believed that albatrosses can sleep while in flight; so Hugo likens Chateaubriand to the bird, for he soars calmly above the turmoil of the earth ("Le Génie" 128–30). Baudelaire, in *L'Albatros*, likens a poet, "exiled on the ground," his wings clipped, to an albatross captured by sailors.

Almond   The almond tree blooms earlier than any other – as early as January in Palestine, March in England; it is *prima omnium*, "first of all," according to Pliny (*Natural History* 16.103). It can thus symbolize spring's arrival, or more precisely a prophecy of its arrival.

The Lord asks Jeremiah what he sees, and he replies, "I see a rod of an almond tree." The Lord says, "Thou hast well seen: for I will hasten my word to perform it" (Jer. 1.11–12). Rather mysterious in English, this passage depends on a Hebrew pun on "almond" (*shaqed*) and "hasten" (or "watch," "be diligent") (*shoqed*): almonds are watchful, hastening to blossom. "'Tis a fair tree, the almond-tree: there Spring / Shews the first promise of her rosy wreath," as

Letitia Landon writes ("Death in the Flower" 1–2). Shelley makes a "lightning-blasted almond-tree" which nonetheless scatters blossoms stand for the renewal of hope after the defeat of the prophetic French Revolution (*PU* 2.1.134–35).

Calderón brings out the notion of premature blossoming. Segismund wants no more false displays "that one gust / Can scatter like the almond tree in flower, / Whose rosy buds, without advice or warning, / Dawn in the air too soon" (*Life is a Dream* 3.3.2330–33; trans. Campbell).

The rod of Aaron is made from an almond tree; when it alone among all the other rods flowers and yields almonds, it is a sign of the Lord's favor: Aaron is chosen to be priest (Num. 17.1–10). This passage lies behind artists' use of an almond-shaped aureole, the mandorla (Italian for "almond"), behind representations of Christ and Mary, the chosen ones.

The white blossoms of the almond tree suggested hair to the author of Ecclesiastes: "the almond tree shall flourish" means "their hair shall turn white" as they grow old (12.5). In the last part of "Of the Four Ages of Man," Anne Bradstreet explains, "Mine Almond tree, grey hairs, doe flourish now" (417).

Amaranth   The amaranth or amaranthus is an eternal flower. The word is a "correction" of the Greek participle *amarantos*, "unfading"; taken as a noun naming a flower the ending was respelled as if it were *anthos*, "flower." Lucian describes a fresco painting of a flowery meadow in spring which, as a painting, is thus "eternal spring and unfading (*amarantos*) meadow" ("The Hall" 9). Peter uses it twice in his first letter: through the resurrection we are begotten again to an inheritance "that fadeth not away" (1.4), and we shall receive "a crown of glory that fadeth not away" (5.4). Milton's angels wear crowns woven with amaranth, "Immortal Amarant, a Flow'r which once / In Paradise, fast by the tree of life / Began to bloom, but soon for man's offence / To heaven removed" (*PL* 3.353–56). Milton made it so distinctively the flower of Paradise (lost) that Tennyson has a painter describe a flower that "only blooms in heaven / With Milton's amaranth" ("Romney's Remorse" 106).

In English poetry, then, it became symbolic of Paradise or eternity and of the Christian hope of salvation. So Cowper writes "Hope . . . // On steady wings sails through th'immense abyss, / Plucks amaranthine joys from bow'rs of bliss" ("Hope" 161–64). Wordsworth claims that the imagination has the power "to pluck the amaranthine flower / Of Faith" (sonnet: "Weak is the will of Man"). The Prometheus of the non-Christian Shelley "waked the legioned hopes / Which sleep within folded Elysian flowers, / Nepenthe, Moly, Amaranth, fadeless blooms" (*PU* 2.4.59–61). So when Coleridge, in his poignant "Work without Hope," writes, "Well I ken the banks where amaranths blow, / . . . / Bloom, O ye amaranths! bloom for whom ye may, / For me ye bloom not," we know it is not an earthly meadow he has lost; he is in spiritual despair.

Sainte-Beuve gives it a somewhat different meaning, as the "symbol of virtue that never fades" (*Causeries du lundi*, vol. 8 [1851–62], p. 142).

Amphisbaena   *see* **Serpent**

Anchor   Any use of a ship as a symbol or metaphor may include the anchor as the sign of safety. In a Christian context, the anchor has become a symbol of hope, especially the hope of salvation. The source is a passage in the Epistle to the Hebrews concerning "the hope set before us" in the sworn promise of God: "Which hope we have as an anchor of the soul, both sure and stedfast" (6.18–19). The cruciform shape of many anchors seconded their connection with the Savior.

Spenser's character Speranza (Hope) has a silver anchor on her arm, upon which she teaches the Redcross Knight "to take assured hold" (*FQ* 1.10.14, 22). Cowper's poem "Hope" includes the anchor among many metaphors: "Hope, as an anchor firm and sure, holds fast / the Christian vessel, and defies the blast" (167–68). The Alpine peasant, according to Wordsworth, is unmoved by perils, "Fixed on the anchor left by Him who saves / Alike in whelming snows and roaring waves" (*Descriptive Sketches* 206–07). Tennyson's Enoch Arden, a sailor, tells his wife, as he departs, "Cast all your cares on God; that anchor holds" (222).

See **Ship**.

Animal   *see* **Beast**

Anointing   *see* **Oil**

Ant (or Emmet)   The ant is known for its wisdom, prudence, or foresight. "Go to the ant, thou sluggard," the Book of Proverbs advises; "consider her ways, and be wise" (6.6). "The ants are a people not strong, yet they prepare their meat in the summer" (30.25).

Hesiod calls the ant the "wise one" for "gathering stores" (*Works and Days* 778). Virgil says the "ant fears a lean old age" (*Georgics* 1.186). Horace expands: "the tiny ant with immense industry... / hauls whatever he can with his mouth and adds it to the heap / he is building, thus making conscious and careful provision for the future" (*Satires* 1.1.33–35, trans. Rudd). In a double simile Ovid cites a column of ants carrying grain and a swarm of bees hovering over thyme (*Ars Amatoria* 1.93–96). Among the gifts each animal gave to man, according to Sidney, the ant gave "industrie" (*Third Eclogues* 66.93). Milton names "The parsimonious emmet, provident / Of future,.../... joined in her popular tribes / Of commonalty" (*PL* 7.485–89). Wild nature, says Wordsworth, "to the emmet gives / Her foresight, and intelligence that makes / The tiny creatures strong by social league" (*Excursion* 4.430–32). The fable of the industrious ant and the improvident grasshopper goes back to Aesop.

The social side of the ant noted by Milton and Wordsworth has a repellent side exploited by Wordsworth himself when he describes London as a "monstrous ant-hill on the plain / Of a too busy world!" (1850 *Prelude* 7.149–50). Baudelaire calls Paris *Fourmillante cité*, "swarming city" (from *fourmi*, "ant") ("Les Sept Vieillards"), in a line T. S. Eliot footnotes in *The Waste Land* (60).

The word "ant" comes from Old English *aemette*, akin to "emmet."

Ape   The Greeks and the Romans considered apes ridiculous, strange, ugly, and somewhat dangerous, and "ape" was a common term of abuse. A passage from Heraclitus, who stressed the superiority of the gods, rests on this contemptuous view of apes: "The handsomest ape is ugly compared with humankind; the wisest man appears as an ape when compared with a god" (in Plato, *Hippias Major* 289a, trans. Wheelwright). In this may lie the germ of the notion that apes imitate people; in any case they resemble us. "The ape [Latin *simia*], that most repulsive animal," said Ennius, "how much it is like [*similis*] ourselves!" (*Saturae*, quoted in Cicero, *De Natura Deorum* 1.35). Horace refers to "that ape of yours who knows nothing but how to imitate Calvus and Catullus" (*Sermones* 1.10.18–19). The word *simia* is not related to *similis* but the connection seemed natural: apes are simulators, imitators. In English and other languages "to ape" is to imitate: "monkey see, monkey do."

An alchemist in Dante's *Inferno*, that is, a counterfeiter, proudly calls himself "a fine ape of nature" (29.139). In Chaucer some musicians begin to watch others and "countrefete hem [them] as an ape" (*House of Fame* 1212). The painter Julio Romano is praised in Shakespeare's *Winter's Tale* as capable of depriving nature of her trade, "so perfectly he is her ape" (5.2.98). Cowper looks forward to a world where "smooth good-breeding" will no longer "With lean performance ape the work of love!" (*Task* 6.853–54).

Not all languages distinguish "ape" and "monkey," but in English literature monkeys as opposed to apes are often taken as lecherous. Shakespeare, for instance, has "lecherous as a monkey" and "hot as monkeys" (*2H4* 3.2.293, *Othello* 3.3.409).

Apple   The most famous apple in western culture, the one from the Tree of Knowledge in the Garden of Eden, has a slender basis in the Bible. In Genesis 3.3 it is simply "the fruit"; perhaps it is a fig, for right after Adam and Eve eat it they stitch together fig leaves for clothing (3.7). It is not certain, in any case, that apples were known in ancient Israel. How the fateful fruit got to be an apple is a long story, complicated by the fact that the Greek word for it (*melon*, or *malon*) meant any sort of tree-fruit; thus the "Armenian *melon*" was an apricot, the "Cydonian *melon*" was a quince, the "Median *melon*" was a citron, and the "Persian *melon*" was a peach; in modern Cyprus a "golden apple" is an apricot; and in English a "melon" is not much like an apple. Latin *pomum* had a similar range, as we see in its daughter languages: French *pomme de terre* ("apple of earth") is a potato, *pomme d'amour* ("apple of love") is a tomato, Italian *pomodoro* ("apple of gold") is a tomato; "pomegranate" comes from Old French *pome grenate*, "seedy apple." When Latin borrowed the Greek word (becoming *malum*), a pun on the common word for "evil" may have influenced Christian speculation. In Milton's influential version of the Fall it is an "apple" (*PL* 9.585, 10.487), though we cannot be sure if he means the common crab-apple or the generic tree-fruit.

It would be enough to suit the biblical story that the "apple" is alluring and tasty, but in both Hebrew and classical tradition the fruit is associated with sexual love, which Adam and Eve discover, in some interpretations, after eating it. Apples are mentioned three times with erotic senses in the Song of Solomon; e.g., "As the apple tree among the trees of the wood, so is my beloved among the sons [young men]" (2.3; cf. 7.8, 8.5) (the Hebrew word *tappuah* also has a broad sense). This passage resembles one in Sappho – "As the sweet-apple reddens on the top of the bough, the top of the topmost; the apple-gatherers have forgotten it – no, not forgotten it but were unable to reach it" – which we are told by Himerius is a simile for a girl (frag. 105 Campbell). Throwing an apple or similar tree-fruit was a signal of readiness to be seduced (e.g., Aristophanes, *Clouds* 997; Virgil, *Eclogues* 3.64). Echoing Sappho, Yeats imagines that Dante became a great poet out of "A hunger for the apple on the bough, / Most out of reach," which must mean his Beatrice ("Ego Dominus Tuus" 24–25). Frost's "After Apple-Picking," with its ladder "Toward heaven," the worthlessness of apples that have fallen, and the coming of winter and sleep, stirs echoes of biblical meanings.

In classical myth another famous apple is the Apple of Discord (or Eris), which she tosses among the three goddesses Hera, Athena, and Aphrodite at the wedding of Peleus and Thetis; it is labeled "For the fairest," and each goddess claims it. The ultimate result is the Trojan War. There are also the golden apples of the Hesperides, guarded by a dragon, whom Heracles slays.

One of the women in Aristophanes' *Lysistrata* recalls that Menelaus, bent on killing Helen, took one look at her "apples" and threw away his sword (155). A girl in Theocritus asks her wooer why he has put his hand on her breasts; he replies, "I will give your downy apples their first lesson" (27.49–50). The breasts of Ariosto's Alcina are "unripe apples" (*Orlando Furioso* 7.14). According to Tasso, in the Golden Age before shame took effect a virgin would reveal "the apples of her breast" ("O bella eta de l'oro"). Spenser compares his beloved's breasts to two golden apples, which surpass those that Hercules found (in the Hesperides) and those that enticed Atalanta (*Amoretti* 77). These latter, Ovid tells us, were picked by Venus herself (*Met.* 10.647–52). In the Walpurgisnight, Faust tells a young witch he had a dream that he climbed a tree to reach two fine apples; she answers that men have wanted apples ever since Paradise, and happily she has some in her garden (*Faust I* 4128–35).

Josephus describes a fruit near the Dead Sea that looks like an apple but is filled with dry, hairy seeds; later it was called a Sodom apple and thought to be filled with the ashes of that sinful city. As fit punishment for leading Eve to eat the forbidden apple, Milton has Satan's legions climb trees to eat fruit "like that which grew / Near that bituminous lake where Sodom flamed," but they "instead of fruit / Chewed bitter ashes" (*PL* 10.561–66). The chorus of women accompanying Helen to Faust's castle finds the boys there attractive, with cheeks like peaches: "I would gladly have a bite, but I shudder before it; / for in a similar case, the mouth was filled, / horrible to say, with ashes!" (*Faust II* 9162–64).

The "apple of the eye" is the pupil, and by extension any intimate or cherished object. The Lord guarded Jacob "as the apple of his eye" (Deut. 32.10). Shakespeare's Oberon, squeezing the love-juice on Demetrius' eyelids, asks it to "Sink in apple of his eye. / When his love he doth espy, / Let her shine as gloriously / As the Venus of the sky" (*MND* 3.2.104–07).

In some accounts of the Crucifixion, Christ, as the antitype of Adam (1 Cor. 15.22), restores the apple Eve plucked. In a witty variant Byron claims that Isaac Newton was "the sole mortal who could grapple, / Since Adam, with a fall, or with an apple." Since Newton's theories, he predicts, will some day show us how to fly to the moon, it can be said that "Man fell with apples, and with apples rose" (*Don Juan* 10.1–16).

April   April is the quintessential month of spring – "Aperil...of lusty Veer [Spring] the pryme," according to Chaucer (*Troilus* 1.156–57) – and most of the traditional imagery of the season has been given to the month.

Ovid gives two etymologies of the month's name. (1) From Latin *aperio* "open": "They say that April was named from the open season, because spring then opens (*aperit*) all things, and the sharp frost-bound cold departs, and earth unlocks her teeming soil" (*Fasti* 4.87–89, trans. Frazer). (2) From Greek *aphros*, the foam of the sea from which Aphrodite was born (*Fasti* 4.61–62). The latter may well be on the right track, for April is the month of Venus (*Fasti* 4.85ff., Horace 4.11.15–16), and the name may derive from Etruscan *apru*, a shortening of *Aphrodite* (as March comes from *Mars* and May from *Maia*, mother of Mercury, god of spring).

The most famous description of April in English literature is the opening of the Prologue to Chaucer's *Canterbury Tales*: "Whan that Aprill with his shoures soote / The droghte of March hath perced to the roote, / And bathed every veyne in swich licour / Of which vertu engendred is the flour..." (1–4). The month's "sweet showers" are a commonplace. The proverb "April showers bring May flowers" has been current at least since 1560; Shakespeare's Iris sings of "spongy April" (*Tempest* 4.1.65); Wordsworth has a character invoke "Ye rains of April" (*Excursion* 7.701).

As the month of Venus it is the month of love. Spenser begins a stanza on the month by calling it "fresh Aprill, full of lustyhed" (*FQ* 7.7.33). Of Octavia weeping at her parting from Caesar, Shakespeare's Antony says, "The April's in her eyes: it is love's spring, / And these the showers to bring it on" (*Antony* 3.2.43–44). Shelley describes a beautiful woman as "A vision like incarnate April, warning, / With smiles and tears, Frost the Anatomy [skeleton] / Into his summer grave" (*Epipsychidion* 121–23). The spring or prime of one's life might be called one's April: "I lived free in the April of my life, / Exempt from care" (Scève, *Délie*, "Dizains" 1).

The other famous description of April begins T. S. Eliot's *The Waste Land*: "April is the cruelest month, breeding / Lilacs out of the dead land, mixing / Memory and desire, stirring / Dull roots with spring rain" (1–4). It is a measure of how far modern life has lost its traditional foundation, in Eliot's view, that we now shrink from the renewal of life and love that April once brought.

See **Spring**.

Armor   In medieval chivalric romances, the armor of the hero, and especially his shield or "escutcheon," is often lovingly described and invested with great significance. The elaborate language of heraldry or armorial bearings – the points, tinctures, bends, chevrons, fesses, pales, piles, and lions couchant, rampant, regardant, or salient – enters the literature, too, but it is beyond the scope of this dictionary. Less technical symbolic meanings of armor, or changes of armor, are usually unique to each work. It is of great significance, for instance, that Achilles' first set of armor belonged to his father Peleus, is then lent to his friend Patroclus, who is killed in it by Hector, and is then worn by Hector, who is killed in it by Achilles, who now wears a new set made by the god Hephaestus. Achilles' shield, extensively described in Book 18 of the *Iliad*, carries a complex set of typical scenes (such as wedding, legal dispute, and siege) in a cosmic setting. The parallel description of Aeneas' shield in book 8 of the *Aeneid* is not typical and cosmic but historical, as if Aeneas shoulders the future history of Rome. In Spenser's *Faerie Queene*, Arthur's "glitterand armour" was made by Merlin (1.7.29–36), while Britomart's once belonged to Angela, the Saxon Queen (3.3.58); both express the virtues of their bearers.

Central to the language of Christianity is the metaphor of "spiritual warfare" and its accompanying armor. It is fully expressed in Paul's Letter to the Ephesians. Since Christians do not fight against flesh and blood but against spiritual wickedness, "Wherefore take unto you the whole armour of God, that ye may be able to withstand in the evil day, and having done all, to stand. / Stand therefore, having your loins girt about with truth, and having on the breastplate of righteousness; / And your feet shod with the preparation of the gospel of peace; / Above all, taking the shield of faith, wherewith ye shall be able to quench all the fiery darts of the wicked. / And take the helmet of salvation, and the sword of the Spirit, which is the word of God" (6.13–17; cf. 2 Cor. 10.3–4). Clement of Alexandria wrote, "If the loud trumpet summons soldiers to war, shall not Christ with a strain of peace to the ends of the earth gather up his soldiers of peace? A bloodless army he has assembled by blood and by the word, to give to them the Kingdom of Heaven. The trumpet of Christ is his Gospel. He has sounded, we have heard. Let us then put on the armor of peace" (*Protrepticus* 11.116). Erasmus continues the tradition: "If we wish to conquer for Christ, let us gird on the sword of the word of the Gospel, let us put on the helmet of salvation and take the shield of faith, and the rest of the truly Apostolic panoply. Then it will come about that, when we are conquered, we are conquerors all the more" (*Dulce Bellum Inexpertis*, in *Adagia*).

Beatrice tells Dante that, "to battle to enkindle faith, / the Gospels served them [the Apostles] as both shield and lance" (*Paradiso* 29.113–14). Milton's Michael tells Adam that God will send a Comforter to the people, "To guide them in all truth, and also arm / With spiritual armour, able to resist / Satan's assaults" (*PL* 12.490–92). Even the atheist Shelley uses these terms: "And from that hour did I with earnest thought / Heap knowledge from forbidden mines of lore, / Yet nothing that my tyrant knew or taught / I cared to learn, but from that secret store / Wrought linked armour for my soul, before / It might walk forth to war among mankind" ("Dedication" of *Laon and Cythna*, 37–42).

Arrow   *see* **Bow and arrow**

Ash   In Greece, where they are plentiful, ash trees were known for their strength and for their excellence as firewood. The centaur Chiron gave Achilles' father Peleus a great spear made of Pelian ash (Homer, *Iliad* 16.143); in his catalogue of trees Ovid calls the ash "useful for spear-shafts" (*Met.* 10.93), and Chaucer perhaps follows him in listing "the hardy asshe" (*Parliament of Fowls* 176). Angry over a trick by Prometheus, Zeus denied the power of fire to ash trees (Hesiod, *Theogony* 563), implying they were the preferred firewood. There were Meliae or ash-nymphs (e.g. *Theogony* 187), but they are not clearly distinguished from the generic Dryads or tree-nymphs.

Hesiod says that the bronze race was made of ash trees (*Works and Days* 145), and a similar tale is found in Norse mythology, where the first man is named Ash (Askr) ("Voluspa" 17 in *The Poetic Edda*). The world tree Yggdrasill, where the fates deal out justice, is an ash ("Voluspa" 19).

In his catalogue of trees Spenser mysteriously names "the Ash for nothing ill" (*FQ* 1.1.9).

Asp   *see* **Serpent**

Asphodel   The asphodel is the flower of Hades. After speaking with Odysseus, the shade of Achilles "stalked away in long strides across the meadow of asphodel" (*Odyssey* 11.539 trans. Lattimore, cf. 11.573). It is a lean, spiky plant with small, pale flowers and gray leaves; it blooms throughout the winter in Mediterranean regions. Pliny says it is planted on graves (*Natural History* 21.68).

Milton names asphodel beside nectar and ambrosia as having the power to confer immortality ("Comus" 838). Pope invokes "those happy souls who dwell / In yellow meads of Asphodel" ("Ode for Music" 74–75). Tennyson more or less translates Homer in his "Demeter and Persephone": "the shadowy warrior glide / Along the silent field of Asphodel" (150–51); in "The Lotos-Eaters" he imagines "others in Elysian valleys dwell, / Resting weary limbs at last on beds of asphodel" (169–70). W. C. Williams takes "asphodel, that greeny flower," as a symbol, or recurring occasion, of memory, poetry, and love in a bleak world. "I was cheered," he says near the opening, "when I came first to know / that there were flowers also / in hell"; he ends: "Asphodel / has no odor / save to the imagination / but it too / celebrates the light. / It is late / but an odor / as from our wedding / has revived for me / and begun again to penetrate / into all crevices / of my world" ("Asphodel, that greeny flower").

Ass   As the preeminent beast of burden and the poor man's horse, the ass deserves a better literary reputation, but since the Greeks at least it has stood for stupidity. A string of insults in Terence gives a handy list of synonyms: *stulto, caudex, stipes, asinus, plumbeus* ("fool, blockhead, stumpwit, ass, leadbrain") (*Self-Tormentor* 877). A shorter list is Shakespeare's "Asses, fools, dolts" (*Troilus* 1.2.241). "What a thrice-double ass / Was I," says Caliban, after his foolish rebellion against Prospero (*Tempest* 5.1.295). When thick-witted King Midas judges Pan's pipes superior to Apollo's lyre, Apollo gives him ass's ears (Ovid, *Met.* 11.144–93); asses are proverbially deaf to music, as to all intellectual things.

As the horse could represent the willful or irrational part of the soul, so the ass, in a humbler way, could stand for the merely physical or bodily side of life. The allegorical dimension of Apuleius' *Golden Ass* (or *Metamorphoses*), in which Lucius is punished for his foolish curiosity and sexual indulgence by being transformed into an ass and made to suffer enormous torments, comes to a climax in his transformation back into the human as he becomes a chaste initiate into the religion of Isis. St. Francis famously calls the body "Brother Ass." Shakespeare reweaves motifs from Apuleius in his "translation" of Bottom into an ass in *A Midsummer Night's Dream*; Bottom is the "shallowest thickskin" of the workers (3.2.13), but like Lucius, to whom Isis comes in a dream, he alone meets the queen of the fairies. So it was that Balaam's ass saw the angel that Balaam himself was blind to (Num. 22.22–35). The satirical side of Apuleius's novel inspired Renaissance satire on the theme of asininity, such as Erasmus' *Praise of Folly*, but something of the emblematic character of the ass as the redeemable lower dimension of life may be found in the braying of the ass that reconciles Prince Myshkin to life in Dostoyevsky's *The Idiot*. Lawrence hears in the braying an agonized cry of love: "He fell into the rut of love, / Poor ass, like man, always in rut" ("The Ass").

See **Horse**.

Attic bird   *see* **Nightingale**

Autumn   Though not as popular as spring, autumn has been a frequent subject of poetry since the classical Roman era, when certain conventions were established. Autumn, of course, has two aspects: it completes summer and it anticipates winter, it celebrates the harvest of the summer's crops and it mourns the death of the year; it is, in Dickinson's words, "A little this side of the snow / And that side of the Haze" (no. 131). Latin poetry usually dwells on its summery side, associating it with harvest and vintage, wealth and corn-ucopias. So Virgil calls autumn "vine-leafed" (*Georgics* 2.5), Horace imagines his head decked with ripe fruit (*Epodes* 2.17–18), Lucretius has Bacchus arrive with him (5.743), Ovid describes a nymph bearing "The horn with all its wealth" (*Met.* 9.88, trans. Melville). Descriptions of "perpetual spring" equally describe perpetual autumn, for as Homer puts it in his account of the garden of Alcinous, "Pear matures on pear in that place, apple upon apple, / grape cluster on grape cluster, fig upon fig" (*Odyssey* 7.120–21, trans. Lattimore). In Eden, according to Milton, "spring and autumn here / Danced hand in hand" (*PL* 5.394–95). (For more examples see under **Spring**.)

Spenser describes Autumn as "Laden with fruits that made him laugh," while he bore "Upon his head a wreath, that was enroll / With ears of corne of every sort" and carried a sickle in his hand (*FQ* 7.7.30). Shakespeare calls it "childing autumn" (*MND* 2.1.112) and "teeming autumn, big with rich increase" (*Sonnets* 97). In his long section on "Autumn" in *The Seasons*, Thomson describes the joyous harvest at length.

Some of the most delicate and convincing of modern descriptions of the season hold both facets of autumn in balance, the fullness and satisfaction of the harvest with the coming on of winter and death. So Goethe calls on the vine and berries to turn greener and swell plumper, as the sun and the moon bring them to fulfillment – and his own tears of love bedew them ("Herb-stgefühl"). Keats ("To Autumn") serenely describes autumn's moment of "mellow fruitfulness" when all seems ready and ripe; he ends with an evening scene where the day is "soft-dying," the "small gnats mourn," and "gathering swallows twitter in the skies" as if preparing to fly south. Pushkin welcomes autumn alone of all the seasons: "How can I explain this? She pleases me / As sometimes, perhaps, you have been drawn to / A consumptive girl.... / She is alive today – tomorrow, not" ("Autumn" 41–48, trans. Thomas). After a brief tableau of November, Pascoli writes, "in the distance you hear / a fragile falling of leaves. It is the summer, / Cold, of the dead" ("Novembre"). After asking God to "Command the fruits to swell on tree and vine," Rilke concludes, "Whoever is alone will long remain so, / will stay awake, read, write long letters / and in the streets up and down / will wander restlessly while leaves are blowing" ("Herbsttag"). Hopkins asks, "Margaret, are you grieving / Over Goldengrove unleaving?" and answers for her, "It is Margaret you mourn for." The title of that poem, "Spring and Fall," reminds us that when the English largely replaced "fall" with the latinate "autumn" they broke up a poetically perfect pair; the original sense of "spring" is now less evident.

Autumn, of course, is a metaphor for the phase of maturity or middle age in a human life. "Then autumn follows," says Ovid, "youth's fine fervour spent, / Mellow and ripe, a temperate time between / Youth and old age, his temples flecked with grey" (*Met.* 15.209–11, trans. Melville). "Nor spring, nor summer beauty hath such grace," Donne writes, "As I have seen in one autumnal face" (*Elegies* 9.1–2). After several stanzas of scenic description, Baratynsky stops to ask, "And you, when in the autumn of your days, / O plowman of the fields of living, / And your own harvest lies before your gaze, / ... / Can you, then, like the farmer, count your hoard?" ("Autumn" 60–71, trans. Myers). Shelley's "Ode to the West Wind" is an ode to autumn; he implores the wind to "Make me thy lyre, even as the forest is: / What if my leaves are falling like its own!" (57–58).

See **Seasons, Spring, Summer, Winter**.

Azure   *see* **Blue**

B

Basilisk   The basilisk is a mythical reptile whose stare is lethal. It is described by Pliny as native to Cyrenaica (Libya), about a foot long, and adorned with a bright mark on its head like a diadem – whence the name *basiliscus*, from Greek *basiliskos*, "little king." It routs all serpents with its hiss; its touch or breath is fatal to all creatures but the weasel, which kills it with the weasel's stench (8.78). In his catalog of snakes Lucan describes "the basilisk which pours forth hisses terrifying all / the beasts, which harms before its poison and orders the entire crowd / far out of its way and on the empty sand is king" (9.724–26, trans. Braund); later he tells how the poison of a dead basilisk traveled up the spear of a soldier and penetrated his hand, which had to be cut off (9.828–33).

The Septuagint (Greek Old Testament) used *basiliskos* for several snakes in the Hebrew, including the well-known messianic passage of Isaiah 11, where the wolf shall live with the sheep, etc., and "the infant shall play over the hole of the asp, and the young child dance over the nest of the *basiliskos*" (11.8). Jerome translated *basiliskos* here and in most other passages into the Vulgate as *regulus*, "little king," but Wyclif and his followers translated it into English as "cockatrice." Blendings of various fabulous reptiles and birds make the history of the cockatrice extremely complex. The word seems to derive from Latin *calcatrix, from *calcare*, "tread" or "track," translating another Greek lizard, the *ichneumon*, meaning "tracker" or "hunter." The French version of "basilisk" was *basilicoc*, the form also used by Chaucer – "the basilicok sleeth folk by the venym of his sighte" (*Parson's Tale* 853) – and so the idea got round that the reptile was generated from an egg laid by a cock but hatched by a toad or snake.

Spenser uses both names to make the same point. A terrible man on a dromedary "secretly his enemies did slay: / Like as the Basiliske, of serpents seede, / From powerfull eyes close venim doth convay / Into the lookers hart, and killeth farre away" (FQ 4.8.39); while in a sonnet Spenser begs his mistress to turn elsewhere her cruel eyes "and kill with looks, as Cockatrices doo" (Amoretti 49). Shakespeare also uses both. Polixenes demands, "Make me not sighted like the basilisk. / I have look'd on thousands, who have sped the better / By my regard, but kill'd none so" (WT 1.2.388–90; see also Cymbeline 3.4.107); Juliet fears the possible news of Romeo's death "shall poison more / Than the death-darting eye of cockatrice" (RJ 3.2.46–47; see also 12N 3.4.196–98). Maurice Scève, in the first of his dizains in Délie, tells that "my Basilisk, with her pointed look / Piercing body, heart, and distraught reason, / Penetrated into the Soul of my Soul."

The Isaiah passage in the Authorized Version reads: "And the sucking child shall play on the hole of the asp, and the weaned child shall put his hand on the cockatrice's den." In his paraphrase of this passage Pope restores "basilisk": "The smiling Infant in his Hand shall take / The crested Basilisk and speckled Snake: / Pleas'd, the green Lustre of the scales survey, / And with their forky Tongue shall innocently play" (Messiah 81–84). Shelley also draws on Isaiah in his description of the future, which includes "a babe before his mother's door, / Sharing his morning's meal / With the green and golden basilisk / That comes to lick his feet" (Queen Mab 8.84–87).

Thomas Browne, in Pseudodoxia Epidemica, has a chapter on the basilisk (3.7), in which he denies that it is the product of a cock's egg and a reptile's incubation, but credits its existence and most of its other attributes. He also distinguishes it from the cockatrice, which has legs and wings and a comb like a cock!

A secondary sense of "basilisk," as the name of a large cannon, arose in the sixteenth century. Marlowe evokes its roaring noise in Tamburlaine I 4.1.2, while Shakespeare puns on the two senses when he has Queen Isabel tell the conquering King Henry V that she is "glad to behold your eyes; / Your eyes, which hitherto hath borne in them, / Against the French, that met them in their bent, / The fatal balls of murdering basilisks" (H5 5.2.14–17).

Bat Until they are examined closely, the most notable features of bats are that they fly at night (though they are visible only at twilight), utter a thin squeak, and often dwell in caves. Though Aristotle knew they were mammals, most ancients took them as a kind of bird. On the Isle of Dreams, according to Lucian, "bats are the only birds to be found" ("A True Story" 2.33), Milton lists "owls, bats, and such fatal birds" (Eikonoklastes, sec. 15), and as late as Saint-Pierre we find "birds of prey, such as the bat, the owl, the eagle owl" (Harmonies de la Nature [1814], p. 268).

In both Greek and Latin their name has an element meaning "night" or "evening": Greek nukteris comes from nukt-, "night," and Latin vespertilio, as Ovid tells us, comes from vesper, "evening" (Met. 4.415).

As caves were evidently entrances into the underworld, bats were thought to be the spirits of the dead. The oldest and most influential literary passage in this respect is the simile in the *Odyssey* (24.6–9), where the souls of the dead suitors, recently killed by Odysseus, are likened to a chain of gibbering bats in a dreadful cave. Plato cites this passage as one that must be expunged so that boys will not learn to be afraid of death (*Republic* 387a).

Homer's verb for the bats' cry, *trizein*, is imitative of the sound, as is the cognate *stridere* in Latin. Ovid describes bats as crying *levi stridore*, "in thin squeaks" (*Met.* 4.413); Virgil gives them a *vocem | exiguam*, "a wispy cry" (*Aeneid* 6.492–93). Hence ghosts, whether or not they are likened to bats in other respects, make batlike cries. In the *Iliad* the ghost of Patroclus goes underground "with a squeak" (23.101). The spirits in Horace's *Satires* 1.8.41 make a similar sound. Shakespeare's Horatio remembers that "the sheeted dead / Did squeak and gibber in the Roman streets" (*Hamlet* 1.1.118–19) and Calphurnia warns Caesar that "ghosts did shriek and squeal about the streets" (*JC* 2.2.24); all four of Shakespeare's verbs imitate the cry.

From their connection with the underworld, features of bats were attributed to the devil. In Dante's *Inferno*, Satan's giant wings "had no feathers but were like those of a bat (*vispistrello*)" (34.49–50). Its infernal and nocturnal character was thus well established before the nineteenth-century vampire stories, notably Polidori's *The Vampyre* and Stoker's *Dracula*.

It became a standard epithet or tag phrase about bats that they were night creatures. Lydgate writes, "No bakke [bat] of kynde [by nature] may looke ageyn the sunne" (*Cock* 43). Among the "fatall birds" Spenser lists is "The lether-winged Batt, dayes enimy" (*FQ* 2.12.36), while Drayton calls it "the Watch-Man of the Night" (*Owl* 502). Only in the early seventeenth century, in English at least, do we find such phrases as "bat-blind" or "blind as a bat" – blind, presumably, in the daylight.

Bay *see* **Laurel**

Bear The Greeks recognized a northern constellation as a bear (*Arktos*, whence English "arctic"), better known to us as Ursa Major ("Great Bear" in Latin) or the Big Dipper (e.g., Homer, *Iliad* 18.487). They also had tales involving bears, such as the one retold in the second book of Ovid's *Metamorphoses* about Jupiter, Callisto, and Arcas. No very definite symbolism, however, attaches to bears. It has been conjectured that a very ancient myth about bears underlies the *Odyssey*, whose hero "hibernates" in caves, and *Beowulf*, the name of whose hero may mean "bee-wolf," a kenning for "bear," but the evidence for the myth is thin. Bears became popular, and populous, in literature in the early nineteenth century with the Grimm brothers' collection of German folktales and Southey's "The Three Bears." Bears can seem attractive and friendly – they are readily humanized – but they are also wild and dangerous. Their alienness as embodiments of the wilderness, but with hints of human or superhuman wisdom, is well brought out in Faulkner's story "The Bear."

Bear-baiting, where dogs attack a tethered bear, was long a popular entertainment, notably in Elizabethan England. Spenser invokes it as a simile: "As chained beare whom cruell dogs doe bait" (*FQ* 1.12.35); Macbeth, facing his final battle, sees himself as a bear: "They have tied me to a stake: I cannot fly, / But, bear-like, I must fight the course [bout or round]" (5.7.1–2).

Beast The animal kingdom has been a lavish source of metaphors, similes, and symbols from the earliest literature to the present. Since beasts come in such great variety, their literary uses are usually specific to the species: lions mean certain things, wolves others things, dogs still others. Even where "beast" or "brute" is used as a general term, there is often an implicit distinction between wild (dangerous) and domestic (tame), a beast of prey or beast of burden.

If the human being is the rational animal, as Aristotle and other ancients defined it, then beasts are "lacking in reason" (Ovid, *Amores* 1.10.25). Yet even "a beast that wants discourse of reason," Hamlet insists, might have acted in more human fashion than his mother (1.2.150). People can be reproached for bestial or brutal behavior, and animals held up as examples for people to follow. Prospero calls Caliban a "beast" (*Tempest* 4.1.140) after his rebellion, but his role has been that of a beast of burden all along; Prince Ferdinand, to prove he is worthy of Miranda, must play a similar part, as if he must sound the depths of his animal or physical nature in order to become fully human, or kingly.

A frequent opposite to beast is god or angel, as when Hamlet contrasts his father to his uncle as "Hyperion to a satyr" (1.2.140); it was a commonplace among Renaissance writers that man occupies a space between beast and angel, sharing traits of both, and liable to sink to the one though capable of rising to the other. The dual nature of humans is a widespread literary theme, perhaps most literally embodied in Stevenson's *Dr. Jekyll and Mr. Hyde*.

The most famous "beasts" in the Bible are the highly symbolic monsters in Revelation, such as the beast from the sea, with seven heads and ten horns (13.1); the seven heads stand for seven kings (17.9–10) and the ten horns for ten more kings (17.12).

Beast entries in this dictionary: **Ape, Ass, Basilisk, Bat, Bear, Crocodile, Deer, Dog, Dolphin, Fox, Frog and toad, Goat, Horse, Leopard, Lion, Lynx, Mole, Pig, Salamander, Serpent, Sheep, Tiger, Whale, Wolf, Worm**.

Bee Bees have been highly prized for their honey and wax for as long as we have record, and much beekeeping lore can be found in ancient literature, notably in book 4 of Virgil's *Georgics*. They are social insects with a highly organized hive "government," they cull nectar from many kinds of flowers, and they are both useful and dangerous to people. These obvious characteristics and others less obvious have made them frequent emblems or analogues in literature.

The Greeks considered the bee (Greek *melissa* or *melitta*, from *meli-*, "honey," and perhaps **lich-*, "lick") a sign of eloquence or poetic gifts, partly perhaps because of its buzzing or murmuring but mainly as a natural extension of idioms still common in English and other modern languages such as "honey-voiced," "sweet-lipped," and "mellifluous." Homer calls the Sirens *meligerus*, "honey-voiced" (*Odyssey* 12.187). There were legends that bees hovered around the mouth of the infant Sophocles, as if to gather the honey he was born with, or perhaps to feed him the honey he will need as the great playwright; the same tale was told of Pindar, Plato, and others who were thought to have a divine gift. A sixth-century AD poem from the *Greek Anthology* is about statues of the great poets; one of them is Homer, and "a Pierian bee wandered around his divine mouth, / producing a dripping honeycomb" (2.343–44). (Pieria, on the slope of Mt. Olympus, was the birthplace of the Muses.) In the opening of his "Elegy on the Death of Ronsard," Garnier wishes that "the bee may always make its honey in your tomb."

Alternatively the poet himself or herself might be called a bee. Aristophanes' birds tell us that Phrynichus, another playwright, resembled a bee who "always sipped from the fruit of our ambrosial song [*ambrosion meleon*], bearing away the sweet ode" (*Birds* 749–51), perhaps punning on *melitta* ("bee") and *melos* ("song"). Pindar makes the same pun in likening his song to honey in *Olymp.* 10.97. Plato writes, "the poets tell us, don't they, that the melodies they bring us are gathered from rills that run with honey, out of glens and gardens of the Muses, and they bring them as the bees do honey, flying like the bees" (*Ion* 534b, trans. Cooper). The *Greek Anthology* poem just cited calls Sappho "the Pierian bee," and also mentions *melos* in the next line (69–70). Theocritus tells the story of Comatas, the goatherd-poet, who was shut alive in a chest but was fed by bees "drawn by the Muses' nectar about his lips" (*Idylls* 7.78–83); Wordsworth retells the tale in the 1805 *Prelude* 10.1021–26. Lucretius opens the third book of *De Rerum Natura* by comparing Epicurus' writings to flowery lawns and his readers to bees (Latin *apis*). Horace turns this tradition to gentle self-deprecation by contrasting Pindar the high-flying swan with himself the hard-working bee (*Odes* 4.2.27–32). The metaphor is found in such modern poets as Foscolo, who calls a musician a "nurse of the bees" ("Spesso per l'altre eta"); Dickinson, who identifies with a bee: "We – Bee and I – live by the quaffing" (no. 230); Darío: "my rhymes go / all around the vast forest / to gather honey and aromas / in the half-opened flowers" ("Primaveral"); and Rilke: "We are the bees of the invisible. We wildly collect the honey of the visible, to store it in the great golden hive of the invisible" (letter to Hulewicz, 13 November 1925).

How a hive governed itself was the subject of much ancient speculation. Aristotle writes about bees in *De Generatione Animalium* (3.10) and *Historiae Animalium* (5.21–23, 9.40); the chief Latin authorities are Varro (3.16) and Pliny, *Natural History* (11.11–70). Virgil draws from these sources in *Georgics*, book 4, which is largely devoted to beekeeping and bee lore. These authors almost invariably used masculine terms – Greek *basileus* and *hegemon*, Latin *rex*, *dux*, and *imperator* – for the "king" bee, to whom the hive is absolutely devoted. The Greeks knew that the Egyptians used the bee as a hieroglyph for the pharaoh, and several modern states, such as France, have used the bee as a symbol of their king. It caused some embarrassment in France and elsewhere when Swammerdam (1637–80) established that the "ruler" bee was really female. In the *Georgics* Virgil goes on at length about bee patriotism, providence, and division of labor, though he also describes a bee civil war. In a famous simile of the *Aeneid*, Virgil likens the building of the city of Carthage, where some lay out streets, others build walls, and still others pass laws, to the activity of bees, who "Hum at their work, and bring along the young / Full-grown to beehood; as they cram their combs / With honey, brimming all the cells with nectar, / Or take newcomers' plunder, or like troops / Alerted, drive away the lazy drones" (1.430–36, trans. Fitzgerald). Shakespeare draws largely from the *Georgics* in Canterbury's speech about the division of human labor: "for so work the honey-bees, / Creatures that by a rule in nature teach / The act of order to a peopled kingdom. / They have a king and officers of sorts; / Where some, like magistrates, correct at home, / Others, like merchants, venture trade abroad, / Others like soldiers, armed in the stings, / Make boot upon the summer's velvet buds;" there are also "civil citizens kneading up the honey" (*H5*, 1.2.187–204). After the evacuation of Moscow, as Tolstoy tells it, the city was empty, "empty as a queenless, dying hive is empty"; then follows a lengthy, detailed description of the behavior of bees when a hive has lost its queen (*War and Peace* 3.3.20).

Bees were often thought of as particularly warlike and their hive as organized like an army. The first simile of Homer's *Iliad* likens soldiers to bees (2.87–90), as does another simile in Aeschylus' *Persians* (126–30). Three of the four times bees are mentioned in the Old Testament, they are associated with armies of enemies (Deut. 1.44, Ps. 118.12, Isa. 7.18), and it may be significant that the name of the warrior-leader Deborah means "bee" in Hebrew.

Virgil and other ancients believed that bees had no sexual intercourse but gathered their young from among the flowers. This idea may account for Plutarch's claim that "bees are thought to be irritable and bellicose towards men who have been with women" (*Advice to Bride and Groom* 44). Others, however, associated bees with love. "O Love...the Muses' bee" begins a song in Aristophanes' *Ecclesiazusae* (973–74). Theocritus said Eros is like a bee, so small yet able to make so great a wound (*Idylls* 19). The two-sidedness of bees, producers of honey and stings, made them good symbols of love. That Melissa or similar terms were common girls' names made the symbol almost inevitable. A fragment of Sappho reads: "[I want] neither honey nor honeybee" (frag. 146 Campbell); it is the oldest trace of the common proverb "Who licks honey will get stung" or "No honey without a bee." Lyly's *Euphues* has "The bee that hath honey in her mouth, hath a sting in her tail" (79).

Valéry's sonnet "L'Abeille" ("The Bee") subtly evokes many classical bee contexts as the female speaker invites a bee to sting her breast so "my sense may be illuminated / by that tiny golden alarm / without which Love dies or falls alseep." It is erotic, but also aesthetic: the bee is also the Muses' bee.

A swarm of bees was considered an unlucky omen. When a swarm settles in the sacred laurel of Latium, in the *Aeneid* (7.65–70), it is a sign that the Trojans will occupy the citadel.

Virgil and others believed that bees generate spontaneously from the carcass of a cow or other animal (*Georgics* 4.285–314), a belief the Hebrews shared, for it underlies the famous riddle of Samson in Judges 14.8–18.

In Latin literature the bee's preferred food or source of nectar is thyme (or wild thyme): *Georgics* 4.31, 112ff., 170, 180; *Aeneid* 1.436; etc. It was so well established that Martial could refer to honey as "Hyblaean thyme," Hybla (in Sicily) being famous for its bees (5.39.3). Theocritus had already written that thyme belongs to the Muses (Epigram 1), no doubt because poets are like bees. By his date Spenser could make "bees-alluring" a routine epithet for thyme (*Muiopotmos* 191). When Marvell in "The Garden" writes, "the industrious bee / Computes its time as well as we" (69–70), he is punning on the plant, which Shenstone called "pun-provoking thyme" (*The Schoolmistress* st. 11).

It has been proverbial since ancient times that bees are busy. Ovid calls them *sedula* (whence English "sedulous") at *Metamorphoses* 13.928. "Busy as a bee" is found in Chaucer (*Merchant's Tale*, Epilogue, 2422, "as bisy as bees").

Marvell calls them "industrious" ("Garden" 69), Thomson "fervent" (*Spring* 508), and so on.

The bee produces honey and wax, that is, "sweetness and light," the famous title of a chapter of Arnold's *Culture and Anarchy* (drawn from Swift's *Battle of the Books*): these are his touchstones of culture.

See **Spider**.

Beech Medieval commentators on Virgil defined a scheme called "Virgil's wheel" (*rota Virgilii*), which linked the three genres established by Virgil (pastoral, georgic, and epic) with sets of three styles, social ranks, locales, animals, plants, etc. The beech was the tree appropriate to pastoral poetry (eclogues or bucolics). Indeed the beech (*fagus*) is mentioned in the first line of the first Eclogue, and early in the next two; it is prized for its shade, the right place to sit and "meditate the sylvan Muse" (1.2). In his pastoral "Summer" Pope addresses "Ye shady beeches, and ye cooling Streams, / Defence from *Phoebus*', not from *Cupid's* beams" (13–14). Shelley called the beech "to lovers dear" (*Orpheus* 111).

The Greek *phagos* (or *phegos*), though cognate with Latin *fagus*, refers to the oak, also welcome for its shade; cf. Theocritus, *Idylls* 12.8. The word "beech" itself is also cognate with *fagus*.

In his catalogue of trees (*FQ* 1.1.9) Spenser lists the "warlike Beech," perhaps because beechwood is hard and useful for weapons. It is not listed in his main source, the catalogue of trees in Chaucer's *Parliament of Fowls* 176–82. Spenser may have been misled by Chapman's translation of Homer's *Iliad* 5.838, where the axle of a chariot is made of "the Beechen tree"; the Greek *pheginos axon* should read "axle of oak."

Bile, choler, gall, spleen In Homer the commonest word for "anger" (*cholos*) is the same except for gender as the common Greek word for "bile" or "gall" (*chole*); once in Homer it seems to have a physiological sense: "Your mother nursed you on *cholos*!" (*Iliad* 16.203). The liver, which secretes bile, was thought to be the seat of deep emotions, perhaps of life itself, though *cholos* and its kindred terms nearly always had the narrower sense of bitter wrath.

Black bile (*chole melaina*) had more or less the same sense at first as bile alone; later, under the term *melancholia*, it was distinguished from it. Another synonym is "choler," from Latin *cholera*, from Greek *cholera*, the disease (which expels bile and other fluids from the body); it came to mean "anger" when its sense was replaced by that of *chole*. A "choleric" person is irascible. Chaucer's Reeve is introduced as "a sclendre colerik man" of whom everyone is afraid (*CT* Pro. 587).

In Latin literature "bile" (*bilis*) also means "anger." Martial speaks of the "heat of my anger" (*bilis…ardor*) (6.64.24); Horace writes, "often your uproar has moved my bile, often my mirth" (*Epistles* 1.19.20). In English "bilious" also means "irascible." Of a woman's brief stormy rage, Byron writes, "Nought's more sublime than energetic bile" (*Don Juan* 5.1076).

More common in English literature than "bile" is "gall" (from Old English, related to "yellow" and *chole*); it tended to mean a bitter, grudging anger rather than a hot, fiery one, and then anything bitter. Chaucer's Criseyde sees her pleasure and joy "al torned into galle" (*TC* 5.732). To Spenser's Envie, "whose nature is to grieve and grudge at all," the sight of something praiseworthy "makes her eat her gall" (*FQ* 5.12.31). Gall and honey are often paired as contrasts. Duessa speaks "With fowle words tempring faire, soure gall with hony sweet" (*FQ* 1.7.3); Ralegh's nymph argues "A honey tongue, a heart of gall, / Is fancy's spring, but sorrow's fall" ("The Nymph's Reply" 11–12).

Even more common is "spleen" (from Greek and Latin *splen*), which by Shakespeare's day could mean violent ill-humor or irascible temper. Spenser's allegorical character Wrath suffers from "swelling Splene" (*FQ* 1.4.35). Shakespeare's Talbot tells how "leaden age" was "Quickened with youthful spleen and warlike rage" (*1H6* 4.6.12–13); "the unruly spleen / Of Tybalt" leads to the fatal fight with Romeo (*RJ* 3.1.155–56). But its earlier and nearly opposite sense of "merriment" or "gaiety" is also found in Shakespeare, as in the phrase "over-merry spleen" (*Shrew* Ind. 136). Its modern sense is much the same as "bile," and the adjective "splenetic" is yet another near-synonym for "choleric."

In the seventeenth and eighteenth century "spleen" tended to mean "dejection" or "melancholy," but with a connotation of oversensitivity or deliberate posturing. Gulliver observes that spleen afflicts only the lazy, luxurious, and rich (Swift, *Gulliver's Travels*, 4.7). It soon seemed to afflict the English more than anyone else. Boswell introduces *The Hypochondriack* to an "England, where the malady known by the denomination of melancholy, hypochondria, spleen, or vapours, has long been supposed almost universal." The French equivalent was *ennui*, borrowed by English, though it is less intense than spleen, closer to boredom or world-weariness. Byron seems to equate the two, and is thus misleading in denying there is a comparable English word: "For *ennui* is a growth of English root, / Though nameless in our language: – we retort / The fact for words, and let the French translate / That awful yawn which sleep can not abate" (*Don Juan* 13.805–08). French for its part borrowed "spleen," which is most notable in the titles of several poems by Baudelaire (e.g., "Le Spleen"). Pushkin's Eugene Onegin suffers from it, as many Russians did: "A malady, the cause of which / 'tis high time were discovered, / similar to the English 'spleen' – / in short, the Russian 'chondria' – / possessed him by degrees" (1.38.1–5).

See **Humor, Liver, Melancholy, Yellow**.

Bird   The symbolism of birds is sometimes metonymical in origin, as when larks represent dawn and nightingales night, or swallows and cuckoos stand for the arrival of spring, because the birds belong to these phenomena. More often it is metaphorical, as when cuckoos stand for cuckoldry, or nightingales and swans symbolize poets, because the birds resemble them. Claude Lévi-Stauss claims that "Birds are given human christian names" (e.g., Polly, Robin, Bob) "because they can be permitted to resemble men for the very reason that they are so different.... they form a community which is independent of our own but, precisely because of this independence, appears to us like another society, homologous to that in which we live: birds love freedom; they build them-selves homes in which they live a family life and nurture their young; they often engage in social relations with other members of their species; and they communicate with them by acoustic means recalling articulated language. Consequently everything objective conspires to make us think of the bird world as a metaphorical human society." Dogs, by contrast, being domesti-cated and therefore metonymical with human life, are typically given special dog names (Fido, Rover, Flush) to set them apart. (See *Savage Mind* 204–05.) Since at least Aristophanes' *The Birds*, western literature has been rich with metaphorical bird-communities; one allegorical variety common in the Middle Ages was the bird conclave, such as Chaucer's *Parliament of Fowls*.

Because they can fly, and seem to link the sky with the earth and sea, birds also resemble gods, so the ancients often considered birds either incarnations of gods or their messengers. In Homer's *Odyssey* Athena is disguised as a "bird" (1.320), a vulture (3.372), and a swallow (22.240); Hermes as a gull or tern (5.51); Leucothea as a shearwater or gannet (5.337). Zeus famously descended as a swan to Leda. Many gods, moreover, had heraldic or familar birds: Zeus the eagle, Athena the owl, Apollo the swan or raven, Aphrodite the dove, and so on. In Christian myth it was a heavenly dove that filled Mary with the Holy Spirit; it is usually depicted as speaking (the Word) into her ear. As messengers of the gods birds spoke sometimes through their flight patterns, and so arose the immemorial art of bird-augury, where an *auspex* (Latin, from *aui-* "bird" + *spek-* "watch") decided whether or not the patterns were "auspicious."

Homer and other Greeks imagined the dead in Hades as birdlike (*Odyssey* 11.605); sometimes souls (*psychai*) are batlike (24.6–9); or the soul (*thymos*) is said to fly (*Iliad* 16.469). Christians likened the rebirth of the soul to that of the phoenix. Visitations of birds were felt to be reappearances of the dead, a thought lying behind Poe's "The Raven." At the same time birds seem to have souls themselves, and to pour them forth when they sing. Thomson imagines that birds in spring "in courtship to their mates / Pour forth their little souls" ("Spring" 619–20) while in autumn they sit "Robbed of their tuneful souls" ("Autumn" 979). Keats tells his nightingale, "thou art pouring forth thy soul abroad / In such an ecstasy!" (57–58). Hardy hears a bird on a winter afternoon: it "Had chosen thus to fling his soul / Upon the growing gloom" ("The Darkling Thrush" 23–24). Contributing to this notion may be the use of "soul" in some dialects of English to mean the lungs of a bird.

In Homer a frequent formula is "winged words," as if speech flies from the mouth like birds. When Penelope does not reply to Telemachus, "her speech stayed wingless" (*Odyssey* 17.57). Plato has Socrates rather playfully compare the mind of a man to a cage and the things he knows to birds (*Theaetetus* 197c ff.). If words can fly, so can a song or poem. Thus Milton's song "with no middle flight intends to soar / Above the Aonian mount" (*PL* 1.14–15). From here we circle back to the identification of poets with songbirds: poets sing like birds, and sometimes they, or their songs, take flight, transcending the mundane life. Thus they often represent freedom or escape from the gravity-bound lower world.

A bird in a cage, or hooded or clipped, might stand for any trapped or exiled person. Ovid in exile likens himself to a nightingale: "Though the cage might be good for the confined daughter of Pandion, / she struggles to return to her own forests" (*Ex Ponto* 1.3.39–40). Baudelaire's clipped bird in *L'Albatros* is a poet. The bird might stand, as in Hopkins, for the soul in a body: "As a dare-gale skylark scanted in a dull cage / Man's mounting spirit in his bone-house, mean house, dwells" ("The Caged Skylark"). It might have spiritual significance in itself, as Blake asserts: "A Robin Red breast in a Cage / Puts all Heaven in a Rage" ("Auguries of Innocence"). See also Yeats's "The Hawk." It has stood in particular for a woman's restricted life in a society dominated by men. The old woman in de Meun's *Romance of the Rose* likens women to caged birds that, no matter how well treated, always search for ways to gain their freedom (13911–36). Spenser tries to persuade his doubting beloved that by marriage she will gain two liberties by losing one, as "the gentle bird feels no captivity / within her cage, but singes and feeds her fill" (*Amoretti* 65). As Mary Wollstonecraft puts it, "Confined, then, in cages like the feathered race, they have nothing to do but to plume themselves, and stalk with mock majesty from perch to perch" (*Vindication of the Rights of Woman*, chap. 4). In *Epipsychidion*, addressed to a young woman confined to a convent until her marriage, Shelley calls her "Poor captive bird! who, from thy narrow cage, / Pourest such music, that it might assuage / The rugged hearts of those who prisoned thee, / Were they not deaf to all sweet melody" (5–8). In *Aurora Leigh*, E. B. Browning describes a woman who "has lived / A sort of cage-bird life, born in a cage, / Accounting that to leap from perch to perch / Was act and joy enough for any bird" (1.304–07).

P. L. Dunbar's poem "Sympathy," which is implicitly about the oppression of black Americans, ends: "I know why the caged bird sings!"

The killing of a bird might be a great sin, as it seems to be in Coleridge's "Rime of the Ancient Mariner"; or it might symbolize the death of a person, as the wild duck in Ibsen's play is linked to Hedvig, who kills herself, or as the seagull in Chekhov's play is associated with Nina, who is seduced and abandoned by the man who has killed the gull.

For catalogues of birds see Aristophanes, *Birds*, passim; Chaucer, *Parliament of Fowls* 330–364; Skelton, *Phyllyp Sparowe* 395–570; Thomson, "Spring" 572–613.

Bird entries in this dictionary: **Albatross, Cock, Cuckoo, Dove, Eagle, Goose, Gull, Hawk, Heron, Lark, Nightingale, Owl, Peacock, Pelican, Phoenix, Raven, Sparrow, Stork, Swallow, Swan, Woodpecker.**

Bird of Jove   *see* **Eagle**

Bird of night   *see* **Owl**

Black   In both Greek and Latin there were several terms for "black" or "dark" with subtle differences among them, but their symbolic associations were similar and almost always negative. The color does not occur frequently in the Bible, but when it does (with one notable exception) it is also negative.

In Homer wine, water, blood, earth, the west, and other things can be black or dark (Greek *melas*) without any particular symbolism, and such applications continue through Greek and Latin literature. More symbolically Death is sometimes black in Homer (e.g., *Iliad* 2.834), as is *Ker*, the spirit of death (2.859). Hades is black in Sophocles' *Oedipus Rex* (29) and Euripides's *Hippolytus* (1388), while Death (personified) is black (Latin *ater*) in Seneca's *Oedipus* (164) and Statius' *Thebaid* (4.528). (For more ancient examples *see* **Death**.) Famine rides a black horse in the Book of Revelation (6.5). Dante's inferno is dark, with "black air" (5.51, 9.6) as well as black devils (21.29) and black angels and cherubim (23.131, 27.113). In Spenser Pluto, the "infernall Furies," and the "Stygian lake" are black (*FQ* 1.1.37, 1.3.36, 1.5.10); in Shakespeare death, hell, Acheron, and Hecate are all black, while we also learn that "Black is the badge of hell, / the hue of dungeons, and the school of night" (*LLL* 4.3.249–51).

Funerals are black in Lucretius (2.580), and Propertius warns of a "black day of funeral at the end" (2.11.4). Hence the custom of wearing black in mourning. Chaucer's Theseus, for instance, meets a procession of widows "clad in clothes blake" (*Knight's Tale* 899). The most famous literary mourner, of course, is Hamlet; when his mother urges him to "cast thy nighted colour off" he claims he feels a deeper mourning that his "inky cloak" and "customary suits of solemn black" cannot express (1.2.68–86).

In Homer and other Greek poets the heart or breast can turn black with anger or grief (e.g., *Iliad* 1.103), as if filled with smoke. Pindar writes that whoever does not love Theoxenus "has a black heart forged from adamant or iron" (frag. 123.5).

Black often means simply "bad" or "evil." Virgil tells of infants whom a "black day" carried down to the underworld (*Aeneid* 6.429; see 11.28). The Romans marked black days on the calendar and forbade business to take place on them. Ovid tells that in former times black pebbles were used to condemn the guilty, white to acquit the innocent (*Met.* 15.41–42). A character in Shakespeare denounces "so heinous, black, obscene a deed" (*R2* 4.1.131), while Macbeth says, "Let not light see my black and deep desires" (1.4.51). Racine's Hippolyte is indignant at "a lie so black" (*Phèdre* 4.2.1087). Milton's Samson feels his griefs fester to "black mortification" (622). A character in Shelley says that one can "stir up men's minds / To black suggestions" (*Cenci* 2.2.157).

As the color of death and mourning, black has been adopted by Christians as a sign of death to this world (mortification) and thus of purity or humility. Spenser's Palmer, a pilgrim who had been to Jerusalem, is "clad in black attyre," and seems "A sage and sobre syre" (*FQ* 2.1.7). Milton claims that black is "staid Wisdom's hue" ("Il Penseroso" 16). Gray echoes Milton when he presents "Wisdom in sable garb arrayed" ("Ode to Adversity" 25).

"I am black but comely," says the female lover of Song of Solomon 1.5, but this translation (the Authorized Version, based on the Latin Vulgate) is almost certainly mistaken about the "but," perhaps deliberately: it should be "I am black and comely," as the Greek Septuagint gives it. The switch in conjunctions bespeaks the history of western prejudice against dark skin, and especially against Africans or Negroes (from Spanish and Portuguese *negro*, from Latin *niger*, "black"). Black writers have had to contend with the almost entirely negative meanings of the color. The American slave Phillis Wheatley accepts the meanings but insists that the color (or its meanings) can be changed: "Some view our sable race with scornful eye, / 'Their colour is a diabolic die'. / Remember, Christians, Negros, black as Cain, / May be refin'd, and join th'angelic train" ("On Being Brought from Africa to America"). Blake, a white sympathetic to oppressed blacks, presents his "Little Black Boy" as in the grip of similar conceptions – "I am black, but O! my soul is white" – but the boy remembers that he has a spiritual advantage over English boys, for the burning love of God (who lives in the sun) has prepared him for heaven. A black character in Harriet Wilson's *Our Nig* asks a white, "Which you rather have, a black heart in a white skin, or a white heart in a black one?" Later writers have rejected the traditional (western) senses of "black" altogether. *Négritude*, a term coined by the Martinican author Aimé Césaire in 1939, was adopted in name or spirit by many African and African-American writers for whom "black is beautiful" and "blackness" is an essence or power.

Gwendolyn Brooks affirms the color-label in the face of euphemisms: "According to my Teachers, / I am now an African-American. / They call me out of my name. / Black is an open umbrella. / I am Black and A Black forever." ("Kojo: 'I am a Black'").

See **White.**

Black sun   When the day of the Lord comes to Babylon, Isaiah prophesies, "the sun shall be darkened in his going forth" (13.10) (see also Joel 3.15). Jesus makes the same prophecy of the final days: the sun and the moon shall be dark, and the stars shall fall (Matt. 24.29). As John of Patmos envisages them, "the sun became black as sackcloth of hair" (Rev. 6.12).

Hugo imagines a dark hell where "a frightful black sun" radiates night (*Les Contemplations* 6.26.186). But Novalis, in his *Hymns to the Night*, welcomes "night's lovely sun" (Hymn 1). Hovering, perhaps, between these two poles, Nerval's outcast prince has a lute that bears "the black sun of melancholy" ("El Desdichado" 4). Alluding to Racine's *Phèdre*, where the queen has harbored a "black flame" (310) and then cannot bear the sight of the sun (1273–74), Mandelstam writes of "the savage sleepless passion of the black sun" of Phaedra, who may represent the murderous stepmother Russia has become (*Tristia*, poem 1). The black sun became a central symbol in Mandelstam's poetry: "I woke in a radiant cradle / Lit by a black sun" (*Tristia*, "This night is irredeemable," trans. Greene).

Blood   "Blood," as Mephistopheles reminds Faust, "is an altogether singular juice" (Goethe, *Faust I* 1740). A substance so vital to human life and so striking in appearance is bound to have many symbolic meanings, but we shall stress three clusters of meanings here: blood as "life" (or "lifeblood"), blood as family or ancestry, and blood as sacrifice.

After the Flood God blessed Noah's family and gave them new dietary laws: they may eat animal flesh, "But flesh with the life thereof, which is the blood thereof, shall ye not eat" (Gen. 9.4; see Deut. 12.23). Life is equated with blood. To "kill" and to "shed blood" are synonymous (Gen. 37.21–22). A murderer is a "man of blood" or (in the AV) "bloody man" (2 Sam. 16.8, Ps. 26.9); he is "bloodthirsty" (Prov. 29.10).

Two words in Homer differing only in accent may well be related, *brótos* ("gore") and *brotós* ("mortal"). Only mortals have blood; the gods do not eat bread and wine like mortals, but nectar and ambrosia, and what flows through their veins is ichor (*Iliad* 5.339–42, 416). Dead mortals are bloodless; to enable them to speak, Odysseus must pour animal blood into a trench for them to drink (*Odyssey* 11.24–50). Horace asks, even if one could play the lyre better than Orpheus, "would the blood return to the insubstantial ghost?" (1.24.15).

From the time of Hippocrates to very recent times blood was taken as one of the four vital fluids or "humors" whose balance is essential to human health and sanity. (*See* **Humor.**) Blood, according to Burton, is "a hot, sweet, temperate, red humour" (*Anatomy of Melancholy* 1.1.2.2); one who has an excess of it is "sanguine," which usually means "cheerful" or "hopeful"; it came also to mean "courageous," as if full of heart (Latin *cor*), the seat of the blood.

Milton describes angels' blood much as Homer describes that of the gods: "A stream of nectarous humour issuing flowed / Sanguine, such as celestial spirits may bleed" (*PL* 6.332–33).

One whose blood is hot is passionate, angry, impetuous. When Byron's Juan gets angry, "His blood was up" (*Don Juan* 1.1471), still a common expression. Cold blood or *sangfroid* is usually thought to be inhuman. "Eager to be held as one of the immortal gods, Empedocles in cold blood leapt into the flames of Etna" (Horace, *Ars Poetica* 464–66); a character in Shakespeare denounces a traitor as a "cold-blooded slave" (*KJ* 3.1.123).

We commonly use "blood" today to mean "ancestry" or "kinship" or "race," though blood has very little to do with it biologically. This usage is not found in the Bible, where "seed" would be used, as in "the seed of Abraham" (e.g., Isa. 41.8), but it is normal in Greek and Latin. In Homer one can say, "You are of good blood" or refer to the "blood of your race" (*Odyssey* 4.611, *Iliad* 19.111); Pindar sings that Aristagoras had "the blood of Peisandros of old" (*Nem.* 11.33–34). Virgil describes "the race [*genus*] of the two branches from one blood" (*Aeneid* 8.142), while Juvenal asks, "What good is it ... to be valued for one's ancient blood?" (8.1–2).

Juno, according to Chaucer, destroyed almost "al the blood / Of Thebes" (*Knight's Tale* 1330–31). Spenser's Red Cross Knight is told he is "borne of English blood" (*FQ* 1.10.64); Spenser equates "noble seed" with "gentle blood" (2.4.1). Shakespeare has the phrase "well-born bloods" (*KJ* 2.1.278), referring not only to their rank but their martial spirit. Racine's play *La Thébaïde*, which is about the war between two brothers born of "incestuous blood" (1.1.33), turns on the value of blood (the word occurs seventy times): Jocaste hopes that common blood will bring peace, but Créon understands that the blood is bad and must be shed.

Occasionally in classical poetry "blood" can refer to a person. "I, blood of poor parents" (=son) (Horace 2.20.5–6); Byblis "hated the name of blood" (=brother) (Ovid, *Met.* 9.466); in a similar vein Neptune is *Nelei sanguinis auctor*, "originator of Neleus' blood" (i.e., his father) (*Met.* 12.558).

Perhaps because "blood" implied relationship, some cultures required that blood be spent in ratifying a bond of brotherhood or any other deep pact among nonkindred; "blood brothers" are not brothers by blood. The devil demands it of Faust, but it is not in fact common in western tradition: the Greeks, for instance, usually poured out wine, not blood, as they swore an oath. There is one biblical case, where Moses concludes a covenant between God and Israel by sacrificing twelve bulls and casting their blood on the altar and the people; this the "blood of the covenant" that creates a new consanguinity among the Israelites (Exod. 24.4–9). Schiller has his Swiss rebels declare "we are one in heart and one in blood" as they take their oath on the Rütli, but they do so by clashing swords and clasping hands (*Wilhelm Tell* 2.2.1202).

Bloodshed demands vengeance. God hears Abel's blood crying to him from the ground and places a curse on Cain (Gen. 4.9–15), though there the vengeance is promised against those who might slay Cain. God tells Noah, "Whoso sheddeth man's blood, by man shall his blood be shed" (Gen. 9.6). "It is law," a chorus of Aeschylus sings, "that bloody drops spilling into the ground demand more blood" (*Choephoroe* 400–02). Macbeth learns that he has, as he feared, taught "Bloody instructions" (1.7.9), which now return to plague him: "It will have blood, they say: blood will have blood" (3.4.121–22).

Christ's blood is the blood of sacrifice, renewing the "blood of the covenant": "This cup [of wine]," he says, "is the new testament in my blood, which is shed for you" (Luke 22.20). The faithful are "justified by his blood" (Rom. 5.9); in him "we have redemption through his blood" (Eph. 1.7). The redeemed in heaven wear white robes, for "they have washed their robes, and made them white in the blood of the Lamb" (Rev. 7.14). Dante sees them as "the holy army / That Christ with his blood took as bride" (*Paradiso* 31.2–3).

See **Purple**.

Blue   Rabelais says "of course blue signifies heaven and heavenly things" (*Gargantua* 1.10). "Blue! – 'Tis the life of heaven – the domain / Of Cynthia," Keats begins a sonnet; "Blue! – 'Tis the life of waters – Ocean / And all its vassal streams"; blue is also the "gentle cousin to the forest green." "The blue of sky and sea, the green of earth," according to Tennyson's "Ancient Sage" (41), are the two great colors of the surface of things.

Because it is the color of the sky (and perhaps because the sea is blue only on sunny days), blue is traditionally the color of heaven, of hope, of constancy, of purity, of truth, of the ideal. In Christian color-symbolism blue belongs to the Virgin. Spenser's Speranza (Hope) is clad in blue (*FQ* 1.10.14). For Shelley, the two hues that nature has made divine are "Green strength, azure hope" ("Ode: Arise" 33). In Chaucer's "Against Women Unconstant" the refrain is "Instead of blue, thus may ye wear all green" – the blue of constancy, the green of the changeable earth. (See **Green**.)

It is so common to see "blue" or "azure" before "sky" or "heaven" – Shakespeare has "blue of heaven," "aerial blue," and "azured vault," Wordsworth has "clear blue sky," "azure heavens" and "blue firmament" – that it takes a feat of phrasing to bring home the blueness and its symbolic resonance. Perhaps Coleridge does so when he claims "saints will aid if men will call: / For the blue sky bends over all" (*Christabel* 330–31); or Shelley, when Beatrice, after her rape, cries "My God! / The beautiful blue heaven is flecked with blood!" (*Cenci* 3.1.12–13).

The Greek word for "blue," *kuaneos* (whence the stem "cyan-" in chemical terms), meant "dark" in Homer and the other early poets. It was the color of mourning: Thetis puts on a *kuaneos* veil when she sees Achilles' fate is near (*Iliad* 24.93–94), Bion calls on Aphrodite to wear a cyan-colored robe ("Lament for Adonis" 4). With Bacchylides and later poets the term seems to have meant "blue" (it is often used of the sea), but its sense "dark" remained traditional (as in the Bion). The Latin term *caeruleus* (whence English "cerulean") modifies sea and sky and other blue things but sometimes also means "dark."

Another Latin word, *lividus*, meant "leaden" or "black and blue," the color of a bruise; we still use "black and blue" in that sense, as Shakespeare did: a character in *Merry Wives* is "beaten black and blue" (4.5.98). It is also the color of death: Virgil uses *livida* for the murky waters of Styx in the underworld (*Aeneid* 6.320), and Milton follows with the "livid flames" of hell (*PL* 1.182). In English "livid" is applied to corpses: Coleridge addresses the dead Chatterton: "thy corse of livid hue" ("Chatterton" 30); Ann Radcliffe writes, "the light glared upon the livid face of the corpse" (*The Italian* 5); while Byron has "thy livid living corse" (*Giaour* 762). It is the living corpse of Gluttony that Spenser describes: "Full of diseases was his carcas blew" (*FQ* 1.4.23). Pestilence was considered blue. Thomson describes the "vapours rank and blue corruption" of "swampy fens" that breed disease ("Summer" 1032); Shelley tells how "blue Plague" fell on mankind (*Revolt of Islam* 3964).

Latin *lividus* also meant "envious" – the hue one turns when filled with spite – and English retains the phrase "livid with envy." A character in Dante's *Purgatorio* confesses, "My blood was so afire with envy that / . . . / the lividness (*livore*) in me was plain to see" (14.82–84, trans. Mandelbaum).

"Azure" has always had nearly the opposite connotation: it is the noble, pure, ideal blue, especially of the clear sky or the Mediterranean Sea. (The word has the same Persian source as "lazuli," as in "lapis lazuli.") It is a favorite word of Shelley's. Leopardi speaks of the *purissimo azzurro* of heaven ("La Ginestra" 162). But some later writers saw the ideal as impossibly distant and indifferent to human suffering. Baudelaire sees a swan turning its neck "towards the ironic and cruelly blue sky" ("Le Cygne"). Mallarmé uses *azur* for the pure ideal toward which his soul sighs ("Soupir"), the "virginal azure" whose air makes his lips hungry ("Don du Poème"), but it is a "cruel ideal" for its "serene irony," its inaccessibility except by glimpses to the tormented poet who tries to apprehend it ("L'Azur"). A blue sky presides over a terrible slaughter in Remarque's *All Quiet on the Western Front*. Darío, on the other hand, tells how a fairy reveals the dawn and a lovely woman's face, filling him with joy, and then "More?...said the fairy. And then I had / fixed my pupils / on the Azure [*Azul*]" (conclusion of "Autumnal," in the book *Azul*). Wallace Stevens uses "blue" and "azure," sometimes in contrast to the green of nature, as the color of imagination and art in such poems as "The Man with the Blue Guitar" and "Sea Surface Full of Clouds"; in the latter he makes five tries at reviving the imagination: "And then blue heaven spread / Its crystalline pendentives on the sea," for instance, or "Then the sea / And heaven rolled as one and from the two / Came fresh transfigurings of freshest blue" (33–34, 88–90). But in the spirit of Baudelaire he also speaks of the sky's "dividing and indifferent blue" ("Sunday Morning" 45).

Blue flower   *see* **Flower**

Boar   *see* **Pig**

Book   That the word "book" occurs over a hundred times in the Old Testament is not surprising given the importance of sacred books to the Hebrews. Books were far less important to the Greeks, who tended to rely more on oral tradition; for all the care given to editing him even "Homer" was never a holy text. Various particular books are named in the Old Testament, some of them otherwise unknown to us, but when the Lord tells Joshua that "This book of the law shall not depart out of thy mouth" (Josh. 1.8) he is referring to the Book of Deuteronomy, whose author uses the same name for it (e.g., Deut. 28.61).

The phrase about Joshua's mouth may have inspired Ezekiel to a more metaphorical usage where the angel in his great vision tells him to eat a scroll written with lamentations – "eat this roll, and go speak unto the house of Israel" – which then tastes as sweet as honey (Ezek. 2.8–3.3); this commissioning of Ezekiel as prophet combines the oral and the "literal" dimension of his culture with revealing awkwardness.

God is the ultimate author. The two tables Moses brings down from Sinai are "written with the finger of God" (Exod. 31.18). There is also a book that names the righteous; the Lord threatens, "Whosoever hath sinned against me, him will I blot out of my book" (Exod. 32.33). This is "the book of the living" of Psalm 69.28 and "the book of life" of Revelation 3.5. In Daniel's vision of the Last Judgment, the Ancient of days sits on a throne "and the books were opened" (Dan. 7.10, elaborated in Rev. 20.12). The names of the rebellious angels, according to Milton, were "blotted out and razed / By their rebellion, from the books of life" (PL 1.361–62). God also writes his law within us, says Jeremiah: the Lord promises "I will put my law in their inward parts, and write it in their hearts" (31.33, echoed by Paul in 2 Cor. 3.3).

The "book of life" easily becomes the book of one's own life. Vigny's Jesus, for instance, pleads with his Father to let him live: "Before the last word do not close my book!" ("Le Mont des Oliviers" 2.2). When we vow to reform ourselves we "turn over a new leaf."

Pindar has the name of an Olympic victor "written on my heart" (Olymp. 10.3). The same metaphor for memory is used six times by Aeschylus; e.g., "the wax-tablets of the mind" in Prometheus 789. Plato likens the memory to a block of wax, which varies from individual to individual in size and softness (Theaetetus 191c). This is the origin of the idea of the tabula rasa (used by Thomas Aquinas), the "blank slate" made commonplace by empiricist philosophers such as Locke. After the Ghost enjoins him to "Remember me," Hamlet vows, "from the table of my memory / I'll wipe away all trivial fond records, / ... / And thy commandment all alone shall live / In the book and volume of my brain" (1.5.98–103).

Mystical Jewish speculation of the Middle Ages imagined the Torah (Pentateuch) as the foundation of the world, and each of the twenty-two letters of the Hebrew alphabet were gates or structural elements in the Creation. In the late Middle Ages the idea arose among Christians that nature or the world is a book to be studied for its truths. That led to the notion of "the two books of God" or "the two revelations" (found also in Islamic thought). As Thomas Browne puts it, "there are two Books from which I collect my Divinity; besides that written one of God, another of His servant Nature, that universal and publick Manuscript, that lies expans'd under the Eyes of all" (Religio Medici 1.15). A soothsayer of Shakespeare's says, "In nature's infinite book of secrecy / A little I can read" (Antony 1.2.10). Milton's Raphael tells Adam that "heaven / Is as the book of God before thee set, / Wherein to read his wondrous works" (PL 8.66–68). Thomson asks, "To me be Nature's volume broad displayed; / And to peruse its all-instructing page, / ... / My sole delight" ("Summer" 192–96).

When the Romantic philosopher Schelling writes, "What we call nature is a poem that lies locked in a secret marvelous script" (Sämtliche Werke [1856–61], 3.628), he is not necessarily invoking God as the author of the script. Coleridge draws from Schelling but takes a more Christian viewpoint: "all that meets the bodily sense I deem / Symbolical, one mighty alphabet / For infant minds"; when the mind grows it shall see God unveiled ("Destiny of Nations" 18–20). Writing of his infant boy, who will grow up in natural surroundings, he prophesies, "so shalt thou see and hear / The lovely shapes and sounds intelligible / Of that eternal language, which thy God / Utters, who from eternity doth teach / Himself in all, and all things in himself" ("Frost at Midnight" 58–62). Wordsworth reverses the relation of poem to nature when he argues that a child who grows up knowing Nature will "Receive enduring touches of deep joy / From the great Nature that exists in works / Of mighty poets" (1805 *Prelude* 5.617–19).

We note finally that the "language of flowers" cult, which flourished in the nineteenth century, could be assimilated to the "book of nature" metaphor. For example, a sonnet by Lassailly quoted in Balzac's *Lost Illusions* has the line, "Each flower speaks a word from the book of nature." *See* **Flower**.

Boreas   *see* **Wind**

Bow and arrow   As the weapon that combines distance, speed, stealth, and piercingness or penetration, the bow and arrow have been recruited since our oldest literature to play figurative parts. Psalm 64, for instance, complains of the "secret counsel of the wicked" (2), who "bend their bows to shoot their arrows, even bitter words" (3), "that they may shoot in secret at the perfect" (4). Shelley enlists this image in his elegy on Keats, whom he thought had been mortally wounded by the bitter words of an anonymous critic: "pierced by the shaft which flies / In darkness" (*Adonais* 11–12).

As the weapon of Apollo, god of sickness and healing, the bow shoots plague upon the Achaeans at the outset of the *Iliad* (1.43–52). Apollo's sister Artemis, an archer like him (she is goddess of the hunt), also has a bow; her association with the moon may have been prompted in part by the shape of the moon as a crescent, "the moon," in Hippolyta's words, "like to a silver bow / New bent in heaven" (*MND* 1.1.9–10). *See* **Moon**, **Silver**.

Because Apollo is also the god of poetry and music, Pindar likens the god's arrows to songs: "from the far-shooting bows of the Muses / shoot a volley of arrows such as these" (*Olymp.* 9.5–8). And so Pindar's own songs are arrows: to honor a victory, for example, "I set my arrow's aim, / As near as I may be to the Muses' mark" (*Nem.* 9.55). And so, again in *Adonais*, the classicist Shelley imagines Byron routing the critics "When like Apollo, from his golden bow, / The Pythian of the age one arrow sped / and smiled" (249–51). Claiming that no peaceful breast ever produced powerful poetry, Lamartine combines Apollo's two sorts of arrows, disease and song: "when Homer's Apollo / Came down from the summit of Eryx / To launch his shafts on the earth, / Flying to infernal shores / He steeped his fatal weapons / In the boiling waters of the Styx" ("Enthusiasm" 65–70).

When Odysseus, disguised as a beggar, finally holds his mighty bow, Homer compares him to a bard with a lyre (*Odyssey* 21.406–11). See **Harp, lyre, and lute**. He then sends his arrow through twelve axe-heads, perhaps symbolizing his twelve adventures or escapades, whereupon he slaughters the suitors. In these climactic deeds Odysseus is revealed as an avatar of Apollo himself, patron of bards and archers, whose feast day this is (20.277–78).

Zechariah prophesies that "the Lord shall be seen over them, and his arrow shall go forth as the lightning" (9.14). This apocalyptic image seems to combine with the climax of the *Odyssey* in Blake's image of the bow which the awakening Albion seizes at the conclusion of *Jerusalem*. It is a bow of spiritual warfare, "a Bow of Mercy & Loving-kindness: laying / Open the hidden Heart in Wars of mutual Benevolence wars of Love" (97.13–14).

In a lower form of metaphorical warfare, of course, "wars of love" have long been fought with "love's sad archery," as Byron puts it (*Childe Harold* 1.72). Io reports to Aeschylus' Prometheus that "Zeus has been inflamed by a shaft of desire" (649–50). The chorus of Euripides' *Hippolytus* sings that neither fire nor stars have stronger arrows than those of Aphrodite sent by the hand of Eros (530–33). Dido, aflame with love for Aeneas, wanders through the city like a doe wounded by an arrow shot from afar (4.69–72). Thus was launched that greatest of clichés, the love-dart, Cupid's bow, the Valentine heart pierced by an arrow. Petrarch exploits it to the full in his *Rime*: Amor takes up his bow and secretly pierces my heart (2), he found the way to my heart through my eyes (3), I might call on him to shoot me with his "pitiless bowstring" again so I might die (36), but I bless the bow and arrows that pierced me (61), yet I shall always hate the window from which love has shot a thousand darts in me (86), and so on, through many contradictions and mood swings. Among petrarchan sonnets in English is Spenser's sonnet 16, which turns entirely on the image of "loves with little wings" "darting their deadly arrows," one of whom aims at his heart. In another, Sidney imagines Cupid, having lost his bow and arrows, receiving two better bows from Stella's brows and infinite arrows from her eyes (*Astrophel and Stella* 17). Desportes makes a vow "by the sweet shafts which Love conceals in your eyes" ("Par vos grâces, ma dame").

Bower   *see* **Garden**

Brass   *see* **Bronze**

Bread   Bread is the fundamental foodstuff of humans. One earns one's bread, begs for bread, prays for "daily bread" (Matt. 6.11), acts the breadwinner, and so on. Bread is the "staff" of life: when the Lord sent famine, "he brake the whole staff of bread" (Ps. 105.16). The Greek word *sitos* meant "grain," "bread," and "food," developing much as English "meal" has; in Homer "eaters of bread" means "humans" (*Odyssey* 9.89), while to be alive is to eat bread (8.222). To "break bread" is a New Testament phrase for eating or feasting (e.g., Acts 2.42). The English words "lord" and "lady" are from *hlafweard* ("loaf-ward") and *hlafdige* ("loaf-kneader").

Even where classical authors tell us that bread was not the original food of humans, they assume bread's priority: Hesiod reports that the terrible bronze race "ate no bread" (*Works and Days* 146), while Ovid claims that "the bread of the first mortals was the green herbs / which the earth gave without solicitation" (*Fasti* 4.395–96).

Bread is thus plain fare, the food of the common people. Horace prefers it to cakes or cookies (*Epistles* 1.10.11), and Don Quixote agrees: "Since we have bread (*hogazas*), let's not look for tarts (*tortas*)" (2.13). All the more perverse for Marie-Antoinette to say, "If they have no more bread, let them eat cake (*brioche*)." She should have known, as the rulers of Rome knew, that the grain supplies must be kept flowing. The cynical Juvenal coins a famous phrase as he observes that the Roman mob no longer meddles in public affairs but "longs for just two things: / bread and circuses (*panem et circenses*)" (10.80–81).

"Bread" in the Old Testament is sometimes used, like "cup," to mean one's portion or lot (*see* **Cup**). The Lord feeds the people with "bread of tears" (Ps. 80.5), and gives them "the bread of adversity, and the water of affliction" (Isa. 30.20). Spenser echoes Isaiah when he has one wandering "in affliction" say, "My bread shall be the anguish of my mind, / My drink the teares which fro mine eyes do raine" (*Daphnaida* 374–76). Shakespeare's Bolingbroke recalls "Eating the bitter bread of banishment" (*R2* 3.1.21). More literal is Dante's description of his own banishment: he knows "how bitter / is the bread of others" (*Paradiso* 17.58–59).

The "unleavened bread" (Hebrew *matzah*) that the Israelites must eat for seven days while awaiting the departure from Egypt (Exod. 12.15) was simply expedient – there was no time to wait for bread to rise – but it also seems to stand for a ritual purification and, re-enacted in the Passover ceremony, a reminder of suffering; it is later called "the bread of affliction" (Deut. 16.3). In the wilderness the starving Israelites remember that they ate "bread to the full" in Egypt, so the Lord promises Moses, "I will rain bread from heaven for you" (Exod. 16.3–4); this is manna (16.15). The Lord "had rained down manna upon them to eat, and had given them of the corn of heaven. / Man did eat angels' food" (Ps. 78.24–25). But Jesus disparages this manna from Moses as not true bread from heaven, "For the bread of God is he which cometh down from heaven, and giveth life unto the world." "I am the bread of life: he that cometh to me shall never hunger" (John 6.33–35). Moreover, at the Last Supper, Jesus passes out bread to his disciples and says, "Take, eat, this is my body" (Matt. 26.26); that, with the wine taken as his blood, is the origin of the Eucharist (*see* **Wine**). Cowper, to give one modern instance, is disgusted with affected preachers who try to "dazzle me with tropes," "When I am hungry for the bread of life" (*Task* 2.423–26).

During the years in the wilderness the people were taught "that man doth not live by bread alone, but by every word that proceedeth out of the mouth of the Lord doth man live" (Deut. 8.3). When Jesus is in the wilderness he tells Satan the same thing (Matt. 4.4). Since Jesus is the Word of God, however, it is he who feeds the faithful – with his word, and with himself as the bread of life.

Breath   Breath is life, and those who draw breath are those who are alive. Homer refers to "all those that breathe on earth or crawl" (*Iliad* 17.447), while Sophocles uses "those who breathe" for "those who live" (*Trachiniae* 1160). Horace equates "breath" (*spiritus*) and "life" (4.8.14), and Statius like Sophocles uses "breathe" for "live" (*Thebaid* 4.559). So Chaucer has "lyf or breth" (*Legend of Good Women* 2031), and Shakespeare has "all the breathers of this world" (*Sonnets* 81). This equation is really metonymy rather than metaphor, since breath is essential to life. The "breath of life" that God "breathed into the nostrils" of Adam (Gen. 2.7) – in Milton's elaboration the "breath of life, the spirit of man / Which God inspired" (*PL* 10.784–85) – is the soul, the *psyche*, the *pneuma*, the *spiritus*, the Greek and Latin terms all connected with "breath." (*See* **Wind**.) "Breath of life" occurs in classical Greek as well (e.g., Aeschylus, *Persians* 507). To die is to "spend breath" (Euripides, *Hecuba* 571); to breathe one's last is to "expire": one of Shakespeare's characters puns, "your breathing shall expire" (*John* 5.4.36). In Spenser a fallen warrior "breathd out his ghost"

(*FQ* 2.8.45). Since in English "death" and "breath" rhyme with each other and with almost nothing else, poet after poet has exploited this accident – Shakespeare for instance several times in *Richard II* – to make points about the fragile evanescent nothing that means life; "life," in Byron's words, is "a mere affair of breath" (*Don Juan* 9.128).

See **West wind, Wind.**

Bronze   The Greek word *khalkos* and the Latin *aes* have been variously translated as "bronze, "brass," and "copper." Probably the usual sense in Homer is "bronze"; the phrase "red bronze" appears once (*Iliad* 9.365), where it may mean "copper" if "red" is not just formulaic. In Greek poetry the word could mean "metal"; Pindar has the phrase "grey bronze" (*Pyth.* 3.48), though "grey" ordinarily belongs with "iron." Apollonius of Rhodes later argued that *khalkos* could mean "iron" as well. Iron was in fact known in Homer's day, but the time he sings of was the "Bronze Age," as scholars now call it (not quite the same as the Bronze Age in classical myth). Even in later settings, where iron was the metal of warfare, battles in literature were often fought with "bronze."

Bronze is the third in the ancient hierarchy of metals. Hesiod names five races, of which the bronze race was third, a race of terrible warriors, while Ovid makes bronze the third of his four ages.

Older English translations are the more confusing because "brass" used to cover what is now meant by "bronze" as well. We now distinguish brass, an alloy of copper and zinc, from bronze, an alloy of copper and tin, but brass once referred to any copper alloy. Pope uses "brass" and "brazen" (the adjectival form of "brass") to translate Homer's *khalkos* and *khalkeos*. "Bronze" was introduced into English in the seventeenth century, from Italian via French (perhaps ultimately from Persian), at first in art-historical contexts and then with reference to its brown color; Pope uses it as a verb: people "bronze their face" in the sun (*Dunciad* 2.10).

As brass is hard and relatively impenetrable, it came to be used of someone impervious to shame. Shakespeare's Kent cries against Oswald, "What a brazen-fac'd varlet art thou, to deny thou knowest me!" (*Lear* 2.2.26–27). Hamlet wants to wring his mother's heart, "If it be made of penetrable stuff, / If damned custom have not braz'd it so, / That it be proof and bulwark against sense" (3.4.36–38; one text has "brass'd"). We still use "brazen" or "brassy" to mean "impudent" or "shameless."

In Rome bronze tablets with laws engraved on them were mounted in public spaces (see Ovid, *Met.* 1.92); such tablets might also record and preserve famous deeds, especially upon tombs. Horace concludes his third book of odes with the famous lines, "I have achieved a monument more lasting than bronze" (3.30.1). In English "brass" is closely associated with the idea of fame. Shakespeare's *Love's Labour's Lost* begins, "Let fame, that all hunt after in their lives, / Live regist'red upon our brazen tombs." The Duke tells Angelo, "your desert ... / ... deserves with characters of brass / A forted residence 'gainst the tooth of time / And razure of oblivion" (*MM* 5.1.9–13). This use is synonymous with "marble," as in Shakespeare's Sonnet 55: "Not marble nor the gilded monuments / Of princes ... "). Ben Jonson thinks his country should have written the name of Lord Mounteagle "in brass or marble" (*Epigrams* 60). Sidney has "brasen fame" (*Astrophel* 28), Pope and Wordsworth both "monumental brass" (*Temple of Fame* 227, *Dunciad* 2.313; *White Doe of Rylstone* 1895). Cowper notes that patriots' names live in "ever-during brass" while martyrs for the truth die unknown (*Task* 5.710); Shelley seems to reply when he claims that fame lodged in human hope will "Survive the perished scrolls of unenduring brass" (*Laon and Cythna* 3747).

See **Metal**.

Butterfly Simply to list the expressive and widely different words for "butterfly" in the European languages is to compose a little poem: *papillon* (French), *farfalla* (Italian), *mariposa* (Spanish), *Schmetterling* (German), "butterfly." The English word evokes the echoing phrase "flutter by"; in Old English it was equally charming: *fifoldara*, probably akin to Latin *papilio*, perhaps from a root meaning "shake" or "flutter."

In Greece there seem to have been few colorful butterflies, and the Greek term for them referred to moths as well, but it is the most interesting of the terms: the "so-called *psyche*," as both Aristotle and Plutarch put it (*Historia Animalium* 551a14, *Moralia* 2.636c), the same as the word for "soul." Greek vase paintings sometimes show a butterfly leaving the mouth of a dying person. Ovid refers to *ferali...papilione*, "funereal butterflies" (*Met.* 15.374), for they were often depicted on graves. The idea is that the soul undergoes a metamorphosis at death, leaving behind its earthbound larval state to take wing in a glorious form. It was adopted in Christian iconography as a symbol of the resurrection. "O Christians," Dante cries, "do you not know that we are worms / born to form the angelic butterfly?" (*Purgatorio* 10.124–25). As Faust's immortal part ascends to heaven, the Blessed Boys sing "Joyfully we receive / this one in chrysalis state" (Goethe *Faust II* 11981–82). The soul ascends to heaven, according to Wordsworth, as "before your sight / Mounts on the breeze the butterfly" (*Excursion* 4.391–92).

The tale of Cupid and Psyche (in Apuleius' *Golden Ass*) does not involve butterfly imagery, though depictions of Psyche as early as the third century BC gave her butterfly wings. In his *Muiopotmos: or, The Fate of the Butterflie*, Spenser has the jealous Venus, remembering her son's earlier love of Psyche, change the nymph Astery into a butterfly. In his "Ode to Psyche" Keats sees "thy lucent fans [wings], / Fluttering among the faint Olympians" (41–42). Shelley reminds us of the traditional symbolism when he describes a cocoon as "an antenatal tomb / Where butterflies dream of the life to come" ("Sensitive-Plant" 2.53–54). As a butterfly vanishes into the seaward October wind, Lawrence cries, "Farewell, farewell, lost soul!" ("Butterfly").

Sometimes a butterfly is a messenger, a kind of angel, that brings grace or a change of heart. Blake's lowly Lilly is "So weak, the gilded butterfly scarce perches on my head. Yet I am visited from heaven" (*Book of Thel* 1.18–19). In two early poems by Frost a butterfly brings him a glad moment amidst gloom ("Tuft of Flowers," "My Butterfly").

It is a commonplace that children chase butterflies. Men follow Coriolanus "with no less confidence / Than boys pursuing summer butterflies" (Shakespeare, *Cor* 4.6.94–95). The sight of a butterfly revives memories in Wordsworth of the time he and his sister chased them ("To a Butterfly").

A fop or fancily dressed courtier is a butterfly. That seems to be what Lear means when he foresees that he and Cordelia will "laugh / At gilded butterflies" (5.3.12–13). Pope declares, "The Fops are painted Butterflies, / That flutter for a Day" (*To Moore* 17–18). Gay asks, "And what's a Butterfly? At best / He's but a Caterpillar, drest" (*Fables* 1.24.41). Shelley scorns "Those gilded flies / That, basking in the sunshine of a court, / Fatten on its corruption!" (*Queen Mab* 3.106–08). One of Byron's characters calls a man "a mere court butterfly, / That flutters in the pageant of a monarch" (*Sardanapalus* 5.90–91).

Occasionally poets have called their poems butterflies. Jean de Sponde addresses his verses as "well-loved butterflies, nurslings of my soul" ("Elegy"). Tennyson reports, "out of painful phrases wrought / There flutters up a happy thought, / Self-balanced on a lightsome wing" (*In Memoriam* 65.6–8). Schumann wrote a set of poems called *Schmetterlinge*, and then composed a set of dance-like piano pieces called *Papillons* (op. 2), which he thought of as a masked ball transformed into music; the German word for "mask" here is *Larve*, which also means "larva." Chopin also wrote an Etude (opus 25, no. 9) called *papillon*. *Papillon* also meant a sheet of paper bound in a book.

C

Cage *see* **Bird**

Castle *see* **Siege**

Caterpillar The caterpillar appears in the Old Testament as a pest that devours crops; it is included with "pestilence, blasting, mildew, locust" (1 Kgs 8.37, 2 Chr. 6.28) and associated with the locust as one of the plagues of Egypt (Pss. 78.46, 105.34). Jeremiah prophesies that Babylon will be filled with men "as with caterpillers" (51.14, 27).

The English name for them probably derives from Old French *catepelose* ("hairy cat"), but it was taken to be a compound with "piller," meaning "pillager": the larvae pillage fields and gardens. As parasites they became symbols of social hangers-on and dependents. Shakespeare's Bolingbroke has it in for King Richard's friends, "Bushy, Bagot, and their complices, / The cater-pillars of the commonwealth, / Which I have sworn to weed and pluck away" (2.3.164–66). Jack Cade and his rebels are more radical: "All scholars, lawyers, courtiers, gentlemen, / They call false caterpillars and intend their death" (*2H6* 4.4.36–37). Blake continues this populist imagery in his attack against priestcraft. "As the caterpiller chooses the fairest leaves to lay her eggs on, so the priest lays his curse on the fairest joys" (*Marriage of Heaven and Hell* 9); in his story of the tree of religion or Mystery Blake means priests when he writes, "And the Catterpiller and Fly, / Feed on the Mystery" ("Human Abstract").

In English poetic diction "worm" sometimes serves for "caterpillar." The cankerworm (sometimes simply "canker") is really a caterpillar, for instance. The loss of Lycidas, says Milton, is "As killing as the Canker to the Rose" ("Lycidas" 45). Blake's "invisible worm" that destroys the rose is the same creature ("Sick Rose"). Some sort of metamorphosis-capable insect must be "the worm" that Byron says "at last disdains her shatter'd cell" (*Childe Harold* 2.45).

See **Butterfly, Worm.**

Cave   Caves in the Bible are burial sites: Abraham buries Sarah in a cave (Gen. 23.19) and Lazarus is buried in one when Christ comes to him (John 11.38). They are also refuges or hiding places: Lot dwells in a cave with his daughters after Sodom is destroyed (Gen. 19.30), the five kings flee to one (Josh. 10.16), the Israelites hide in them to avoid the Philistines (1 Sam. 13.6), and Isaiah prophesies that on the day of the Lord "they shall go into the holes of the rocks, and into the caves of the earth, for fear of the Lord" (Isa. 2.19). In these caves there seems to be little symbolic resonance. The cave that David flees to, "the cave Adullam" (1 Sam. 22.1), is sometimes alluded to; a character in Scott's *Old Mortality* (chap. 43) says, "I like my place of refuge, my cave of Adullam."

In classical epic, however, caves are so common as to be a defining feature of the epic and romance landscape ever since. Calypso and the Cyclopes live in them, for instance, and Odysseus stores his gifts in the cave of the Naiads (*Odyssey* 5.57, 9.400, 13.357). In the *Aeneid* there are caves of Aeolus, Scylla, the Cyclops, the Sibyl, Vulcan, Cacus, and others, as well as the cave where Aeneas and Dido consummate their love (4.124, 165). There are a dozen caves in *The Faerie Queene*, including several that are entirely allegorical, such as the caves of Error (1.1.11), Despair (1.9.33–35), Mammon (2.7.28ff.), and Guile (5.9.8ff.). In Milton Death has a "grim cave" (*PL* 11.469). Caves are where things go when they are not visible or active. In Spenser, Night has a cave where she hides during the day (*FQ* 1.5.20–21); when the moon is absent, according to Milton, she hides "in her vacant interlunar cave" (*Samson Agonistes* 89). Personified abstractions also withdraw to caves. So in Shelley's poetry Famine, Pity, and Poesy all have caves, in Keats's poetry Quietude has one, and so on.

Probably the most important symbolic cave is Plato's in *Republic* 7.514ff. In this cave sit shackled prisoners with their backs to the opening; they have never seen the sun or even sunlight. Behind them in the cave's mouth is a fire that casts the shadows of passing people and objects against the cave's inner wall, which is all the prisoners can see. It is an allegory about the knowledge most people possess; only a few escape to see the sun and real objects. This image of epistemological darkness seems to contribute to Blake's image of the human skull as a cave. In the modern age "Man has closed himself up, till he sees all things thro' narrow chinks of his cavern" (*Marriage of Heaven and Hell* 14). Yet caves might also suggest the depth and not just the opacity of thought or perception. Byron says "thought seeks refuge in lone caves" or "in the soul's haunted cell" (*Childe Harold* 3.43–45); Tennyson speaks of "the Temple-cave of thine own self" ("Ancient Sage" 32). What Shelley calls "the dim caves of human thought" (*PU* 1.659) are also "prophetic caves" (1.252) from which our bright future shall come (see "Ode to Liberty" 49–50). In both Blake and Shelley these caves are dormant volcanoes. Behind this image too is the Romantic notion of the poet as retreating to a cave. Wordsworth remembers "poets who attuned their harps / In wood or echoing cave" (1850 *Prelude*

11.456–57); the prototype was the legendary Ossian, the Gaelic bard who took refuge in "Fingal's mystic Grot" or "tuneful Cave," to quote from two of Wordsworth's three sonnets entitled "Cave of Staffa." A cave is a refuge for Julien Sorel in Stendhal's novel *The Red and the Black*, and a site of primitive mystery and unconscious fears in Forster's *A Passage to India*.

Cedar   Because the cedar, especially the cedar of Lebanon, is very tall but with wide branches, in the Bible it is sometimes an emblem of pride or arrogance. "For the day of the Lord of hosts," says Isaiah, "shall be upon every one that is proud and lofty, and upon every one that is lifted up; and he shall be brought low: / And upon all the cedars of Lebanon, that are high and lifted up" (2.12–13). Ezekiel warns Egypt by telling of Assyria: "Behold, the Assyrian was a cedar in Lebanon with fair branches" whose "height was exalted above all the trees of the field," but God delivered him to the heathen and he was ruined; the nations shook at the sound of his fall (chap. 31).

So Spenser calls the cedar "proud and tall" (FQ 1.1.8) and makes it one of the emblems of vanity in "Visions of the World's Vanitie" (7). Sidney's character Dorus, after pondering the symbolic meaning of many other trees, turns at last to "the Cedar, Queene of woods," as most resembling his disdainful mistress, and prays to her (*First Eclogues* 13.141–54). Jonson's Sejanus boasts that he "did help / To fell the lofty cedar of the world, / Germanicus" (*Sejanus* 5.241–43). A cryptic oracle in Shakespeare's *Cymbeline* claims, "when from a stately cedar shall be lopped branches which, being dead many years, shall after revive, be jointed to the old stock, and freshly grow," then shall Britain flourish (5.4.140–43); a soothsayer explains that the "lofty" and "majestic" cedar is Cymbeline (5.5.452–57).

Chaff   *see* **Wind**

Chariot   *see* **Moon, Night, Sun**

Chess   Chess is the game of kings in two senses: it was for centuries a royal and aristocratic game, and its object is to "check" the opposing king. The name, moreover, is really the plural of "check," from Old French *eschecs*, from Persian (via Arabic) *shah*, "king." "Checkmate" means "the king is dead," from *shah* plus Arabic *mat*, "dead." One of the pieces, the rook, also has a Persian name (*rukh*, of uncertain meaning). We are reminded of the Persian origin of chess in Fitzgerald's translation of *The Rubaiyat of Omar Khayyam*: "But helpless Pieces of the Game He plays / Upon this Checker-board of Nights and Days; / Hither and thither moves, and checks, and slays, / And one by one back in the Closet lays" (st. 69).

The symbolic resonance of chess depends, of course, on whether people are taken to be players of the game or, as in the Omar Khayyam passage, pieces on the board. As it is the royal game, it is appropriate that Ferdinand and Miranda are discovered playing chess in the final act of Shakespeare's *The Tempest* (5.1.171); there they are the happy master and mistress of the game. The black knight of Chaucer's *Book of the Duchess* bewails the fact that he lost his beloved queen at a game of chess against "fals Fortune," who played with "false draughtes [moves] dyvers" (618, 653); it is surprising that Fortune, who ought to be playing roulette or another game of chance, should be playing a game entirely based on skill.

The Old French *Romance of the Rose* describes a battle in chessboard terms (662off.). Sancho Panza seems to have been reading Omar Khayyam, for he describes life as a game of chess: "so long as the game lasts, each piece has its special office, and when the game is finished, they are all mixed, shuffled, and jumbled together and stored away in the bag, which is much like ending life in the grave" (Cervantes, *Don Quixote* 2.12, trans. Starkie). Middleton bases a whole play, *A Game at Chess*, on the pieces, gambits, and goals of chess; it is "the noblest game of all" (Ind. 42), but it is the vehicle of a very current political satire, involving foreign Catholic plots against the English royal house. The "White Queen's Pawn," for example, may stand for Princess Elizabeth, daughter of James I. Some of the characters seem to be both pieces manipulated by others and players themselves. Two later works based on the game are Lewis Carroll's *Through the Looking-Glass* and Nabokov's *The Defence*.

T. S. Eliot names the second part of *The Waste Land* "A Game of Chess," where the game represents a way to kill time – "And we shall play a game of chess, / Pressing lidless eyes and waiting for a knock upon the door" (137–38) – while the queenly figure whose "nerves are bad" dominates a man who thinks he is, or wishes he were, dead. Allusions to *The Tempest* evoke the ideal young couple at their game.

Beckett's play *Endgame* (French *Fin de partie*), named for the final moves of chess, might be taken as a working out of Omar Khayyam's fatalistic stanza, only there is no God to make the moves. The first words of the "king" character, Hamm, are "Me – (*he yawns*) – to play," for he is both player and the least mobile of the pieces, but there are few moves left, and they only bring closer the inevitable checkmate.

Choler   *see* **Bile**

Chough   *see* **Raven**

Cicada   The insect that the Greeks called *tettix* and the Romans called *cicada* is not always distinguished from the cricket, grasshopper, or locust, which have various symbolic connotations in English. In classical literature, however, the "cicada" has quite distinct and consistent associations.

However it may strike our ears, to the ancients the shrill stridulation of the cicada was a pleasant sound. Though there were specialized verbs for its sound in both Greek and Latin, the cicada was often said to "sing" like any bird. A hymn to Apollo by Alcaeus, according to Himerius, tells that when Apollo returned to Delphi in the middle of summer he was greeted by the songs of the nightingale, swallow, and cicada. Socrates in the *Phaedrus* praises the setting of his conversation for its fresh air and "the shrill summery music of the cicada choir" (230c). He later warns that he and Phaedrus must beware of "their bewitching siren song" and tells the legend that cicadas were once human: they are descendants of humans who were so enchanted with music when they first heard it that they sang continually, without stopping to eat and drink, until they died. So cicadas need no sustenance, and when they die they report to the Muses on which mortals honored the Muses' gifts (259a–d).

Theocritus' goatherd in *Idyll* 1 praises Thyrsis by saying "you outsing the cicada" (1.146), and Meleager addresses the cricket (*akris*) as "the Muse of the grainfields" (*Anthology* 7.195).

The cicada's first appearance in literature comes in a simile in Homer's *Iliad*, where the old men of Troy are said to be fine speakers "like cicadas, who through the woods / settle on trees and send forth their lily-like voice" (3.150–52). Just what "lily-like" might mean here is unclear, but Hesiod uses the same epithet for the voice of the Muses (*Theogony* 41); perhaps it means "delicate." Hesiod establishes the cicada's link to summer in *The Shield of Heracles*: "When the dark-winged whirring cicada, perched on a green shoot, begins to sing of summer to men" (393–94; see also *Works and Days* 582–85). Virgil's *Eclogues* (2.12) and *Georgics* (3.328) both tie the cicada to summer's heat. Indeed its link to summer was so obvious that it could be used as a synecdoche for summer: Juvenal writes, if you're cold in the winter, then *durate atque expectate cicadas*, "hold on and wait for the cicadas" (9.69).

Hesiod says that cicadas eat dew (*Shield* 395), and that too became a commonplace. About an underfed calf one of Theocritus' herdsmen asks, "She doesn't feed on dew like the cicada?" (4.16). Cicadas were also thought to be dry and bloodless; that characteristic may lie behind Homer's simile, for old age was taken to be a kind of drying out of the body. The modern Greek poet Sepheris likens an old man to "an empty sheath of a cicada on a hollow tree" ("The Old Man" 12).

Cicada lore comes to a culmination in a charming poem among the *Anacreontea* (34), called *eis tettiga*, "To the Cicada": "drinking a little dew / you sing like a king /...sweet prophet of summer, / the Muses love you, / Apollo himself loves you, / and gave you clear song." Among others Goethe translated it into German ("An die Zikade") and Abraham Cowley and Thomas Moore into English. Richard Lovelace's "The Grasse-Hopper" is based on it.

Several recent poets have taken up Socrates' identification of the cicada with the singer or bard. Dario describes a moment when "The old cicada / tries out its hoarse, senile guitar, / and the cricket begins a monotonous solo / on the only string of its fiddle" ("Symphony in Gray Major" 28–32, trans. Kemp). In an early poem Lorca envies the insect's poetic death: "But you, cicada, / die enchanted, spilling music, / transfigured in sound / and heavenly light" ("Cicada!" 30–33, trans. Brown). Montale in several poems feels at one with a lone cicada, fragile and short-lived, chirring on a treetop.

In English literature one may find "cicala" and "cigale" as variant forms, derived from Italian and French.

See **Dew.**

Clay   The main symbolic sense of clay is human flesh, what Spenser calls "living clay" (*FQ* 3.4.26) or Blake calls "mortal clay" (*Jerusalem* 27.59).

In Genesis "the Lord God formed man [Hebrew *adam*] of the dust of the ground [*adamah*]" (2.7); the Hebrew pun may be duplicated in English with "human" and "humus" (from the same Latin root): man is an "earthling," a creature of earth or clay. A phrase in Job, "them that dwell in houses of clay" (4.19), means "mortals." Isaiah prays, "O Lord, thou art our father; we are the clay, and thou our potter" (64.8). Paul asks, "Nay but, O man, who art thou that repliest against God?... / Hath not the potter power over the clay...?"

(Rom. 9.20–21). In some versions of the Prometheus myth the Titan also made men out of earth (cf. Ovid, *Met.* 1.82–84).

"Mould" is sometimes used in a similar way, as in Shakespeare's Pistol's plea, "Be merciful, great duke, to men of mould," meaning "mortal men" (*H5* 3.2.22). In the coming age of gold, according to Milton, "leprous sin will melt from earthly mould" ("Nativity" 138). Emerson refers to "the Creator of our human mould" ("Naples" 2).

Echoing Job, Cowper believes that "An heav'nly mind / May be indifferent to her house of clay" (*Task* 2.457–58). Writing of broken hearts, Byron varies the potter image: "happy they! / Thrice fortunate! who of that fragile mould, / The precious porcelain of human clay, / Break with the first fall" (*Don Juan* 4.81–84). Remembering those who have died, the mind, says Dickens, can recall "the beaming of the soul through its mask of clay" (*Oliver Twist* chap. 11). When in the body, in Tennyson's phrase, the spirit is "claspt in clay" (*In Memoriam* 93.4).

Blake invokes the root sense of Hebrew *adamah*, "red," in his image of reviving life: "And on the bleached bones / Red clay brought forth" (*Marriage of Heaven and Hell* 2.12–13). For him a "clod of clay" is both death and life; a clod happily sacrifices itself under the cattle's feet ("Clod and Pebble"), while another is a mother to an infant worm (*Book of Thel* 4.7ff.). The title "Clay" to one of Joyce's *Dubliners* stories makes one incident resonate: Maria, blindfolded in a game, touches "a soft wet substance" and provokes an embarrassed silence and whispering, as if she has revealed death in the midst of the game of life.

Clod   *see* **Clay**

Cloud   A cloud can be anything that prevents vision. Since in Greek terms life is seeing the light, as well as being seen in the light, death comes as a cloud: "the black cloud of death concealed him" (Homer, *Iliad* 16.350); Statius imitates the phase in *Thebaid* 9.851. So Spenser writes, "on those guilefull dazed eyes of his / The cloude of death did sit" (*FQ* 1.3.39), and Shakespeare, "Dark cloudy death o'ershades his beams of life" (*3H6* 2.6.62). As sleep resembles death, it also comes in a cloud: a Stygian sleep escapes from the box Psyche carries and "pervades all her limbs in a thick cloud" (Apuleius, *Met.* 6.21), and Spenser has "cloudes of deadly night / A while his heavy eyelids cover'd have" (*FQ* 2.8.24). Perhaps because one is blinded by griefs or sorrows they come in clouds as well: "the dark cloud of sorrow closed over Hektor" (*Iliad* 17.591 trans. Lattimore); a cloud fills Ovid's mind as he must leave his wife (*Tristia* 1.3.13); Chaucer elaborates: "right as when the sonne shyneth brighte / In March, that chaungeth ofte tyme his face, / And that a cloude is put with wynd to flighte, / Which oversprat the sonne as for a space, / A cloudy thought gan thorugh hire soule pace, / That overspread her brighte thoughtes alle" (*Troilus* 2.764–69).

Homer also has the phrase "cloud of war" (*Iliad* 17.243), as do Pindar (*Nem.* 9.38), Statius (*Thebaid* 4.840), and other ancient writers; one can imagine the literal dustcloud stirred up by battle or the almost literal cloud of flying weapons, but perhaps this phrase is an extension of "cloud of death." It too has become a modern commonplace ("warclouds"). Blake makes good use of the image in *America*, where Orc, the spirit of revolution, rises in red clouds and is surrounded by "myriads of cloudy terrors" (4.10), Albion sends a cloud of plagues (war) (14.4), and Urizen conceals Orc from English eyes by sending down clouds and mists (16.13).

The sky gods of the Greeks, Romans, and Hebrews dwell among clouds. Zeus is called "cloud-gatherer" in Homer, and Jehovah has a "secret place," a "pavilion" of clouds; "clouds and darkness are round about him" (Pss. 18.11, 97.2). As Zeus comes down in disguise lest his naked glory annihilate the mortal that beholds him (Semele's fate), Jehovah "came down in a cloud, and spake unto him [Moses]" (Num. 11.25; cf. Exod. 19.9, 34.5), while at Christ's Transfiguration "there was a cloud that overshadowed them: and a voice came out of the cloud" (Mark 9.7). One might think that the glory of the Lord would be revealed by a parting of the clouds, as if the Lord were the sun shining with "all-cloudless glory" (in Byron's phrase, *DJ* 9.61), but in this life, at least, we need the clouds, which are glorious enough. It is in a pillar of cloud that the Lord leads the Israelites out of Egypt (Exod. 13.21) and at the Second Coming we shall see "the Son of man coming in the clouds of heaven with power and great glory" (Matt. 24.30). According to Milton, God dwells in "his secret cloud" (*PL* 10.32); as Mammon elaborates, "How oft amidst / Thick clouds and dark doth heaven's all-ruling sire / Choose to reside, his glory unobscured, / And with the majesty of darkness round / Covers his throne" (2.263–67). Even to the Seraphim God appears only through a cloud (3.378); his only cloudless manifestation is through his Son, "In whose conspicuous countenance, without cloud / Made visible, the almighty Father shines" (3.385–86).

It is an ancient trope that the face is like the sky over which clouds may pass and from which tears may rain. Sophocles' Ismene has "a cloud on her brow" (*Antigone* 528), and so does Euripides' Phaedra (*Hippolytus* 173). Horace advises a friend, "Lift the cloud from your brow" (*Epistles* 1.18.94). "Clear up," one of Shakespeare's characters echoes, "that cloudy countenance" (*Titus* 1.1.266). "Let clouds bedimme my face," Sidney asks, "breake in mine eye" (*Astrophil* 64). Spenser likens his lady's smile to "sunshine when cloudy looks are cleared" (*Amoretti* 40). And so on, as late as Frost: "A cloud shadow crossed her face" ("Cloud Shadow").

In 1803 Luke Howard established the modern nomenclature of clouds and inspired a great deal of interest in them: Constable, Turner, Friedrich, and other painters studied them carefully, and among other writers Goethe and Shelley took note of Howard's terms. One of them, "cirrus," Latin for "lock" or "curl," may have led to Shelley's description of "The locks of the approaching storm" as "the bright hair uplifted from the head / Of some fierce Maenad" ("Ode to the West Wind" 20–23); see also his poem "The Cloud."

See **Rain, Sun**.

Cock   The cock, or rooster (Greek *alectruon*, Latin *gallus*), is the herald of dawn. Theognis speaks of "dawn, at the sound of the rousing roosters" (864); Simonides calls them "day-sounding" (frag. 80B). Theocritus concludes his epithalamion to Helen by promising to return when "the first singer" crows, perhaps a decorative phrase for cock (18.56). "Before the cocks sing" means "early" in Plautus' *Miles* 689. The cock is not found in epic – it may have been thought too homely, or out of place in a military camp; the birds whose "morning songs" awaken Evander in Virgil's *Aeneid* may be martins (8.455–56).

Chaucer charmingly lists "The kok, that orloge is of thorpes lyte" ("the clock of little villages") (*Parliament of Fowls* 350). In Spenser, "chearefull Chaunticlere with his note shrill" warns of dawn (*FQ* 1.2.1). Horatio explains that "The cock, that is the trumpet to the morn, / Doth with his lofty and shrill-sounding throat / Awake the god of day," and repeats the ancient belief that ghosts withdraw at his crowing (*Hamlet* 1.1.155–61); moreover at Christmas "This bird of dawning singeth all night long," as if heralding the divine Sun (1.1.165). (See **Sun**.)

Aristophanes has the phrase, "the second cock sounded" (*Ecclesiazusae* 390). Chaucer writes, "When that the first cok hath crowe" (*Miller's Tale* 3687) and "Til that the thridde [third] cok bigan to synge" (*Reeve's Tale* 4233). Macbeth's Porter explains, "we were carousing till the second cock" (2.3.24), while Edgar explains the Flibbertigibbet "walks till the first cock" (*Lear* 3.4.113). It hardly seems possible that these numbers mean anything precise, but conventionally the three crowings take place at midnight, three, and an hour before dawn. So Tolstoy writes, "The cocks were crowing for the third time and the dawn was breaking" ("Family Happiness" sec. 3).

The most famous cock-crow in the Bible is the one Jesus predicts will end the night in which Peter betrays him: "this night, before the cock crow, thou shalt deny me thrice" (Matt 26.34); just when Peter denies for the third time that he knew Jesus, "immediately the cock crew" and Peter "wept bitterly" (26.74–75).

Cock-fighting was common in ancient Athens, Rome, and most European cities until quite recently. In Aristophanes "the Persian bird" (cock) is the "nestling of Ares" (*Birds* 833–35). Cocks were noted for their pugnacity and pride.

A "coxcomb" (cock's comb or crest) is a fool's cap and then a foolish, conceited person (who struts vainly). Shakespeare's Kate and Petruchio pun on "crest" as well as "cock" in their badinage: "What is your crest, a coxcomb?" "A combless cock, so Kate will be my hen." "No cock of mine, you crow too like a craven" (*TS* 2.1.225–27).

Cockatrice   *see* **Basilisk**

Color   *see* **Black, Blue, Green, Purple, Red, Scarlet, White, Yellow**

Comet   The first comet in western literature may be the plunging star found in Homer's simile for Athena's flashing descent from Olympus: "As when the son of devious Cronus [Zeus] throws down a star, / a portent to sailors or to large armies of men, / blazing and sending out many sparks, / in such a likeness Pallas Athena sped to the earth" (*Iliad* 4.75–78). Homer does not use the word "comet," and what he describes sounds more like a meteor or what we call a shooting star or falling star. Later translators have taken it to be a comet, however, as we see in this expansive version by Chapman: "as Jove, brandishing a starre (which men a Comet call), / Hurls out his curled haire abrode, that from his brand exhale / A thousand sparkes (to fleets at sea and everie mightie host / Of all presages and ill haps a signe mistrusted most): / So Pallas fell twixt both the Camps" (4.85–89). The "hair" of Chapman's comet is implicit in the word "comet" itself, Greek *kometes*, which literally means "hairy" or "long-haired" and is understood to modify "star" (*aster*). (Less frequent Greek terms included "bearded star" and "sword-shaped star.") The Romans translated (*aster*) *kometes* as (*sidus*) *crinitum* or (*stella*) *crinita*, occasionally (*stella*) *cincinnata*.

The Romans took comets, especially red ones, as signs of impending war or civil commotion. As the stars in their orderly motions represented the normal course of government, a new and striking "star" with a tail or beard must portend disorder or disaster. Cicero writes of "what are called by the Greeks *comets* and in our language 'long-haired stars,' such as recently during the Octavian War [87 BC] appeared as harbingers of great calamities" (*De Natura Deorum* 2.14). During the Civil War between Caesar and Pompey (49–45 BC), according to Lucan, there were many celestial portents, including "the hair of the baleful / star, the comet that portends a change of reign (*mutantem regna*) on earth" (1.528–29).

A particularly famous comet was the Star of July (or Julius), the *sidus Iulium*, which appeared four months after the death of Julius Caesar and during the month named after him; it was taken as a sign that he had been deified as well as an apocalyptic portent. Ovid tells how Venus took up the soul of Caesar, which glowed as it rose, leaving a fiery train (*Met.* 15.849–50). It remains a star, protector of Caesar's adopted son Augustus, who wears it, according to Virgil, on his crest (*Aeneid* 8.681); see also Horace, *Odes* 1.12.46–47. Shakespeare's Calphurnia tells her husband Caesar, "When beggars die there are no comets seen; / The heavens themselves blaze forth the death of princes" (*JC* 2.2.30–31), and Horatio tells Barnardo that just before Julius fell there were such portents as "stars with trains of fire" (*Hamlet* 1.1.120). At the time of Nero, according to Tacitus, "a comet blazed, of which vulgar opinion is that it portends a change in reigns (*mutationem regnis*)" (*Annals* 14.22).

Tasso echoes Lucan's and Tacitus' phrases: "with its bloody streaming locks a comet shines through the parching air, which changes reigns (*i regni muta*) and brings fierce pestilence, an ill-omened light for princes of the purple" (*Jerusalem Delivered* 7.52). Shakespeare's Bedford opens the *Henry VI* plays by calling on "Comets, importing change of times and states, / [To] Brandish your crystal tresses in the sky" (*1H6* 1.1.2–3). Milton, following Tasso, likens Satan to a comet that "from his horrid hair / Shakes pestilence and war" (*PL* 2.710–11); behind that simile also lies Virgil's simile for Aeneas, whose shield spouts flames "as when bloody mournful comets shine red in the clear night" (*Aeneid* 10.272–73).

Copper   *see* **Bronze**

Cricket   *see* **Cicada**

Crocodile   "Crocodile tears" (French *larmes de crocodile*, German *Krokodils Tränen*, etc.) are false or hypocritical tears. In a simile Spenser shows where this odd phrase comes from: "As when a wearie traveiler, that strayes / By muddy shore of broad seven-mouthed Nile, / Unweeting of the perillous wandring wayes, / Doth meete a cruell craftie Crocodile, / Which, in false griefe hyding his harmefull guile, / Doth weepe full sore, and sheddeth tender teares …" (*FQ* 1.5.28). Travellers in the Middle Ages had reported "tears" on crocodiles, and since they could not project human pity onto so ferocious a beast they projected human hypocrisy instead. In a terrible moment Othello, having struck the innocent Desdemona, scorns her tears: "If that the earth could teem with women's tears, / Each drop she falls would prove a crocodile" (4.1.240–41). Dryden's Ventidius foretells that Caesar, when he learns his rival Antony is dead, "will weep, the crocodile will weep" (*All for Love* 1.224). Hypocrisy, looking like Viscount Sidmouth, rides a crocodile in Shelley's *The Mask of Anarchy* (24–25).

Crocus   *see* **Saffron**

Crow   *see* **Raven**

Cuckoo   The cuckoo, like the swallow and the nightingale, is a harbinger of spring. "When the cuckoo first calls in the leaves of the oak," Hesiod tells us, we know it is March (*Works and Days* 486). The medieval "Cuckoo Song" is famous: "Sumer is ycomen in, / Loude sing cuckou!" ("summer" referring here to what we call spring and summer together). Spenser calls it "The merry cuckow, messenger of Spring" (*Amoretti* 19); Wordsworth the "Darling of the Spring" ("To the Cuckoo"). "I should learn spring by the cuckooing," according to Dylan Thomas ("Here in this Spring").

Its call is so distinctive that its name in every European language is imitative: Greek *kokkux* or *koukkos*, Latin *cucullus*, French *coucou*, etc. Germanic forms such as Old English *geac* and German *Gauch*, as they deviated from an original "gook-" sound, yielded to "cuckoo" and "Kuckuck," as if the bird itself gave lessons in pronunciation (though "gowk" survives in northern England and Scotland). In Greek *kokku!* meant "Go!" or "Quick!" perhaps because the sound of the bird in spring meant "back to work" to farmers. In a comment on his "Cuckoo" poem, Wordsworth speaks of "the seeming ubiquity of the voice of the Cuckoo" which "is almost perpetually heard throughout the season of Spring" but "seldom becomes an object of sight" (1815 *Preface*).

But the bird has another distinctive feature: as Aristotle and other ancients noted, it lays its eggs in other birds' nests, and its hatchlings push the other eggs out. As Shakespeare writes, "hateful cuckoos hatch in sparrows' nests" (*Lucrece* 849). (This is not true of the American variety.) Such behavior seemed unnatural; as Chaucer puts it, "the cukkow [is] ever unkynde" (*Parliament of Fowls* 358). It also seemed symbolic of adultery, especially by a married woman who deceives her husband. The word "cuckold" comes from "cuckoo" and refers only to the husband; its equivalent in German and sometimes in French refers, more logically, to the adulterous man. So the famous sound of the cuckoo became a source of fear in husbands, and of merriment in onlookers. Clanvowe calls the bird "the lewde cukkow" ("The Cuckoo and the Nightingale") and Milton "the rude Bird of Hate" ("O Nightingale!"). A character in Machiavelli's *Mandragola* explains that Saint cuckoo is "the most honored saint in France" (4.9). The song with which Shakespeare ends *Love's Labour's Lost* celebrates the delights of spring, but adds: "The cuckoo then, on every tree, / Mocks married men; for thus sings he, / Cuckoo; / Cuckoo, cuckoo: O, word of fear, / Unpleasing to a married ear!" (5.2.898–902).

Cup The most frequent symbolic sense of cup, one's portion or lot in life, is biblical; it is usually God who fills the cup. "Upon the wicked he shall rain snares, fire and brimstone, and an horrible tempest: this shall be the portion of their cup" (Ps. 11.6), but "Thou preparest a table before me in the presence of mine enemies; thou anointest my head with oil; my cup runneth over" (23.5). The prophets often speak of the cup of fury, of consolation, of astonishment and desolation. The Lord tells Jeremiah, for instance, "Take the wine cup of this fury at my hand, and cause all the nations, to whom I send thee, to drink it" (25.15). The cup might be a source of good or ill to others. "Babylon hath been a golden cup in the Lord's hands, that made all the earth drunken" (51.7); "And the woman [Babylon]...[had] a golden cup in her hand full of abominations and filthiness of her fornication" (Rev. 17.4).

In the Garden of Gethsemane Jesus prays, "O my Father, if it be possible, let this cup pass from me" (Matt. 26.39).

In modern literature, except for direct allusions to the overflowing cup of Psalm 23, the "cup" is most often bitter. Shakespeare's Albany promises, "All friends shall taste / The wages of their virtue, and all foes / The cup of their deservings" (*Lear* 5.3.303–05; but see *Pericles* 1.4.52). "How many drink the Cup / Of baleful Grief," Thomson asks, "or eat the bitter Bread / Of misery" ("Winter" 334–36). As he meditates on an autumn scene, Lamartine, feels, "Now I would drain to the lees / This chalice mixed with nectar and gall: / At the bottom of this cup where I drank my life / Perhaps there would remain a drop of honey" ("Autumn" 21–24). "Life's enchanted cup but sparkles near the brim," says Byron; "His [Childe Harold's] had been quaff'd too quickly, and he found / The dregs were wormwood" (*Childe Harold* 3.72–74). In this spirit is Pushkin, in the final stanza of *Eugene Onegin*: "Blest is he who left life's feast early, / not having drained to the bottom / the goblet full of wine" (8.51).

See **Wine**.

Cypress A distinctive feature of the Greek and Italian landscape, the tall, cone-shaped cypress is mentioned only once in Homer, as one of the trees in Calypso's grove. But it early became associated with funerals and tombs, in part because it is evergreen and thus naturally suggests eternal life, and perhaps because, as Byron fancies, "'tis / A gloomy tree, which looks as if it mourn'd / O'er what it shadows" (*Cain* 3.1.3–5). It became, as Spenser puts it, "the sign of all sorrow and heaviness" and "signe of deadly bale" (note to "November" of *Shepheardes Calendar*, and *Virgils Gnat* 216). Virgil mentions altars to the dead with black cypress on them (*Aeneid* 3.64); see also Ovid, *Tristia* 3.13.21; Claudian, *Rape of Proserpine* 2.108; Spenser, *FQ* 2.1.60). Lucan gives the cypress social status when he writes that it is "witness to no plebeian grief" (3.442–43). Horace reminds us that, when we die, none of the trees we have cultivated on our estate will follow us to the grave, "except the hated cypress" (*Odes* 2.14.23). That may have inspired Byron's cynical line that the cypress is "the only constant mourner o'er the dead" (*The Giaour* 287). When Feste in Shakespeare's *Twelfth Night* sings, "Come away, come away death, / And in sad cypress let me be laid" (2.4.51–52), he may be referring to a coffin of cypress wood rather than a bier strewn with cypress branches.

Corneille's Chimène vows, "with my cypress I will overwhelm his laurels" (*Le Cid* 4.2.1196). Tennyson, imagining that if his friend Hallam had not died he would have married Tennyson's sister, remembers: "But that remorseless iron hour / Made cypress of her orange flower, / Despair of hope, and earth of thee" (*In Memorium* 84.14–16). (A bouquet of orange blossoms was often carried by brides in Victorian England.)

In his *Metamorphoses* (book 10), Ovid tells the story of the boy Cyparissus who loved a sacred deer but accidentally killed it, and who in his grief was transformed into a cypress, to stand wherever there are mourners.

D

Daffodil Throughout Europe and North America the daffodil is among the first flowers of the year, often appearing while snow remains on the ground and gone before many other signs of early spring arrive. Shakespeare's Perdita calls for "daffodils, / That come before the swallow dares, and take [charm] / The winds of March with beauty" (*WT* 4.4.118–20). As "Daffadowndillies" they show up in "April" of Spenser's *Shepheardes Calendar* (140). Herrick laments their brevity: "Faire Daffadills, we weep to see / You haste away so soone" ("To Daffadills" 1–2).

Milton bids "Daffadillies fill their cups with tears" for drowned Lycidas (150), though they would not have been blooming when he drowned (in August). The most famous daffodils in English literature are the ten thousand flowers dancing in the breeze along a lake that Wordsworth comes upon; when he recollects them later, "then my heart with pleasure fills, / And dances with the Daffodils," but they seem to have no more specific symbolism ("I wandered lonely as a Cloud").

The name is misleading. It derives from *asphodel*, a very different flower; for a time both "affodil" and "daffodil" were in use. Now the latter is restricted to the Yellow Narcissus (Narcissus pseudo-Narcissus). Its symbolic resonances, such as they are, should not be confused with those of either the asphodel or narcissus.

See **Asphodel.**

Daisy Chaucer correctly explains the etymology of "daisy" in *The Legend of Good Women*: "wel by reson men it calle may / The 'dayesye' [day's eye], or elles the 'ye of day'" (F text 183–84); in Old English it appears as *daeges ege*. The flower resembles a conventional depiction of the sun, often called the day's eye itself, and when the sun sets the "ray" of the daisy closes round the yellow "eye."

Chaucer says he loves the daisy most of all the flowers in the meadow (41–42), and in the first of his "legends" he identifies it with Alceste (Alcestis), the most faithful of wives. Perhaps because some of the other good women were betrayed by their lovers, the daisy might have acquired the connotation of unfaithfulness; Robert Greene mentions "the dissembling daisy, to warn such light-of-love wenches not to trust every fair promise bachelors make them" (*A Quip for an Upstart Courtier*); that connotation may account for Ophelia's giving away a daisy, among several other flowers, though she says nothing about its meaning (*Hamlet* 4.5.181).

Wordsworth calls the daisy "The Poet's darling" ("To the Daisy" / "In youth from rock to rock" 32), and it is true that English poets, at least, have often mentioned daisies, though usually without a consistent symbolism. Wordsworth devoted four poems to them, having sensed in them "some concord with humanity" ("To the Same Flower" 6).

In fourteenth-century France there was a brief cult of poetry, from which Chaucer drew, mainly by Machaut, Froissart, and Deschamps, that praised the *marguerite* (French for "daisy"), where the flower, as in Chaucer, also stands for a woman, named Marguerite. The name comes from Greek *margarites* (from Persian), meaning "pearl"; presumably the flower's color struck French observers as pearly.

Dance In ancient literature as in modern almost any regular movement can be called a dance. The goddess Dawn has dancing floors (Homer, *Odyssey* 12.3–4), perhaps because the beams from the hidden sun seem to dance on clouds. War is a dance: Ares dances "in the dance that knows no music" (Euripides, *Phoenissae* 791) and warriors are the "dancers of Enyo" (Nonnus 28.275). But Peace is also "queen of the dance" (Aristophanes, *Peace* 976).

The best established symbolic dance is the great cyclical pattern of the heavenly bodies. Time is a movement, according to Plato, and the stars dance in an intricate pattern (*Timaeus* 40c); the Athenian in *Epinomis*, attributed to Plato, tells how the stars "move through the figures of the fairest and most glorious of dances" (982e, trans. Taylor). Lucian's "The Dance" extends the metaphor (7). The fullest elaboration in English is Davies's *Orchestra, or, a Poem of Dancing*, which explains how Love formed the "turning vault of heaven," "Whose starry wheels he hath so made to pass, / As that their movings do a music frame, / And they themselves still dance unto the same" (130–33); "Who doth not see the measure of the moon? / Which thirteen times she danceth every year, / And ends her pavan thirteen times as soon / As doth her brother" (281–84). Milton speaks of the "starry dance" and the "wandering fires that move / In mystic dance" (PL 3.580, 5.177–78; see *Comus* 112–14). The traditional "dance of the Hours" is the course of the seasons, but it is an eternal dance; so Milton imagines that "universal Pan / Knit with the Graces and the Hours in dance / Led on the eternal spring" (4.266–68). Emerson calls it "the mystic seasons' dance" ("Monadnoc" 63). "Once the hungry Hours were hounds / Which chased the Day, like a bleeding deer," Shelley writes, "But now –" in the eternity of love, "Oh weave the mystic measure / Of music and dance and shapes of light, / Let the Hours, and the Spirits of might and pleasure / Like the clouds and the sunbeams unite" (PU 4.73–79).

Greek drama included dancing, and indeed probably arose from the dance; our theatre term "chorus" meant "dance," while "orchestra" meant the "dance floor" before the stage. As dancing has always been a part of weddings – we see this as early as the description of Achilles' shield (*Iliad* 18.491–96) – and as Shakespeare's comedies end in weddings, they also often end in dancing; Benedick concludes *Much Ado* by calling "Strike up, pipers,"

Jacques absents himself from the weddings of *As You Like It* by saying "I am for other than for dancing measures," and even the mechanicals' play in *Midsummer Night's Dream*, though a tragedy of sorts, ends with a "bergomask" (5.1.347). Dancing in these instances is choral, communal, and thus an obvious symbol of the uniting of the community around the couple. An almost opposite meaning resonates from the Capulets' masked ball, where Romeo meets and dances with Juliet at the risk of his life.

In modern novels dances are often occasions for courtship, for coming of age, and for significant discoveries, especially for the heroine. Natasha's development in Tolstoy's *War and Peace* can be traced in part through her dancing partners Pierre (1.20), Denisov (4.12), and, at the great ball, André (6.14–17). There are several significant recognitions and misrecognitions, for instance, at the balls of Jane Austen's novels; the ball at Vaubyessard makes a gap in Emma Bovary's life in Flaubert's *Madame Bovary*.

The solo dance of a woman, perhaps most beautifully rendered in Florizel's rapt praise of Perdita – "when you do dance, I wish you / a wave o' th' sea, that you might ever do / Nothing but that, move still, still so, / And own no other function" (*WT* 4.4.140–43) – became emblematic of what Yeats calls "unity of being," an unselfconscious harmony of mind and body, during the nineteenth-century "aesthetic" movement. An interest in Salome's dance (from Matt. 14.6–11) can be traced through Mallarmé, Flaubert, Wilde, Symons, and Yeats, who ends "Among School Children" with a rhetorical question: "O body swayed to music, O brightening glance, / How can we know the dancer from the dance?"

For the Dance of Death, see under **Death**.

See **Time**.

Darkness   *see* **Light and darkness**

Daw   *see* **Raven**

Dawn   Poets since Homer have delighted in describing dawn in all its glory. Perhaps as a reflection of a religious cult common to Indo-European cultures, dawn has been personified as a young woman, *Eos*, *Heos*, or *Auos* in Greek, *Aurora* in Latin; the names are related to English "east" and "Easter." In the Greek myths she is variously the daughter of Hyperion and Theia, the daughter of Helios, the sister of Helios, the mother of the four winds and of Eosphoros (or Lucifer) the morning star, and lover of Tithonos, Orion, Kleitos, or Ganymede. In classical poetic descriptions her connection with Tithonos has prevailed, but for the most part she is described with her own attributes: rosy fingers, a saffron robe, dew, a golden throne, a chariot with two white horses, and so on.

Twenty-two times, mainly in the *Odyssey*, Homer describes Dawn with the identical line: "When the early-born rosy-fingered Dawn appeared." The epithet *rhododaktylos* is perhaps the most famous in Homer. Another fine one is *krokopeplos*, "saffron-robed": "At that time when the dawn star [Heosphoros] passes across the earth, harbinger / of light, and after him dawn of the saffron mantle is scattered / across the sea ..." (*Iliad* 23.226–27, trans. Lattimore). In the *Odyssey* once (12.4) Dawn has "dancing floors," perhaps referring to clouds and mists through which sunbeams seem to dance. She is throned in gold at *Odyssey* 22.197. Tithonos, granted immortality but not eternal youth, remains in bed when Dawn arises: "Now Dawn rose from her bed, where she lay by haughty Tithonos, / to carry her light to men and to immortals" (*Iliad* 11.1–2, trans. Lattimore).

Virgil transfers the saffron color from robe to bed: "Soon early Dawn, quitting the saffron bed / Of old Tithonus, cast new light on earth" (*Aeneid* 4.584–85, trans. Fitzgerald; identical to 9.459–60); "with pallid cheek Aurora / Rises to leave Tithonus' saffron bed" (*Georgics* 447, trans. Wilkinson). Aurora has a red chariot in Virgil: "When Dawn tomorrow, borne from the Ocean stream / On crimson chariot wheels, reddens the sky..." (*Aeneid* 12.76–77, trans. Fitzgerald). Euripides imagines Dawn with a single horse (*Orestes* 1004), while Sappho seems to conceive her as on foot, and gives her golden slippers (123). Ovid once (*Met.* 3.184) calls Dawn "purple" (*purpureae Aurorae*). (See **Purple, Saffron**.)

Modern writers influenced by the classics liked to emulate the ancients in dawn-descriptions. Here is Spenser, dutifully trying to get it all in: "Now when the rosy fingred Morning faire, / Weary of aged Tithones saffron bed, / Had spred her purple robe through deawy aire . . ." (*FQ* 1.2.7). Shakespeare achieves some freshness with "the morn in russet mantle clad / Walks o'er the dew of yon high eastward hill" (*Hamlet* 1.1.166–67). The hill is also a frequent convention in morning descriptions, as in Spenser's "Phoebus fiery carre / In hast was climbing up the Easterne hill" (*FQ* 1.2.1) and Pope's "The Dawn now blushing on the Mountain's Side" ("Spring" 21). Collins has an "oriental" variant of the Dawn goddess in his *Persian Eclogues* (1.13–14): "When sweet and odorous, like an eastern bride, / The radiant morn resumed her orient pride...." It neatly reminds us that "orient" comes from a Latin verb meaning "rise." (See **East and west**.)

Classical writers seem not to have personified evening or sunset, and there are few ancient descriptions of it. Many modern writers, such as Shelley, have been fascinated by it.

In Job 41.18, and in a note to the Authorized Version of Job 3.9, dawn is called "the eyelids of the morning"; the "eye" must be the sun. (See **Sun**.) Blake echoes this phrase when he has spring look down "Thro' the clear windows of the morning" ("To Spring").

From the equation of a lifespan to a day, dawn or morning is infancy or youth. Shakespeare imagines his love in old age, "when his youthful morn / Hath traveled on to age's steepy night" (*Sonnets* 63). (More examples at **East and west**.)

Dawn may stand for the moment of illumination, as when we say "it dawned on me." Wordsworth describes his struggle to compose a poem: "gleams of light / Flash often from the east, then disappear, / And mock me with a sky that ripens not / Into a steady morning" (1805 *Prelude* 1.134–37). Tieck writes, "Like dawn [*Morgenrot*] a blessed memory / Arises out of the dark, silent night" ("Improvised song" 4–5).

The "dawn song" is a genre that expresses the regret of lovers that the day has come that must part them. It arose in twelfth-century Provençal poetry: the *alba*, French *aube* or *aubade*, all from Latin *alba*, "white," presumably modifying *lux*, "light"; in German it is called the *Tagelied*, "day song."

Day   *see* **Dawn, East and west, Sun**

Day star   *see* **Star**

Death   Death is one of the great themes of literature, perhaps more frequent even than love. The myths of many ancient peoples centered on death and the afterlife. Egyptian guidebooks, such as *The Book of the Dead* (not the Egyptian name for it), and the Sumerian story of the descent of the goddess Inanna to the underworld, are the earliest written records. The Mesopotamian epic of Gilgamesh deals largely with the king's quest to find his dead friend Enkidu, while Homer's *Iliad* turns on Achilles' grief for his friend Patroclus. Much ancient poetry is lamentation or elegy. One of the most common terms for "human" is "mortal"; what makes gods gods is their immortality. Descents to the land of death are common epic features since the *Odyssey*; drawing on the descent in book 6 of Virgil's *Aeneid*, Dante devotes the whole of his *Divine Comedy* to a journey through death's three realms.

Death may occasionally symbolize something else, but much more often death is itself represented symbolically, usually as a person. In the brief space of this dictionary we can trace only a few of the more common symbolic features.

In Greek literature death (*thanatos*) is dark. The epithet *melas* ("dark" or "black") modifies *thanatos* several times in Homer, and is found in Hesiod, Pindar, and the other early poets. Death is a dark cloud (*Iliad* 16.350) or shadow (a dozen times) or night: "dark night covered over his eyes" (5.310). A dead soul is a "shade." In Euripides death is "dark-robed" (*Alcestis* 843); in Sophocles the "dark eyes" of Eurydice mean she is dead (*Antigone* 1302). Hades (the realm) is dark as well (Sophocles, *Oedipus Tyrannus* 29); no sun shines in it (*Odyssey* 12.383). To die is to leave the light (Hesiod, *Works* 155, and see under **Sun**).

Death is not fully personified in Homer except once where he and his brother Sleep remove Sarpedon from the battlefield and spirit him off to Lycia (*Iliad* 16.672–83). The god Hades usually supplies this personification, though he is not death strictly but the lord of the underworld; but death can also be called the "lord of corpses" (*Alcestis* 843–44).

In Latin literature death (*mors*) is also sometimes dark, and sometimes pale (e.g., Horace 1.4.13–14). (Orcus, god of the underworld, is also pale in Virgil's *Georgics* 1.277.) In Tibullus Death's head is shrouded in darkness (1.1.70). The phrase "black clouds of death" appears in Statius (*Thebaid* 9.851), and clouds continue to be a characteristic into modern times: "the cloude of death" sits on the eyes of someone in Spenser (*FQ* 1.3.39), in Shakespeare "Dark cloudy death o'ershades his beams of life" (*3H6* 2.6.62), and Tennyson's Oenone calls out, "O death, death, death, thou ever-floating cloud" (*Oenone* 234).

Death is more frequently personified in Latin poetry, and is even considered a god by Seneca and Lucan. From Homer and Hesiod (*Theogony* 756) comes the idea that Death and Sleep are brothers, as in *Aeneid* 6.278. Death has a dwelling and can be summoned from it; so Lucan: "Unbar the Elysian abodes and summon Death / herself" (6.660–01, trans. Braund). Statius imagines Death counting the dead shades for its master (*Thebaid* 4.528–29).

In the Bible, of course, death is not a god, and it is only glancingly personified. Death has an abode, *sheol* (translated as "Hades" in Greek), but it is not described much beyond its having gates (e.g., Isa. 38.10, Matt. 16.18). The Lord asks Job, "Have the gates of death been opened unto thee? or hast thou seen the doors of the shadow of death?" (38.17) ("shadow of death" occurs nine times in Job). Homer has the phrase "gates of Hades" (*Iliad* 5.646, 9.312), Lucretius has "gates of death" (3.67), Virgil gives Orcus a "vestibule" (*Aeneid* 6.273). "To be at death's door" remains a cliché today.

Sheol is personified in Isaiah: "Therefore hell hath enlarged herself, and opened her mouth without measure" (5.14). Hell and Death are never satisfied (Prov. 27.20, Hab. 2.5). Orcus has a throat (*fauces*) in Virgil (*Aeneid* 6.273), and jaws in Apuleius (*Met.* 7.7.4). These passages are the origin of the commonplace "the jaws of hell" and the notion of death as ravenous. "Death the devourer of all the worlds delight" is Spenser's description (*Clorinda* 49); he also writes of the "dreadfull mouth of death, which threatned sore / Her to have swallow'd up" (*FQ* 5.4.12). Death is a major character in Milton's *Paradise Lost*, and one of his prominent traits is his hunger for flesh: "he snuffed the smell / Of mortal change on earth (10.272–73), he pines with "eternal famine" (597) and yearns "To stuff this maw" (601). Tennyson's Light Brigade charges "Into the jaws of Death, / Into the mouth of hell" (24–25).

The "second death," an expression found only in Revelation (e.g., 2.11, 20.6), is equivalent to the "lake of fire" or hell. The shade of Virgil tells Dante that he shall hear howls of despair as each damned soul laments his second death (*Inferno* 1.117). Christ, however, "hath abolished death" (2 Tim. 1.10). John of Patmos envisages the time when "death and hell were cast into the lake of fire. This is the second death" (Rev. 20.14). If death swallows the living, God "will swallow up death in victory" (Isa. 25.8; see 1 Cor. 15.54). "One short sleep past," Donne writes, "we wake eternally, / And death shall be no more, Death thou shalt die" ("Death be not proud").

The final chapter of Ecclesiastes has several striking images of dying and death: "man goeth to his long home, and the mourners goeth about the streets: / Or ever the silver cord be loosed, or the golden bowl be broken [two parts of an oil lamp], or the pitcher be broken at the fountain, or the wheel broken at the cistern. / Then shall the dust return to the earth as it was" (12.5–7).

Death, a character in Euripides' *Alcestis*, bears a sword to cut off the hair of Alcestis (73) (normally done to a mourner rather than the dead). In later literature it is usually a spear or "deathes eternall dart" (*FQ* 3.10.59); "And over them triumphant death his dart / shook" (*PL* 11.491–92). Byron calls him "The old archer" (*Don Juan* 4.95).

Since the Middle Ages death has often been portrayed in ghastly terms, as a skeleton or mouldering corpse. Schiller, following Lessing's essay "How the Ancients Pictured Death," writes that in Greece "No appalling skeleton was standing / At the bedside of the dying one: / By a kiss the final breath was taken / While a Genius let sink his torch" (1800 version 65–68).

It was during the Middle Ages that the "dance of death" or *danse macabre* became a popular theme, probably in response to the bubonic plague or "Black Death"; in it Death leads a dance of people of all ranks to the grave. Scott sets "The Dance of Death" at Waterloo: on the eve of the battle "phantoms wheeled a revel dance / And doomed the future slain" (57–58). Beddoes ends his play *Death's Jest-Book* with a death dance. See also the poems by Goethe and Anatole France and the play by Strindberg, all called *The Dance of Death*. Paul Celan's famous poem "Death-Fugue," about the German death camps, was first titled "Death-Tango."

"Death circles on black wings," Horace writes (*Satires* 2.1.58), and thus enlists the imagery of ravens or vultures, "death-birds," as Shelley was to call them (*Hellas* 1025), for death itself. Statius expands: "Death, sent forth from the Stygian dark, / Enjoyed the sky and as he flew o'erspread / The battle field and called the warriors / To his black maw" (*Thebaid* 8.376–81, trans. Melville). Milton likens the scenting of Death to "a flock / Of ravenous fowl" lured to a battlefield by the scent of "living carcasses" (10.273–77). (*See* **Raven**).

An evocative simile in Job has had a long legacy. "Thou shalt come to thy grave in full age, like as a shock of corn cometh in in his season" (5.6); also man "cometh forth like a flower, and is cut down" (14.2). "All flesh is grass," Isaiah adds, which will wither (40.6–8). The lines from Job, if not Isaiah, would seem to imply that death is a harvester, the Grim Reaper, and so he is commonly portrayed as a skeleton with a scythe. (*See* **Time**.) Byron philosophizes: "All things that have been born were born to die, / And flesh (which Death mows down to hay) is grass" (*Don Juan* 1.1755–56).

Death is the great leveller: mighty conquerors are laid low no less than the wretched of the earth. Horace's pale Death "with impartial foot knocks at poor men's hovels and princes' castles" (1.4.13–14). In this life, writes Spenser, "death is an equall doome / To good and bad, the common In of rest" (*FQ* 2.1.59). In the graveyard Hamlet ponders this fact: "Alexander died, Alexander was buried, Alexander returneth to dust, the dust is earth, of earth we make loam, and why of that loam whereto he was converted might they not stop a beer-barrel?" (5.1.201–05). Shirley writes, "Sceptre and Crown, / Must tumble down, / And in the dust be equal made / With the poor crooked scythe and spade" ("The glories of our blood and state," from *Ajax and Ulysses*). As Gray famously puts it, "The paths of glory lead but to the grave" ("Elegy" 36). Byron wittily combines the agricultural imagery of the Bible with the political connotation of leveling: "Death, the sovereign's sovereign" is the "Gracchus of all mortality, who levels, / With his Agrarian laws, the high estate / ... / Death's a reformer, all men must allow" (*Don Juan* 10.193–200).

As Sophocles' Antigone prepares for her death, she laments that she is to have no wedding song; "I shall marry Acheron" (816); she cries, "O tomb, O wedding chamber" (891). Shakespeare's Capulet tells Paris, "the night before thy wedding day / Hath Death lain with thy wife.... // My daughter he hath wedded" (*Romeo* 4.5.35–39). "Death is the supple Suitor," says Dickinson, "That wins at last" (no. 1445). In "Behind the Coffin," Blok describes a woman in a black veil following the coffin of her betrothed, "As though ... she arrayed herself in a bridal veil against the dust and awaited another Bridegroom" (trans. Obolensky).

Deer Deer have appeared in literature primarily as the object of the hunt, whether literal or metaphorical. (*See* **Hunting**).

"Deer" is the generic term, but many more specific terms arise in English literature: "hart" or "stag" is the mature male (especially of the red deer), "hind" is the mature female, "fawn" is the young (especially of the "fallow" or pale brown deer), "buck" and "doe" are the male and female of the fallow deer; "roe" is a species of small deer. In works devoted to the "love chase" this ample vocabulary allowed for many puns, notably on "hart" and "heart" (and the Middle English form of "hurt") and on "deer" and "dear." Chaucer's *Book of the Duchess*, much of which takes place during a literal hunt, uses "hert" or "herte" 41 times in 1334 lines, usually with at least two senses. Marvell's "Nymph Complaining for the Death of her Fawn" has these perhaps overly clever lines: "Look how your huntsman here / Hath taught a fawn to hunt his *dear*" and "quite regardless of my smart, / Left me his fawn, but took his heart" (31–32, 35–36).

A striking if implicit use of the woman-as-deer metaphor, without a hunting context, comes in Wyatt's poem that begins: "They flee from me that sometime did me seek / With naked foot stalking in my chamber. / I have seen them gentle, tame, and meek / That now are wild and do not remember / That sometime they put themselves in danger / To take bread at my hand." He remembers a wondrous moment in the arms of his beloved, when she asked, "Dear heart, how like you this?"

The stricken deer that dies apart from the herd sometimes carries symbolic meanings. Shakespeare's Jacques moralizes over "a poor sequest'red stag / That from the hunter's aim had ta'en a hurt / ... / The wretched animal heaved forth such groans / That their discharge did stretch his leathern coat / Almost to bursting" (*AYLI* 2.1.33–38). In a Christian allegory Cowper writes, "I was a stricken deer, that left the herd / Long since; with many an arrow deep infixt / My panting side was charg'd, when I withdrew / To seek a tranquil death in distant shades. / There was I found by one who had himself / Been hurt by th'archers" (i.e., Christ) (*The Task* 3.108–13). The stricken deer is a favorite image of Shelley's, who applies it to himself; e.g., "then, as a hunted deer that could not flee, / I turned upon my thoughts, and stood at bay, / Wounded and weak and panting" (*Epipsychidion* 272–74; cf. *Adonais* 297). James Joyce told a friend that the animal he most resembled was a deer. In *Ulysses* Stephen Dedalus, as a dog runs towards him, thinks of himself as a deer: "I just simply stood pale, silent, bayed about" (chap. 3).

Desert *see* **Forest**

Dew In the dry lands of the Old Testament dew is always welcome, as rain is welcome (indeed dew is taken as a kind of rain); both fall from heaven, and are taken as gifts or blessings of God, like manna. When Isaac blesses Jacob (in disguise), he prays, "God give thee of the dew of heaven" (Gen. 27.28); Moses' dying blessing includes, "Blessed of the Lord be his [Joseph's] land, for the precious things of heaven, for the dew" (Deut. 33.13). Zechariah at the end of the Old Testament has the Lord promise that "the seed shall be prosperous; the vine shall give her fruit, and the ground shall give her increase, and the heavens shall give their dew" (8.12). (Dew is not mentioned in the New Testament.)

Dew was thought of as life-giving, indeed as life itself, death being dry, as bones are dry. A phrase from Psalm 110.3, "thou hast the dew of thy youth," might be based on the equation of youth with morning, when dew is found, but it also suggests that dew is something young people have within them. There is a parallel in Greek thought. Homer once calls newborn kids *hersai*, "dews" or "dewdrops" (*Odyssey* 9.222), and Aeschylus, perhaps in imitation of Homer, once refers to the "tender dews (*drosoi*) of lions," meaning their young (*Agamemnon* 141). A famous passage of Isaiah seems to rest on the notion that dew is a vital force: "Thy dead men shall live, together with my dead body shall they arise. Awake and sing, ye that dwell in dust: for thy dew is as the dew of herbs, and the earth shall cast out the dead" (26.19).

In Greek cosmological myth, dew is both generative and nurturing: it seems to fertilize flowers and pasturage, insects were thought to spring from it, the cicada feeds on it. According to Hesiod the Muses pour "sweet dew" on the tongues of princes at their birth to make them eloquent (*Theogony* 81–84). In Euripides and other authors various things can be "dewy," such as spring water, if they are pure or blessed by the gods.

It is but a step from the blessing of dew to blessing *as* dew. So Shakespeare's Belarius asks, "The benediction of these covering heavens / Fall on their heads like dew" (*Cym.* 5.5.350–51). As a symbol of grace from on high dew could be ascribed to any lofty giver, as when Spenser hopes that Love "will streame / some deaw of grace, into my withered hart" ("Hymn in Honour of Beauty" 26–27).

One of the great restorative blessings is sleep, which normally happens during the night as dew falls, so not surprisingly sleep is sometimes likened to dew. Spenser has "sweet slombring deaw" (*FQ* 1.1.36), Shakespeare "the golden dew of sleep" (*R3* 4.1.83) and "the honey-heavy dew of slumber" (*JC* 2.1.230), and Milton "the timely dew of sleep / Now falling with soft slumbrous weight inclines / Our eyelids" (*PL* 4.614–16).

Dew is usually thought of as silver, in part because of its association with the moon. So Spenser: "Cynthia [the moon] still doth steepe / In silver deaw his ever-drouping hed" (*FQ* 1.1.39). The assocation with the moon goes back at least to the Greek lyrist Alcman, who in different fragments calls dew (*ersa*) the daughter of Zeus and Moon and (as *drosos*) the son of Moon and Air.

If the moon brings dew, it was thought that the sun drinks it in the morning. This notion underlies the allegory of Marvell's "On a Drop of Dew," where the sun takes pity on a homesick drop of dew and "exhales" it back to the skies; it is also the basis of some of the imagery of Blake's *The Book of Thel*.

In poetry dew seems to have a special affinity for the rose, though the sheer number of roses in poetry may be one reason for it; there is sometimes an implicit pun on the Latin word for "dew," *ros*. "I'll say she looks as clear / As morning roses newly washed with dew," says Shakespeare's Petruchio (*TS* 2.1.172–73).

In Greek and Latin poetry dew is often a metaphor for tears. "Thickly fall the tears whose pale dew she sheds," writes Sophocles (*Trachiniae* 847–48). Ovid has the phrase "the dew of tears" (*lacrimarum rore*) (*Met.* 14.708; see 10.360), and Seneca writes, "her cheeks are made wet with constant dew" (*Phaedra* 381–82). In an elaborate conceit Shakespeare combines tears with rose: "but see ... / My fair rose wither – yet look up, behold, / That you in pity may dissolve to dew, | And wash him fresh again with true-love tears" (*R2* 5.1.7–10). Milton develops the conceit a little differently: Dalila "with head declin'd | Like a fair flower surcharg'd with dew, she weeps" (*Samson Agonistes* 727–28). Shelley frequently identifies tears with dew, notably in *Adonais*.

Also common in Greek and Latin poetry is the comparison of dew with blood. Agamemnon's blood is a dew, in Clytemnestra's wild imagination, and she is the sown field (Aeschylus, *Agamemnon* 1390–92). In Virgil's *Aeneid* "the rapid hooves scatter bloody dews" (12.339–40), while in Lucan's *Civil War* there is a "bloody dew from the gore of the dripping Medusa head" (9.698).

"Dew" and "dewy" became such staples of Romantic and Victorian poetry – Keats has "etherial dew," "pearliest dew," and "nectarous dew" among nearly thirty instances in *Endymion* alone – that rebellion was inevitable. In "The Man on the Dump" Wallace Stevens discards the traditional imagery of lyric poetry, including his own early poems, and especially dew: "how many men have copied dew | For buttons, how many women have covered themselves | With dew, dew dresses, stones and chains of dew, heads | Of the floweriest flowers dewed with the dewiest dew. | One grows to hate these things except on the dump."

See **Cicada, Rain**.

Dice A die, or pair of dice, can represent both chance and fate: chance if the emphasis is on the throw (assuming the dice are not "loaded"), fate if on the result, which is unalterable. The word "die" comes via French *dé* from Latin *datum*, "what is given" or "fate." "Human life is like shooting dice [*ludas tesseris*]," a character in Terence's *Adelphoe* says; "If the dice don't turn up as you hoped, you have to make the most of how they did" (739–41). As he crossed the Rubicon, Julius Caesar famously said, "The die is cast" (*see* **River**). Since then the image has seemed especially appropriate to the hazard and fatefulness of battle. Spenser's Knight describes his victory over a foe: "his harder fortune was to fall | Under my speare: such is the dye of warre" (*FQ* 1.2.36). Shakespeare's Richard III, in the midst of his final battle, defiantly cries, "I have set my life upon a cast, | And I will stand the hazard of the die" (5.4.9–10).

Coleridge imagines Death and Life-in-death dicing for the ship's crew in *The Rime of the Ancient Mariner*: "the twain were casting dice; | 'The game is done! I've won! I've won!' | Quoth she, and whistles thrice" (1834 version 196–98), thus dooming the mariner to a purgatorial life amidst the dead fellow sailors. Mallarmé's mysterious poem, *Un coup de dés jamais n'abolira le hasard* ("A throw of dice will never abolish chance") seems to be about the act of thinking, or writing a poem: like the captain of a ship on a stormy sea, the poet cannot rely on skill or control alone but must yield to unpredictable chance.

Dog Dogs have long aroused contradictory feelings. Words for "dog" in Hebrew, Greek, and Latin literature frequently served as terms of abuse, as they still do in modern languages. Abishai calls someone a "dead dog" in 2 Samuel 16.9; Jesus enjoins us to "Give not that which is holy unto the dogs" (Matt. 7.6; see also 1 Sam. 17.43, Rev. 22.15). A disgusting canine habit inspired the still common saying, "As a dog returneth to his vomit, so a fool returneth to his folly" (Prov. 26.11, 2 Pet. 2.22). A similar habit led to Horace's report that a man known for eating rotten olives and drinking sour wine was rightly called "the Dog" (*Satires* 2.2.56).

The indiscriminate mating often seen among dogs gave another edge to insults. In Deuteronomy 23.18 "dog" means "sodomite." In Homer dog-terms are applied mainly to women or goddesses, with the distinct suggestion of sexual looseness. In the *Iliad* Helen calls herself a "horrible dog [or bitch]" (6.344), Zeus tells Hera "there is nothing more doglike than you" (usually translated "shameless") (8.483), Hera for her part later calls Artemis a "brazen dog" (21.481). In the *Odyssey* Helen calls herself "dog-faced" (4.145), and Agamemnon uses the same term for the faithless Clytemnestra (11.424). According to Hesiod, Pandora was given the mind of a bitch (*Works and Days* 67). In later Greek "dog" was a common term for "prostitute" (e.g., Aristophanes, *Knights* 765). Catullus wants a "dirty adulteress" to blush on her "dog's face" (42.16–17).

To go to the dogs, to die like a dog, to lead a dog's life – these and similar phrases are common expressions of the miserable status of dogs. Many of Shakespeare's characters resort to dog-terms to express contempt and anger: "Out, dog! Out, cur!" (*MND* 3.2.65); "you bawling, blasphemous, incharitable dog!" (*Tempest* 1.1.40); "You ruinous butt, you whoreson indistinguishable cur" (*TC* 5.1.28–29). "Bitch" and "son of a bitch" are such frequently heard insults in English today that "bitch" has almost lost its original sense.

On the other hand, the dog has always been treasured for its loyalty. "Fido" (Italian for "faithful") is still considered the typical dog's name, though it is in fact rare. The first named dog in western literature is Odysseus' dog Argus, who provides perhaps the most touching recognition scene in the *Odyssey*: "There the dog Argos lay in the dung, all covered with dog ticks. / Now, as he perceived that Odysseus [in disguise] had come close to him, / he wagged his tail, and laid both his ears back; . . . // But the doom of dark death now closed over the dog, Argos, / when, after nineteen years had gone by, he had seen Odysseus" (17.300–02, 326–27, trans. Lattimore). Many ancient heroes and even gods had dogs for hunting or just for companionship.

Both wild and domesticated dogs notably hunt in packs. Over a dozen similes in Homer's *Iliad* compare battle situations to hunting with dogs, the quarry being a lion, a boar, or a hapless fawn. Ares and Mars are sometimes portrayed as having dogs. Shakespeare's Antony prophesies that Caesar's spirit will "Cry 'Havoc!' and let slip the dogs of war" (*JC* 3.1.273).

As both hounds that harry sinners and as symbols of the bestial side of fallen human nature dogs belong to hell: Milton refers to "dogs of hell" and "hell hounds" (*PL* 10.616, 630), and his character Sin, like Scylla, is partly made of dogs: "about her middle round / A cry of hell hounds never ceasing barked / With wide Cerberian mouths full loud" (2.653–55); Milton is alluding to Cerberus, the classical watchdog of Hades. In medieval allegories the devil is sometimes likened to a dog, usually black. Wittily suggesting the urbanity of the modern devil, Goethe has his Mephistopheles emerge from a poodle (*Faust I* 1147ff.). If the devil is the hound of hell, God might be, as Francis Thompson titles his best known poem, "The Hound of Heaven."

Dog star   *see* **Star**

Dolphin   Homer mentions dolphins (Greek *delphis* or *delphinos*) only twice, once as prey for Scylla (*Odyssey* 12.96) and once as a devouring sea-beast in a simile for Achilles (*Iliad* 21.22), quite untypical of its later benign associations. The Homeric *Hymn to Apollo* connects the dolphin, one of Apollo's guises, with the god's oracle at Delphi (495–96); the etymology is questionable, though it is possible that both words are related to *delphys*, "womb." The *Hymn to Dionysus* tells how the pirates who captured that disguised god leapt overboard when he turned himself into a lion, whereupon they were turned into dolphins; it is retold by Ovid in *Metamorphoses* (3.607–86).

The Greeks believed that dolphins like music – Euripides calls them "oboe-lovers" (*Electra* 435–36) – and so they escort ships on which music is playing. With more plausibility, it was thought that a person might be saved from drowning at sea by a dolphin, as Plato notes (*Republic* 453d). The most famous example is the poet Arion, who, when about to be tossed overboard by thieves, begs and gains the privilege of singing a last song, which attracts the dolphins, who then rescue him; it is told by Herodotus (1.23–24) and Ovid (*Fasti* 2.79–118), and cited by Spenser (*FQ* 4.11.23), Shakespeare (*12N* 1.2.15), Shelley (*Witch of Atlas* 484), and many others. Another example is that of Palaemon, son of Leucothea (Ovid, *Met.* 4.31; Statius, *Thebaid* 1.121, 9.331). The sea nymph Thetis rides a dolphin (*Met.* 11.237); in Shakespeare it is a singing mermaid (*MND* 2.1.150).

In Christian symbolism the dolphin means salvation or resurrection and is sometimes linked with the whale of Jonah, himself a type of Christ; in iconography the souls of the dead were portrayed as riding on the backs of dolphins. Milton evokes both the Christian symbol and the classical link with poets as he asks, "O ye dolphins, waft the helpless youth," that is, Lycidas, the drowned poet ("Lycidas" 164). Keats imagines Lycidas in a cave of the Hebrides, where dolphins come to pay devotion ("Staffa" 31–33).

Perhaps because Nereids ride them (Plato, *Critias* 116e), or because the beautiful nymph Galatea's shell-chariot is portrayed as drawn by them, or because they swim in groups, or because the sea itself is seen as the source of life (and of Venus), dolphins are sometimes associated with love or generation. Ovid calls the dolphin a "go-between in love's intrigues" (*Fasti* 2.79). Gellius claims that dolphins form amorous passions for attractive boys (6.8). Goethe makes much of the erotic and generative connotations in *Faust Part II* where Proteus changes himself into a dolphin and bids Homunculus climb aboard (8316–20); after Galatea passes by, Homunculus throws himself into the sea in a kind of sexual ecstasy. In Blake "jealous dolphins," representing a jealous lover, sport round his beloved (*Visions of the Daughters* 1.19). Yeats adopts the dolphin as escort of dead souls but seems to take it also as the body or fleshly vehicle of the soul, which may be purged and reincarnated in the sea: "Astraddle on the dolphin's mire and blood, / Spirit after spirit!" riding on the "dolphin-torn" sea ("Byzantium" 33–34, 40; see also "News for the Delphic Oracle").

Dove   It is a happy accident that "dove" rhymes with "love" in English, for the dove has been the bird of love for as long as we have record. It was the bird of Ishtar and Astarte, the Babylonian and Syrian love-goddesses, as well as of

Greek Aphrodite and thus of Roman Venus. Their gentle cooing and apparent faithfulness to their mates made doves, and especially turtle-doves, inevitable symbols not only of love but of the kindred virtues of gentleness, innocence, timidity, and peace.

The return of turtle-doves to Palestine in April was a sure sign (and sound) of spring, as we see in Song of Solomon 2.12: "The flowers appear on the earth; the time of the singing of birds is come, and the voice of the turtle is heard in our land." "Turtle" by itself means the turtle-dove, not the reptile; its names in Hebrew (*tor*), Greek (*trugon*), and Latin (*turtur*, whence "turtle") seem derived from its call. In the same chapter of the Song (2.14) the beloved is summoned as "my dove, that art in the clefts of the rock," alluding to its preference for dwelling on cliff-sides and in caves; it may be a different bird (*yonati* in Hebrew, probably the rock dove) but it has much the same connotation. As a term of endearment "dove" is found in Greek and Latin as well.

The earliest references to Aphrodite in Greek literature say nothing about doves (and vice versa); in fact the birds that accompany the goddess in Sappho's great *Ode to Aphrodite* (early sixth century) are sparrows. In Homer doves bring ambrosia to Zeus (*Odyssey* 12.63). But doves were associated with the sites of the Aphrodite cult (especially Paphos and Amathus on Cyprus) much as owls were with Athens. The "timid dove" who escapes a hawk in Apollonius' *Argonautica* (3.541–50) is identified as the "gentle bird" of Cypris (a standard name for Aphrodite).

In Latin literature the link is routine. When two doves lead Aeneas to the golden bough he knows them to be his mother Venus' birds (*Aeneid* 6.190ff.). Near the end of the *Metamorphoses* Ovid lists three gods' birds, Juno's peacock, Jove's eagle, and "Cytherea's doves" (15.385–86) (Cytherea is another common alternative for Venus/Aphrodite). Martial mentions "Paphian doves" (8.28.13), Propertius the "doves of my lady Venus" (3.3.31), and so on. They are yoked to Venus' chariot in Apuleius (*Met.* 6.6.2). Chaucer describes doves flitting about the head of Venus (*Knight's Tale* 1962), Spenser has "Venus dearling dove" (*FQ* 4 Proem 5), and Shakespeare has "Venus' doves" (*MND* 1.1.171), "Venus' pigeons" (*MV* 2.6.5), and, like Martial, a "dove of Paphos" (*Per* 4 Gower 32). In the final stanza of Shakespeare's *Venus and Adonis*, Venus, weary of the world, "yokes her silver doves" to her chariot and flies to Paphos (1189–94). Ancient lovers gave doves to their beloveds (e.g., Theocritus 5.96–97). As the bird of Venus the dove occasionally represents lechery (as in Catullus 29.7–8), but that role is usually played by Aphrodite's other bird, the sparrow.

Aristotle wrote that doves are monogamous (*Historia Animalium* 9.7.612b33ff.), and faithfulness to one mate became part of the lore of doves, especially of turtle-doves. Chaucer names "the wedded turtil, with hire herte trewe" (*PF* 355). "As true as turtle to her mate" was a proverb by the Renaissance; "so turtles pair / That never mean to part" (Shakespeare, *WT* 4.4.154–55).

When it is named in Homer, the dove (*peleia*) is usually accompanied by the epithet "fearful" or "trembling" (*treron*), as it is in Apollonius much later. (But it is possible that *treron* is an old word for "dove" itself, related to *trugon*, "turtle," and so on.) In Homer and tragedy, too, the dove is often linked with the hawk, eagle, or another bird of prey. When Hector loses his nerve and flees Achilles, "As when a hawk in the mountains who moves lightest of things flying / makes his effortless swoop for a trembling dove...// so Achilles went straight for him in fury" (*Iliad* 22.139–43; trans. Lattimore). A typical omen is the sight of "a high-flown eagle, [which] carried a tremulous dove" (*Odyssey* 20.243). The chorus of Aeschylus' *Seven Against Thebes* fears the besieging army as an ever-timorous (*pantromos*) dove fears serpents for her nestlings' sake (292–94). In Euripides' *Andromache*, the Trojans turn their backs in flight "like doves seeing a hawk" (1140–41).

It is a widespread image in Latin literature. Omen and simile combine in Virgil's *Aeneid*: "So easily / A hawk ... / Will strike a soaring dove high in a cloud / And grip her as he tears her viscera / With crooked talons" (11.721–23). Ovid has "thus the lamb the wolf, the deer the lion, / the doves on trembling wing flee the hawk" (*Met.* 1.505–06).

Another connotation derives from the Bible. Noah sends a dove forth three times to find out how far the waters of the Flood have receded (Gen. 8.8–12); the second time the bird returns with a fresh olive leaf in its beak, a sign that the waters have shrunk enough to reveal olive groves. In classical tradition the olive came to represent peace, and so had the dove – Horace calls it *inbellem...columbam*, "unwarlike dove" (Odes 4.4.31–32) – and that symbolism seconded the connotation of the dove in the Noah story as confirming the new covenant of the Lord. Thus hope was joined with peace. (*See* **Olive**.)

Jesus enjoins his followers to be "wise as serpents, and harmless as doves" (Matt. 10.16). The Church father Tertullian called the dove the "animal of simplicity and innocence" (*De Baptismo* 8). In passages of great future importance to Christian imagery, all four Gospels describe the spirit of God as "descending like a dove" on Jesus at his baptism (e.g., Matt. 3.16). The dove came to symbolize the Holy Spirit, the third person of the Trinity, as we see in countless medieval and Renaissance paintings of the Trinity or the Annunciation. In Genesis "the Spirit of God moved upon the face of the waters" (1.2). To those Christians inclined to take the Spirit of God as dovelike it was significant that the Hebrew verb translated as "moved" (AV) occurs later (Deut. 32.11) as "fluttereth," used of an eagle over her young; that led to the idea that the Spirit incubated the face of the waters. That idea underlies Milton's famous address to the Spirit, who "with mighty wings outspread / Dove-like sat'st brooding on the vast abyss / And madest it pregnant" (PL 1.20–22). Hopkins's sonnet "God's Grandeur" ends, "the Holy Ghost over the bent / World broods with warm breast and with ah! bright wings."

Two passages from the Psalms – "Oh that I had wings like a dove! for then I would fly away, and be at rest" (55.6) and "Though ye have lien among the pots, yet shall ye be as the wings of a dove covered with silver, and her feathers with yellow gold" (68.13) – inspired the title of Henry James's novel *The Wings of the Dove*, whose main character, Milly Theale, is dovelike in her gentleness and power to comfort.

Dragon   *see* **Serpent**

Dream   Dreams are a ubiquitous feature of ancient, medieval, and modern literature beginning with Enkidu's dream in the *Epic of Gilgamesh*. Agamemnon and Achilles have dreams in the *Iliad*, Penelope and Nausicaa in the *Odyssey*, Aeneas and Dido in the *Aeneid*; Jacob dreams of the ladder to heaven and the promise of the Lord; the stories of Joseph and Daniel turn on dreams and the art of dream interpretation; three of Aeschylus' surviving plays have significant dreams; we could add examples endlessly. In older literature dreams are very often prophetic, and their message may be straightforwardly literal or couched in a dark symbolism that demands a decipherer. Very often they are sent by the gods. It is thus often impossible to distinguish between a dream and a vision, which in turn might be either a waking dream (or trance) or a real heaven-sent revelation.

The symbols in a dream or vision may draw from any of the traditional meanings that this dictionary presents, or they may refer to particular situations unique to the dreamer and interpretable only in context. Dreams are the occasions for interpolated tales within larger narratives; the tales may be told in a different mode, usually more symbolic or allegorical, and they may bear oblique and subtle connections to their frameworks. As dreams are seldom symbols in themselves, but rather gates into the realm of symbols, this entry will be much briefer than the subject might seem to deserve.

In the Middle Ages many whole works were dreams, notably the dream allegories, of which the French *Romance of the Rose* by Guillaume de Lorris and Jean de Meun is the leading example; it begins with a defense of the truth of dreams, and the rest of the long poem is, in Chaucer's translation, "such a swevenyng [dream] / That lyked me wonders wel" (26–27). Dream allegories in English include *Pearl*; Langland's *Piers Plowman*; Chaucer's *Book of the Duchess*, *House of Fame*, and *Parliament of Fowls*; and Bunyan's *Pilgrim's Progress*. The most influential ancient source of dream narratives is Cicero's *Somnium Scipionis*, "The Dream of Scipio," along with a commentary on it by Macrobius.

The formulaic phrase for introducing a dream in English literature was "methinks" or "methought," which does not quite mean "I think" or "I thought" but rather "it seems/seemed to me," hence "I see/saw as in a dream or vision" (sometimes "me seems/seemed" was used). Chaucer, for example, introduces the dream within *The Book of the Duchess*: "thys was my sweven. / Me thoghte thus: that hyt was May" (290–91). Eve uses "methought" four times in recounting her dream to Adam in Milton's *Paradise Lost* (5.35–91).

There are ancient conventions about dreams and where they come from. They are often sent by gods, as when Zeus sends a destructive dream to Agamemnon in Homer's *Iliad* (2.1–34); the Dream is personified and obeys Zeus's command like any servant, and then takes the form of Nestor *in* the dream. Athena sends a dream-figure to Penelope in the guise of her sister (*Odyssey* 4.795–841). In Homer also we find the two mysterious gates of dreams, the gate of ivory (*elephas*), though which deceptive dreams pass, and the gate of horn (*keras*), through which true ones pass (*Odyssey* 19.560–67); the gates are "explained" through puns on *elephairomai*, "deceive," and *kraino*, "fulfill." Virgil adds to the mystery by having Aeneas and the Sibyl depart the underworld (Hades) through the gate of ivory. Since the underworld is the realm of Death, brother of Sleep, it may be appropriate that it has those gates, but it raises questions about the truth of the prophecies Aeneas hears in the underworld that he should leave by the dubious exit. Perhaps, since he and the Sibyl are not dreams, or shades, but still alive, they may be considered false dreams themselves, that is, not really dreams.

Ovid has an elaborate description of the Cave of Sleep, where empty dreams lie about in great number; at Iris' behest Sleep summons Morpheus ("Shaper," from Greek *morphe*) to impersonate Ceyx in his wife Alcyone's dream (*Met.* 11.592–675). This account is the main source of Spenser's similar story, where Archimago sends a sprite down through the bowels of the earth to Morpheus' house to wake him and order a false dream; Morpheus summons one from his "prison dark" and the sprite returns with it through the ivory gate (*FQ* 1.1.38–44).

It is tempting to speculate that there is a deep similarity between the experience of dreaming and the rapt state of attentiveness that ancient oral poetry and song elicited, the "charm" or "spell" (*kelethmos*) that Odysseus casts over his audience (*Odyssey* 11.334); if that is so then the fact that dreams play so large a part in literature should not surprise us. The notion that a play enacted on a stage is a kind of dream, an "insubstantial pageant," is evoked by Shakespeare and other playwrights (*Tempest* 4.1.155). Robin Goodfellow concludes *A Midsummer Night's Dream*, for instance, by calling himself and his fellow actors "shadows" ("shadow" and "shade" were often synomyms for "dream") and inviting the audience to take the whole play as a dream (5.1.414–19). Since a play or any other work of literature was an imitation of life, life itself could be taken as a dream. "We are such stuff / As dreams are made on," Prospero says, "and our little life / Is rounded with a sleep" (*Tempest* 4.1.156–58).

It does not need the analogy with story and drama, of course, to set one thinking that life is a dream; looked at from one's old age, life's brevity and the evaporation of life's illusions readily suggest the equation. Pindar wrote, "man is a shadow's dream" (*Pyth.* 8.95–96); "shadow" (*skia*) might mean "shade" here, a shade being a ghost, in which case there is a suggestion that our lives are dreamt by the dead. Walther von der Vogelweide wondered if he had dreamt his own life: "ist mir mîn leben getroumet?" ("Owê war sint verswunden" 2). Petrarch wrote in a letter to Colonna that his life seemed "a light dream, a most fleeting phantasm." Calderón gave his view in his most famous play, *La Vida es Sueño* ("Life is a Dream"): its leading character, Segimundo, concludes that "all of life is a dream, / and dreams are dreams" (2.2186–87). Poe went one better by concluding (and echoing his title) that "*All* that we see or seem / Is but a dream within a dream."

Poe in part expressed the Romantic view, inherited by psychoanalysis, that dreamers enter a deeper or truer reality than the world of consciousness or reason, that "gleams of a remoter world / Visit the soul in sleep," as Shelley put it in "Mont Blanc" (49–50). Shelley wonders if death, that resembles sleep, might be the portal to truth. After his entranced hearkening to the nightingale, Keats asks, "Was it a vision or a waking dream? / Fled is that music: – Do I wake or sleep?" The first of Yeats's collected poems laments the loss of the ancient world of dreams, "old earth's dreamy youth" ("Song of the Happy Shepherd" 54), and one of the last poems reviews his works and concludes "when all is said / It was the dream itself enchanted me" ("The Circus Animals' Desertion" 27–28). In conferring great, if equivocal, value on the dream in the face of rationalist disparagement, the Romantics were restoring it to its ancient prestige, though without the divine agency that guaranteed it. In the wake of Freud, many twentieth-century writers (notably the surrealists) have exploited the dream in many ways; Joyce's *Finnegans Wake*, for instance, is (perhaps) one long dream.

Dust   *see* **Clay**

E

Eagle   In classical literature the eagle is the king of birds and the bird of the king of gods. Homer calls it "dearest of birds" to Zeus (*Iliad* 24.311); Pindar calls it "king of birds" and "eagle of Zeus...leader (*archos*) of birds" (*Olymp.* 13.29, *Pyth.* 1.9–11); Aeschylus also calls it "king of birds" (*Agamemnon* 113); Euripides calls it the "herald of Zeus" (*Ion* 159). Theocritus names the eagle "the aegis-bearer of Zeus" (26.31); Virgil and Ovid call it "Jove's armor-bearer" (*Iovis armiger*, *Aeneid* 5.255, 9.563, *Met.* 15.386), the armor here referring to the lightning bolt; Horace dubs the bird "minister of lightning" (*ministrum fulminis*, 4.4.1). (Pliny in *Natural History* 10.4.15 says that the eagle is immune to thunderbolts.)

Homer also says that the eagle is the "most perfect" (*teleiotaton*) of birds (*Iliad* 8.247, 24.315), by which he probably means most perfect for omens, Zeus being the "perfecter" or "accomplisher" of events. Several omens involving eagles are sent by Zeus in the *Iliad* (e.g., 12.200ff.) and the *Odyssey* (e.g., 2.146ff.) and eagle omens are common in Greek and Latin literature thereafter.

According to Ovid, it is in the guise of his own eagle that Jupiter abducts Ganymede (*Met.* 10.157ff.), whereas in Virgil (*Aeneid* 5.255) and Apuleius (*Met.* 6.15.2) Jupiter sends the eagle to do it.

The eagle, particularly the sea-eagle (*haliaietos*), by which the ancients may have meant the osprey, was thought to be particularly keen-sighted. We still say "eagle-eyed"; Shakespeare has "eagle-sighted eye" (*LLL* 4.3.226). Pliny tells how eagles can stare at the sun: they force their young to look at it and if they flinch or weep they are expelled from the nest (*Natural History* 10.3.10). Many Latin writers, such as Lucan in his *Civil War* 9.902ff., repeat this legend, as does Thomson in "Spring" (1728 version) 702–09. The "royal egle," according to Chaucer, "with his sharpe lok perseth the sonne" (*PF* 330–31); Spenser writes of the "Eagles eye, that can behold the Sunne" (*FQ* 1.10.47); Blake bids us ask "the wing'd eagle why he loves the sun" (*Visions* 3.12).

Psalm 103 contains the cryptic line, "so that thy youth is renewed like the eagle's" (5); combined with classical passages associating the eagle with the sun, this line led to the legend in medieval bestiaries that eagles in old age fly toward the sun to singe their wings and burn the film from their eyes and then plunge into a fountain or sea. "As Eagle, fresh out of the ocean wave, / Where he hath lefte his plumes all hory gray, / And deckt himselfe with fethers youthly gay, / Like Eyas [young] hauke mounts up unto the skies" (Spenser, *FQ* 1.11.34). A famous passage of Milton's *Areopagitica* varies the legend to make the sun and fountain one: "Methinks I see her [England] as an eagle muing [moulting] her mighty youth, and kindling her undazzled eyes at the full midday beam; purging and unscaling her long-abused sight at the fountain itself of heavenly radiance." Blake follows Milton: the eagle "lifts his golden beak to the pure east; / Shaking the dust from his immortal pinions to awake / The sun that sleeps too long" (*Visions* 2.26–28); so does Shelley: "the eagle, who…could nourish in the sun's domain / Her mighty youth with morning" (*Adonais* 147–49).

One of Homer's omens is the sight of a flying eagle carrying a struggling serpent (*Iliad* 12.200ff.). In that struggle the snake wins, as it does in the related simile in Aeschylus, *Choephoroe* 247ff. Virgil gives a different outcome in his simile: "As when a golden eagle flapping skyward / Bears a snake as prey – her feet entwined / But holding fast with talons, while the victim, / Wounded as it is, coils and uncoils / And lifts cold grisly scales and towers up / With hissing maw; but all the same the eagle / Strikes the wrestler snake with crooked beak / While beating with her wings the air of heaven" (*Aeneid* 11.751–56; trans. Fitzgerald). Ovid has a similar image twice in the *Metamorphoses* (4.36ff., 714ff.), and Spenser has a "Gryfon" and a dragon struggling in flight at *FQ* 1.5.8. The image is central to the symbolism of Shelley's *Revolt of Islam*; see also his *Alastor* 227–32. Blake engraved a drawing of it on plate 15 of *The Marriage of Heaven and Hell*. According to the Norse legend told in the *Prose Edda* of Snorri, an eagle perched in the great tree of Yggdrasill defends it against a great serpent lying among the roots.

The eagle is frequently contrasted with the dove. According to Horace, "fierce eagles do not hatch unwarlike doves" (4.4.31–32). "Our songs avail against the weapons of Mars," one of Virgil's shepherds sings, "as much, they say, as Chaonian doves when an eagle comes" (*Eclogues* 9.11–13). Their incompatibility is so well established by Chaucer's time that his Criseyde can say that "everich egle [shal] ben the dowves feere [mate or companion]" before she forgets Troilus (*Troilus* 3.1496). Shakespeare's Coriolanus boasts "That like an eagle in a dove-cote, I / Flutter'd your Volscians in Corioles" (*Cor* 5.6.114–15). (Frequently, however, it is the hawk that preys on the dove, as at *Aeneid* 11.721ff.)

Sometimes in Greek literature it is not clear if the eagle or the vulture is meant. The bird associated with Prometheus' torment is sometimes taken to be a vulture, though of course it is Zeus who sends his "winged hound" (Aeschylus, *Prometheus* 1022).

In 104 BC Gaius Marius assigned the eagle to the legions as their special badge, whereupon it became the emblem of the Roman Empire; they are mentioned by Propertius (4.1.95). The Soothsayer in Shakespeare's *Cymbeline* reports a vision in which "I saw Jove's bird, the Roman eagle," sign of the "Roman host" (*Cym* 4.2.346–52). It has been adopted by many armies and states since then, including the United States. When Dante ascends to the sphere of Jupiter, he sees a vast eagle composed of shining souls and symbolic of divine justice as well as the universal terrestrial empire (*Paradiso* cantos 18–20).

The eagle also stands for John the Evangelist, based on the correspondence of the four gospel-writers to the four "living creatures" of Ezekiel chapter 1, one of which is an eagle; John is the most soaring and visionary of the four evangelists. As D. H. Lawrence puts it in the opening of "St John," "John, oh John, / Thou honourable bird, / Sun-peering eagle. / Taking a bird's-eye view / Even of Calvary and Resurrection."

For the same reasons the eagle was adopted by Romantic poets as a symbol of the poet himself, or of his imaginative powers. Shelley's soul "in the rapid plumes of song / Clothed itself, sublime and strong; / As a young eagle soars the morning clouds among" ("Ode to Liberty" 6–8). Lamartine addresses "Enthusiasm, conquering eagle," as "I tremble with a holy zeal" ("L'Enthousiasme"); Hugo opens an ode by exclaiming, "The eagle, it is genius" ("Ode 17"). "No sooner does the divine word touch his keen hearing," according to Pushkin, "than the poet's soul starts like an eagle that has been roused" ("The Poet," trans. Obolensky).

Earth   *see* **Nature**

East and west   East is the direction or the quarter of the sky where the sun, moon, and stars rise; west is where they set. Terms for these directions in other languages often reflect these definitions. The Homeric word for "east," *eos*, also means "dawn," while "west," *zophos*, means "gloom" or "dusk"; Odysseus says Ithaca lies "toward the *zophos*," while the neighboring islands lie "toward the *eos* and the sun" (Homer, *Odyssey* 9.26). A later Greek word for "east," the noun *anatole*, also means "rising"; the verb *anatello* can mean "give birth to" or "bring to light"; "Anatolia" is still in use in English to refer to Asia Minor (Turkey), so called because it lies to the east of Greece. Greek *hesperos* and Latin *vesper* mean both "evening" and "west." The Latin participle *oriens* means "rising (sun)" and "east" (whence English "orient"), while *occidens* means "falling" or "setting (sun)" and "west" (whence "occident"). The "firmament," says Chaucer, "hurlest al from est til occident" (*Man of Law's Tale* 295–97); evoking the Latin sense, Pope has "Aurora heav'd her orient head" (*Iliad* 19.1). German *Morgenland* ("morning-land") means the "East" or "Orient," while *Abendland* ("evening-land") means the "West" or "Occident." In English, to "orient" or "orientate" oneself is, literally, to find the east. "North" is akin to words in other European languages meaning "left," which is where north is when one is oriented.

If humans are seen as ephemeral beings, creatures of a day, then their life follows the pattern of the sun. One infers from the sailing directions in the *Odyssey* that to reach Hades, the realm of the dead, one sails westward, or northwestward, following the path of the setting sun into the *zophos*; in Hades there is no sun. Tennyson captures the metaphor nicely in his "Ulysses" – "my purpose holds / To sail beyond the sunset, and the baths / Of all the western stars, until I die" (59–61) – though the last clause is almost redundant. A character in Theocritus asks, "Do you think my sun has set?" (1.102). Shakespeare rather pedantically correlates one's age with the stages of the sun by attributing age *to* the sun: at noon the sun resembles "strong youth in his middle age" but later "Like feeble age he reeleth from the day" and sets (*Sonnets* 7); in a greater sonnet he writes, "in me thou seest the twilight of such day / As after sunset fadeth in the west, / Which by and by black night doth take away" (73). Gray writes, "Thy sun is set, thy spring is gone" ("Spring" 49). Arnold brings out the mythical dimension in his phrase, "western shores, death-place of the day" ("Cromwell" 112).

What Thomson calls the "cheerful morn of life" (*Winter* 7) begins in the east, in "Birth's orient portal," as Shelley puts it (*Hellas* 202). Henry King laments, "At night when I betake to rest, / Next morn I rise neere my West / Of life, almost by eight houres saile, / Then when sleep breath'd his drowsie gale" ("Exequy" 97–100). Wordsworth's "Intimations" ode exploits the full diurnal cycle: our soul is "our life's Star" that "Hath had elsewhere its setting" (59–60), but we must travel "daily farther from the East" until we see our natal light "fade into the light of common day" (71, 76); at the conclusion the speaker still appreciates "The innocent brightness of a new-born Day" but notes that "The clouds that gather round the setting sun / Do take a sober colouring from an eye / That hath kept watch o'er man's mortality" (197–201). Byron, with his usual breezy deflation, speaks of the coming of coughs and wrinkles before "the sun / Of life reach ten o'clock" (*Don Juan* 10.60–61).

There is tradition with ancient roots of the "westering" of empire or the spirit, as if they followed the celestial bodies. The orient is the origin – *ex oriente lux*, as the proverb has it – but light and power have been passing westward, from Asia, to Greece, to Rome, to France or England, to America. Virgil's *Aeneid*, a prime source of this myth, tells how Aeneas leads a remnant of Troy, the city of Anatolia destroyed by the Greeks, past Greece to the destined homeland of Italy or Hesperia, the Western Land. Medieval legends made descendants of Aeneas into founders of other European states, such as Brutus the eponymous founder of Britain. As stars stand for the glory of states or their leaders (*see* **Star**), Queen Elizabeth was celebrated as "that bright Occidental star" (Dedicatory Epistle to the King James Bible). Berkeley's line, "Westward the course of empire takes its way," has often been quoted, especially in America ("Verses on the Prospect of Planting Arts and Learning in America"). Timothy Dwight believed in it: "All hail, thou western world! by heaven design'd / Th'example bright, to renovate mankind. / Soon shall thy sons across the mainland roam; / And claim, on far Pacific shores, their home" (*Greenfield Hill* 2. 707–10).

In his long poem *Liberty*, Thomson traces liberty's progress from Egypt, Persia, and Phoenicia to Greece and Rome, then to the heavens (during the dark ages), then back down to Italy, then through northern Europe to Britain; Britons, "with star-directed prow," will conquer the oceans (4.424). Collins's "Ode to Liberty" briefly rehearses a similar itinerary and ends, "Thou, Lady, thou shalt rule the West!" (144). Gray notes the rather abrupt westering of poetry from Greece, to Rome, and then to Albion ("Progress of Poesy").

Herbert expounds the westering of the Church, from Egypt, to Greece, to Rome, to Germany, and to England. "The course was westward, that the sunne might light / As well our understanding as our sight" (17–18). But sin has followed the same path, corrupting the Church, till "Religion stands on tip-toe in our land, / Readie to passe to the American strand" (235–36).

See **Dawn, Sun, West wind**.

Elm The elm tree is mentioned in Homer (*Iliad* 21.350), though with no particular significance, and it often appears in Latin, European, and English poetry as a prominent, dignified, shady tree. Gray speaks of the "rugged elms" of the country churchyard (*Elegy* 13).

The elm's main symbolic meaning depends on its use as a support for vines: Chaucer calls it "The piler [pillar] elm" (*PF* 177), and Spenser makes that more explicit with "The vine-prop Elme" (*FQ* 1.1.8). Elm and vine together stand for husband and wife. It has been the practice in Italy for millennia to train vines up elms (see Virgil, *Georgics* 1.2, 2.221), and it seems to have been a common expression in Latin to "marry" (*maritare*) the vine to a tree. Two wedding songs by Catullus are the prime source for this image in poetry. Addressing the new bride, he writes "just as the limber vine / Enfolds trees planted beside it, / He will be enfolded in / Your embrace" (61.102–05). In the second song, the young men's chorus sings to the maidens: "Just as the unwed vine (*vidua...vitis*) that grows on naked ground / Can never raise herself, never produce ripe grapes, ...// But if she happens to be joined to a husband elm (*ulmo...marito*)" she will be tended and fruitful, so a maiden must find a husband (62.49–58, trans. Lee). (Ben Jonson included a translation of this passage in his masque *Hymenaei* 749–64.)

Horace (e.g., 2.15.4), Juvenal, Ovid, and other Latin poets used the same metaphor, and it became commonplace in European poetry after the Renaissance. Shakespeare's Adriana says to the man she thinks is her husband, "Thou art an elm, my husband, I a vine" (*CE* 2.2.174). Shakespeare alters the vine to ivy once, where Titania, winding Bottom in her arms, says, "the female ivy so / Enrings the barky fingers of the elm" (*MND* 4.1.42–43). Garcilaso has a disillusioned variant, where a spurned lover complains that his ivy is clinging to another wall and his vine to another elm ("Egloga primera" 136–37); and so does Góngora: "That lovely vine / that you see embracing the elm / divides its leaves discreetly / with the neighboring laurel" ("Guarda corderos" 17–20). Milton has Adam and Eve, before the Fall, doing their rural work: "they led the Vine / To wed her Elm; she spous'd about him twines / Her marriageable arms, and with her brings / Her dow'r th'adopted Clusters, to adorn / His barren leaves" (*PL* 5.216–20). As late as Tennyson we find the image: "we two / Were always friends, none closer, elm and vine" (*The Princess* 2.315–16).

See **Ivy, Oak**.

Emmet   *see* **Ant**

Evening   *see* **East and west**

Evening star   *see* **Star**

Eye   The most prominent and expressive of facial features as well as the organs of sight, eyes appear in literature more often than any other parts of the body. Their appearances are most often literal or metanymical (e.g., "in their eyes" means "in their sight"), especially in love poetry, where for centuries the convention reigned that love enters through the eyes of the lover, very often because (now metaphorically) the eyes of the beloved "darted" a killing or inflaming glance. "Those eyes of yours have inveigled themselves through my own eyes into the depths of my heart," says a character in Apuleius, "and are kindling in my marrow the keenest of flames" (*Met* 10.3, trans. Walsh). Guillaume de Lorris describes the god of love as shooting him "through my eye and into my heart" (*Romance of the Rose* 1692). Petrarch tells how "Love found me altogether disarmed, / And the way open through my eyes to my heart" (*Rime* 3). Sidney's Astrophil is full of praise for Stella's eyes – Nature's chief work (7), where Cupid shines (12), which make infinite arrows for Cupid beneath two bows (brows) (17), whose beams are joys (42), and so on. After centuries of this image, all we know for truth, as Yeats has it in "Drinking Song," is that "Wine comes in at the mouth / And love comes in at the eye." So susceptible are eyes that Puck in *A Midsummer Night's Dream* can apply a juice to them to make their owners fall in love with the next creature they behold.

Eyes express thought and feeling. "Your eyes were not silent," Ovid writes (*Amores* 2.5.17); Medea has "crime in her eyes" (*Tristia* 2.526); "Her eyes flashed lightning," says Propertius (4.8.55). A warrior in Spenser casts his "eye flaming with wrathfull fyre" (*FQ* 1.5.10). A sonnetizing character in Shakespeare nicely names "the heavenly rhetoric of thine eyes" (*LLL* 4.3.55). Eyes not only flash lightning but display all weathers, shining like the sun, clouding over, raining tears. They express jealousy if they turn green – Shakespeare has "green-eyed jealousy" *MV* 3.2.110) (see other instances under **Green**) – or if they turn "whally," Spenser's unusual word: Lechery's goat has "whally eies (the signe of gelosy)" (*FQ* 1.4.24); looking askance, with "wanton eyes," may have a similar rhetoric (*FQ* 3.1.41). Disdain for death casts a "cold eye" in Yeats's "Under Ben Bulben."

Plato writes of "the eye of the soul" (*Republic* 533d; cf. 527e), and Aristotle uses that phrase to define "intelligence" (*Nicomachean Ethics* 1144a30). Ovid says of Pythagoras that the "things that nature kept from mortal sight / His inward eye explored" (*Met.* 15.63–64, trans. Melville). Hamlet and Horatio each use the phrase "mind's eye" (1.2.185, 1.1.115); "my soul's imaginary sight / Presents thy shadow to my sightless view" (*Sonnets* 27; cf. 113).

Blindness, then, sometimes bespeaks wisdom or inner sight. Homer is said to have been blind, and blind Milton invokes him and others as precedents for himself: "Blind Thamyris, and blind Maeonides [Homer], / And Tiresias and Phineus prophets old" (*PL* 3.35–36). Oedipus, famous for his perspicacity, defies the blind Tiresias, but when he learns the soothsayer was right, Oedipus plucks out his eyes. Lear is spiritually blind, but it is Gloucester in the parallel plot whose eyes are stamped out.

Eyes are central to Hoffmann's tale "The Sandman": a man said to be the sandman, who puts sand in the eyes of a child to make it sleep, is really an evil magician, who demands the eyes of the child; later he turns up as a telescope salesman, and he has a hand in making a lifelike automaton whose false eyes seem to speak.

The sun, the moon, and occasionally the stars are said to be, or to have, eyes: see **Sun, Moon**. Dante calls the island of Delos the place where "the two eyes of the sky" were born, i.e., Apollo and Artemis/Diana, the sun and the moon (*Purgatorio* 20.132).

F

Falcon   *see* **Hawk**

Fall   *see* **Autumn**

Fame or glory   Like a few other entries in this dictionary (e.g., **Death, Dream**), fame or glory is a concept that seldom serves as a symbol of something else but is itself often symbolized in distinctive conventional ways in western literature.

Words meaning "fame" are usually derived from roots meaning "hear" or "say," since before modern times a person's fame depended almost entirely on the heard or spoken word. Homer's term for it, *kleos*, derives from the Indo-European root *kleu-*, which also yields Greek *kluo*, "I hear," *klutos*, "heard-of, famous," Kleio (whence Latin Clio), the muse of epic poetry, and several other words. The English derivatives of *kleu-* are "loud" and "listen." In Sanskrit the same root generates *sravah*, "fame" (in the *Rigveda*), while in Slavic it produces *slava*, "fame" (and *slovo*, "word, epic tale"). These words are closely associated with epic poetry, which was the chief vehicle of glory in ancient times. Latin *fama*, which passes through French into English as "fame," is related to *fari*, "to speak," and *fatum*, "utterance, something spoken by a god or oracle," which yields English "fate." An Old English word for "fame" is *blaed* (as in *Beowulf* 1761), which can mean "breath" as well; it is related to *blawan*, "blow," and *blaest*. Latin *gloria* is of uncertain origin.

Unlike *kleos* in Homer, *fama* in Virgil is sometimes a debased version of poetic fame. Virgil personifies Fama, usually translated as "Rumor," as a bird with an eye on every feather and just as many tongues and ears (*Aeneid* 4.181–83). Shakespeare follows him in the Induction to *2 Henry 4*, where Rumor is "painted full of tongues." Fame may also be dismissed as mere breath, fickle and evanescent air, at least on earth. "Worldly renown is nothing other than / a breath of wind," Dante writes, "that blows now here, now there, / and changes name when it has changed its course" (*Purgatorio* 11.100–02, trans. Mandelbaum). If an enemy speaks one's praise, Shakespeare's Aeneas says, "That breath fame blows" (*TC* 1.3.244). "What's Fame?" Pope asks: "a fancy'd life in others' breath" (*Essay on Man* 4.237). Byron notes that "love of glory's but an airy lust" (*Don Juan* 4.101.2). Great fame may require that breath be blown through a trumpet. Spenser speaks of the "trump of fame" and "fame in her shrill trump" (Sonnets 29 and 85); Beattie disdains the "obstreperous trump of Fame" (*Minstrel* 1.2.6); Dryden writes, "Fame is the trumpet, but your smile the prize" (Epistle 4.18). Clio is also a trumpeter. See under **Trumpet** for more examples.

Poets have claimed the privilege of conferring true fame on those who deserve it, including themselves. The bard Demodocus in Homer's *Odyssey* sings the *klea andron*, the "famous deeds of men" (8.73). Some of these deeds, in fact, were brought about by the gods so that bards might sing them: Troy was destroyed, according to Alcinous, "for the sake of a song for those to come" (8.580), while Helen says that Zeus brought misery to her and Paris so they will be the subject of song (*Iliad* 6.357). Sappho warns a woman that she will be forgotten because she has no share in "the roses of Pieria" (the Muses) (Frag. 55). Virgil hopes his poem will preserve the memory of Nisus and Euryalus (*Aeneid* 9.446–49). Horace notes that many brave men lived before Agamemnon but, lacking a Homer, they descended unmourned into the darkness (*Odes* 4.9). Petrarch claims that "our study" (poetry) makes men immortal through fame (*Rime* 104). In Sonnet 8 Milton offers to requite a gentle act of a conquering soldier by employing the "charms" of poetry to grant him fame. Poetry, says Foscolo, "defeats the silence of ten thousand years" ("On Sepulchers" 233–34).

In Homer, Virgil, and other classical poets, fame rises to heaven, and the famous one becomes a star. Several examples of this imagery are given under **Star**. We may then speak of "the clear sky of fame," as Falstaff does (*2H4* 4.3.49), or "the heaven of fame," as Shelley does ("Ode to Liberty" 10).

Fame or Rumor, usually personified as female, may have a house; as Ovid describes it, it stands on the highest peak, has a thousand openings, and is built throughout of reverberating bronze (*Met.* 12.39–63). Chaucer develops this idea at length in *The House of Fame*. A grander and nobler version is Shelley's temple in Canto 1 of *Laon and Cythna*, where the great poets and thinkers of the past dwell together.

The word "glory" has lent itself more readily to Christian redefinition – heavenly glory, to go to glory, and so on – than "fame" has. In English, at least, "glory" often suggests a heavenly light, as it does in Wordsworth's "Intimations" ode, and has served as a synonym of "halo." The haloes over the saints in paintings, then, represent their fame in heaven.

Field   *see* **Plow, Seed**

Fire   Fire is so important to human life and comes in so many forms – the sun and stars, lightning, volcanoes, sparks from flint, burning logs on a hearth, candles, oil lamps, conflagrations of a city or forest – that its symbolic meanings in literature are as manifold as the forms a flame may take. Indeed to Heraclitus its ever-changing shapes suggested that it is the *arche* or fundamental substance of the world, the fire that Hopkins celebrates in "That Nature is a Heraclitean Fire": "Million-fuelèd, nature's bonfire burns on." The meanings of fire are not only manifold but sometimes ambiguous: what warms can burn, what illuminates can dazzle and blind. Fires are found on earth, in heaven, in hell, and in purgatory; they bring life and death; they can kill by burning up or by burning out.

Here we shall detail only a few senses: the fire of the Lord in the Bible, the fire of purgatory, the Promethean fire of culture or intellect, and the fire of passion (lust and anger).

Like Zeus and Jupiter, the God of the Old Testament sends lightning, "fire from the Lord out of heaven" (Gen. 19.24), but he is much more intimately linked to other forms of fire. He descends upon Mt. Sinai in fire (Exod. 19.18), the sight of his glory was like "devouring fire" (24.17), his angel speaks in a burning bush (3.2) while the Lord himself "spake unto you out of the midst of the fire" on the mountain (Deut. 4.12), "For the Lord thy God is a consuming fire, even a jealous God" (4.24). The wrath of the Lord shall burn the wicked, says Isaiah, "as the fire devoureth the stubble, and the flame consumeth the chaff" (5.24), "and the people shall be as the fuel of the fire" (9.19). From this it is but a step to the "hell fire" with which Jesus threatens one who calls his brother a fool (Matt. 5.22), the "lake of fire" which is the "second death" (Rev. 20.14–15). These fires of wrath are also purifying, for they destroy only the wicked, the chaff. Daniel and his companions are unsinged in the "burning fiery furnace" (Dan. 3.26). Jesus, John the Baptist prophesies, "shall baptize you with the Holy Ghost, and with fire"; he will purge the threshing floor and "burn up the chaff" (Matt. 3.11–12). A more benign fire is in the flames of Pentecost, "cloven tongues like as of fire," that descended on the polyglot crowd and let them speak with "other tongues" to each other (Acts 2).

It is a commonplace that hell is full of fire, but it is worth noting that the most celebrated literary hell, Dante's *Inferno*, is not fiery at its center; it is icy cold, for the worst sins, those of malice rather than passion, are cold-blooded. On the highest terrace of his *Purgatorio*, however, the lustful walk in fire, but this is "the fire that refines" (26.148), a line that Eliot quotes in *The Waste Land* (427). Eliot also strikingly combines the fires of Pentecost with those of purgatory in "Little Gidding": "The dove descending breaks the air / With flame of incandescent terror / Of which the tongues declare / The one discharge from sin and error. / The only hope, or else despair / Lies in the choice of pyre or pyre – / To be redeemed from fire by fire." The fire that destroys Rochester's house, and blinds Rochester himself, in Charlotte Brontë's *Jane Eyre* completes a long skein of significant fire imagery; it is purgatorial, cleansing the Byronic hero of his past sins.

Prometheus is the "Fire-Bringer" in Greek mythology, fire stolen in a fennel stalk from Olympus and given to the miserable mortals below, Prometheus' creatures, who had lived like ants in dark caves. Fire is thus both a real boon, crucial for a truly human life, and a synecdoche for all cultural attainments, spelled out by Aeschylus in *Prometheus Bound*: star-lore, numbers, letters, domestication of animals, seamanship, medicine, divination, mining, indeed "every art of mortals is from Prometheus" (447–506). The Promethean fire in mortals should lead them to scholarly study, but as Berowne and his friends in Shakespeare's *Love's Labour's Lost* discover, it is women's eyes that "sparkle still the right Promethean fire; / They are the books, the arts, the academes" (4.3.347–49).

The fire of passionate love and jealousy is one of the most widespread symbols in literature. Perhaps its earliest appearance is in a fragment (31) by Sappho, quoted by Longinus, in which she says "a subtle fire has crept beneath my flesh" at the sight of her beloved with a man. In Catullus' imitation of this poem (51) a "thin flame" penetrates his limbs. Horace also imitates it, in *Odes* 1.13, where he is "consumed by slow fires within." At Venus' command Cupid "inflames" (*incendat*) Dido with love for Aeneas (*Aeneid* 1.660); fire imagery recurs until it becomes literal at her suicide's pyre. Ovid's Medea conceives a powerful fire for Jason (*Met.* 7.9). Seneca has Phaedra's nurse urge her to control her flames for Hippolytus (*Phaedra* 165). The metaphor is amusingly elaborated in Guillaume de Lorris's *Romance of the Rose*: "The more a man gazes on what he loves, the more his heart is fried and basted with lard" (2345–46). With more decorum one of Spenser's characters tells of a time "when corage hott / The fire of love, and joy of chevalree, / First kindled in my brest" (*FQ* 1.2.35). After the Fall, Adam feels Eve's beauty "inflame my sense / With ardor to enjoy thee" (Milton, *PL* 9.1031–32). In Racine's *Phèdre* the queen "recognized Venus and her terrible flames" but could not repel her; now she wishes to hide her "flame so black" from the light (277, 310). Keats's Porphyro rides across the moors "with heart on fire / For Madeline" (*Eve of St. Agnes* 75–76).

As early as Callimachus "fire" (*pyr*) could also mean the object of one's passion (*Epigrams* 27.5). Horace tells a young man in the throes of love that he is "worthy of a better flame" (*flamma*) (*Odes* 1.27.20); this ode may have inspired

Petrarch to address his beloved *dolce mio foco* ("my sweet fire") (*Rime* 203) and Boccaccio to name his lady Fiammetta ("Little Flame") in some of his sonnets. The same use of "flame" is found in a few English poems of the seventeenth and eighteenth centuries, as in this from Marvell's "The Garden": "Fond lovers, cruel as their flame, / Cut in these trees their mistress' name" (19–20). We still use the phrase "old flame" for a former lover.

In Greek and Latin literature one could also burn with anger or pride. The chorus of Sophocles' *Oedipus at Colonus* warns Antigone and Ismene "not to burn too much" over the fate of their father (1695). The youth of Aristophanes' *Clouds* are enjoined to "burn" (with shame and anger, presumably) when they are mocked (992). Since then the flames of wrath are almost as common as those of love.

In the *Iliad* warriors are fiery. "They saw Idomeneus like a flame in his strength" (13.330); "Thus they fought in the guise of a bright fire" (18.1). Fire images blend with images of brightness, such as dazzling light from helmets and shields (13.341–42) or the glare of a baleful star (5.5–6), and come to a brilliant climax with the simile that likens Achilles' appearance to a signal flare sent up by a beleaguered city (18.207–14) – an obvious foreshadowing of Troy's fate. Fire is even personified as Hephaestus, who fights on behalf of Achilles against the River Scamander (book 21).

A Latin phrase *ferrum flammaque*, "iron and flame," means "total destruction"; we would say "fire and sword." Priam, for instance, sees Asia falling in fire and sword (Juvenal 10.266).

Fire might symbolize passion of any sort, any warmth of feeling, even human life itself. Both Jane Eyre and Rochester are fiery characters – Rochester appreciates Jane's "soul made of fire" (chap. 24) – whereas the virtuous St. John Rivers is "cold as an iceberg" (chap. 35); many of the novel's intimate and emotional moments take place by the fireside. When Gradgrind, in Dickens's *Hard Times*, asks his daughter Louisa if she is willing to marry Bounderby, she has been so defeated by his educational methods that she agrees, but as she agrees she notices the "languid and monotonous smoke" from the Coketown chimneys, a symbol of her life, and she adds, "Yet when the night comes, Fire bursts out, Father!" (1.15). (*See* **Salamander, Volcano**).

Flood   *see* **Sea**

Flower   Flowers, first of all, are girls. Their beauty, their beauty's brevity, their vulnerability to males who wish to pluck them – these features and others have made flowers, in many cultures, symbolic of maidens, at least to the males who have set those cultures' terms. The most obvious evidence is girls' names. Daisy, Heather, Iris, Lily, Rose, and Violet remain common in English today; Susan comes from Hebrew *Shoshannah*, meaning "lily"; less common are Flora (Latin for "flower") and Anthea (Greek for "flowery"). Plant names, whether a flower is implied or not, are also frequent: Daphne (Greek for "laurel"), Hazel, Holly, Ivy, Laurel, Myrtle, Olive. With rare exceptions, such as Hyacinth and Narcissus (from the Greek myths), boys are not given flower names. "Custom hath been, time out of mind / With Rose or Lily to compare / Our favourite maid!" So George Crabbe begins "The Flowers," which likens a dozen more flowers to different types of maids.

Two of the earliest Greek poems, the Homeric *Hymn to Demeter* and the Hesiodic *Catalogues of Women*, make the connection between girls as flowers and their being plucked, raped, or snatched away. In the *Hymn*, Persephone is gathering flowers of various kinds and sees a "marvelous radiant flower," the narcissus, and as she reaches for it she is abducted by Hades; she herself has a "flower-like face" (8). According to the *Catalogues* (19), Zeus sees Europa gathering flowers in a meadow, disguises himself as a bull, and tricks her by breathing forth a crocus. Moschus in *Europa* repeats the flower-picking motif, as Ovid does in *Metamorphoses* 5 when tells the story of Proserpina (Persephone).

In Euripides' *Ion*, Creusa tells Apollo, who has abducted her: "You came with hair flashing / Gold, as I gathered / Into my cloak flowers ablaze / With their golden light" (887–90, trans. Willetts). Similarly Helen is gathering flowers when Hermes snatches her away (Euripides, *Helen* 243–46). So is Oreithyia when Boreas abducts her, according to a fragment of Choerilus.

Milton makes the metaphor explicit when he compares Eve to Proserpina: "where Proserpin gath'ring flow'rs / Herself a fairer Flow'r by gloomy Dis / Was gather'd" (*PL* 4.269–71). Later, some distance from Adam, Eve is supporting the drooping flowers, "Herself, though fairest unsupported Flow'r, / From her best prop so far, and storm so nigh" (9.432–33), when Satan appears as the serpent. When Adam sees that she has fallen he drops the garland of roses he has made for her (9.892) and tells her she has been "deflow'r'd" (9.901).

The word "deflower" for "deprive of virginity" has been in English since the Middle Ages (from Late Latin *deflorare*), and in many languages "flower," "rose," "cherry," and the like are terms for the hymen or maidenhead.

Another prominent source of this symbolism is Catullus' choral wedding song: "Just as a flower that grows in a garden close, apart, / Unbeknown to sheep...; / Many boys have longed for it and many girls: / But when its bloom is gone [*defloruit*], nipped off by a fingernail, / Never boy has longed for it and never girl: / A maid too while untouched is dear the while to kin; / But when with body smirched she loses her chaste bloom [*florem*], / She's neither pleasing then to boys nor dear to girls" (62.39–47, trans. Lee). Ben Jonson incorporated a translation of this passage in his masque *Hymenaei*.

Ovid advises young women to pluck the flower before age overtakes them (*Art of Love* 3.79–80). At the end of *All's Well that Ends Well* the King asks Diana, "If thou beest yet a fresh uncropped flower / Choose thou thy husband and I'll pay the dower" (5.3.327–28). During the Golden Age, according to Lovelace, "Lasses like Autumn Plums did drop, / And Lads indifferently did crop / A Flower, and a Maiden-head" ("Love Made in the First Age" 16–18).

Blake in "The Sick Rose" succinctly restates the metaphor, with echoes of Milton's version of Eve's fall. In his *Visions of the Daughters of Albion*, the brave heroine Oothoon accepts an invitation by a marigold to pluck it, whereupon she herself is raped by Bromion; like the plucky marigold, however, she recovers from the rape and remains a virgin in her spirit.

Robert Frost finds life in the girl-plucked-while-plucking-flowers motif in "The Subverted Flower."

We speak of the "bloom" of youth of either sex, though more frequently of girls. The transience of a girl's beauty is frequently stated in floral terms, as in Herrera's advice: "Don't be proud, Leucippe, of your beauty, / For you will not be lovely always, / For the lily loses its colors, / The rose loses its beauty and its fragrance, / And the green tree its blossoms" (*Egloga* 77.301–05). According to Spenser, "that faire flowre of beautie fades away, / As doth the lilly fresh before the sunny ray" (*FQ* 3.6.38). It is a proverb that the fairest flower soonest fades; Milton invokes it in the opening of "Death of a Fair Infant": "O Fairest flower, no sooner blown but blasted."

And of course anything not eternal, such as life itself, can seem no more lasting than a flower. "A life was but a flower," as the pages sing in *As You Like It* (5.3.28). The prime source of this thought is Isaiah: "All flesh is grass, and all the goodliness thereof is as the flower of the field: / The grass withereth, the flower fadeth: because the spirit of the Lord bloweth upon it" (40.6–7; cf. 1 Peter 1.24). The metaphor is reversed in Hugo's line, "the flower passes like life" ("Regret" 23).

All these themes appear together in Capulet's cry over the young Juliet, apparently dead: "There she lies, / Flower as she was, deflowered by him [death]" (*RJ* 4.5.36). They are united in a different way in the "gather ye rosebuds" theme common in Cavalier poetry. (*See* **Rose**.)

"Flower" can also mean the highest or most excellent of a type, as when one speaks of a "flower of courtesy" or "the flower of Europe for his chivalry" (Shakespeare, *RJ* 2.5.43, *3H6* 2.1.71). As the "choice" or "pick" of a kind, "flower" came to refer to select short poems gathered into a bouquet or posy (itself from "poesy") and circulated as an anthology. "Anthology" is from Greek *anthologia*, "gathering of flowers"; it was translated into Latin as *florilegium*, occasionally used in English. The Greek poet Meleager compiled a set of epigrams that he called *Stephanos*, "Garland," and likened each poet to a flower. A collection of excerpts from Apuleius was called *Florida*. Gascoigne wrote a collection called *A Hundred Sundry Flowers*; a sixteenth-century French anthology bore the typical title *Les Fleurs de Poésie Françoyse*. In an elaboration of this metaphor, Shelley offers his poem *Epipsychidion* to Emily: "Lady mine, / Scorn not these flowers of thought, the fading birth / Which from its heart of hearts that plant puts forth / Whose fruit, made perfect by thy sunny eyes, / Will be as of the trees of Paradise" (383–87). Baudelaire's deliberately shocking if mysterious title, *Les Fleurs du Mal* ("Flowers of Evil"), plays not only on the equation of poem to flower but evokes Christian devotional works where flowers are virtues or prayers.

There is a traditional language of flowers and herbs, with various dialects, according to which each flower is assigned a meaning. Some of these meanings, if they are prominent in literature, may be found under various plant names in this dictionary. Shakespeare's Ophelia knows them well, even in her madness: "There's rosemary, that's for remembrance – pray you, love, remember. And there is pansies, that's for thoughts," and so on (*Hamlet* 4.5.175–77). Perdita passes out appropriate flowers at the sheep-shearing festival in *The Winter's Tale* 4.4.73 ff.). In the eighteenth century Lady Mary Wortley Montagu wrote about a secret flower code for sending love messages in the Turkish harem, and the notion appealed to many writers of Europe. The Romantics sometimes looked on flowers as nature's speech, or as speakers themselves, with silent messages intelligible only to those initiated in nature's mysteries. Friedrich Schlegel begins a poem, "Flowers, you are silent signs" ("Variations"). The most famous Romantic flower is the mysterious "blue flower" of Novalis's novel *Heinrich von Ofterdingen*, which seems to symbolize a primordial harmonious realm, accessible only in dream, as well as a woman's face. Not just poems but a poet might be a flower, as in Lamartine: "The flower falls while yielding its odors to the zephyr; / To life, to the sun, these are its farewells; / As for me, I die; and my soul, at the moment it expires, / Is emitted like a sad and melodious sound" ("L'Automne").

Another tradition may be singled out as the "Flowers of Paradise," lists or catalogues of flowers growing in a garden or bower of love. The earliest is in the *Iliad*, where Zeus and Hera make love on a bed of clover, crocus, and hyacinth (14.347–49). Spenser's Garden of Adonis has a myrtle grove with "wanton ivy," eglantine, caprifole, hyacinth, narcissus, amaranthus, and other flowers into which lovers were transformed (*FQ* 3.6.43–45; for Spenser's other flower catalogues see *Virgil's Gnat* 665–80 and *Muiopotmus* 187–200). In the "blissful bower" of Milton's Paradise are found laurel, myrtle, acanthus, iris, rose, jessamine (jasmine), violet, crocus, and hyacinth (*PL* 4. 690–703).

Classical rhetoricians recognized a level of style they called "flowery" (*antheron* or *floridum*). An embellishment or ornament of speech has been called a flower, as in the phrase "flowers of rhetoric." An orator is "one that hath phrases, figures and fine flowers / To strew his rhetoric with" (Jonson, *Sejanus* 2.419–20). We still speak of a flowery speech or florid prose.

Flower entries in this dictionary: **Almond, Amaranth, Asphodel, Crocus, Daffodil, Daisy, Hyacinth, Lily, Marigold, Mistletoe, Pansy, Poppy, Purple flower, Rose, Sunflower, Violet**.

See also **Garden, Seed**.

Flute   *see* **Pipe**.

Fly   Flies, not surprisingly, are usually considered unpleasant, disease-ridden, and evil. A swarm of flies is the fourth of the ten plagues Moses sends upon the Egyptians (Exod. 8.21–31). Egypt was known for its flies, especially when the Nile was in flood, and Isaiah even calls Egypt itself a fly (7.18). One of the terms for Satan, or "the prince of the devils," was Beelzebub (Matt. 12.24), which has been translated as "lord of the flies" (whence the title of Golding's novel about the source of evil).

Homer brings out another feature of the fly: "the boldness of the fly / which, even though driven away from a man's skin, / persists in biting out of relish for human blood" (*Iliad* 17.570–72). In Renaissance emblem books the fly is sometimes a symbol of persistence or pertinacity. That sense may lie behind Sartre's decision to substitute flies for the relentless Eumenides or Furies in his play about Orestes, *Les Mouches* ("The Flies")

In English poetry "fly" is the generic term for any winged insect, and as such (like "insect") it symbolizes ephemerality. Indeed, as Bacon writes, "There are certain Flies that are called Ephemera that live but a day" (*Sylva* sec. 697). The chorus of Milton's *Samson Agonistes* speaks of "the common rout" of men who "Grow up and perish, as the summer fly" (675–77). Tennyson in an even bleaker mood sees in "men the flies of latter spring, / That lay their eggs, and sting and sing / And weave their petty cells and die" (*In Memoriam* 50.10–12). Its ephemerality makes it a poignant presence in Dickinson's "I heard a Fly buzz – when I died" (no. 465). (*See* **Insect**.)

The fly could also mean any insignificant thing, as in Chaucer's "I counte hym nat a flye" (*Reeve's Tale* 4192). "As flies to wanton boys, are we to th' Gods," says Shakespeare's Gloucester; "They kill us for their sport" (*Lear* 4.1.36–37). But if people are like flies in the brevity of their life, then perhaps flies are like people in their interior lives, which might seem long to them. So Blake asks a fly whom he has brushed away, "Am not I / A fly like thee? / Or art not thou / A man like me? / ... / If thought is life / And strength & breath; / And the want of thought is death; // Then am I / A happy fly, / If I live, / Or if I die" ("The Fly"). Shelley speculates in a note to *Queen Mab* (8.203) that time is subjective, a function of our consciousness. "Perhaps the perishing ephemeron," he concludes, "enjoys a longer life than the tortoise."

Shelley also once likens his verses, ill received, to a fly: "What hand would crush the silken-winged fly, / The youngest of inconstant April's minions, / Because it cannot climb the purest sky / Where the swan sings, amid the sun's dominions?" (*Witch of Atlas* 9–12). (*See* **Swan**.) For other examples of this metaphor see under **Butterfly**.

Folding star   *see* **Sheep**

Foot   *see* **Path**

Forest   Forests used to be places of danger to a degree difficult to appreciate today, when for modern city-dwellers they are retreats or playgrounds; perhaps only arctic forests or tropical jungles retain something of the fearful vastness and strangeness they once implied. Forests are traditionally dark, labyrinthine, and filled with dangerous beasts.

The earliest literature is sometimes structured on the contrast between city and wilderness. The *Gilgamesh* epic, for instance, moves from the walls of Uruk to the pastures of Enkidu and thence to the great cedar forest of the monster Humbaba. Euripides' *Bacchae* sets the civic order of Thebes, in the person of King Pentheus, against the wooded mountain Cithaeron, where the maenads dance to the alien god Dionysus.

To be "lost in the woods," or "not yet out of the woods," remain common phrases. It is there that one loses one's way or path, which taken allegorically has meant to wander in error or sin. So Dante finds himself in a *selva oscura* or dark wood at the opening of the *Inferno*, and Spenser sends the Redcross Knight and Una into "the wandring wood," the den of Error, where the trees shut out heaven's light (*FQ* 1.1.7,13). Bunyan's pilgrim progresses through "the wilderness of this world"; Shelley, following Dante, goes forth "Into the wintry forest of our life" (*Epipsychidion* 249). Hawthorne's character "Young Goodman Brown" leaves his wife, Faith, to go into the forest where he has an experience that leaves his faith shattered. The natural basis of this symbolism is seconded by the ancient notion that "wood" (Greek *hyle*, Latin *silva*) is fundamental matter, the lowest stuff – hence Dante's punishment of suicides, who treated their bodies as mere matter, is to imprison them in, or change them into, trees (*Inferno* 13).

Roman writers treated their country estates as restorative havens from the corruption and pettiness of urban life, but those estates were not primarily forests, which remained forbidding. Shakespeare in several plays uses the natural world – the forest of Athens in *A Midsummer Night's Dream* or the forest of Arden in *As You Like It* – as sites of reversal of city relationships and restoration of right order. With Romanticism a new appreciation of wildness emerges, especially forests, mountains, and seashores, sometimes with religious intensity. Coleridge recalls how he pursued "fancies holy" through untrodden woods and there found "The spirit of divinest Liberty" ("France: An Ode" 11, 21). Wordsworth claims "One impulse from a vernal wood / May teach you more of man; / Of moral evil and of good, / Than all the sages can" ("The Tables Turned" 21–24). In Germany the forest, especially the Black Forest, became a symbol not only of the true naturalness of life but also of the "roots" of the German nation. Wanderers and huntsmen abound in the poems and stories of the period. The Grimm Brothers' fairy tales often turn on forest adventures; dwarves and gnomes and other woodland creatures know things and do things townsfolk cannot. The Grimms published a journal called *Old German Forests*, which linked the forests to the true German culture.

In ancient times the myth of Arcadia countered the more frightening and realistic image of the forest. In book 8 of Virgil's *Aeneid* Aeneas meets the Arcadians at the site of future Rome, and their simple forest life stands, perhaps, both for the natural roots of Rome and for what has been lost with the building of the great city. Much of American literature deals with the theme of the "virgin land," through which brave (usually male) explorers and fighters penetrate, leaving civilization behind; their more primitive life serves as a standard for judging the life of (usually female) settled society; but sometimes there is a feeling that the conquest of the American wilderness is a rape of the land and an unjust slaughter of the "savages" (the word comes ultimately from Latin *silva*), or that to "go native" is itself false or dangerous.

See **Nature**.

Fort   *see* **Siege**

Fountain   In classical literature, fountains or springs (Greek *krene*, Latin *fons*) are sacred to the Muses and sources of poetic inspiration. According to Hesiod, the Muses on Mt. Helicon "dance about the violet-colored spring" and bathe in "the Horse's Spring [Hippocrene]" or the streams of Permessus and Olmeius (*Theogony* 3–6); Hesiod, whose home was the village of Ascra on Helicon's slopes (in Boeotia), was later reputed to have drunk from the Hippocrene himself. A later story had it that the Hippocrene was created by Pegasus' stamping hoof (Callimachus, *Aitia* frag. 2.1; Ovid, *Met.* 5.256–64). (*See* **Horse**.) Moschus claims that Homer and Bion were both nourished by fountains, Homer by Pegasus' spring, Bion by Arethusa ("Lament for Bion" 77); Arethusa is in the harbor of Syracuse in Sicily, the homeland of pastoral poetry.

Lucretius says "I love to draw near the untouched fountains [of Pieria] and drink from them" (1.927–28); Pieria, on the north slope of Olympus in Macedonia, was the original home of the Muses, whence they moved to Helicon. Horace addresses the Muse "who delights in clear springs" (1.26.6–7). Virgil tells how Gallus had wandered by the Permessus but one of the Muses led him to Helicon, where he was taught to sing like Hesiod (*Eclogues* 6.64–73). Propertius makes this distinction of sources more explicit when he turns from love poetry and vows to sing of warfare in the epic mode, "But as yet my songs are ignorant of Ascran springs: / Love has but laved them in Permessus' stream" (2.10.25–26, trans. Shepherd).

Theocritus, after drinking from a spring in the muse-like Nymphs' cave somewhere in Sicily, gratefully addresses them as "Castalian Nymphs, who hold steep Parnassus" (*Idylls* 7.148) – Castalia being yet another spring, also sacred to Apollo and the Muses, on Parnassus near Delphi; Milton calls it "th'inspir'd / Castalian Spring" (*PL* 4.273–74).

Jonson's "clear Dircaean fount / Where Pindar swam" is the river Dirce at Thebes, where Pindar was a swan ("Ode Allegoric" 19–20). (*See* **Swan**.)

If holy springs confer fame on a poet, at least one poet, Horace, promised to confer fame on an unknown spring, in the ode beginning "O fountain of Bandusia" (3.13); the spring has never been located! And if Homer was nourished by a fountain, he has become one himself for all succeeding poets: "Maeonides [Homer], from whose perennial fount / The mouths of poets are moistened with Pierian waters" (Ovid, *Amores* 3.9.25–26). (*See* **River**.)

Although just what spring belonged to what genre of poetry was not consistently sorted out by the ancients, it is a little odd that the anthology *Englands Helicon* (1600) should be devoted to pastoral poetry. Milton is safer in addressing "O Fountain Arethuse" in his pastoral elegy "Lycidas" (85); he remains vague, however, in *Paradise Lost*, where he says he still wanders "where the Muses haunt / Clear spring, or shady grove, or sunny hill" (3.27–28), and later where he mentions "th' inspired / Castalian spring" (4.273–74) without saying what it inspired. Pope gives his famous advice to young poets: "A little Learning is a dang'rous Thing; / Drink deep, or taste not the Pierian Spring" (*Essay on Criticism* 215–16), "Pierian" here referring to the Muses, wherever the spring may be. Gray rightly invokes "Helicon's harmonious springs" in "The Progress of Poetry: A Pindaric Ode" (3).

See **Sea**.

Fox As a symbol of cunning or trickery the fox is inscribed in our language: Old English *foxung* meant "wile" or "craftiness," while today we try to "outfox" an opponent. It goes back, of course, to the Greeks. Solon accuses his political opponents of walking "with the steps of the fox" (Loeb 10.5); Pindar praises the wrestler Melissos for the boldness of a lion "but in skill he is a fox, which rolls on its back to check the eagle's swoop" (*Isth.* 4.47–48, trans. Race); Aristophanes several times uses "foxiness" to mean "trickery" (e.g., *Lysistrata* 1270). The lion-fox contrast becomes standard. Lucretius asks why lions are innately violent and foxes cunning (3.742); Horace describes someone as a "crafty [*astuta*] fox masquerading as a noble lion" (*Satires* 2.3.186). Mocking the part of the timorous lion in the mechanicals' play, Shakespeare's Lysander says, "This lion is a very fox for his valour" (*MND* 5.1.231). Another famous contrast comes from Archilochus: "The fox knows many things, the hedgehog one – a big one" (118 Edmonds).

Chaucer and Spenser call the fox "false," Spenser also "wily" and "maister of collusion" (*SC*, "May" 219). Shakespeare's Venus urges Adonis to hunt "the fox which lives by subtlety" rather than the dangerous boar (*Venus and Adonis* 675). The title character of Jonson's *Volpone, or, The Fox* is as cunning as his name suggests (from Italian *volpe*, from Latin *vulpes*). It is as an emblem of cunning that Dante introduces the fox in his allegorical pageant of the history of the church in *Purgatorio*; there it stands for heresy, a greater danger than forthright violence (32.118–23).

Foxes are protagonists in many fables from Aesop to modern times; the most famous is the fox and the grapes, the origin of the phrase "sour grapes." There is a rich tradition of medieval tales about Reynard the Fox (French *Renard*, German *Reinecke*).

The Bible does not bring out the cunning of foxes – the Hebrew word for it might also mean "jackal" – but a passage from the Song of Solomon, "Take us the foxes, the little foxes, that spoil the vines" (2.15), has bred many allegorical interpretations, and might also lie behind Dante's fox (taking the garden–vineyard in the Song as the church). *The Little Foxes* is the title of a play by Lillian Hellman.

Frankincense and myrrh

Frankincense is an aromatic gum resin drawn from the frankincense tree. The word means "best incense": the adjective was applied to plants and trees of highest quality ("frank-myrrh" is attested). That sense of "frank" derived from its sense "free (of impurities)" or "noble," both in turn from the ethnic word "Frank" (Latin *Francus*), for the Franks were the freemen or nobles of Gaul, which they had conquered. Its Hebrew name *lebonah* (whence Greek *libanos*, *libanotos*) means "white (stuff)," as the best incense was white when crushed into a powder. It was burned during sacrifices (Lev. 2.1–2; Herodotus 1.183; Aristophanes, *Clouds* 426). Its main source in ancient times was Arabia Felix, especially the region of modern Yemen and Oman. When the Queen of Sheba (in Yemen) visited Solomon she brought great quantities of spices (1 Kgs 10.10); Jeremiah refers to "incense from Sheba" (6.20), while Virgil imagines Venus' temple in Paphos warm with "Sabaean incense" (*Sabaeo | ture, Aeneid* 1.416–17). Milton compares the perfumes of Eden with "Sabaean odours from the spicy shore | Of Arabie the blest" (*PL* 4.162–63).

Ovid says the phoenix feeds on the "tears [gum] of frankincense" (*turis lacrimis*) and "juice of amomum" (*Met.* 15.394); repeated by Dante (*Inferno* 24.110).

Myrrh (Hebrew *mor*, Greek *smyrna*, *murra*) is an aromatic gum produced by the myrrh tree, which also grew in Arabia, among other places. According to the Bible it was used as incense, as perfume, and in embalming corpses. Its taste is bitter, but it was sometimes mixed into wine; such a mixture was offered to Jesus on the cross (Mark 15.23). Frankincense and myrrh appear together three times in the Song of Solomon, and they make two of the three gifts the wise men bring to the infant Jesus (Matt. 2.11). That gold is the third indicates how costly the two resins were. Its use in embalming lies behind the metaphor with which Scève addresses his beloved: "you will be for me the incorruptible Myrrh | against the worms of my mortality" ("La blanche aurore," *Délie*).

See also Ovid's tale of Myrrha (*Met.* 10.298–518).

Frog and toad

If frogs and toads are distinguished at all, frogs are usually distinctively raucous, though benign, while toads are distinctively ugly, venomous, and evil.

There is something of a tradition in classical literature where frogs are a kind of comic chorus, notably in Aristophanes' *The Frogs*, where they are, in fact, the chorus. (Two other Greek comedies, now lost, had the same title.) Moschus laments that Bion the poet is now silent while "it was decreed by the Nymphs that a frog may sing forever" ("Lament for Bion" 107). Virgil notes that among the signs of a storm we hear "the frogs in the mud croak their ancient quarrel" (*Georgics* 1.378), possibly an allusion to Aristophanes' frogs, who mocked Dionysus with their croaking skills.

Frogs are one of the ten plagues Moses brings upon Egypt (Exodus 8.1–15). John of Patmos sees "three unclean spirits like frogs come out of the mouth of the beast"; they are "the spirits of devils" (Rev. 16.13–14). Horace describes a witch's potion that includes "the blood of a hideous toad" (or "frog": Latin *rana*) (*Epodes* 5.18). "Toad" by itself (Latin *rubeta*) is used by Juvenal to mean its poison (Satires 1.69–72). A venomous toad is the first ingredient to be tossed into the three witches' pot in *Macbeth* (4.1.6–9). The biblical and classical sources combined in the Middle Ages to make toads (and sometimes frogs) symbols of the devil or of several sins, especially gluttony and avarice. Milton's Satan was found "squat like a toad, close at the ear of Eve" (*PL* 4.800). Three times Shakespeare's Richard III is called a poisonous toad, and of these twice a "bunch-backed toad" (*R3* 1.2.245, 1.3.245, 4.4.81).

In folktales, especially German, princes and occasionally princesses are enchanted as frogs until the spell is broken by a kiss or another act of love. As small animals, frogs and toads have lent themselves to allegories and fables (Aesop, La Fontaine, and others), as well as to the comic epic attributed to Homer, *The Battle of the Frogs and the Mice*.

Fruit   *see* **Apple**

G

Gall   *see* **Bile, Wormwood**

Garden   The two most influential gardens in western literature are both biblical: the garden of Eden and the "garden enclosed" of the Song of Solomon (4.12).

"And the Lord God planted a garden eastward in Eden" (Gen. 2.8) – "Eden" by tradition means "delight" or "luxury" – with a river and pleasant trees bearing edible fruit (9–10). When Adam and Eve ate of the tree of knowledge they were expelled from the garden, and human history began. Nothing is said about regaining the garden until Isaiah writes, "For the Lord shall comfort Zion . . . and he will make her wilderness like Eden, and her desert like the garden of the Lord" (51.3), whereafter it looms large in messianic hopes.

Nowhere in the Hebrew Bible is this garden called Paradise. "Paradise" comes from Greek *paradeisos*, which the writers of the Septuagint (Greek Old Testament) used to translate "garden" in Genesis; the Greek word comes from Old Persian *pairi-daeza*, "around-wall," "enclosure," and then "park" or "garden." Late Hebrew *pardes*, borrowed from Persian, is used three times in the Old Testament for various other gardens or orchards, including the one in the Song of Solomon (4.13). In the New Testament "paradise" is the heavenly kingdom. Jesus tells one of those crucified with him, "Today shalt thou be with me in paradise" (Luke 23.43). John of Patmos is told by Christ to say, "To him that overcometh will I give to eat of the tree of life, which is in the midst of the paradise of God" (Rev. 2.7).

The garden of the Song is metaphorical and erotic: "A garden enclosed is my sister, my spouse; a spring shut up, a fountain sealed" (4.12); "I am come into my garden, my sister, my spouse" (5.1); "My beloved is gone down into his garden, to the beds of spices, to feed in the gardens, and to gather lilies" (6.2). Perhaps as far back as Sumerian literature the word for "garden" has stood for the body of a woman; Greek *kepos* and Latin *hortus* were occasionally used to refer to a woman's sexual parts. The frank eroticism of the Song, however, was a difficulty for both Jewish and Christian theologians. Though it was thought to be a wedding song of Solomon and a Shulamite woman, it was taken allegorically as the wedding of God with Israel or of Christ with the soul, the church, or the Virgin Mary. "Thou, O Virgin, art a garden enclosed," St. Ambrose wrote, "preserve thy fruits." Some Protestant theologians were so embarrassed by the Song as to argue that it had only an allegorical meaning, like a code or rebus. The sensual language of the song, in any case, entered into Christian liturgy and then into literature. A poem attributed to Donne, for example, addressed to the Virgin, begins "O Frutefull garden, and yet never tilde."

But the garden continued its literary life as both setting for and symbol of love encounters. Shakespeare makes the ancient equation explicit when he urges his friend to have children: "many maiden gardens, yet unset [unplanted], / With virtuous wish would bear your living flowers" (*Sonnets* 16); and more elaborately his Venus invites Adonis: "I'll be a park, and thou shalt be my deer: / Feed where thou wilt, on mountain or in dale; / Graze on my lips; and if those hills be dry, / Stray lower, where the pleasant fountains lie" (*Venus and Adonis* 231–34). Many other literary gardens stand for the erotic or sensual life without such explicit mappings, such as the Garden of Pleasure in *The Romance of the Rose*, the Bower of Bliss in Spenser's *Faerie Queene* (2.12), or, less explicitly, the garden where Julien seduces Mme de Re nal in Stendhal's *The Red and the Black*. As Guyon violently eradicates the Bower of Bliss, the boy Wordsworth violates the "dear nook" where hazels grow, a "virgin scene" ("Nutting" 16–21). A larger context for this symbolism, of course, is the ancient tradition of a "married land" (Hebrew *beulah*), or "virgin land" to be conquered and "planted." (*See* **Nature**.)

The significance of gardens also overlaps with that of bowers, groves, orchards, and other pleasant places. In a tradition beginning with the garden of Alcinous in Homer's *Odyssey* 8, the *locus amoenus*, Latin for "pleasant place" or "pleasance," is given increasingly elaborate descriptions. Some of the conventions (shady trees, a spring or brook, flowers, birds) entered Christian accounts of the garden of Eden.

Isaiah's prophecy that Zion will become the garden of the Lord seems ultimately to lie behind the scene in Shakespeare's *Richard II* where the Gardener uses terms from statecraft to describe his duties, after which his assistant asks why they should keep the garden orderly "When our sea-walled garden, the whole land, / Is full of weeds, her fairest flowers chocked up, / Her fruit trees all unpruned, her hedges ruined, / Her knots [flower beds] disordered, and her wholesome herbs / Swarming with caterpillars?" (3.4.43–47). To Hamlet this world (and Denmark in particular) is "an unweeded garden / That grows to seed. Things rank and gross in nature / Possess it merely [entirely]" (1.2.135–37).

The "plot" of the Bible – from the loss of the earthly Eden in the third chapter of Genesis to the promise of the heavenly Jerusalem in the final chaper of Revelation – is also the plot, much more succinct, of Milton's *Paradise Lost*. "Of man's first disobedience," it begins, "and the fruit / Of that forbidden tree whose mortal taste / Brought death into the world, and all our woe, / With loss of Eden, till one greater Man / Restore us, and regain the blissful seat" (1.1–5); it ends, after Michael tells Adam, "[thou] shalt possess / A Paradise within thee, happier far," as Adam and Eve "Through Eden took their solitary way" (12.586–87, 649). This pattern, with the interiorization of the lost Eden, governs the plots of many works of modern literature. Wordsworth's autobiographical epic *The Prelude* begins with an Edenic moment – "O there is blessing in this gentle breeze / That blows from the green fields" (1.1–2) – and soon describes his Edenic childhood in gardenly terms: "Fair seed-time had my soul, and I grew up / Fostered alike by beauty and by fear, / Much favoured in my birthplace, and no less / In that beloved vale to which erelong / I was transplanted" (1.305–09). He passes through the wilderness of political com-mitments and disaffections, loses and regains his imagination (book 11), and ends by vowing that he and Coleridge will teach others "how the mind of man becomes / A thousand times more beautiful than the earth / On which he dwells" (13.446–48; all 1805 version). Coleridge's "Kubla Khan" draws heavily on Milton's Eden (book 4) for the description of Xanadu, the emperor's walled pleasure garden, which is lost (it seems) through warfare, but which might be regained in music by a poet who has "drunk the milk of Paradise." Keats's many bowers for escaping the fever and fret of the world include poetry itself, "All lovely tales," things of beauty that "still will keep / A bower quiet for us" (*Endymion* 1.1–24). Burnett's *The Secret Garden* is not alone among children's books that center on a secret paradise. T. S. Eliot's *Four Quartets* begins with an evocation of a rose-garden, "our first world," where "the leaves were full of children," ("Burnt Norton" sec. 1) and concludes with the hope that we may hear again "the children in the apple tree" and "arrive where we started / And know the place for the first time" ("Little Gidding" sec. 5).

A contributor to this pattern is the classical tradition of retirement from the tumult of civic affairs to the quiet solitude of farm or garden. Virgil's description of an ideal garden and a worthy old gardener who feels as wealthy as kings (*Georgics* 4.116–48) has had a large influence. Probably the greatest meditation on gardens in English is Marvell's "The Garden," where the speaker turns his back on the "uncessant Labours" of public endeavor, embraces repose, solitude, and the "wond'rous Life" of lovely green and luscious fruits that drop about his head, and feels like Adam in "that happy Garden-state" before the Fall. In the famous ending of Voltaire's *Candide* this tradition culminates: abandoning the world about which he had philosophized in vain, Candide insists, *Il faut cultiver notre jardin*, "We must dig in our garden."

Candide labors, whereas Marvell's speaker just picks up fallen fruit: this contrast in effect repeats the debate between nature and art (artifice) that often took place in and about gardens. A brief but charming example is the exchange between Perdita and Polixenes in Shakespeare's *Winter's Tale* (4.4.79–103). How to lay out a real garden was much debated as well, from the Renaissance through the Romantic era, and a good deal of cultural history is refracted in the development from the more "artificial" and geometrical style of the Italian and (especially) the French gardens to the more "natural," less "planned" look of the English garden.

A book of poems, finally, might be called a "garden," as the individual poems are "flowers". (*See* **Flower**.) Examples range from one of Goethe's *Roman Elegies*, which introduces the set – "Here my garden is planted, here I tend the flowers of Love" – to Stevenson's *A Child's Garden of Verses*.

See **Seed, Serpent**

Ghost   *see* **Bat**

Glass   *see* **Mirror**

Glory   *see* **Fame or glory**

Goat   The pastoral economies of the ancient Mediterranean depended on goats as well as sheep, especially for milk. It was a goat, or goat-nymph, Amaltheia, that nursed the infant Zeus, and one of Zeus's epithets in Homer, *aigioxos*, usually translated "aegis-bearing," may instead be derived directly from *aix*, "goat" (Pope translates it "goat-nurs'd" at *Odyssey* 9.330 = 9.275 in the Greek). Goat's milk is still a common food in Greece and elsewhere in the region.

Aside from nourishing Zeus, goats have another claim on literary history, for the word "tragedy," Greek *tragoidia*, seems to mean "goat-song," or "performance by a goat-singer." Just how goats came into it remains a mystery: perhaps men in goat dress sang and danced, or a goat was sacrificed to Dionysus the patron of tragedy, or a goat was given as a prize for the best performance (the opinion of Horace in *Ars Poetica* 220).

In classical as well as Hebrew culture goats were offered as sacrifices. The most symbolically interesting of these was the scapegoat. As it is explained in Leviticus, the priest is to take two goats and decide by lot to sacrifice one as a sin offering but let the other live and "let him go for a scapegoat into the wilderness"; before it is let free "Aaron shall lay both his hands upon the head of the live goat, and confess over him all the iniquities of the children of Israel, and all their transgressions in all their sins, putting them upon the head of the goat, and shall send him away by the hand of a fit man into the wilderness" (16.10, 21). There is reason to believe that some of the abuse of Christ during the Passion is derived from scapegoat rituals in use at the time. "Scapegoat" is used by literary critics to refer to characters such as Malvolio in Shakespeare's *Twelfth Night* or Shylock in *Merchant of Venice* who are banished from society, or at least excluded from the comic reconciliation, at the end.

Goats are proverbially lecherous. Horace calls one *libidinosus* (*Epodes* 10.23). Spenser depicts Lechery riding on a bearded goat (*FQ* 1.4.24). A "lecherous" "whoremaster," according to Shakespeare's Edmund, has a "goatish disposition" (*Lear* 1.2.124–28); Iago links goats with monkeys and wolves as exemplars of lust (*Othello* 3.3.403–04; see also 4.1.263).

Pan, the Greek goat-god, was notably randy, and he seems to have lent some of his physical and moral traits to Christian depictions of the devil, such as his beard, the "goatee."

"To separate the sheep from the goats" means to "distinguish the good from the evil." The phrase comes from Matthew 25.31–46, which describes the Last Judgment; the goats are the sinners, and are damned. (*See* **Left and right, Sheep**.)

"Goat," now the generic term, once meant the female, with "buck" reserved for the male; in the fourteenth century "he-goat" and "she-goat" came into use, then "billy-goat" and "nanny-goat"; a young goat is a kid.

Gold   Gold is the first of metals. "Gold, like fire blazing / in the night, shines preeminent amid lordly wealth," says Pindar (*Olymp.* 1.1–2). Its beauty and purity gave it divine status in biblical as well as classical culture; untarnishable and thus immortal, it belongs to the gods – "gold is the child of Zeus" (Pindar, frag. 222). Hera, Artemis, and Eos (Dawn) have golden thrones, Hera a golden chariot, Zeus and Apollo golden whips, Iris golden wings, Zeus golden scales, Artemis and Ares golden reins, Calypso and Circe golden "zones" (girdles), and Aphrodite herself is golden, all in Homer. The gods sit in council on a golden floor, drinking out of golden cups (*Iliad* 4.2–3), Aphrodite leaves her father's golden house (Sappho, "Ode" 8), "Ye golden gods" is an interjection in Aristophanes (*Frogs* 483). The tabernacle of the Israelites is to have "a mercy seat of pure gold" and "two cherubims of gold" (Exod. 25.17–18), while the New Jerusalem is "pure gold," and "the street of the city was pure gold" (Rev. 21.18, 21).

"Golden" is applied to whatever is best or most excellent, such as the golden rule, the golden verses of Pythagoras, or the golden mean. The last of these is found first in Horace, who recommends neither daring the deep nor hugging the shore but cultivating the *auream…mediocritatem* (2.10.5). There was a golden race, who "lived like gods, with carefree heart, remote from toil and misery," according to Hesiod (*Works and Days* 112–13); in Ovid the time this race lived becomes the golden age. (*See* **Metal**.)

The sun is golden – Pindar again has "the golden strength of the sun" (*Pyth.* 4.144), while Shakespeare has the sun's "gold complexion" (*Sonnets* 18) – whereas the moon is silver. "Sol gold is, and Luna silver we threpe [assert]," says Chaucer's Canon Yeoman (826). Yeats ends his "Song of Wandering Aengus" with "The silver apples of the moon, / The golden apples of the sun." It was an ancient belief that gold was begotten by the fire of the sun and that veins of gold in the earth slowly burned what they touched. Blake demands, "Bring me my Bow of burning gold" (*Milton* 1.9).

Gold burns in another sense, for it is a spiritual danger, a cause of wickedness. The faithless Israelites built a golden calf, idolators made idols of gold. Propertius observes that "Religion is vanquished, all men worship gold" (3.13.47). Aeneas cries, "To what, accursed lust for gold, do you / not drive the hearts of men?" (Virgil, *Aeneid* 3.56–57). Horace notes that gold has broken through city gates where force failed (3.16.9–18). Shakespeare's Romeo calls it "saint-seducing gold" (1.1.214) and "worse poison to men's souls" than the drug he has just bought from the apothecary (5.1.80). In King Lear's view, "Plate sin with gold, / And the strong lance of justice hurtless breaks"

(4.6.165–66). "Judges and Senates have been bought for gold," says Pope (*Essay on Man* 4.187). Byron observes that the Age of Gold was the age "When gold was yet unknown" (*Don Juan* 6.436).

A medieval Latin saying, "All that shines is not gold," is repeated by Chaucer's Canon Yeoman: "But al thyng which that shineth as the gold / Nis nat gold" (962–63); Cervantes' Sancho Panza (*Don Quixote* 2.33); the scroll in the golden casket of Shakespeare's *Merchant of Venice* (2.7.65); and many others.

Goose   Wild migrating geese are mentioned casually twice by Homer, and once he likens a warrior among enemies to a vulture among geese (*Iliad* 17.460). Domestic barnyard geese, however, play a significant symbolic part in the *Odyssey*. While visiting Menelaus and Helen, Telemachus sees a mountain eagle carrying a white goose from a yard; Helen interprets the omen to mean that Odysseus will return home and take revenge on the suitors (15.160–78). The same meanings are elaborated in Penelope's dream, in which twenty tame geese are killed by a mountain eagle, who then speaks, telling her he is her husband and the geese her suitors (19.535–53). The suitors have been fattening themselves idly in Odysseus' house; they will be no match for the eagle.

Geese may seem foolish, hapless, or helpless. "Goose" means "fool" or "silly one" in several modern languages, and Chaucer uses the adjective "goosish" of people who dream things that never were (*Troilus* 3.583). But the Romans were grateful to the geese of the Capitol, whose honking warned the citizens of a surreptitious attack by the Gauls in 390 BC. The event is alluded to in Virgil's *Aeneid* 8.655; Ovid mentions it in *Metamorphoses* 2.539 and *Fasti* 1.453. Ovid also refers to geese as good guards: they are "more sagacious than dogs" (*Met.* 11.599; see also 8.684). In his catalogue of birds Chaucer lists "The waker goos" (*Parliament of Fowls* 358); and Sidney may suggest this virtue when he names "the Goose's good intent" as characteristic (*First Eclogues* 10.80).

Since at least the seventeenth century the phrase "all his geese are swans" has meant "he sees his things or deeds as greater than they are." It lies behind Byron's quip about the poet Landor, who "has taken for a swan rogue Southey's gander" (*Don Juan* 11.472), and perhaps behind Stevens' "Invective against Swans," which begins, "The soul, O ganders, flies beyond the parks." (See **Swan**.)

The source of nursery rhymes called "Mother Goose" can be traced to seventeenth-century France ("Mère Oye") and perhaps farther back to a German "Fru Gosen."

When Joyce's Stephen Dedalus muses on his time in France he recalls a young Irishman who was a "Son of a wild goose" (*Ulysses*, "Proteus"). The wild geese were Irishmen who emigrated to France or Spain after defeats by the English, especially the Battle of the Boyne in 1690.

Grain   *see* **Bread**

Grape   *see* **Wine**

Grasshopper   *see* **Cicada**

Green The Greek word translated as "green" or "yellow-green," *chloros* (whence English "chlorophyll"), had a broader range of meanings than the color, just as our "green" can mean "unripe" or "naïve" without a color reference. Though it is cognate with English "yellow" and "gold," the primary sense of Greek *chloros* may have been "sappy" or "having sap," and hence "vital" or "vigorous." The Greeks associated life and youth with moisture (water, blood, juice, sap, semen, and so on) and old age and death with dryness. Homer calls freshly cut or unseasoned wood *chloros* as we call it green (e.g., *Odyssey* 9.379). Euripides speaks of "green flowers" (*Iphigenia at Aulis* 1297), and in other Greek poets we find dew, tears, honey, wine, and even blood all modified by *chloros*.

The Latin word for "green," *viridis* (whence English "verdant"), could also mean "youthful" or "vigorous" as well as "naïve," but it does not seem to have had the wide range of *chloros*. On the other hand its likely kinship to other Latin words suggests an older sense like "sappy" or "juicy": *vir*, "man" or "male" (whence English "virile" and "virtue") as source of semen; *ver*, "spring" (whence English "vernal") as the season of sap or moist life; *virga*, "green twig," whence *virgo*, "virgin." Virgil speaks of "green youth" (*viridique iuventa*) in *Aeneid* 5.295, and Catullus worries about a "girl in her greenest flower" (*viridissimo...flore puella*) who might go astray (17.14).

English "green" itself is related to "grow" and "grass."

The primary association of the color green, of course, is the herbage and foliage of nature, especially in spring and summer. In April, Chaucer says, the mead is clothed "With newe grene" (*TC* 1.157). Thomson cries, "gay *Green*! / Thou smiling Nature's universal Robe!" (*Spring* 83–84). Gardens are green, as Marvell's "The Garden" memorably reports: "No white nor red was ever seen / So am'rous as this lovely green"; withdrawn into the garden, the poet's meditating mind reduces everything "To a green thought in a green shade" (17–18, 48). (Virgil also has a "green shade" in *Eclogues* 9.20.) "'Tis the green wind of May time / That suddenly wakes," according to Clare ("Spring Wind"). Dylan Thomas's famous opening lines, "The force that through the green fuse drives the flower / Drives my green age," begin an account of a more violent kinship with nature. Midsummer, according to Wallace Stevens, "is the natural tower of all the world, / The point of survey, green's green apogee" ("Credences of Summer"); in several poems Stevens plays the green of nature against the blue of art or imagination. (*See* **Blue**.) The prominence of green in the medieval poem *Sir Gawain and the Green Knight* may derive from a popular belief in a "green man" representing the cycle of the seasons.

Spenser says that "greene is for maydens meete" (*SC* "August" 68), as a sign of their youth and unripeness. From here it is a step to the meaning of "green" as "naïve," "gullible," or "foolish," as we found in the Catullus passage above. Shakespeare's Polonius tells his daughter Ophelia, "Pooh, you speak like a green girl" (*Hamlet* 1.3.101); Cleopatra recalls "My salad days, / When I was green in judgment" (*AC* 1.5.73–74); Iago connects "folly and green minds" (*Othello* 2.1.244). Shelley writes of a disease that pierced "Into the core of my green heart" (*Epipsychidion* 263).

A disease called "green sickness" (*chlorosis*) in the sixteenth century afflicted young people, usually girls, at puberty; unhealthy desires were attributed to it, and hence frustration. It seems to have been a kind of anemia, and the pale green was perhaps mainly due to the absence of a healthy reddish color.

When Juliet resists her father's plan to marry her to Paris, he shouts "Out, you green-sickness carrion! out, you baggage!" (*RJ* 3.5.156), and shouts more truly than he knows. Falstaff thinks failure to drink strong wine produces "a kind of male green-sickness" (*2H4*, 4.3.93). Viola tells the Duke that Olivia "never told her love . . . : she pin'd in thought, / And with a green and yellow melancholy / She sat like Patience on a monument, / Smiling at grief" (*12N* 2.4.111–16). Perhaps this is why Armado says "Green indeed is the color of lovers" (*LLL* 1.2.86).

Consonant with this sense is the connection of green with envy and jealousy. Romeo thinks of the "envious moon" as a pale maid, "sick and green" before Juliet's sun (*RJ* 2.2.4–8). Portia speaks of "green-eyed jealousy" (*MV* 3.2.110), while Iago brings it about by warning Othello: "O, beware my Lord of jealousy; / It is the green-ey'd monster, which doth mock / The meat it feeds on" (*Othello* 3.3.165–67). Blake's nurse in *Songs of Experience* ("Nurse's Song") listens to the children at play and "The days of my youth rise fresh in my mind, / My face turns green and pale." Envy and jealousy, according to the humor theory, are a function of yellow bile or gall, Greek *chole* (related to *chloros*), but the origin of this use of "green" may be Homer's use of *chloros* as a frequent epithet of *deos*, "fear" – "Green fear took hold of them" (*Iliad* 7.479). As with the green sickness, green seemed the right color for a man when the blood drained from his face.

Because it is the color of young vegetation and springtime, green is sometimes also the color of hope, especially the Christian hope of salvation (though more often hope is blue). Green is found in Dante's *Purgatorio*, the realm of hope (as opposed to hell, where hope is abandoned, and heaven, where hope is unnecessary). Even in this life, Dante says, no one is so lost that eternal love cannot return, "as long as hope has a green flower" (3.135). Two angels appear in garments "as green as newborn leaves" and with green wings to guard the valley of the rulers (8.28–29), and when Beatrice appears at the top of the mountain she wears a green cape (30.32). Sor Juana de la Cruz dismisses worldly hope as delusory, but it is also green, and those who are in its grip look through "green spectacles" ("A la esperanza").

Green is often the color of the sea. Shakespeare's Macbeth despairs that the sea will not wash off Duncan's blood but rather the blood will make "the green one red" (2.2.62). Antony vaunts that he has sent ships to found cities "o'er green Neptune's back" (*AC* 4.14.58). Neptune is "green-ey'd" in Milton's early *Vacation Exercise* (43); in *Paradise Lost* fish "Glide under the green Wave" (7.402).

Perhaps because it is the color of vegetation, which changes with the season, green is sometimes the color of inconstancy, as we find in Chaucer's "Against Women Unconstant," and in the *Squire's Tale* (646–47), in both places contrasting with the blue of faithfulness. Spenser's Lechery wears "a greene gowne" (*FQ* 1.4.25).

Grotto   *see* **Cave**

Gull   A gullible person is a gull; he can be gulled or duped or tricked. The relation of this set of words with the name of the seabird is unclear. "Gull" some-times meant a young unfledged bird of any sort (Shakespeare uses it in this sense occasionally), hence perhaps a naïve person, easily fooled. The verb "gull" could also mean "cram" or "gorge" (into someone's gullet), hence perhaps to feed falsehoods to a dupe, to make a dupe swallow something. Shakespeare's Malvolio is called a gull by those who "practice" on him (*12N* 3.2.66) and by himself: he was "made the most notorious geck [fool] and gull / That e'er invention play'd on" (5.1.342–43). Emilia screams at Othello "O gull, O dolt," after he has strangled Desdemona (*Othello* 5.2.164). A character in Dickens is described as "the blundering cheat – gull that he was, for all his cunning" (*Martin Chuzzlewit*, chap. 28).

The Italian verb for "gull" is *uccellare*, from *uccello*, "bird." Machiavelli uses it in *Mandragola* 1.3, where Callimaco plots to "bird" Nicia so he can bed his wife.

Joyce implicitly evokes the verb as he has Leopold Bloom throw a crumpled paper ball among the gulls looking for a meal. But they don't go for it. "Not such damn fools," Bloom thinks. The ball was made of a leaflet advertising a religious revivalist. Neither Bloom nor the gulls are so easily gulled (*Ulysses* 8.152 Random House).

H

Hair Cutting off or tearing off a portion of one's hair is a sign of grief or mourning in classical literature. At the news of Patroclus' death Achilles tears his hair (Homer, *Iliad* 18.27), and at Patroclus' funeral Achilles' companions all drop a lock of their hair onto the corpse (23.135–36); as she witnesses Hector's death Hecuba tears out her hair (22.405–06), and she and Andromache tear their hair when his body is brought back to Troy (24.710–11). Orestes leaves two locks of hair, for the river Inachus and his father, in the opening of Aeschylus' *Libation Bearers* (6–8); early in Sophocles' *Electra*, Orestes announces that he will leave cuttings from his hair at Agamemnon's grave (51–53); see also Euripides' *Electra* 90–91. In Euripides' *Alcestis*, Death himself tells Apollo he will cut off Alcestis' hair as he takes her to Hades' house (73–76), a speech that may have inspired the famous moment in Virgil's *Aeneid* when Iris descends to Dido on her pyre and cuts off a lock of her hair to take to the underworld (4.698–99).

The Bible is less clear about this custom, but it seems to be implicit in a few passages, e.g., where the Lord forbids men to mourn for those "in this land" and to "make themselves bald for them" (Jer. 16.6), or where the Lord calls on Jerusalem: "Cut off thine hair, O Jerusalem, and cast it away, and take up a lamentation on high places" (Jer. 7.29).

Behind this tradition lies the widespread belief that hair is an expression of life, youth, strength, or fertility. The secret of Samson's strength is his long hair (he is a Nazorite who has taken a vow not to cut it); only when his seven locks are removed can he be subdued (Judges 16). It was, and remains, a sign of willing humility or unwilling humiliation to shave the head of a man or a woman. A gift or theft of a lock of a woman's hair is an obvious symbolic act, one which Pope exploits in his mock-epic *The Rape of the Lock*. Ibsen's Hedda Gabler, cold and destructive, envies Thea Elvsted's abundant hair and threatens to burn it; she does burn Thea's "child," the book manuscript of Thea's lover.

If abundant hair is a sign of fertility, women in most western societies have been expected to cover or tie up their hair when appearing in public lest they be taken as sexually licentious. The loosening of hair, deliberate or not, and the tying or dressing of it, have been exploited by many writers to reveal inner states or future actions of their heroines. Racine's Phèdre asks who has tied up her hair in "knots" (1.3.159–60), knots that stand for her impossible and illicit passion for Hippolyte; near the end, her guilt at causing his death makes her hair stand on end (4.6.1268). Shelley's Beatrice Cenci, staggered by her rape at her father's hands, asks, "How comes this hair undone? / Its wandering strings must be what blind me so, / and yet I tied it fast" (*Cenci* 3.1.6–8); at the play's conclusion, calmly facing execution for her father's murder, she asks her stepmother to "bind up this hair / In any simple knot" (5.4.160–61). Escaping ringlets may signify innocent sexual exuberance, as it does with Pauline in Balzac's *La peau de chagrin* (p. 253 Pléiade), though later her dishevelled (*épars*) hair will express something less innocent. Maggie Tulliver's undisciplined hair in George Eliot's *Mill on the Floss* – "But her hair won't curl all I can do with it," her mother complains (1.2) – expresses her natural and impetuous personality. A prototype of this hair is Eve's in Milton's *Paradise Lost*: she "Her unadorned golden tresses wore / dishevelled, but in wanton ringlets waved" (4.305–06).

Like Eve's, a woman's hair in literature is often golden, whereby it may represent not only sexuality but beauty and wealth. Spenser complains of his lady's guile in dressing her golden tresses under a net of gold in order to entangle men's eyes "in that golden snare" (*Amoretti* 37). Bassanio describes Portia's hair as "A golden mesh t'entrap the hearts of men" (*MV* 3.2.122). It may suggest an angelic nature, as Lucie Manette's does in Dickens's *A Tale of Two Cities*, or it may be deceitful, as Rosamond Vincy's "wondrous" hair traps Lydgate in Eliot's *Middlemarch*.

Phaedrus' description of *occasio* or opportunity as "bald, hairy on the forehead, nude at the back" (*Fables* 5.8), gave rise to the advice to seize time or opportunity "by the forelock." Rabelais reports that "Chance wears all her locks in front, and once she has passed you by, you cannot recall her. For the back of her head is bald, and she never turns back" (*Gargantua and Pantagruel* 1.37, trans. Cohen). Spenser asks the spring to tell his love "the joyous time will not be staid / Unlesse she doe him by the forelock take" (*Amoretti* 70). Othello will "take the safest occasion by the front" to be reconciled with Cassio (3.1.50). To quote *The Cenci* again, a plotter urges "we take fleet occasion by the hair" (5.1.38), a disturbing echo of Beatrice, "whom her father sometimes hales / From hall to hall by the entangled hair" (3.1.44–45). But Goethe playfully announces that lovers worship one goddess above all the gods and goddesses, *Gelegenheit* or Opportunity: "one day she appeared to me, as a dark-haired / Girl: an abundance of locks tumbled down over her brow, / Shorter ringlets entwined her delicate neck, and unbraided / Hair rose boldly in waves over the crown of her head. / And I knew her, I seized her as she went hurrying by me..." (*Roman Elegies* 6.127–31, trans. Luke).

Halcyon   The halcyon is a semi-mythical Greek seabird with a plaintive cry, identified with the kingfisher. The original form of the name in Greek is *alkuon*, but the *h* got attached when it was thought that the word was made of two roots, *hal-* ("sea") and *kuo-* ("breed"); that surmise derives from the belief that the bird builds its nest on the sea. To do so it must have calm weather, and so, as Simonides puts it, "in the winter months Zeus / admonishes fourteen days, / the wind-forgetting season / mortals call it, the holy time of childrearing for the dappled / halcyon" (508). Aristotle quotes these lines where he explains that the halcyon builds its nest and breeds during the week before and after the winter solstice (*Historia Animalium* 542b15); these two weeks became known as the *alkuonides hemerai* or "halcyon days" – a period of tranquillity. When Poseidon proposes peace to the birds of Aristophanes, he offers them "rainwater in the pools / and halcyon days forever" (*Birds* 1593–94). Theocritus predicts "halcyons shall lay the waves and sea to rest" (7.57).

Ovid devotes much of book 11 of the *Metamorphoses* to the story of Ceyx and Alcyone. Changed into halcyons, they still mate and raise their young; for seven days Alcyone broods on her nest floating on the waters. The seas are calm, for Aeolus forbids the winds to go abroad (11.743–49). Several other poets mention them, e.g., Virgil, who calls them "pleasing to Thetis" the sea-nymph (*Georgics* 1.399).

Shakespeare's Joan of Arc predicts, "Expect Saint Martin's summer [in November], halcyon days, / Since I have entered into these wars" (*1H6* 1.2.131–32). Halcyons are the "Birds of Calm" that "sit brooding on the charmed wave" at the birth of Christ (Milton, "Nativity" 68).

Harbor *see* **Sea, Ship**

Harp, lyre, and lute There has been a good deal of confusion for centuries over just what stringed instruments were meant by several Hebrew, Greek, and Roman words. We will not attempt to sort it all out here, as for our purposes the associations of certain words are more important than philological accuracy.

Angels play harps: that seems well established. "Harp" is the usual word in English Bible translations for Hebrew *kinnor* and Greek *kithara*. Yet the former probably and the latter certainly were kinds of lyre, that is, the strings passed partly parallel to a box or shell sounding board. "Lyre" does not appear in either Testament of the Authorized Version.

According to Genesis the *kinnor* was invented by Jubal, son of Lamech (4.21). David was "a cunning player on an harp" (1 Sam. 16.16), and the Psalms attributed to him are to be sung to the harp, or sometimes to a harp and another instrument called a *nebel* in Hebrew. The *nebel* is usually translated as "psaltery" but may well have been a harp! ("Psalm" and "psaltery" are derived from a Greek verb meaning "pluck" or "twang.") It was common for prophets to prophesy with a "harp" (e.g., 1 Chro. 25.6). The *kithara*, rendered "harp" in the Authorized Version, is the instrument of the angels, as we read at several points in Revelation (5.8, 15.2); with characteristic thoroughness its author writes, "and I heard the voice of harpers harping with their harps" (14.2).

The lyre was one of several similar stringed instruments of ancient Greece. The *lyra*, the standard lyre, is not named in the *Iliad* or *Odyssey*, where the bards and Apollo play a *phorminx*, and others play a *kitharis*, both usually translated as "lyre" in English. Both probably had four strings, whereas the later *lyra* usually had seven. Sappho sometimes calls her lyre a *barbiton*, which had longer strings; Horace refers to the "Lesbian *barbiton*" in his first ode. They may all have been plucked with a pick or *plektron*; none was bowed. The Homeric *Hymn to Hermes* tells in detail how the clever young Hermes "was the first to make a singer of a tortoise" by turning its shell into the sounding board of the first lyre (24–54), which he eventually gave to Apollo. Horace calls Mercury the "father of the curved lyre" (1.10.6), but Apollo becomes its patron god (see Plato, *Republic* 399d–e). "Tortoise" (Greek *chelys*, Latin *testudo*) was a common synecdoche for the lyre among both Greek and Roman poets (Sappho 18, Euripides' *Alcestis* 446–47; Virgil's *Georgics* 4.464, Horace 1.32.14). This is "the corded Shell" of Dryden's "Song for St. Cecilia's Day" (17) and the "Enchanting shell!" of Gray's "Progress of Poesy" (15).

"Lyric" poetry was originally poetry sung to the lyre, and occasionally to the oboe or shawm (Greek *aulos*). Alexandrian scholars settled on a canon of nine great lyric poets: Alcman, Sappho, Alcaeus, Stesichorus, Ibycus, Anacreon, Simonides, Pindar, Bacchylides; sometimes Corinna was added. Lyric song might be choral, such as the songs between episodes of tragedy, or it might be solo, a monody. It could be set in a great variety of meters and be about a great variety of subjects; it might be a song of praise for a victor in the games, a wedding hymn (*epithalamion*), a love song, an inspirational patriotic anthem, or even a story, if it is brief. The greatest lyric poet was the legendary Orpheus, who was so skillful on his lyre that he could charm animals and make trees and rocks move.

In the opening of his First Pyth., Pindar praises his lyre as the pacifier of all violence: "Even Ares the violent / Leaves aside his harsh and pointed spears / And comforts his heart in drowsiness" (10–12; trans. Bowra). (Gray imitates these lines in "Progress" 17–19). By contrast, according to Aeschylus, war is "danceless, lyreless" (*Suppliants* 681). Horace could refer to his "unwarlike lyre" (*imbellisque lyrae*) (1.6.10), and in his final ode he tells how Apollo rebukes him with his lyre for wishing to speak of battles and conquered cities (4.15.1–2); many poets found "lyric" fitter to express love or other personal feelings than for rousing young men to their martial duty. It is a little jarring, then, to find Byron, who admired Horace, speaking of "the warlike lyre" ("Elegy on Newstead" 89).

At times, indeed, the lyre stood for a certain genre of poetry in opposition to that of the flute, trumpet, or other instrument. So Marino, in his sonnet in honor of Torquato Tasso, gives pipe, lyre, and trumpet as the three kinds of poetry Tasso wrote.

The word "harp" is Germanic in origin, and first appears in a Latin text by the sixth-century bishop Venantius Fortunatus: "the Roman lyre and the barbarian harp praise you" (*Carmina* 7.8.63). In *Beowulf* the *scop* or bard sings to the *hearpe*. But Fortunatus' distinction was often blurred: Aelfric glossed "hearpe" as *lyra*, and in medieval Latin *cithara* was used to translate both. In later English poetry "harp" is still preferred as the instrument of the angels and of David, but occasionally we find "David's lyre" (e.g., Cowley, *Davideis* 1.26). Byron begins one of his *Hebrew Melodies* with "The harp the monarch minstrel swept," but soon it also becomes "David's lyre." Orpheus is usually given his proper lyre, his "Orphean lyre" (Milton, *PL* 3.17; Wordsworth, 1805 *Prelude* 1.233), but sometimes it is "Orpheus' lute" (Shakespeare, *2GV* 3.2.77). Even Apollo gets a lute in *Love's Labours Lost* (4.3.340), while in the Athens of

Theseus a eunuch offers (in vain) to sing to a harp (*MND* 5.1.45). Coleridge gives harps to angels and lyres to the muse and to Alcaeus, but he translated Pindar's *phorminx* as "harp," no doubt to alliterate with "hymn" (trans. of Second Olympic). Bowles's poem "The Harp, and Despair, of Cowper" makes Cowper's instrument a lyre, and once even "Fancy's shell," never a harp.

The word "lute" is ultimately from Arabic; the instrument became fasionable from the fourteenth to seventeenth centuries. There were ancient equivalents (the strings, often just two or three, passed over a long neck where they could be stopped), but they were less common than lyre and harp.

As interest in Germanic and Celtic bards grew in the eighteenth century it was understood that "harp" was the better term for their instrument, but even in "The Bard" Gray used "harp" (28) or "lyre" (22) as the rhyme or alliteration dictated. Blake's bards are almost always harpers, but once in a while they get a lyre. Scott generally gave his Scottish minstrels harps. After the distinction between "romantic" and "classic" spread from Germany to England, Wordsworth in effect returned to Fortunatus' distinction: in his 1815 Preface he writes of "the classic lyre or romantic harp," and in "To the Clouds" he asks, "Where is the Orphean lyre, or Druid harp, / To accompany the verse?" (60–61).

Victor Hugo stages a debate between "La Lyre et la Harpe" for the soul of the young poet, the classical lyre urging him to withdraw from the world's miseries and pursue poetic fame, beauty, and pleasure, the Christian harp summoning him to comfort the afflicted and praise God; the result is a compromise wherein the poet will write in a classic manner on Christian themes.

However unwarlike, the lyre struck more than one early bard as rather like a bow. (Indeed the earliest harps are bows with several strings.) When the disguised Odysseus finally gets to handle his bow, he "looked it all over, / As when a man, who well understands the lyre and singing, / easily, holding it on either side, pulls the strongly twisted / cord of sheep's gut, so as to slip it over a new peg, / so, without any strain, Odysseus strung the great bow. / Then plucking it in his right hand he tested the bowstring, / and it gave him back an excellent sound like the voice of a swallow" (*Odyssey* 21.405–11, trans. Lattimore). The philosopher Heraclitus offers "the bow and the lyre" as models for the nature of things, held together through contrary tensions (frag. 51, cited in Plato, *Symposium* 187a). Pindar, in the ode quoted above, tells his lyre that "Your shafts enchant the souls even of the gods" (12).

See **Aeolian harp, Pipe, Trumpet.**

Harvest *see* **Autumn**

Haven *see* **Sea, Ship**

Hawk In the traditional hierarchy of birds the hawk, falcon, and kindred predators rank just below the eagle. In Chaucer's *Parliament of Fowls* "the royal egle" is named first among the "foules of ravyne," followed by the "tiraunt" or "goshauk," the "gentyl faucoun [falcon]," the "sperhauk [sparrowhawk]" and the "merlioun [merlin]" (a kind of falcon) (323–40). In the absence of an eagle, Spenser suggests, the hawk is king: "the soring hauke did towre, / Sitting like the King of fowles in majesty and powre" (*FQ* 6.10.6). (*See* **Eagle**.)

Hamlet can tell a hawk from a handsaw (2.2.379), but in literature by and large there is little difference between a hawk and a falcon, and the sport of falconry is also called hawking.

Homer once calls the hawk (Greek *kirkos*) the swift messenger of Apollo (*Odyssey* 15.526); Virgil once calls the hawk (Latin *accipiter*) "holy" and his commentator Servius explains it was sacred to Mars. Little has been made, however, of these divine connections.

Hawk and falcon are emblems of swiftness. When Achilles begins his pursuit of Hector, Homer likens him to a hawk "who moves lightest of things flying" (*Iliad* 22.139). The Argo sails "like a hawk which rides the breeze swiftly through the high air" (Apollonius, *Argonautica* 2.935, trans. Hunter). Sidney describes a flight as "More swift then falcon's stoope to feeding Falconer's call" (*Fourth Eclogues* 73.58).

The typical prey of the hawk is the dove. In the *Iliad* passage Hector is compared to one; in another simile Aeschylus imagines "hawks not far behind doves" (*Prometheus* 857); for yet another chase Ovid offers this: "As doves on fluttering wings flee from a hawk, / And as a hawk pursues a fluttering dove, / So did I run, so fiercely he gave chase" (*Met.* 5.604–606, trans. Melville). In a version of the peaceable kingdom, Spenser has the lion and the lamb consort, "And eke the Dove sate by the Faulcons side" (*FQ* 4.8.31). (*See* **Dove**.) But other prey will do: Chaucer's sparrowhawk is "The quayles foo" while the merlin seeks the lark (338–40), in Spenser "A fearfull partridge" flees "the sharpe hauke" (*FQ* 3.8.33), while in both authors the heron is also a quarry: Chaucer calls a falcon a "heroner" (*TC* 4.413), Spenser has "a cast of Faulcons make their flight / At an Herneshaw [heron]" (*FQ* 6.7.9).

Certain technical terms from falconry are common in Renaissance writers. "To tower" is to mount up in preparation for a strike, "stoop" means "swoop" (noun or verb) onto a quarry or descent (descend) to the lure, the "pitch" is the height the bird towers, the "place" is the highest pitch, and the "point" is the position to the windward of the quarry around which the falcon circles. In one of the eerie portents of Macbeth's murder of Duncan, "A falcon, towering in her pride of place, / Was by a mousing owl hawk'd at, and kill'd" (2.4.12–13). In another metaphorical scene, Henry tells Gloucester, "what a point, my lord, your falcon made / And what a pitch she flew above the rest" (*2H6* 2.1.5–6). At the fall of nature, according to Milton, "The bird of Jove, stooped from his airy tower, / Two birds of gayest plume before him drove" (*PL* 11.185–86). Hawks and falcons are usually kept hooded until they are loosed for the chase; Byron makes wicked use of this practice among his bird similes for contemporary poets: "And Coleridge, too, has lately taken wing, / But like a hawk encumber'd with his hood" (*Don Juan* Dedication 13–14).

The opening of Yeats's "The Second Coming" is justly famous: "Turning and turning in the widening gyre / The falcon cannot hear the falconer." It is an omen, an augury, of the coming anarchy as the aristocracy loses its command.

Heliotrope   *See* **Sunflower**

Heron   A heron is sent by Athena as a sign of success to Odysseus and Diomedes on their night foray (*Iliad* 10.275), and the sight or sound of the bird (Greek *erodios* probably referred to several species) remained a good omen in the ancient world (cf. Plutarch, *Moralia* 405D). In the Bible, however, it is named only in lists of unclean "abominations" (Lev. 11.19, Deut. 14.18).

The heron does not seem to have acquired a consistent range of symbolic meanings in literature; indeed it is featured in literature only seldom. Its striking appearance, its slow and solitary hunting in marshes, and its graceful flight have sometimes suggested nobility, freedom, and the beauty of nature. The German poet Platen writes, "Wine, that sets us free, fledges our hearts; / A heron [*Reiher*] I fly off" ("O nimm die Rosen auf" 8). In Jewett's well-known story "A White Heron," the girl Julie offers to find the heron's nest for a hunter–ornithologist, but in the end, perhaps inspired by its freedom, she cannot bring herself to do so. Jeffers, in "People and a Heron," likens a swarm of people on the beach to gulls, but when they leave a heron comes, "a lone bird," "dearer to me than many people." Herons (or hernes) frequent Yeats's poems and plays, notably in the brief play *Calvary*, where it may stand, mysteriously, for Christ, though "God has not died for the white heron."

Holly   There are several types of holly, including "male" and "female" varieties; in combination with other plants (mistletoe, ivy) they may have been used in pagan fertility ceremonies. But its chief distinctive trait is that it is evergreen: as the author of *Sir Gawain and the Green Knight* has it, the "holyn bobbe" or holly cluster carried by the Green Knight is "goodliest in green when the groves are bare" (206–07). As such it was thought appropriate to Christmas and New Year's Day, the season of death and renewal of life. For centuries it has been the distinctive Christmas plant, at least in Britain, as the carol "The Holly and the Ivy" reminds us; there the blossom, berry, prickle, and bark of the holly all stand for characteristics of Jesus Christ. It was so common by the mid-nineteenth century that Dickens's Scrooge wishes everyone who says "Merry Christmas" were "buried with a stake of holly through his heart" (*A Christmas Carol*, "Stave I"), while the Ghost of Christmas Past has "a branch of fresh green holly in its hand" ("Stave II").

Its evergreen character also suits funerals or graves. Don Quixote comes across a group of mourners carrying holly branches (1.13), while Victor Hugo announces to his dead daughter that he will bring heather and green holly (*houx vert*) to her grave ("Demain, dès l'aube," from *Les Contemplations*).

Honey   *see* **Bee**

Horn   *see* **Dream**

Horse   It is difficult to appreciate today how thoroughly we depended on horses before the railways of the nineteenth century and especially the automobile of the twentieth. The horse was the chief beast of travel, work, hunting, and war. Even the vehicles which displaced it were described in equine terms – "iron horse" and "horseless carriage" – while "horsepower" is still the measure of engines. Many proverbial phrases, such as "ride a high horse," "ride roughshod over," "flog a dead horse," "look a gift horse in the mouth," "spur someone on," "horse of a different color," "dark horse," and "straight from the

horse's mouth," are still in common use; in America many say "Hold your
horses" or even "Whoa!" who have never ridden a horse.

Horses are ubiquitous in literature until recent times. Greek and Roman
warriors fight from horse-drawn chariots, knights ride on steeds and do
chivalrous deeds ("chivalry" is from Old French *chevalerie*, from *cheval*, "horse"),
the cavalry charges enemies or rescues friends ("cavalry" has a similar
etymology), and every hero's horse has a name, from Achilles' horse Xanthos,
who speaks (*Iliad* 19.404ff.), to Don Quixote's "hack" Rosinante. In more recent
literature horses (and unicorns) have been the heroes of their own stories: e.g.,
Anna Sewell's *Black Beauty*.

The most common metaphorical horses are those that draw the chariot of
the sun, the moon, etc. (*See* **Dawn**, **Moon**, **Night**, and especially **Sun**.)
Probably the most influential symbolic horses are those that Plato describes in
his simile for the soul. The soul is a union of three parts, a charioteer
(judgment or reason) and two horses, one of which is noble and obedient
(honor or mettle), the other base and disobedient (appetite or will) (*Phaedrus*
246a–b, 253c–54e); the charioteer must learn the difficult art of managing two
different steeds ("manage" in its earliest English sense referred only to horses).
Whether driving several or riding one, the reason could be disobeyed or
overthrown by the willful, bestial, or irrational part of the soul. So Euripides'
Hippolytus, whose name means something like "horse-looser," is killed when
his horses bolt at the sight of a monster, ultimately the doing of Aphrodite,
whom Hippolytus had scorned. Marlowe's enamored Leander chaffs at the bit:
"For as a hot, proud horse highly disdains / To have his head controlled, but
breaks the reins, // . . . so he that loves, / The more he is restrained, the worse
he fares" (*Hero and Leander* 625–29). "Most wretched man," Spenser writes,
"That to affections does the bridle lend!" (*FQ* 2.4.34); Guyon learns to resist
temptation, "brydling his will" (2.12.53). Milton has the phrase, "give the reins
to grief" – to let an emotion have its head, as it were (*Samson Agonistes*
1578).

It is thus a witty decision on Swift's part to make his rational beings horses
(the Houyhynhnms) and his bestial ones humans (the Yahoos) (*Gulliver's Travels*,
book 4). The traditional equation remains common nonetheless, even in Swift:
the narrator of his *Tale of a Tub* confesses he is "a Person, whose Imaginations
are hardmouth'd, and exceedingly disposed to run away with his Reason,
which I have observed from long Experience, to be a very light Rider, and
easily shook off" (sec 9). Rochester reads Jane Eyre's face and tells her, "Reason
sits firm and holds the reins, and she will not let the feelings burst away and
hurry her to wild chasms" (Charlotte Brontë, *Jane Eyre* chap. 19). But Dickens
plays with it in *Hard Times*, as Bitzer, the boy who embodies the "rational"
teaching methods of Gradgrind, defines a horse correctly as "Quadruped.
Graminivorous. Forty teeth," etc., in the opening, but in the end, having
grown up all head and no heart, he is outwitted by a real horse who refuses
to obey him.

A variant of this image is the "manage" of government, where the leader
rides the city or populace. Jupiter assigns the winds to Aeolus, who knows
"when to tighten and when to loosen their reins" (Virgil, *Aeneid* 1.63; see
Lucan 7.124ff.). Dante denounces abject Italy for its empty saddle, even though

Justinian has mended its bridle (codified its laws): "see how this beast turns fierce / because there are no spurs that would correct it" (*Purgatorio* 6.88–96, trans. Mandelbaum). Shakespeare's Claudio wonders whether "the body politic be / A horse whereon the governor doth ride, / Who, newly in the seat, that it may know / He can command, lets it straight feel the spur" (*MM* 1.2.159–62). When Richard II submits to Bolingbroke he invokes a mythical precedent of bad horsemanship: "Down, down I come, like glist'ring Phaeton, / Wanting the manage of unruly jades" (*R2* 3.3.178–79); it is a symbolically charged moment when Bolingbroke rides Richard's favorite horse (5.5.77–94). Vigny's Moses asks God, "Let someone else bridle the steed of Israel" ("Moses" 55, trans. Blackmores). The hero of the "western" is typically a lone horseman who is at one with an extraordinary horse; his enemies, though they also ride horses, are typically horse-thieves.

According to the myth, Pegasus the flying horse was beloved of the Muses because he created the spring Hippocrene on Mt. Helicon by stamping the ground with his hooves, after which he flew up to heaven. Propertius calls the Muses the daughters of Pegasus (3.1.19); Dante addresses one of the Muses as Pegasea as he invokes her aid (*Paradiso* 18.82). In the Renaissance the horse became an emblem of the poet's ambition, a symbol common enough for ambitious Milton to claim, "above the Olympian hill I soar, / Above the flight of Pegasean wing" (*PL* 7.3–4). Concerning poetry Pope recommends judgment as a balance to wit or imagination: "'Tis more to guide than spur the Muse's steed; / Restrain his Fury, than provoke his speed; / The winged Courser, like a gen'rous Horse, / Shows most true Mettle when you check his Course" (*Essay on Criticism* 1.84–87).

There is a striking recurrent trope about the Trojan horse, the "wooden horse" by which the Greeks infiltrated and destroyed Troy (*Odyssey* 8.493). Aeschylus calls the Greeks the "young of the horse" (*Agamemnon* 825) and Virgil says the horse "bore armed infantry in its heavy womb" (*Aeneid* 6.516) – or in Dryden's translation, the horse was "pregnant with arms" (see also 9.152). Dante varies the trope in saying that the horse caused a breach through which "the noble seed of the Romans escaped" (*Inferno* 26.60).

See **Ass.**

Hours *see* **Seasons**

Humor The Greeks and other ancients considered life to depend on fluids in the body; youth is moist, age is dry, death is desiccation. Homer speaks of a liquid called *aion*, which is occasionally indistinguishable from tears (e.g., *Odyssey* 5.152) and is more often something like "vital juice" or "life fluid"; it later acquired more abstract meanings: "life," "age," "eternity" (English "eon" is a derivative).

Blood, sweat, semen, and milk were all taken as potent with human life, and life could be enhanced by anointing with oil, rubbing with the sweat of an animal, drinking wine, and bathing in blood. Urine and other secretions such as bile or phlegm became indices of human health.

Hippocrates, in *The Nature of Man* 4, describes four *chumoi* or fluids – blood, phlegm, yellow bile, and black bile – the balance or proportion of which determines human health and sickness. Pain or illness is the excess or defect of one of them. They were correlated with the four elements – earth, water, air, and fire – and with the four qualities – hot, cold, moist, dry; phlegm, for example, is coldest and wettest, and thus related to water.

In Latin the term for *chumos* is *umor* or *humor*, and "humor" is the English term (its original sense as fluid remains in another English borrowing, "humid"). The medical theory, elaborated by Latin and medieval European writers, held sway well into the nineteenth century, as Byron's death by medicinal bleeding may remind us.

Many terms still current in English, or only recently obsolete, depend on the theory. One's "temperament" is one's particular mixture of humors; "temper" can mean "temperament" but more often "proper temperament" or "composure," as when one is "out of temper" or "loses one's temper." A "distemper" is a disease or disorder: Milton speaks of "distempers foul" (*PL* 4.118). A synonym of "temperament" is "complexion": Chaucer writes of his Frankeleyn, "Of his complexioun he was sangwyn" (*CT* Pro. 333); later it was thought that skin color reflected one's inner complexion.

"Sanguine" is still in use today to mean "cheerful" or "hopeful," sometimes "courageous"; a sanguine temperament is dominated by blood (Latin *sanguis*), which is hot and wet, and marked by a ruddy appearance; it is associated with air. Besides the Frankeleyn Shakespeare's Mercutio and Beatrice are sanguine. (*See* **Blood**.)

"Phlegmatic" still means "dull" or "sluggish," but also "calm" or "even–tempered"; a phlegmatic character has too much phlegm (Greek and Latin *phlegma*). Sidney complains to Patience, with her "leaden counsels," that he can never take "In thy cold stuff a phlegmatic delight" (*Astrophel* 56). Jane Austen's character Mary Bennett might be taken as phlegmatic.

"Choleric" means "irascible," "hot-tempered," from "choler" (Greek and Latin *cholera*) or bile (hot and dry, hence fiery). Synonyms are "bilious" and "splenetic" (from "spleen"). (*See* **Bile**.)

"Melancholic" means "sullen," "sad," or "dejected"; it comes from an excess of melancholy or black bile (cold and dry, hence earthy). The "humors black" of Milton's *Samson Agonistes* 600 are melancholy. (*See* **Melancholy**.)

In the 1590s in England "humor" seems to have been in great fashion, a fad Shakespeare mocks through his character Nym, whose every line has the word in it (*MW* 1.3). "Humor" could mean "temperament." To be in "good humor" (or just "in humor") is to be in good temper, in proper balance. Ben Jonson wrote two comedies, *Every Man in his Humour* and *Every Man out of his Humour*, whose titles remind us that comedies since Menander have turned on characters of a particular temperament or humor: the miser, the grouch, the angry old man, the braggart soldier, the passionate lover, the cowardly servant. Literary critics sometimes use "humor" to refer to such characters themselves. The pattern in most comedies is the return of the "humorous" character to his or her proper humor, or the expulsion of the bad humor; "humor" is thus the comic counterpart of the tragic *hamartia*, "flaw" or (more properly) "error."

Hunting   The hunt or chase has been a male preoccupation for thousands of years. It not only provided food and excitement, but (as Xenophon argued in his *Cyropaedia*) it was the best training for war. Indeed some of the acts of warfare in epic seem little different from hunting, as the similes tell us: Achilles chases Hector three times around Troy, "chasing him, as a dog in the mountains who has flushed from his covert / a deer's fawn follows him through the folding ways and the valleys" (Homer, *Iliad* 22.189–90, trans. Lattimore), and Aeneas pursues Turnus as a hunting dog pursues a stag (Virgil, *Aeneid* 12.750–51). Siegried is a great hunter (in the Old High German *Nibelungenlied*), but he is killed by Hagen whose sign or device is a boar. (The stag and the boar are the two highest or noblest quarries.) "As the stag flees before the dogs / The pagans took flight before Roland," according to the Old French *Song of Roland* (1874–75).

Hunting, and the scars that come of it, may be rites of passage into manhood or marks of personal identity. The scar that almost betrays the disguised Odysseus, for instance, came from a boar that he killed even as it gored him (*Odyssey* 19.388–466). Or hunts may be occasions of fateful or fatal events, as when Dido and Aeneas, seeking shelter from a storm during a hunt, make love in a cave (*Aeneid* 4.160–72), or when the Calydonian boar hunt, which the maiden Atalanta wins, leads to the death of Meleager (told by Ovid, *Met.* 8.260–444). Ahab's maniacal pursuit of the white whale, to which many symbolic meanings accrue, leads to catastrophe (Melville, *Moby-Dick*).

The theme of the hunter hunted is common, in part for its satisfying formal turn or reversal. Agamemnon, who angered Artemis (goddess of the hunt) by hunting down her sacred stag, and who then propitiated her by sacrificing his daughter, is caught in a hunting net and murdered by his wife and lover when he returns home (Aeschylus, *Agamemnon*). Pentheus in Euripides' *Bacchae* wants to hunt down the uncontrollable maenads, but he himself becomes their quarry; his mother, still in a trance, boasts that she has brought back the trophy of her chase – her son's head. When Actaeon the hunter comes upon Artemis bathing, he is transformed into a stag and killed by his own dogs (Ovid, *Met.* 3.131–255). Tristan becomes the master of the hunt for King Mark, but is caught in nets of love for Isolde; they both become "love's huntsmen," laying nets and snares for each other (Gottfried von Strassburg, *Tristan and Isolde* 11930–32).

Hunting metaphors since ancient times have been deployed for many states and actions. Plato has Socrates propose that not only generals but geometers, astronomers, and calculators are hunters of a kind, for they try to find things out (*Euthydemus* 290b–c). Sophocles' *Oedipus Tyrannus* is filled with hunting metaphors, as Oedipus leads the investigation into the unknown murderer: another case of the hunter hunted. Ovid, who seems to have inadvertently come across something he should not have seen, and was sent in exile for it, likens his indiscretion to Actaeon (*Tristia* 3.103–07). In Christian allegories sometimes the hunter is the devil, or sin, and the quarry is everyman. In Chaucer's translation from a French poem, "An ABC," the speaker appeals to the Virgin to save him, though he has been a "beste in wil and deede," and to "make oure foo to failen of his praye [prey]." (45, 64). Arthur and Guyon set out "To hunt for glory and renowmed prayse" (Spenser, *FQ* 3.1.3), while King Ferdinand begins Shakespeare's *Love's Labour's Lost* by asking, "Let fame, that all hunt after in their lives, / Live regist'red upon our brazen tombs."

The most widespread metaphor, however, is the love hunt, as shown in the image of Eros (Cupid) with his bow and arrows. In one of his earliest appearances, however, Eros hunts with nets; so Ibycus (6): "Eros, looking at me languishingly under his dark eyebrows, by all manner of enchantments casts me into the nets of Cypris [Aphrodite], from which there is no escape" (trans. Kenney). Euripides' Helen was one of the first to complain that someone "hunts her in marriage" (*Helen* 63). Lucretius warns us to shun "the hunting nets of love" (4.1146). The love-struck Dido wanders through the city "like an unsuspecting hind hit by an arrow, whom a shepherd pursuing with weapons has shot from afar" (*Aeneid* 4.69–71). Horace pleads, "You avoid me, Chloe, like a fawn / seeking its mother on the pathless / mountain and starting with groundless / fears at the woods and winds (1.23.1–4, trans. Shepherd). Petrarch echoes Ovid on Actaeon: "Not so much did Diana please her lover / When, by a similar chance, all naked / he saw her in the midst of the cold waters, / Than the cruel mountain shepherdess pleased me" (*Rime* 52). In a sonnet (*Rime* 190) Petrarch describes a white doe with a sweet and proud look but with a sign about her saying "Let no one touch me, for Caesar set me free." Wyatt's version is justly admired: "Whoso list to hunt, I know where is an hind, / But as for me, helas, I may no more..."

Hyacinth   Just what flower the classical "hyacinth" (Greek *hyakinthos*) referred to is uncertain, perhaps the wild hyacinth (bluebell), wild iris, or blue larkspur, but it was "dark" (Theocritus 10.28) or "purple" (Persius 1.32). Greeks thought they saw the letters AI inscribed on the petals (hence the iris and larkspur are likelier candidates); it is one of the flowers that laments for Bion in Moschus' elegy – "now hyacinth, let your lettering speak" (3.6), "AI" being a cry of grief. Ovid tells the story of the boy Hyacinth, beloved of Apollo, and accidentally killed by the god's discus (*Met.* 10.167–219): from Hyacinth's blood grows a purple flower like a lily, with AIAI on it, which also suggests Ajax (Aias) (see *Met.* 13.394–98). The "sanguine flower inscrib'd with woe" of Milton's "Lycidas" (106) is the hyacinth. Shelley describes blown blossoms with the message "follow" on them "as the blue bells / Of Hyacinth tell Apollo's written grief" (*PU* 2.1.139–40).

Apart from the myth of Hyacinth, the flower is found among those in ideal gardens or fields. Zeus makes love with Hera on a bed of herbs and flowers, including the hyacinth (*Iliad* 14.348); it is one of the flowers plucked by Persephone when she is plucked by Hades (*Hymn to Demeter* 7, 426). The crucial scene of the hyacinth garden in Eliot's *The Waste Land*, where the girl says "You gave me hyacinths first a year ago; / They called me the hyacinth girl" and the poet fails to speak or even look at her (35–41), may evoke both Homeric sexuality and elegists' dead beloved.

Another passage in Homer has had a long progeny – his description of Odysseus' hair as having locks that hung "like the hyacinth flower" (*Odyssey* 6.231). It has usually been taken to refer to the flower's blue-black color, though it could refer to its shape. Pope has it both ways in his translation: "His hyacinthine locks descend in wavy curls" (6.274). Milton gives Adam "hyacinthine locks" (*PL* 4.301), Byron's Leila's hair falls "in hyacinthine flow" (*Giaour* 496), Poe praises Helen's "hyacinth hair" ("To Helen" 7), and Hetty's hair in George Eliot's *Adam Bede* has "dark hyacinthine curves" (chap. 15).

I

Incense   *see* **Frankincense and myrrh**

Insect   The symbolic meaning of the generic term "insect" is usually ephemerality or brevity of life. Gray notes how the "insect youth" have peopled the air and draws a moral: "Such is the race of man: / And they that creep, and they that fly, / Shall end where they began. / Alike the busy and the gay / But flutter through life's little day" ("Ode on the Spring" 25–36). See also Thomson, *Summer* 342–51. Shelley thinks his song ends "as a brief insect dies with dying day" ("Ode to Liberty" 280); when the sun sets, "each ephemeral insect then / Is gathered unto death" (*Adonais* 254–55). "What are men?" Tennyson asks; "Insects of an hour, that hourly work their brother insect wrong" ("Locksley Hall Sixty Years After" 202). Addressing Mt. Monadnoc Emerson says, "Hither we bring / Our insect miseries to thy rocks; / And the whole flight, with folded wing, / Vanish, and end their mumuring" ("Monadnoc").

"Fly," used as the generic term for any flying insect, often has the same sense. (*See* **Fly**.)

It is not clear what insect Kafka's Gregor Samsa is transformed into ("The Metamorphosis") – perhaps a cockroach or a dung beetle – but it is a metamorphosis not from a larva to a flying insect such as a butterfly but rather the reverse, from human to bug. The story has been thus interpreted, or overinterpreted, to be a kind of parody of a spiritual transformation or resurrection. (*See* **Butterfly, Caterpillar**.)

Insect entries in this dictionary: **Ant, Bee, Butterfly, Caterpillar, Cicada, Fly, Locust, Scorpion, Spider, Wasp**.

Iron   The last and worst of the races or ages, the one that now prevails, according to Hesiod, Ovid, and other ancient authors, is symbolized by iron (*see* **Metal**). Iron was chosen not only because it stood lowest on the hierarchy, after gold, silver, and bronze, but probably also because the ancients remembered the shift from bronze to iron as the most useful metal during the third and second millennia BC. By the time of Hesiod, too, most weapons and armor were made of iron, and it was associated with Ares the god of warfare (Roman Mars); since the present is (always) a time of warfare and other violence, the present is an iron age. About to have his eyes burnt out with hot irons, Shakespeare's Arthur cries, "Ah, none but in this iron age would do it!" (*King John* 4.1.60). Ovid, however, notes that gold was a greater bane than iron, and that men used both to slaughter each other (*Met.* 1.141–42).

Homer gives to iron (Greek *sideros*) such epithets as "gray," "violet-colored," "dark," and "gleaming"; it is also "wrought with toil" because of its hardness (*Iliad* 6.48). As a sign of hardness, "iron" sometimes modifies "spirit" or "heart": Hector tells Achilles, "Your spirit is of iron" (*Iliad* 22.357); "your heart is of iron," Hecuba and Achilles each tell Priam (24.205, 512). Such phrases passed through Latin poetry into all the vernaculars – Shakespeare has "Bear witness, all that have not hearts of iron" (*H8* 3.2.424) – into modern speech.

In Latin, iron (*ferrum*) by itself could mean "sword" or "spear" (as at Virgil, *Aeneid* 8.648). Similarly in Shakespeare: "Come, my young soldier, put up your iron" (*12N* 4.1.39). As an epithet of "war" it is both synecdoche (the weapons of war) and synonym for "remorseless" or "cruel": Shakespeare, again, has "iron wars" at *1H4* 2.3.48. See also "wrathful iron arms" (*R2* 1.3.136).

As a sign of inexorability or inflexibility "iron" could of course modify many other nouns. Ovid writes that even the gods could not break the "iron decrees" of the Fates (*Met.* 15.781). In Virgil death is an "iron sleep" (*ferreus somnus*) because one cannot break its bands (*Aeneid* 10.745) (the phrase translates Homer's *chalkeos hypnos*, "bronze sleep," at *Iliad* 11.241). Marvell writes of "the iron gates of life" ("To his Coy Mistress" 44).

See **Metal**.

Ivory The material of elephant tusks ("ivory" in Greek is *elephas*), ivory is precious and a sign of wealth. King Solomon made a great ivory throne overlaid with gold (1 Kings 10.18), and Nestor's court in the *Odyssey* is filled with objects of gold, silver, amber, and ivory (4.73). But the chief literary use since antiquity is as a metonym for whiteness or purity. A simile in the *Iliad* likens the look of Menelaus' blood on his skin to a purple dye on an ivory cheek-piece for horses (4.141–42), while Penelope is transformed by Athena to appear "whiter than sawn ivory" (18.196). The Song of Solomon compares the neck of the beloved to "a tower of ivory" (7.4), almost certainly for its whiteness. To give just a pair of modern examples, Spenser describes a maid who, "seeing her selfe descryde, / Was all abasht, and her pure yvory / Into a cleare Carnation suddeine dyde" (*FQ* 3.3.20); and Shakespeare's Venus makes her linked white arms into "an ivory pale [fence]" around Adonis (*Venus and Adonis* 230).

For "ivory tower" see **Tower**. For the "gate of ivory" see **Dream**.

Ivy Ivy (Greek *kissos*) is the distinctive plant of Dionysus (Bacchus), the god of life's regenerative energy and of such vital fluids as wine, milk, honey, blood, and semen. In one of the Homeric Hymns to Dionysus the god is "ivy-crowned"; in another ivy magically twines about the mast of the ship carrying the captive god. "Ivy-crowned" becomes a standard epithet of Bacchus or Dionysus, as in Milton's "L'Allegro" 16. Ivy (Latin *hedera*) is "most pleasing to Bacchus," Ovid writes (*Fasti* 3.767), because ivy hid him from the jealous Hera. The natural basis for the symbolism may be that, as an evergreen plant, it represents the victory of life over death (winter). Dionysus' followers, the maenads or bacchantes, wore ivy crowns and so did the *thyrsoi* (wands) they carried. In at least one local cult Dionysus was simply called Ivy (*Kissos*).

The ivy was an emblem of tenacious emotional clinging, as in Hecuba's defiant vow to hold onto her daughter: "Ivy to oak, that's how I'll cling to her" (Euripides, *Hecuba* 398; see also *Medea* 1213). (Ivy clings to oak, in literature, as vine clings to elm.) Often, however, ivy took on a sexual connotation quite apart from its Dionysian associations. In his wedding song Catullus enjoins Hymen to "bind her mind with love / as clinging ivy [*tenax hedera*] entwines the tree, / wandering here and there" (61.33–35), while Horace reminds the faithless Neaera of her pledge of loyalty, clinging to him more closely than an ilex is girdled by ivy (*Epodes* 15.5–6), and describes another woman, Damalis, as like "wanton ivy" (*lascivis hederis*) (*Odes* 1.36.20). In the Renaissance the "lascivious" sense predominates. Bacon says ivy is Bacchus' sacred tree because passion coils itself around human actions like ivy (*Wisdom of the Ancients* chap. 24). Spenser calls it "wanton" and gives it "lascivious armes" (*FQ* 2.5.29, 2.12.61). In Romantic poetry, however, ivy without disapproval decorates such love bowers as Shelley's cave of Prometheus and Keats's cave of Endymion.

Among Roman writers, ivy seemed the appropriate plant for the lighter genres of literature – such as pastoral and love lyrics – as opposed to the oak and laurel (bay). (Apollo, god of poetry, wore the laurel crown.) In his *Eclogues* Virgil calls on the Arcadian shepherds to "crown with ivy your rising bard" (7.25–26), and of the military conqueror Pollio he asks, "Accept the songs begun at your bidding, and let this ivy creep among the laurels around your brow" (8.11–13). (Pope repeats this gesture in "Summer" 9–10.)

Horace claims that "the ivy, the reward of poets' brows, links me with the gods above" (1.1.29–30); in using the word *doctorum* for "poets" Horace began a tradition that ivy was appropriate for the "learned" victors, leaving the other plants for those who win military or athletic contests. Pope extends this idea in his *Essay on Criticism*, where he contrasts "The Poet's Bays and the Critick's Ivy" (706), while in *The Dunciad* he denounces all those who "Mix'd the Owl's ivy with the Poet's bays" (3.54).

Pope may have drawn his pejorative meaning of ivy, which puzzled some of his early readers, from another of its features, noted by the ancients, that it may destroy the tree which holds it up; it can thus represent ingratitude. Shakespeare's Prospero invokes this sense in describing his usurping brother: "he was / The ivy which had hid my princely trunk, / And suck'd my verdure out on't" (*Tempest* 1.2.85–87). Adriana in *Comedy of Errors* plays the vine to her husband's elm, and dismisses whatever might dispossess her as "usurping ivy" (2.2.177). Pope's point, then, is that critics are parasites on poets, and ungratefully hide them under commentaries until they suffocate.

See **Laurel, Oak, Myrtle, Elm.**

J

Jackdaw   *see* **Raven**

K

Kestrel   *see* **Hawk**

Kingfisher   *see* **Halcyon**

L

Labyrinth A sonnet of Petrarch's tells how desire, love, pleasure, habit, and blind hope have trapped him; it concludes: "One thousand three hundred twenty-seven, exactly / at the first hour of the sixth day of April, / I entered the labyrinth, nor do I see where to get out" (*Rime* 211). That was the moment he met Laura.

The original labyrinth of classical mythology was the vast maze under the palace of King Minos of Crete, inside which was the Minotaur, product of the monstrous lust of the queen for a bull. It was built by Daedalus and finally entered and exited (after he slew the monster) by Theseus, with the help of Ariadne and her ball of string. Aeneas learns the story as he examines the doors of a temple that Daedalus himself built, just before Aeneas must descend into another labyrinth, Hades (Virgil, *Aeneid* 6.14–41). Ovid tells the story briefly in *Metamorphoses* 8.152–82, Catullus at greater length in 64.50–266; see also Plutarch, *Life of Theseus* 15–16. Ovid's *Heroides* 10 is a letter from the abandoned Ariadne to Theseus, a version that lies behind Chaucer's "Legend of Ariadne" and Gower's *Confessio Amantis* 5.5231–5495.

The name Daedalus comes from Greek *daidalos*, "cunningly wrought." Taken into Latin, the adjective is used by Virgil, for instance, to refer to beehives, *daedala ... tecta*, "intricate (or labyrinthine) dwellings" (*Georgics* 4.179). Lucretius' phrase *daedala tellus* (1.7), meaning something like "manifold (or variegated) earth," has had many imitators: Spenser has "Then doth the daedale earth throw forth to thee / Out of her fruitfull lap aboundant flowres" (*FQ* 4.10.45); and Shelley, "The daedal earth, / That island in the ocean of the world, / Hung in its cloud of all-sustaining air" ("Ode to Liberty" 18–20). In French the noun *dédale* means "maze" or "labyrinth."

The first metaphorical use of "labyrinth" is found in Plato's *Euthydemus*, where Socrates likens a fruitless philosophical inquiry to falling into a labyrinth, where we think we are at the finish but the path turns and we are back at the beginning (291b). Boethius uses the same trope in *Consolation of Philosophy* 3p12; in Chaucer's charming translation, thou "hast so woven me with thi resouns the hous of Dedalus, so entrelaced that it is unable to ben unlaced."

Anything impenetrable or inextricable might be called a labyrinth. For Christians, sin is a wandering off the path of righteousness into labyrinthine tangles. "Leaving the public road," Ambrose writes, sinners "often run into labyrinths of error and are punished for having left the road" (*Exposition of Psalm 118.59*). Dante does not mention the labyrinth in his *Inferno* (though the Minotaur is there), but the concentric circles, walls, broken bridges, and "pouches" make hell a great labyrinth itself. Chaucer compares the House of Rumor, full of error and confusion, with the "Domus Dedaly, / That Laboryntus cleped [called] ys" (*House of Fame* 1920–21). Spenser's "shadie grove" of Error is a labyrinth of many paths and turnings (*FQ* 1.1.11). Milton's Satan seeks the serpent and finds him with symbolically resonant coils: "him fast sleeping soon he found / In labyrinth of many a round self rolled" (*PL* 9.182–83).

Petrarch's labyrinth of love becomes the theme of many Renaissance works, such as Boccaccio's *Laberinto d'Amore*, part of *Il Corbaccio*, a place where men are trapped by the illusions of passion and turned into animals. Cervantes wrote a comedy, *El Laberinto de Amor*. Mary Wroth begins a sonnet, "In this strange labyrinth how shall I turn?" Rejecting every possible step, she is moved "to leave all, and take the thread of love." In one of the phases of Blake's "Mental Traveller" a desert is planted with "Labyrinths of wayward Love" (83).

In more recent literature labyrinthine settings are common: passageways of castles in gothic novels, forests, caves, and so on. Cities are labyrinthine in Eugène Sue's *Mysteries of Paris* and Hugo's *Notre Dame of Paris*; Hugo gives an elaborate account of the labyrinth of sewers under Paris in *Les Miserables*. London is a labyrinth in Dickens's *Oliver Twist* and *Bleak House*. Detective novels presume the impenetrability of cities, impenetrable to all but the detective. Chapter 10 of Joyce's *Ulysses* ("Wandering Rocks") has been described as labyrinthine in the way it follows the movements of a dozen characters through the streets of Dublin; the whole novel might be well described as a labyrinth, and indeed one of its leading characters is named Stephen Dedalus. One of Borges's collections of stories, called *Labyrinths* in its English version, presents several literal and metaphorical labyrinths, including a mysterious and seemingly chaotic novel called *The Garden of the Forking Paths*, which is about time and eternity. A literal labyrinth is central to Eco's *The Name of the Rose*, a metaphorical one to Marquez's *The General in his Labyrinth*.

There is a technical distinction between a labyrinth and a maze, the labyrinth being "unicursal" (with one path), the maze "multicursal" (with branching paths); one can get lost only in a maze. This distinction, however, is seldom observed in literature.

Land   *see* **Nature**

Lark   The lark, also called the laverock, is one of the most popular birds in post-classical European poetry. The crested lark appears occasionally in Greek literature, but not the skylark, with its distinctive literary characteristics. Latin had a word for the skylark, *alauda* (perhaps borrowed from Gaulish), giving French *alouette* and Italian *allodetta*, but the bird seldom appears in Latin literature. In English, "lark" by itself (from a Germanic root) usually refers to the skylark (*Alauda arvensis*). This little brown bird is known for the loud, merry, musical song that it sings only in flight and notably early in the morning; it soars so high it disappears in the light, though its song might still be heard.

"Alas, near all the birds / Will sing at dawn," Elizabeth Barrett Browning reminds us (*Aurora Leigh* 1.951–52), but in literature the lark is *the* dawn bird, the one who begins the singing and rouses the others. "Hark, hark, the lark at heaven's gate sings, / And Phoebus gins arise," according to the famous song in Shakespeare's *Cymbeline* (2.3.19–20); "the lark at break of day arising / From sullen earth, sings hymns at heaven's gate" (*Sonnets* 29.11–12); twice elsewhere Shakespeare calls it "the morning lark" (*MND* 4.1.94, *TS*, Ind. 2.44). In Spenser: "The merry Larke her mattins sings aloft" (*Epithalamium* 80) and "With merry note her [Aurora] loud salutes the mounting larke" (*FQ* 1.11.51). To get up early is to "rise with the lark" (*R3* 5.3.56; Wordsworth, *Excursion* 4.491). Milton's description is definitive: "Thus wore out night, and now the

Herald Lark / Left his ground-nest, high tow'ring to descry / The morn's approach, and greet her with his Song" (PR 2.279–81).

The sound of the song is conventionally "tirra-lirra" (e.g., Shakespeare, WT 4.3.9); in French it is "tire-lire."

The lark is often paired with the nightingale, most famously in *Romeo and Juliet* 3.5. Wordsworth contrasts the "Lark of the dawn, and Philomel of night" ("Liberty" 82); Tennyson contrasts "the morning song of the lark" and "the nightingale's hymn in the dark" ("The First Quarrel" 33–34). (*See* **Nightingale**.)

The heights to which the lark mounts – "mounting" is in fact a common adjective since Spenser at least (FQ 1.11.51) – gave it religious associations, as if it were a chorister or angel. It is charmingly expressed in the medieval Welsh poet Dafydd ap Gwilym's phrase "a *cantor* from the chapel of God" ("The Skylark"). Dante mentions it once, in a simile in the *Paradiso* (20.73–75). In both his "Skylark" poems Wordsworth calls "divine" some feature of the bird. In an earlier work he writes of the "gay lark of hope" (*Descriptive Sketches* 528), while in the first "To a Skylark" he takes the contrast between the lark's joyous flight and song with his own weary plodding through life as an occasion to express "hope for higher raptures, when life's day is done."

That this bird among others triggers yearnings in human listeners is explained by Faust to his student: "And yet inborn in all our race / Is impulse upward, forward, and along, / When overhead and lost in azure space / The lark pours forth its trilling song" (Goethe, *Faust I* 1092–95, trans. Passage). Shelley in "To a Sky-Lark" yearns to become as capable as the bird, which he compares to a "Poet hidden / In the light of thought" (36–37).

Perhaps the most astonishing and elaborately symbolic treatment of the lark is found in Blake's poem *Milton*. Just as the morn appears the lark springs from the corn-field and "loud / He leads the Choir of Day! trill, trill, trill, / Mounting upon the wings of light into the Great Expanse: / Reechoing against the lovely blue & shining heavenly Shell: / His little throat labours with inspiration; every feather / On throat & breast & wings vibrates with the effluence Divine[.] / All Nature listens silent to him & the awful Sun / Stands still upon the Mountain looking on this little Bird" (31.30–37).

Laurel   The laurel (or bay) was sacred to Apollo, god of prophecy, poetry, and music, perhaps originally because chewing them or inhaling their aroma seemed to induce a prophetic trance. The pythoness or priestess of Apollo was crowned with laurel (Greek *daphne*), as were the victors in the Pythian games, celebrated by Pindar. Hesiod reports that the muses gave him a shoot of laurel as a staff and then breathed a divine voice in him (*Theogony* 30–32). Laurel grew in the sacred grove of Delos, the island dedicated to Apollo (Euripides, *Hecuba* 459); and his temples were decked with it (*Ion* 80, 103). Before long it became conventional that Apollo and his nine muses wore laurel; as Spenser was to put it, "The Muses...were wont greene bayes to weare" (SC "November" 146).

The myth of Apollo and Daphne is memorably told by Ovid. After Daphne is changed into a laurel tree, Phoebus (Apollo) vows, "Since thou canst not be my bride, thou shalt at least be my tree! My hair, my lyre, my quiver shall always be entwined with thee, O laurel. With thee shall Roman generals wreathe their heads..." (*Met.* 1.557–60). Ovid also reminds us that laurel is "unfading" or evergreen (*Tristia* 3.1.45), as befits a symbol of fame.

Victors in battle were indeed sometimes crowned with laurel; to quote Spenser again, it was "the meed of mightie conquerours" as well as of "Poets sage" (*FQ* 1.1.9). See Virgil, *Eclogues* 8.11–13, quoted under Ivy.

After the Italian poet Petrarch was made the first modern poet laureate (crowned with the laurel) in 1341 at the Capitol in Rome, he explained that he chose laurel for his crown not only for its associations with prophecy and Apollo but for its fragrance (fame), its evergreen leaves (eternity), and its supposed immunity from lightning. He seems not to have known that the victors of the ancient Capitoline poetry contests were crowned with oak leaves. "The crown / Which Petrarch's laureate brow supremely wore," in Byron's words (*Childe Harold* 4.57), became the prototype for the wreath of all poets laureate, or "the lauriat fraternity of poets," in Milton's phrase (*Apology for Smectymnuus*).

Milton opens his pastoral elegy *Lycidas* with three plants associated with poetry: "Yet once more, O ye laurels, and once more / Ye Myrtles brown, with Ivy never sere, / I come to pluck your Berries . . ." He is in part alluding to Virgil's "Second Eclogue" – "You too, O laurels, I will pluck, and you, their neighbor myrtle" (54–55) – the plants of Apollo and Venus, appropriate to a song about love. (See also Horace 3.4.18–19.) Petrarch wrote that ivy and myrtle would also have been appropriate for his crown, and another account of his coronation reports that all three were used.

Byron once pointedly contrasts laurel (fame or glory) with myrtle and ivy (love): "And the myrtle and ivy of sweet two-and-twenty / Are worth all your laurels, though ever so plenty" ("Stanzas Written on the Road between Florence and Pisa" 3–4).

See **Ivy, Myrtle, Oak.**

Lead   The heaviest common metal, pale and dull in appearance, lead sits on the bottom of the traditional hierarchy of metals. In the Old Testament it is included among the baser metals in prophetic visions of God's testing the "mettle" of his people: Jeremiah says the rejected people are brass, iron, lead, and "reprobate" or spurious silver (6.28–30); Ezekiel says they are dross: "all they are brass, and tin, and iron, and lead, in the midst of the furnace; they are even the dross of silver" (22.18). Its heaviness is the reason for a simile in the Song of Moses – Pharaoh's host "sank as lead in the mighty waters" (Exod. 15.10) – which has remained a commonplace; e.g., the albatross slips off Coleridge's Ancient Mariner "and sank / Like lead into the sea" and later "The ship went down like lead" ("Rime of the Ancient Mariner" 290–91, 549).

Alchemists strove to transform the base or vile metal lead into gold. As it is the heaviest it was considered the "slowest" metal, and was thus connected with slowest planet Saturn. Spenser calls it "sad lead" (*FQ* 3.11.48) and twice uses the phrase "sad as lump of lead," once of a melancholy person, once of a literal weight (2.1.45, 2.8.30); "sad" meant "heavy," as "saturnine" meant "slow" or "gloomy." Shelley once calls it "sullen lead" (*PU* 4.541). It was not among the traditional four races or ages, which were gold, silver, bronze, and iron, but it was available to characterize a really dull and heavy time. In *The Dunciad* Pope sees "Dulness" "hatch a new Saturnian age of lead" (b 1.28), cleverly reversing the usual association of Saturn with the golden age. Byron writes of "Generals, some all in armor, of the old / And iron time, ere lead had ta'en the lead" (*Don Juan* 13.553–54) – not only implying that the present time is worse than "iron" but that lead bullets and shot, which penetrate iron, have made it so.

The paradox that the heaviest metal flies swiftest on the battlefield was irresistible. So Shakespeare's Moth and Armado have this exchange: "As swift as lead, sir." "Is not lead a metal heavy, dull, and slow?...I say, lead is slow." "You are too swift, sir, to say so. Is that lead slow which is fired from a gun?" (*LLL* 3.1.57–63).

"Leaden" in Latin (*plumbeus*) occasionally meant "oppressive" or "dull." In English it often meant "slow," as in Shakespeare's "leaden age, / Quickened with youthful spleen" (*1H6* 4.6.12–13) or Sidney's "leaden eyes" that miss "sweet beautie's show" (*Astrophil* Song 7). Milton's "lazy leaden-stepping hours, / Whose speed is but the heavy Plummet's pace" ("On Time" 2–3), wittily reminds us that the plummet of a clock is made of lead (from Latin *plumbum*). It often went with sleep, as in Shakespeare's "leaden slumber" (*R3* 5.3.105); Pope's "leaden slumbers press his drooping eyes" (*Odyssey* 4.610); or this from Young: "Night.../...stretches forth / Her leaden Scepter o'er a slumbering world" (*Night Thoughts* 1.18–20). Melancholy walks "with leaden eye" in Gray's "Ode to Adversity" (28).

It had a particular association with death because of the common use of lead-lined coffins. Spenser uses the formulaic phrase "wrapt in lead" three times in *The Shepheardes Calender* to mean "dead," twice rhyming with it. Byron has "laid in lead" (*Vision of Judgment* 550), Keats has "hears'd up in stifling lead" (*Otho* 4.1.58).

The association with death, added to its low rank among metals, makes lead suitable for the third casket in Shakespeare's *Merchant of Venice*: the superficial suitors choose the gold or silver caskets, but deeper Bassanio rejects "gaudy gold" and silver for "meagre lead," whose "paleness moves me more than eloquence," and wins Portia (3.2.101–07). It was with similar symbolism that Dante imagined the hypocrites in hell wearing cloaks gilded on the outside but inside all of lead (*Inferno* 23.64–67).

See **Metal**.

Leaf   Three of the most striking facts about leaves are that there are vast numbers of them, even on a single tree, that they are born in the spring and die in the fall, and that they rustle or fly off in the wind. These features, mainly, make them favorite images in poetry.

The familiar contrast between the annual coming and going of leaves on deciduous trees and the near-permanence of the trees themselves prompts Homer's famous simile in the speech of Glaucus to Diomedes: "High-hearted son of Tydeus, why ask of my generation? / As is the generation of leaves, so is that of humanity. / The wind scatters the leaves on the ground, but the live timber / burgeons with leaves again in the season of spring returning. / So one generation of men will grow while another / dies" (*Iliad* 6.145–50; trans. Lattimore). Glaucus goes on to tell his genealogy, what we would now call his "family tree," as befits a poem in which patronymics are as prominent as given names (here, for example, each hero is named only as the son of someone). That this perspective may seem too godlike for a young warrior, himself a leaf likely to fall, is confirmed by the reappearance of the simile on the lips of

Apollo, who tells Poseidon there is no point in contending over "insignificant / mortals, who are as leaves are, and now flourish and grow warm / with life, and feed on what the ground gives, but then again / fade away and are dead" (21.463–66). It is part of the poignancy of the *Iliad* that its heroes occasionally achieve the detachment to see their own life as the brief thing it is.

Homer's comparison is repeated by Mimnermus: "we, like the leaves that grow in the flowery springtime…like them we enjoy the flower of youth for a brief span" (2.1–4); by Sophocles: man is as "shortlived as the leaves of a slender poplar" (frag. 593); and by Aristophanes in *Birds* 686: humans are "feeble-lived, much like the race of leaves" – an appropriate simile to be drawn by a bird.

Shelley elaborates the simile in *Queen Mab* 5.1–15 and takes an even longer view, imagining the trees falling as well as the leaves, while from the rotting trunks a new forest springs "Like that which gave it life, to spring and die" (his note cites *Iliad* 6.146ff.).

Homer also mentions leaves (and flowers) as types of multitudinousness in his flurry of similes for the mustering armies outside Troy (*Iliad* 2.468), a comparison used by many poets ever since, such as this by Apollonius of Rhodes: the Colchians thronged to the assembly, and "like the waves of the stormy sea / or as the leaves that fall to the ground from the wood with its myriad branches / in the month when the leaves fall" (*Argonautica* 4.215–17). Marlowe uses the image with a Homeric allusion to Mt. Ida: "Here at Aleppo, with an host of men, / Lies Tamburlaine, this king of Persia, / In number more than are the quivering leaves / Of Ida's forests" (2 *Tamburlaine* 3.5.3–6).

The numerousness of leaves, their mortality, and their susceptibility to wind made them perfect emblems for the dead in the underworld. According to Bacchylides, when Heracles descended to Hades he saw the souls of mortals "like leaves the wind shakes" (*Epinician* 5.63). Virgil's Aeneas in the realm of Dis meets "as many souls / As leaves that yield their hold on boughs and fall / Through forests in the early frost of autumn" (*Aeneid* 6.309–10; trans. Fitzgerald). Seneca uses the leaf simile among several others (flowers, waves, migrating birds) to bring out the vast number of shades summoned by Tiresias (*Oedipus* 600). Dante sees the dead on the shore of Acheron: "As, in the autumn, leaves detach themselves, / first one and then the other, till the bough / sees all its fallen garments on the ground, / similarly the evil seed of Adam / descended from the shoreline one by one" (*Inferno* 3.112–16; trans. Mandelbaum). With this tradition before him, and a passage from Isaiah about the day of vengeance – "all their host [of heaven] shall fall down, as the leaf falleth off from the vine" (34.4) – it was almost inevitable that Milton would use it for the recently fallen legions of Lucifer, "angel forms, who lay entranced / Thick as autumnal leaves that strew the brooks / Of Vallombrosa" (*PL* 1.301–03).

Isaiah also likens an individual life to a leaf: "we all do fade as a leaf; and our iniquities, like the wind, have taken us away" (64.6). This too became a commonplace. To take some modern examples: Lamartine likens himself to "une feuille morte" ("a dead leaf"), and prays the wind to carry him like the leaf ("L'Isolement"); Ibsen's Hedda Gabler, home from her honeymoon, gazes at the withered golden leaves and feels she is "already into September" (Act 1);

Hopkins's Margaret is grieving over the "unleaving" of the grove, while the leaves, "like the things of man," express "the blight man was born for" ("Spring and Fall").

A tree may be personified and given feelings, leaves then becoming hair, as in Ovid: "The woods grieved for Phyllis, shedding their leaves" (*Ars Amatoria* 3.38); the cutting of hair was the common rite of mourning.

Sometimes a person is compared to a tree that may or may not lose its leaves. In the Bible: "he shall be like a tree planted by the rivers of water, that bringeth forth his fruit in his season; his leaf also shall not wither" (Ps. 1.3); "ye shall be as an oak whose leaf fadeth, and as a garden that hath no water" (Isa. 1.30). Ovid and other ancient poets compared the life of a man to the passing seasons (as in *Metamorphoses* 15.199–216). Drawing on these comparisons, Shakespeare begins one of his best known sonnets (73), "That time of year thou mayst in me behold / When yellow leaves, or none, or few, do hang / Upon those boughs which shake against the cold, / Bare ruined choirs where late the sweet birds sang." In the garden scene of *Richard II*, which is one elaborate simile for the condition of England, a servant, thinking of Richard, says, "He that hath suffered this disordered spring / Hath now himself met with the fall of leaf" (3.4.48–49). As he faces his doom, Macbeth says, "I have liv'd long enough: my way of life / Is fall'n into the sere, the yellow leaf" (5.3.22–23). Byron felt "My days are in the yellow leaf" in "On This Day I Complete My Thirty-Sixth Year" (5). In his "Ode to the West Wind," Shelley (like Lamartine above) imagines that he is a dead leaf the wind might bear, but (like Shakespeare) also imagines that he *has* leaves: "make me thy lyre, even as the forest is: / What if my leaves are falling like its own!" (57–58).

In several languages "leaf" also serves for the page, or double-page, of a book (e.g., French *feuille*, *feuillet*, German *Blatt*), as we say when we "turn over a new leaf" – an irresistible meaning for writers to exploit. Du Bellay imagines his verses as dead leaves (*feuillards*) scattered by the wind ("Non autrement que la prêtresse folle"). In Sonnet 17 Shakespeare considers "my papers, yellowed with their age" like old men. Shelley asks the West Wind to "Drive my dead thoughts over the universe / Like withered leaves to quicken a new birth!" (63–64). Perhaps a distant source of this metaphor is Horace's simile likening the changing words (vocabulary) of a language to the shedding and regrowing of leaves (*Ars Poetica* 60–62).

Pindar uses the evocative phrase "leaves of song" (*Isth.* 4.27). Among the Romantics it became a commonplace that poetry should come spontaneously, as if it grew organically from the poet. Keats wrote, "if Poetry comes not as naturally as the Leaves to a tree it had better not come at all" (letter to Taylor, 27 February 1818). Hugo dismisses as of no importance the fact that "some autumnal blast of bitter air / With its unsettled wings may sweep along / Both the tree's foliage and the poet's song" ("Friends, a last word!" 6–8). This metaphor, combined with the near-punning sense of "page," lies behind such titles as Leigh Hunt's *Foliage*, Hugo's *Feuilles d'automne*, Whitman's *Leaves of Grass*, and Rosalia de Castro's *Follas Novas*.

Left and right As about seven-eighths of the population of all cultures are right-handed, it is not surprising that in most of them "right" has positive meanings and "left" negative. In the European languages terms for "right" have consistently favorable senses: Greek *dexios* also meant "lucky," particularly in augury, where the augur stood facing north and a flight of birds to his east was propitious (see *Iliad* 12.239–40), and it meant "clever" or "dextrous"; Latin *dexter* had the same meanings; French *droit* (from Latin *directum*) has many of the same senses as English "right," and yields English "adroit," synonymous with "dextrous." One of the Greek words for "left" (*skaios*) could mean "ill-omened" or "clumsy"; Sophocles writes of Agamemnon's "*skaion* mouth" (*Ajax* 1225) and how willfulness leads to *skaiotes* or folly (*Antigone* 1028). Latin *sinister* meant "wrong" or "perverse" (whence English "sinister"); *laevus* meant "foolish"; both could mean "unfavorable"; in Roman augury, however, the left was often propitious, as if the augur faced south. French *gauche*, which may come from a Frankish word meaning "turn aside" (from the "right" way), also means "clumsy," as it does in English. English "left" may come from word meaning "useless." Two Greek words for "left" (*aristeros*, "best," and *euonumos*, "good-named") are obvious euphemisms, perhaps evidence of a taboo on saying "left."

There are a few mysterious passages in the Old Testament that suggest a disparagement of "left." "A wise man's heart is at his right hand," says Ecclesiastes, "but a fool's heart at his left" (10.2); "heart" here seems an unwise translation in the light of human anatomy (the NEB has "mind"). Ezekiel lies on his left side to make a point to the city of Jerusalem (4.4), but it is not clear what the point is. The right hand, on the other hand, symbolizes power: "Thy right hand, O Lord, is become glorious in power" (Exod. 15.6); the Lord will use "the saving strength of his right hand" (Ps. 20.6). To be at one's right hand is to protect or support: "because he is at my right hand, I shall not be moved" (Ps. 16.8); "he shall stand at the right hand of the poor" (109.31).

In Plato's myth of Er we hear that the souls of the just journey to the right and upward to heaven while those of the unjust go to the left and downward (*Republic* 614c–d). At the final judgment, according to Jesus, the Son of man shall separate the sheep from the goats, "And he shall set the sheep on his right hand, but the goats on the left"; those on the right are the "righteous" (a revealing pun in the AV) and shall inherit the kingdom, while those on the left shall go into everlasting fire (Matt. 25.31–46). In one description of the cosmos Milton has "on the left hand hell" (*PL* 10.322). The Nicene Creed claims that Christ "ascended into the heavens, and sitteth on the right hand of the Father." Milton makes much of this fact, reporting it at least five times in *Paradise Lost* (e.g., 3.279, 5.606); the Messiah leaves "the right hand of glory where he sat" (6.747) to lead the battle against the rebel angels, Victory sits at his right hand in the chariot (762), the rebels are defeated, and he returns to sit "at the right hand of bliss" (892).

Leopard The leopard, the pard, the pardal, the panther, and the lynx are not consistently distinguished from each other in literature, and indeed they are sometimes indiscriminately grouped with other cats as emblems of cruelty or ferocity. As its name suggests, the leopard was thought to be a hybrid of the lion (Latin *leo*) and the "pard" (Latin *pardus*, from Greek *pardos*, from *pardalis*), which was thought to be a kind of panther; "pard" then came to be a poetic equivalent of "leopard."

A passage in Jeremiah gives one symbolic or proverbial meaning of the leopard as symbol of unchangeableness or the indelibility of sin: "Can the Ethiopian change his skin, or the leopard his spots? then may ye also do good, that are accustomed to do evil" (13.23). When Shakespeare's Richard II tries to halt the quarrel between Bolingbroke and Mowbray, he invokes his authority as the king of beasts – "lions make leopards tame" – to which Mowbray responds, "Yea, but not change his spots" (R2 1.1.174–75). Kipling's story "How the Leopard Got his Spots" (which includes the Ethiopian), is a jocular response to Jeremiah.

The leopard is one of the four beasts of Daniel's dream, where it has four heads (7.6); it reappears in the description of the seven-headed beast of Revelation: "And the beast which I saw was like unto a leopard, and his feet were as the feet of a bear, and his mouth as the mouth of a lion" (13.2). These visions are the basis of the later Christian iconographic meaning of the leopard as sin, Satan, or the Antichrist.

Another passage in Jeremiah, where he prophesies that a lion, a wolf, and a leopard will tear in pieces those who break the yoke of the Lord (5.6), stands behind the most thoroughly discussed leopard in literature, if it is a leopard, the *lonza*, "covered with a spotted hide," that confronts Dante as he struggles vainly up the hill in canto 1 of the *Inferno*. It is finally neither the *lonza* nor the *leone* (lion) but the *lupa* (she-wolf) that defeats Dante. Countless allegorical meanings have been proposed for these three alliterating beasts, but the likeliest theory has it that the leopard represents the sins of fraud, deeper and crueler sins than those of violence (lion) and incontinence (she-wolf). Richard of St. Victor had commented on Daniel 7.6: "Rightly is the fraudulence of dissemblers symbolized by the pard which is speckled with spots over its whole body. For dissemblers indeed make a show of holiness." Dante may be confessing that his own sins, which block his climb to salvation, are not of the cold-blooded leopard-like sort but more impulsive and thoughtless.

From late classical sources the leopard or panther emerged as the distinctive beast of Dionysus or Bacchus. Captured by pirates, Dionysus transforms their ship by magic, grape vines grow around the oars and sails, and "tigers, lynxes, and fierce spotted panthers" appear on board (Ovid, *Met.* 3.669); in his triumphal procession, a pair of lynxes draw his chariot (4.24–25), or it is panthers and lions (Nonnus, *Dionysiaca* 14.261). By the time of Schiller, his chariot is drawn by "majestic panthers in a team" ("Gods of Greece" 58), while Keats imagines himself "charioted by Bacchus and his pards" ("Ode to a Nightingale" 32).

In English poetry the pard/panther was seen as the characteristic enemy of the hind (doe). Shakespeare's Cressida lists the proverbial predators and prey: "as false | ... | As fox to lamb, as wolf to heifer's calf, | Pard to the hind, or stepdame to her son" (TC 3.2.191–94). Dryden's poem *The Hind and the Panther* deploys these beasts and many others in a complex religious allegory.

See **Lion, Wolf.**

Leviathan   *see* **Whale**

Light and   Light and darkness are probably the most fundamental and inescapable
darkness   terms, used literally or metaphorically, in the description of anything in life

or literature. It seems almost superfluous to include them in a dictionary, and almost circular to try to shed light on them. What follows will be highly selective.

Light is traditionally linked with goodness, life, knowledge, truth, fame, and hope, darkness with evil, death, ignorance, falsehood, oblivion, and despair. When all was darkness, the first thing God created was light (Gen. 1.3), as if light is a precondition of creating anything, of bringing a hidden thing "to light" (as in Job 28.11). To "see light" is to be born (Job 3.16); in fact light is life itself (3.20): "the light of the wicked shall be put out" (18.5). The Lord is our light and salvation (Ps. 27.1); he shall be "an everlasting light" (Isa. 60.19). "The people that walked in darkness have seen a great light," says Isaiah (9.2), and Matthew quotes him as a prophet of Christ (4.16). John, for whom light is a dominant image, makes Christ "the light of men" (1.4), "the true Light, which lighteth every man that cometh into the world" (1.9); "men loved darkness rather than light" (3.19), but Jesus says, "I am the light of the world: he that followeth me shall not walk in darkness, but shall have the light of life" (8.12). Jesus tells his followers, "Ye are the light of the world" (Matt. 5.14), "the children of light" (Luke 16.8); Paul repeats it: "Ye are all the children of light, and the children of the day; we are not of the night, nor of darkness" (1 Thess. 5.5). When Christ was crucified, there was darkness at noon (Matt. 27.45).

Hell is dark, as far as possible from the light of God. Dante calls it "the eternal dark" and "the blind world" (*Inferno* 3.87, 4.13). Milton, drawing on St. Basil, describes hell as full of flames, "yet from those flames / No light, but rather darkness visible / Served only to discover sights of woe" (*PL* 1.62–64). In absolute contrast, Dante concludes *The Divine Comedy* with a vision of "the Highest Light," whom he addresses twice as God and praises as the ultimate and ineffable truth (*Paradiso* 33.50ff.). Heaven in Milton is "the happy realms of light" (1.85), and Milton opens book 3 by invoking Light itself: "Hail, holy Light, offspring of heaven first-born, / Or of the eternal co-eternal beam / May I express thee unblamed? since God is light, / And never but in unapproached light / Dwelt from eternity, dwelt then in thee, / Bright effluence of bright essence increate" (3.1–6).

The image of light emerging from darkness becomes an important symbol in Aeschylus' *Oresteia*, from the relay beacon-fires that the guard sees in the opening of the *Agamemnon* – "Oh hail, blaze of the darkness, harbinger of day's / shining" (22–23 trans. Lattimore) – to the torchlight processional that concludes *The Eumenides*; the herald of Agamemnon, for instance, greets both the land and the light of the sun (508) and with dramatic irony announces that his lord will bring light into the gloom (522).

Light and dark imagery pervades *Beowulf*. The monster Grendel is dark, a "shadow-walker" (703), from whose eyes comes a "horrible light" (727); the dragon is also dark, though it belches fire; Herot the hall of Hrothgar shines brightly, as do Beowulf and his men.

We could easily multiply examples from works of all periods, but we shall end with the notion of "enlightenment." In the Gospel of John, Jesus is not only the light but the "truth" (14.6). Truth gives us light to see or understand, and it seems to shine with its own light. Spenser speaks of "the light of simple veritie" (*Ruins of Time* 171); his character Error hates the light and prefers to dwell in darkness, "Where plain none might see her, nor she see any plaine" (*FQ* 1.1.16). Pope's epigram "Intended for Sir Isaac Newton" is justly famous for its succinct celebration of that hero of the Enlightenment (who wrote a book on optics): "Nature and Nature's laws lay hid in Night: / God said, Let Newton be! and all was Light." The Enlightenment put an end to the "Dark Ages." Thomas Paine writes, "But such is the irresistible nature of truth, that all it asks, and all it wants, is the liberty of appearing. The sun needs no inscription to distinguish him from darkness" (*Rights of Man*, Part 2, Intro.). Blake, a foe of the Enlightenment, nonetheless deploys the indispensable terms: "God Appears & God is Light / To those poor Souls who dwell in Night / But does a Human Form Display / To those who Dwell in Realms of day" ("Auguries of Innocence" 129–32).

See **Black, Night, Sun, White**.

Lightning   The sky gods of the Hebrews, Greeks, and Romans manifested themselves in lightning and thunder. When the Lord descends on Mt. Sinai, "there were thunders and lightnings, and a thick cloud upon the mount" (Exod. 19.16). David's song of thanksgiving tells that "he sent out arrows, and scattered them [the enemies]; lightning, and discomfited them" (2 Sam. 22.15); Psalm 144.6 also sets arrows and lightning in parallel (see 77.17), for lightning is the Lord's arsenal. At the Day of Judgment there shall be plenty of thunder, lightning, and earthquake (Rev. 4.5, 8.5, etc), and the Son of Man shall come "as the lightning cometh out of the east" (Matt. 24.27).

The lightningbolt is Zeus's characteristic weapon (Homer, *Iliad* 11.66) and one of his Homeric epithets is "lightning-gatherer" (16.298). In Hesiod he has three weapons, if that is possible: thunder, lightning, and "bright thunderbolt" (*Theogony* 854). Pindar calls Zeus "driver of thunder" and "lord of lightning and thunder" (*Olymp.* 4.1, *Pyth.* 6.24). Roman Jupiter also terrifies with lightning (Virgil, *Aeneid* 1.230); his eagle is the "winged plyer of the thunderbolt" (Horace 4.4.1). In both Greek and Latin the verbs "thunders" and "lightens" can take either an impersonal form ("it thunders") or Zeus/Jupiter as the personal subject. (*See* **Rain**.) When Semele begged Zeus to manifest himself without disguise, he came as a lightningbolt and destroyed her (Euripides, *Bacchae* 3).

This theophanic or god-revealing character of lightning seems natural enough to believers in gods, but it is interesting that we retain the word "thunderstruck" in English even when nothing divine is in question. Our words "astonish" and "stun" derive from Latin *tonere*, "to thunder." Lightning now can represent any revelation, though something of its numinous character remains. Liberty gleams like lightning in Shelley's "Ode to Liberty" and scatters "contagious fire" (4). Byron imagines that if he could "unbosom now / That which is most within me" and express it in one word, "And that one word were Lightning, I would speak" (*Childe Harold* 3.905–11). A flash of lightning reveals something in the face of the lover that breaks the spell in Lawrence's "Lightning": "the lightning has made it too plain!"

As lightning is often forked – Cowper, for instance, writes, "forky fires / Dart oblique to the Earth" ("A Thunder Storm" 28–29) – Dickinson can both wittily domesticate it by saying, "The Lightning is a yellow Fork / From Tables in the sky / By inadvertent fingers dropt," and restore its awesome aura by calling it "The Apparatus of the Dark / To ignorance revealed" (no. 1173).

As organs of revelation, eyes "glance" or "flash" or "dart lightning" in love or anger at least as far back as Sophocles, who writes, "Such is the magic charm of love, a kind of lightning of the eyes" (frag. 474). In Aristophanes a warrior has "glances of lightning" (*Acharnians* 566). Shakespeare's Imogen "like harmless lightning throws her eye / On him, her brother, me, her master, hitting / Each object with a joy" (*Cym* 5.5.394–96). Reversing vehicle and tenor, Byron sees a night storm as lovely "as is the light / Of a dark eye in woman!" (*Childe Harold* 3.862–63). (*See* **Eye**.)

Lilac   *see* **Purple flower**

Lily   After the rose, the lily is the most prominent of literary flowers. Indeed it is often paired with the rose, not least as a pleasing contrast of colors, for the lily has long been a synonym for "white." The Greek *leirion* was almost certainly the *Lilium candidum*, the white lily or Madonna lily; adjectives derived from it often meant "white." "White as a lily" and "lily-white" are ancient commonplaces. Propertius begins a list of deliberate love-clichés with "Lilies are not whiter than my mistress" (2.3.10).

The epic form of the adjective (*leirioeis*) seems to have meant "soft" or "delicate." Perhaps in mockery, Hector threatens to rend Ajax's "lily-like flesh" (*Iliad* 13.830). The voices of cicadas are "lily-like" (*Iliad* 3.152), as are those of the Muses (Hesiod, *Theogony* 41–42) and the Sirens (Apollonius 4.903); perhaps it also means "clear" or "bright." The Hesperides are "lily-like" in Quintus Smyrnaeus (2.419–20), perhaps the source of "the lily maid of Astolat," Elaine, in the Arthurian cycle (see Tennyson's "Lancelot and Elaine").

In Latin literature lilies stood for the brevity of life or beauty. Horace with characteristic brevity calls the lily "brief" (*breve lilium*) (*Odes* 1.36.16), but Valerius Flaccus spells it out at length: "as white lilies gleam brightly through the colors of spring, / whose life is short and their honor / flourishes for a moment and already the dark wings of the south wind approach" (*Argonautica* 6.492–94).

Lilies are prominent in the Song of Songs, of which the most famous and influential verses are these: "I am the rose of Sharon, and the lily of the valleys. / As the lily among thorns, so is my love among the daughters" (2.1-2). Both "rose" and "lily" are unlikely translations of the Hebrew terms ("lotus" would be better for the latter, *shoshannah*), but they have entered the European languages and shaped Christian allegorizings of the Song. The lily's whiteness suggests purity, its beauty suggests perfection, but since it is unclear who speaks these verses the lily has been assigned to Christ, to the Church, and above all to the Virgin Mary. Paintings of the Annunciation, where the archangel Gabriel brings the news to the Virgin that she shall bear a son (Luke 1.26–38), almost always include a lily, either in a vase or in Gabriel's hand. This association presumably lies behind Howe's evocative but mysterious line, in "The Battle-Hymn of the Republic": "In the beauty of the lilies Christ was born across the sea."

The lily can then represent virginity in any woman. Chaucer's nun makes St. Cecilia another lily, "'hevenes lilie,' / For pure chaastnesse of virginitee" (*Second Nun's Tale* 87–88). Shakespeare's Cranmer prophesies that the young Elizabeth will live and die "a virgin, / A most unspotted lily" (*H8* 5.5.60–61). As for the flower itself, there is "the virgin Lillie" of Spenser ("Prothalamion" 32), Pope has a garden where "lilies smile in virgin robes of white" ("Imitation of Cowley" 5), and Blake's Thel addresses a lily as "thou little virgin of the peaceful valley" (*Book of Thel* 2.3). Rimbaud imagines that the drowning Ophelia "floats like a great lily" ("Ophélie" 28–29).

Linden   The linden, like the oak and beech, is appreciated for its shade; in Europe it is often planted near homes and in village greens, while in England it often lines avenues on estates. It is also called the lime tree: "lime" is probably a variant of "line," itself a variant of "lind," and has nothing to do with the citrus fruit. The tree in Coleridge's "This Lime-Tree Bower My Prison" is the linden. Its name in older English literature is "lind"; the more common modern form "linden" may come from German. The tree is also known for its yellow flowers and attractive fragrance, "the lime at dewy eve / Diffusing odours" (Cowper, *Task* 1.316–17).

In Ovid's tale of the hospitable old couple Philemon and Baucis, Philemon (the husband) is turned into an oak, while Baucis (the wife) is turned into a linden (*Met.* 8.620). In Baltic pagan lore, men are to sacrifice to the oak, women to the linden.

In Middle English poetry "lind" or "line" might refer to any tree, especially in the phrase "under lind" or "under the lind." A proverbial saying about the tree (or generic tree) is found in Chaucer's *Clerk's Tale*: "Be ay of chiere as light as leef on lynde" (1211).

The linden was distinctive of German village centers and so it appears often in German poetry, notably in the famous love poem by Walther von der Vogelweide that begins "Under der linden / An der heide / da unser beider bette was..." ("Under the linden by the heath where we two had our bed..."). It becomes a conventional resort of lovers, and often a symbol of faithful love. Eichendorff remembers mournfully the many times he sat with his beloved under a linden ("The Vespers"). The best-known linden poem is "Der Lindenbaum" from Müller's cycle *Die schone Mullerin*, set by Schubert. Heine writes, "We sat under the linden tree / And swore eternal faithfulness" ("I dreamt the old dream again," from *Lyrical Intermezzo*). Heine notes elsewhere that "the linden plays a leading role in [*The Boy's Magic Horn*, by Brentano and von Arnim]; in its shade lovers talk in the evenings; it is their favorite tree, perhaps because the linden leaf has the shape of a human heart" (*The Romantic School* 3.1). Since many trysts under the linden take place at night, nightingales are often heard singing in its boughs.

Lion   Lions are rampant in both biblical and Greek literature from the beginning. They are the strongest and most dangerous of predatory beasts, whose roaring alone is terrifying, and they loom large in the minds of ancient authors. "Thou huntest me as a fierce lion," says Job (10.16). "Their roaring shall be like a lion, they shall roar like the young lions: yea, they shall roar" (Isa. 5.29). In the *Iliad* lions appear about thirty times, nearly always in similes. "As among cattle a lion leaps on the neck of an ox or / heifer, that grazes among the wooded places, and breaks it, / so the son of Tydeus hurled both from their horses / hatefully"; "And as herdsmen who dwell in the fields are not able to frighten / a tawny lion in his great hunger away from a carcass, / so the two

Aiantes, marshals of men, were not able / to scare Hektor, Priam's son, away from the body" (5.161–64, 18.161–64, trans. Lattimore). Nearly every warrior is likened to a lion during his display of prowess. Tyrtaeus enjoins the Spartan soldiers to place "a tawny lion's spirit in your breast" (frag. 13).

The lion thus became a byword for ferocity, strength, and terror. In Chaucer, for instance, lions are called "crewel," "fel," "fiers," "grym," "wild," and "wood" (mad or furious). In Spenser they are also "dredd," "ramping," and "ravenous." Shakespeare's Bottom and his friends rightly worry that whoever plays the lion must not frighten the ladies, because "a lion among ladies is a most dreadful thing; for there is not a more fearful wild fowl than your lion living, and we ought to look to't" (*MND* 3.1.30–33).

As fighter and roarer the lion is an emblem of anger. "The king's wrath is as the roaring of a lion" (Prov. 19.12). When the system of the seven deadly sins was established during the Middle Ages, the lion often stood for *ira*, "anger"; so in Spenser's procession of the sins "fierce revenging Wrath" rides on one (*FQ* 1.4.33). Less explicit is the lion Dante meets at the opening of the *Inferno*, the second of three beasts (1.45–48). If the leopard stands for fraud, the worst category of sin, and the she-wolf stands for incontinence, the least bad category, then the lion may represent the sins of violence, which Dante places midway in his hell. (*See* **Wolf, Leopard**.) The lion is also sometimes linked to pride (*superbia*), the first of the seven sins, since pride often goes with irascibility. Since the fifteenth century "pride" has been the term for a company or family of lions.

In the Middle Ages also the lion was crowned king of beasts, though it was long considered a regal emblem. Spenser calls him "mighty Lyon, Lord of all the wood" ("Vanitie" 10.1) and "Lyon Lord of everie beast in field" (*FQ* 1.3.7) and speaks of its "imperiall powre" (2.5.10). Marlowe also has "imperial lion" (*Edward II* 5.1.11), while Shakespeare calls it "imperious" (*Othello* 2.3.275). Richard II, demanding obedience, proclaims "lions make leopards tame" (*R2* 1.1.174); deposed, he is reminded by his queen that he is "a lion and the king of beasts" (5.1.34).

When Jacob gives his blessings on his sons, he pronounces that "Judah is a lion's whelp:...he couched as a lion, and as an old lion," and prophesies that he shall hold the scepter (Gen. 49.9–10). John of Patmos makes "the Lion of the tribe of Juda" a title of Christ (Rev. 5.5). Ezekiel has an allegory where the captured princes of Israel are lions and the sons of a lioness (19.1–9). Despite these connotations lions also came to represent enemies of the faithful: Daniel in the lions' den was the prototype for the fate of many Christians in the Roman empire. The four faces of the living creatures of Ezekiel's vision (1.10) include a lion's; Christians assigned the lion to St. Mark, and as he is the patron saint of Venice the lion became a symbol of that city.

The best-known biblical lion is the one that supposedly lies down with the lamb in the peaceable kingdom. Misled by the alliteration of "lion" and "lamb," however, most people muddle the famous passage from Isaiah, which reads: "The wolf also shall dwell with the lamb, and the leopard shall lie down with the kid; and the calf and the young lion and the fatling together; and a little child shall lead them. And the cow and the bear shall feed; the young ones shall lie down together: and the lion shall eat straw like the ox" (11.6–7; see 65.25). Virgil's "Fourth Eclogue," adopted by Christianity, makes a similar prophecy of a time when "cattle will not fear the great lions" (22). If such harmony will reign in the messianic kingdom, Milton imagines that it reigned before the fall as well: "Sporting the lion ramped, and in his paw / Dandled the kid" (*PL* 4.343–44); but when Satan enters the garden Milton likens him to a (fallen) lion and tiger, seeking prey (401–08), an allusion to 1 Pet. 5.8, comparing Satan to a roaring lion. In heaven, according to Blake, the lion will weep tears of pity and say, "And now beside thee bleating lamb, / I can lie down and sleep; / Or think on him who bore thy name, / Grase after thee and weep" ("Night" 41–44). Shelley foresees a transformation in this world, where "The lion now forgets to thirst for blood: / There might you see him sporting in the sun / Beside the dreadless kid" (*Queen Mab* 8.124–26). Wordsworth imagines a place in the past where meekness tempered pride, where "The lamb is couching by the lion's side, / And near the flame-eyed eagle sits the dove" (*Ecclesiastical Sonnets* 2.7).

The Asiatic goddess Cybele was depicted in Latin literature as riding a chariot pulled by lions (Virgil, *Aeneid* 3.113, 10.253), as if to say she tames wild nature; Lucretius has the same image for mother Earth (2.601ff.); both may be traceable to the Sumerian goddess Inanna, who is shown seated on a lion throne. Kings, if they are not called lions themselves, or "lion-hearted" like Richard I, have often been symbolized as hunters or tamers of lions; and the lion is a frequent heraldic animal and national symbol, as it is of Britain. Another old tradition is that a lion will not harm a true prince or princess – an excuse Falstaff makes to account for his cowardice before the disguised Prince Hal (1H4 2.4.267–71). A lion rushes suddenly upon Spenser's Una, but then "he kist her wearie feet, / And lickt her lilly hands with fawning tong" (*FQ* 1.3.6).

In Latin literature lions are associated with Africa (i.e., North Africa), particularly Libya (Seneca, *Oedipus* 919), Gaetulia (Horace 1.23.10), or the land of the Carthaginians ("Punic lions" in Virgil, *Eclogues* 5.27). These places became "decorative adjectives" for lions, and lasted into modern poetry.

Liver The most celebrated literary liver belongs to the Titan Prometheus, whose punishment for stealing fire from the gods was to have his liver (Greek *epar*) devoured each day by a vulture or eagle (it was restored each night) (Hesiod, *Theogony* 523–25). The Greeks traced certain emotions and faculties to various bodily organs, but it is not clear what function the liver serves in the Prometheus myth; perhaps his torture is meant simply to be excruciating and intimate. In Homer's *Iliad*, Hecuba, the mother of Hector, wishes she could attach herself to his killer Achilles and eat at his liver (24. 212f.), perhaps because Achilles is known for his ferocious anger (*cholos*, "bile"), which was sometimes thought to be a liver product (*see* **Bile**). It was not until Aeschylus that the liver was generally taken to be the seat of the passions. The chorus of the *Agamemnon* sings that "many things touch the liver" (432); in Sophocles' *Ajax* the chorus says, "True grief, I know, goes to the liver" (938); in both cases, modern translators make the liver into the "heart," a more familiar seat of feeling and courage ("courage" comes from the French word for "heart").

By the Renaissance the liver was usually taken as the seat of sexual desire. It is frequently so used by Shakespeare. Tarquin seeks Lucrece "To quench the coal which in his liver glows" (*Rape of Lucrece* 47). Ferdinand assures Prospero, "The white cold virgin snow upon my heart / Abates the ardour of my liver" (*Tempest* 4.1.55–56). As the seat of courage or martial valor the liver is the occasion of insults, as when Macbeth dismisses a servant as a "lily-liver'd boy" (5.3.15) or Goneril taunts Albany as a "Milk-liver'd man" (*Lear* 4.2.50), the proper color of the liver being dark red with blood. Hamlet blames himself for being "pigeon-liver'd" and lacking gall (2.2.573), for the notoriously timid pigeons were thought to lack that source of bitter anger. (*See* **Dove**.)

Livid   *see* **Blue**

Locust   In parts of North Africa and the Middle East locusts come in vast swarms and devour all vegetation. They are one of the plagues sent upon Egypt (Exod. 10.12–19), and if Israel disobeys the laws of God they will come again (Deut. 28.38, 42). Locusts are included with famine, pestilence, caterpillars, etc., as typical disasters (1 Kgs 8.37, Pss. 78.46, 105.34). John of Patmos prophesies they shall come in the last days from the bottomless pit: they shall sting like scorpions and look like horses with human faces (Rev. 9.3, 7).

Fortunately it is permitted to eat them (Lev. 11.22), and John the Baptist famously does so, along with honey, in the wilderness (Matt. 3.4) (see Dante, *Purgatorio* 22.151–52).

Locusts make good similes and metaphors. Milton likens Satan's legions to the locusts of Egypt (*PL* 1.338–46); Wordsworth saw that France "all swarmed with passion, like a plain / Devoured by locusts" (1805 *Prelude* 9.178–79); Byron laments that Spain has been overrun by "Gaul's locust host" (*Childe Harold* 1.215). Nathanael West invokes the biblical apocalypse in the final scene of violent riot in his novel *The Day of the Locust*.

Lode star   *see* **Star**

Lute   *see* **Harp**

Lynx   The lynx is proverbially sharp-eyed. It is invoked twice in the *Romance of the Rose* as the keenest-sighted animal (8023, 8901). A troop of monsters in Spenser is the more dangerous because "every one of them had Lynces eyes" (*FQ* 2.11.8). As "modes of sight betwixt each wide extreme," Pope would have us admire "The mole's dim curtain, and the lynx's beam" (*Essay on Man* 1.211–12). "I did look," says a character of Browning's, "sharp as a lynx" ("Youth and Art" 41). Ezra Pound dwells on lynxes in an insistent but mysterious way in one of his "Pisan Cantos," written while in detention by the US army; perhaps tranfiguring his guards into the watchful lynxes, he prays to one as to a god, "O Lynx keep watch on my fire," "O Lynx, guard my vineyard" (*Cantos* 79).

One of the Argonauts is named Lynceus, after the cat: "beyond all mortals else his eye was sharpest," according to Pindar (*Nem.* 10.61–62); he "had the sharpest eyes of any mortal, if the report is true that without trouble he could see even down beneath the earth" (Apollonius 1.153–54, trans. Hunter; cf. 4.1477–79). Lynceus became proverbial too. Horace advises us not to examine bodily perfections with the eyes of Lynceus (*Satires* 1.2.90–91). Goethe mentions him in *Faust* (7377) and then names two watchmen after him (9218ff., 11143ff.); the first says, "Eye-beam [*Augenstrahl*] is given me / like the lynx at the top of the tree" (9230–31). Galen describes an eye-salve called "lynceus" (12.778).

Ovid describes Bacchus as driving a pair of lynxes (*Met.* 4.25); Propertius imagines Ariadne borne to the sky by them (3.17.8); Virgil speaks of "Bacchus's colorful lynxes" (*Georgics* 3.263). Elsewhere Bacchus drives tigers or leopards.

Lyre   *see* **Harp**

M

Maggot   *see* **Worm**

Mandrake   The mandrake is a plant native to the Mediterranean, a member of the potato family, with thick roots, often forked, and thought to resemble male or female genitals, or the legs of a human being. The name comes from Latin *mandragora*, from Greek *mandragoras*, of unknown origin; the English word was misinterpeted to be a compound of "man" and "drake" (from Latin *draco*, "dragon").

Mandrakes (Hebrew *duda'im*) are mentioned twice in the Old Testament. Rachel asks Leah for the mandrakes her son Reuben has gathered, presumably as a fertility drug (Gen. 30.14–16). By extension it may have been used as an aphrodisiac, and thus it appears in the Song of Solomon (7.13). The Greeks also knew of it as a love philtre; *mandragoritis* was an epithet of Aphrodite. The seducer Callimaco in Machiavelli's play *La Mandragola* tells the gullible husband of the woman he wants: "there is no more certain way to get a woman pregnant than to give her an infusion of mandragora to drink" (Act 2). When Donne demands the impossible, "Get with child a mandrake root," he is wittily reversing one of its functions ("Go, and catch a falling star" 2). Some ancient readers thought the "miserable drugs" by which Circe transformed Odysseus' men into swine were mandrakes (*Odyssey* 10.236).

The main effect of eating mandrakes is narcotic or soporific. Apuleius says it produces a sleep very like death (*Met.* 10.11). It is sometimes mentioned with the poppy, as in Shakespeare's *Othello*: "not poppy, nor mandragora, / Nor all the drowsy syrups of the world, / Shall ever medicine thee to that sweet sleep / Which thou owedst yesterday" (3.3.330–33) (see also *AC* 1.5.4). Marino calls it the "stupid and heavy mandragora" (10.95).

Aelianus and other Latin writers report that the plant was extremely dangerous to uproot: the approved ritual was to tie it, at night, to a black dog, who would die in the process of pulling it up. It was also believed that the mandrake shrieks terribly as it comes out. So Juliet imagines that in the Capulet tomb she will hear "shrieks like mandrakes torn out of the earth, / That living mortals, hearing them, run mad" (4.3.47–48).

See **Poppy**.

Manna *see* **Bread**

Marble *see* **Bronze**

Marigold Though the name of this hardy yellow or orange flower seems to mean "Mary's gold," its usual symbolic meaning has to do with its heliotropic or sun-following character. It "opens and shuts with the sun," according to Nashe (*Unfortunate Traveller* 9). One name for it in modern Latin was *solsequium*, "sun-follower," whence French *souci*. Shakespeare invokes it in a simile for the transitory glory of courtiers dependent on the favor of the monarch: "Great princes' favourites their fair leaves spread / But as the marigold at the sun's eye" (*Sonnets* 25). Ronsard compares himself to a "Soucy" "who dies and hangs her languishing head / when she is no longer enjoying the sun" but is reborn at dawn, when the sun – his beloved's eye – shines on him ("Fantaisie à sa Dame" 39–50 in *Premières Poésies*).

The marigold's heliotropism was inevitably figured as the love between the female flower and the male sun. As Shakespeare's Perdita passes out flowers she includes "The marigold, that goes to bed wi' th' sun / And with him rises, weeping" (*WT* 4.4.105–06), while Drayton names "marigold, Phoebus' beloved friend" (*Endimion and Phoebe* 63). Carew elaborates the conceit: "Mark how the bashful morn, in vain / Courts the amorous Marigold, / With sighing blasts, and weeping rain; / Yet she refuses to unfold. / But when the Planet of the day, / Approacheth with his powerful ray, / Then she spreads, then she receives / His warmer beams into her virgin leaves" ("Boldness in Love"). Keats addresses "Ye ardent marigolds!" in "I stood tiptoe" (48). Though she is not a marigold, Ovid's description of Clytie after she becomes a plant lies behind these modern passages (*Met.* 4.259–270).

Erasmus Darwin writes in canto 3 of *The Loves of the Plants* that marigolds sometimes emit flashes of light at evening, as if returning the rays they have received all day. Coleridge concludes his "Lines written at Shurton Bars" by alluding to this phenomenon: "'Tis said, in Summer's evening hour / Flashes the golden-color'd flower / A fair electric flame: / And so shall flash my love-charg'd eye / When all the heart's big ecstasy / Shoots rapid through the frame!" (91–96). Gosse may be referring to the flash in his "Flower of the Marigold": "And I have found the flower she loves, / Whose burning leaves shut in the sun; / All day to watch his path it moves, / And dreams of him when day is done" (13–16).

The *Romance of the Rose* describes Jealousy as wearing a *chapel de soussie*, a "garland of marigolds" (21741–42); Chaucer imitates this in *Knight's Tale* (1928–29). Yellow is a traditional color of jealousy, and this sense is seconded by the pun on *souci*, "care" or "worry." (See **Yellow**.)

Blake makes use of the well-known hardiness and regenerative powers of the garden marigold when his amorous heroine Oothoon encounters one who tells her, "pluck thou my flower Oothoon the mild / Another flower shall spring" (*Visions of the Daughters of Albion* 8–9); she does so, and is thus fortified against the rape she shortly suffers. She then becomes the emblem of unjealous love.

Mask *see* **Theatre**

Matzah   *see* **Bread**

Maze   *see* **Labyrinth**

Melancholy   Melancholy, from Greek *melancholia*, "black bile," was once thought to be caused by an excess of that fluid, produced by the liver. It was not at first clearly distinguished from yellow bile (Greek *chole*), but in Hippocrates and other ancient physiologists melancholy is taken as one of four "humors" or fluids, alongside yellow bile, blood, and phlegm.

Its dominant constituent element is the earth, its qualities are cold and dry, it is sympathetic to nighttime, to the color black, and to the slowest of the planets, Saturn. Its Latin term, *atra bilis*, entered English as "atrabile" and the adjective "atrabilious"; it was also called "choler adust" (from Latin *adustus*, "burnt, scorched," hence "blackened"). In German it has been called *Schwarzgalligkeit*, "black-gallishness."

Its link with choler (bile) is shown in Chaucer's *Nun's Priest's Tale*, where Pertelote, who knows a lot about humors, advises Chauntecleer to purge himself "bothe of colere and of malencolye" (2946). A letter from Shakespeare's verbose Armado supplies the appropriate epithets: "So it is, besieged with sable-colored melancholy, I did commend the black-oppressing humor to the most wholesome physic of thy health-giving air" (*LLL* 1.1.231–34). It became associated with meditation, introspection, study, and the idle imagination. Sidney connects the "fumes of melancholy" with "dull pensiveness" (*Astrophel* 23); Dürer's famous engraving, though mysterious in certain details, connects it with intellectual contemplation. Spenser's character Phantastes is "full of melancholy," with a dark complexion and mad or foolish eyes, as if he were born under Saturn; in his chamber are flying swarms of "idle thoughtes and fantasies" (*FQ* 2.9.50–52). Hamlet, a student, seems to be in its grip as well. Robert Burton, who suffered from the scholar's version of it, wrote an immense treatise on it, *The Anatomy of Melancholy*.

Love-melancholy is common: Romeo has it, and so does Duke Orsino in *Twelfth Night*, whom the Clown commends to the protection of "the melancholy god" (Saturn) (2.4.73); in that play Viola speaks of a girl whose love is not requited and who pines "with a green and yellow melancholy" (2.4.113).

Melancholy gains prominence in eighteenth-century "sensibility" literature, and then in Romanticism, where a poet typically visits a graveyard or a ruined abbey and has "night thoughts." Milton's *Il Penseroso* is a prime source for this mode. Coleridge started a poem called "Melancholy" and completed one called "Dejection," Mary Robinson wrote "The Progress of Melancholy," Keats wrote an "Ode on Melancholy"; Schiller wrote "Melancholie," Tieck "Melankolie"; Darío wrote "Melancolia," in which he blames poetry itself for his suffering. Much of Byron's *Childe Harold* is composed of gloomy meditations among ruins and the "blight and blackening" of the mind (4.211). Peacock was prompted by it to write his novel *Nightmare Abbey*, about which he said, "I think it necessary to 'make a stand' against the 'encroachments' of black bile" (letter to Shelley 30 May 1818); it has a character based on Byron called Mr. Cypress.

Gérard de Nerval poses as a bereaved prince in a ruined tower, whose lute bears "the black sun of Melancholy" ("El Desdichado").

See **Bile, Humor**.

Merlin   *see* **Hawk**

Metal   The traditional hierarchy of metals – gold, silver, bronze, iron, and perhaps lead – is ancient. One of the earliest recorded uses of the hierarchy is to characterize the succession of races or ages of humankind. Thus Hesiod, in *Works and Days* 109–201, describes five races, four of them assigned a metal. The golden race "lived like gods, with carefree heart, / remote from toil and misery," taking what they wished from a plenteous earth. The silver race was "much inferior": they were witless and given to crime and impiety; Zeus removed them. The bronze race was "terrible and fierce, occupied with the woeful works of Ares." The fourth race were the demigods (Greek *hemitheoi*), a "godly race of heroes" who fought at Thebes and Troy and destroyed themselves. The race now on earth is the iron race, which "will never cease from toil and misery by day or night." Hesiod predicts it will behave worse and worse until Zeus destroys it. (Translations from M. L. West.)

There are parallels in Zoroastrian myth for the correspondence of metals to ages. In Daniel 2.31–45 there is Nebuchadnezzar's dream of a huge statue with golden head, silver breast and arms, bronze belly and thighs, iron legs, and feet part clay and part iron. Daniel interprets it to refer to the succession of kingdoms to follow Nebuchadnezzar's (gold); it will culminate in a new everlasting kingdom, which among later Christians was called the Fifth Monarchy.

Ovid recasts the Hesiodic story in *Metamorphoses* 1.89–150. In the golden age (not race) everyone did what was right, without laws; earth was bounteous and spring was perpetual. This was the age of Saturn (corresponding to Greek *Kronos*), who was banished by his son Jove (or Jupiter). The silver race came in along with seasons and agriculture. Then followed the bronze or brazen race, which was savage but not yet impious. Then the age of "hard iron" arrived and all evil burst forth, including private property, war, plunder, murder, and marital hatred; "Baneful iron came, and gold more baneful than iron" (141).

In his famous "Fourth Eclogue" Virgil names three ages, gold, heroic, and iron, and announces they will repeat, an idea not found in Hesiod or Ovid.

The metallic hierarchy was applied to individuals as well as races or ages. Plato in his *Republic* divides citizens into three classes or castes according to what innate metal they possess. God, he wrote, mingled gold in the composition of the rulers, silver in that of the auxiliaries or helpers, and iron and bronze in that of the farmers and the other craftsmen (3.415a). This use is the origin of the English word "mettle," meaning temperament or innate character; it is simply a respelling of "metal." "To try one's mettle" is to test one's character or spirit; "mettlesome" means "spirited" or "brave." The full original sense is alive in Shakespeare's line, "They have all been touched, and found base metal" (*Timon* 3.3.6), the word "touched" meaning "tested by the touchstone," which reveals the nature of the metal. (If mineralogical terms are used of social distinctions, the reverse is also true, for we still speak of "base" metals and "noble" gases.)

The process of refining or purifying precious metals has long lent itself to metaphoric uses, as we find in the Hebrew prophets. Isaiah quotes the Lord as saying, "I will turn my hand upon thee, and purely purge away thy dross, and take away all thy tin" (1.25). The New English Bible version reads: "Once again I will act against you to refine away your base metal as with potash and purge all your impurities." Ezekiel has God say, "As they gather silver, and brass, and iron, and lead, and tin, into the midst of the furnace, to blow the fire upon it, to melt it; so I will gather you in mine anger and in my fury, and I will leave you there, and melt you" (22.20). See also Jeremiah 6.27–30 and Malachi 3.3.

Metal entries in this dictionary: **Bronze, Gold, Iron, Lead, Silver**.

Milk Milk, like snow, is a standard of whiteness: "white as milk" is a commonplace, and "milkwhite" lambs and doves abound in older poetry. "Milkwhite" is doubly appropriate for lambs and doves because milk, the drink of infants, is also an emblem of innocence. In Pope's translation of the *Iliad* there is a tribe that "from Milk, innoxious, seek their simple Food" (13.12). A mother's breasts are filled with "innocent milk" (Wordsworth, 1805 *Prelude* 5.272). It is thus often associated with female tenderness and mercy. Lady Macbeth coins a famous phrase to describe her husband's mild nature, "the milk of human kindness" (1.5.17; the Folio has "humane kindness"); she herself calls on spirits to "Come to my woman's breasts / And take my milk for gall" (1.5.47–48). If Byron's Lambro were to lose his daughter it would "wean / His feelings from all milk of human kindness" (*Don Juan* 3.454–55). Sin "turns Heaven's milk of mercy to revenge," according to a character in Shelley's *Charles I* (1.65). One in Tennyson's *Princess* speaks of "The soft and milky rabble of womankind" (6.290).

"Milk," of course, might be metaphorical for any beneficent drink. "Wine," says Jonson, "it is the milk of Venus" ("Over the Door" 12). The poet in Coleridge's "Kubla Khan" has drunk "the milk of Paradise" (54).

The Promised Land is "a land flowing with milk and honey" (Exod. 3.8) – a formula that recurs many times in the Old Testament. In the final days "the mountains shall drop down new wine, and the hills shall flow with milk" (Joel 3.18). When Dionysus appears, according to Euripides, the earth flows with milk, wine, and honey (*Bacchae* 142–43). During the golden age, Ovid tells us, "streams of milk and springs of nectar flowed / And yellow honey dripped from boughs of green" (*Met.* 1.111–12, trans. Melville).

Milk's whiteness, innocence, and maternal and paradisal associations make it all the more terrible that what the Jews in the death camp drink, in Celan's words, is "black milk": "black milk of daybreak we drink it at nightfall / we drink it at noon and the morning we drink it at night / we drink it and drink it" ("Death-Fugue").

Mirror The symbolism of mirrors depends not only on what things cause the reflection – nature, God, a book, drama – but also on what one sees in them – oneself, the truth, the ideal, illusion.

As early as Roman times real mirrors were instruments of vanity or "narcissism" and soon came to stand for it. The myth of Narcissus, indeed, is the first great mirror tale, told in full by Ovid (*Met.* 3.339–510). In the *Amores* Ovid reminds a vain girl that she has ruined her hair by constantly curling it with irons; now "you lay aside the mirror with sorrowful hand" (1.14.36). Petrarch calls Laura's mirror "my adversary" because it has driven him away, and he warns her to remember Narcissus and his fate (*Rime* 45); in the next sonnet he blames his miserable state on "those murderous mirrors / which you have tired out by gazing fondly at yourself" (46). Spenser's proud Lucifera "held a mirrhour bright, / Wherein her face she often vewed fayne, / And in her selfe-lov'd semblance took delight" (*FQ* 1.4.10).

But we might profit from watching others as potential mirrors. A character in Terence tells a friend "to look at other men's lives as in a mirror" (*Adelphoe* 415–16). Certain people are models or ideals and serve as mirrors for everyone. "Mirror of X" had become a common phrase by Chaucer's time. In Chaucer one's lover is the "mirour of goodlihed" (*Troilus* 2.842); Shakespeare has "mirror of all Christian kings" (*H5* 2 Prologue 6), "mirror of all martial men" (*1H6* 1.4.74), "mirror of all courtesy" (*H8* 2.1.53), while Ophelia calls Hamlet "The glass of fashion and the mould of form" (3.1.153); Waller calls Ben Jonson the "Mirrour of Poets" ("Upon Ben Jonson").

By extension a book can be a mirror. Jean de Meun says his *Romance of the Rose* might be called a *Mirror of Lovers*, "since they will see great benefits in it for them" (10620–22). Hundreds of books, in fact, were titled *Mirror of X* or *Mirror for Y*, beginning with Augustine's *Speculum*; there have been mirrors of the world, of faith, of astronomy, of alchemy, of sin, of fools, of drunkenness, and for magistrates, all calculated to instruct and admonish.

The ancient idea that the arts imitate nature or the world led sometimes to an analogy with a mirror, as in Plato, *Republic* 596d–e. Donatus attributed to Cicero the opinion that comedy is a "mirror of custom" (*Commentum Terenti* 1.22). Skelton refers to his own play *Magnyfycence*: "A myrrour inclerd [made clear] is this interlude, / This lyfe inconstant for to beholde and se" (2524–25). Marlowe invites his audience to "View but his picture in this tragic glass" (1 *Tamburlaine* Prologue 7). Hamlet's speech on acting is justly famous: the end of playing is "to hold as 'twere the mirror up to nature; to show virtue her feature, scorn her own image, and the very age and body of the time his form and pressure" (3.2.21–24). Shortly after Don Quixote likens a play to a mirror (2.12), he encounters the Knight of the Mirrors, sent by his friends to defeat him and bring him home (2.15). The mirror became a common analogue in neoclassic aesthetic theory, according to which art imitates reality, but even after the Romantic analogue lamp or fountain took hold, the mirror could still be invoked (with a difference); so Shelley: "A story of particular facts is as a mirror which obscures and distorts that which should be beautiful: poetry is a mirror which makes beautiful that which is distorted" (*Defence of Poetry*). With the advent of realism the mirror again assumed a central role; so Stendhal: "a novel is a mirror being carried down a highway. Sometimes it reflects the azure heavens to your view; sometimes, the slime in the puddles along the road" (*The Red and the Black* 2.19, trans. Parks).

Many romances and fairy tales have magic mirrors. Spenser's Merlin has a "looking glasse, right wondrously aguiz'd [fashioned]," which could show everything in the world (*FQ* 3.2.18); Britomart's adventure begins when she sees Artegall in "Venus looking glas" (3.1.8). The mirror of Snow White's stepmother is both a means of magic and a mundane tool of vanity. Lewis Carroll's Alice begins a tale by stepping *Through the Looking-Glass*. Wilde's *Picture of Dorian Gray* is about a portrait as "the most magical of mirrors" (chap. 8): it reveals the inner degradation of its subject.

Mist   *see* **Cloud**

Mistletoe   The Icelandic *Poetic Edda* alludes to the death of Balder the son of Odin by mistletoe ("Voluspa" st. 31). Snorri Sturluson tells how the mistletoe, which had been overlooked when all things on earth took an oath not to harm him, was thrown at Balder by an enemy. (See also Matthew Arnold's "Balder Dead" 6.) Pliny records that the Druids of Gaul venerated the mistletoe, which grew on sacred oaks from which they cut it down with a golden sickle and used as a potion for fertility (*Natural History* 16.95).

The Greeks and Romans noted the affinity of the mistletoe for the oak – a fragment of Sophocles has the phrase "mistletoe-bearing oaks" (frag. 403) – but seem not to have regarded it with much awe. Propagated through bird-droppings, especially by the missel-thrush, mistletoe grows green in winter while the host tree itself (not necessarily an oak) seems dead or dormant. These facts underlie the famous simile in Virgil's *Aeneid* (6.205–09) for the "golden bough," which Aeneas is led to by birds; the bough looks like mistletoe, but it is a dead thing growing on a live tree, whereas mistletoe is apparently the opposite; the bough lets the living Aeneas enter the realm of the dead, where no birds may fly.

Mistletoe was also used to make birdlime to capture birds. Marcus Argentarius warns a blackbird away from an oak, for "the oak bears mistletoe, the foe of birds" (*Greek Anthology* 9.87). Since it is spread by birds in the first place, it seems poetically just that it should catch them.

Sidney wishes that a wedded couple may live "Like Oke and Mistletoe. / Her strength from him, his praise from her do growe" (*Third Eclogues* 63.51–52). It was widely thought to be poisonous, as Shakespeare seems to note when he calls it "baleful mistletoe" (*Titus* 2.3.95), unless he is alluding to old Germanic legends. Keats imagines it as an ingredient of a deadly potion (*Endymion* 3.514).

Since at least the seventeenth century mistletoe has been a feature of Christmas customs, perhaps because, as an evergreen, it represents life in the season of death.

Mold   *see* **Clay**

Mole   The mole is an emblem of blindness. Virgil says moles are "robbed of sight" (*Georgics* 1.183). Sidney, withdrawn from his beloved's light, likens himself "to the Mowle with want of guiding sight, / Deepe plunged in earth, deprived of the skie" (*Certain Sonnets* 21). It is contrasted with the lynx: Coleridge addresses a penetrating man as "Lynx amid moles!" ("No more twixt conscience" 5) (see more under **Lynx**); and to the eagle: "Does the Eagle know what is in the pit?" Blake asks, "O wilt thou go ask the Mole" ("Thel's Motto"), while Yeats wonders about "toils of measurement / Beyond eagle or mole / Beyond hearing or seeing" ("A woman's beauty" 9–11). He may have good ears, however, as Yeats's line may imply; Shakespeare's Caliban thinks so: "Pray you, tread softly, that the blind mole may not hear a foot fall" (*Tempest* 4.1.194–95).

The mole is a miner or burrower in the ground. When the ghost keeps moving underground, Hamlet cries, "Well said, old mole. Canst work i' th' earth so fast? / A worthy pioner! [miner]" (1.5.162–63). Nature tells man, according to Pope, "Learn of the mole to plow" (*Essay on Man* 3.176). Cowper, however, takes the mole as a symbol of destructive greed: noting the hillocks "Raised by the mole, the miner of the soil," he comments, "He, not unlike the great ones of mankind, / Disfigures earth; and, plotting in the dark, / Toils much to earn a monumental pile, / That may record the mischiefs he has done" (*Task* 1.273–77).

As for the hillocks, a character in Sidney is so depressed "that molehilles seem high mountaines" (*Fourth Eclogues* 71.23), and Shakespeare's Coriolanus compares "Olympus to a molehill" (5.3.30).

A toast by a Scotsman in Scott's *Waverley* "to the little gentleman in black velvet who did such a service in 1702" almost leads to bloodshed, for the little gentleman was the mole whose hill caused the horse of William III to stumble and kill him (chap. 11).

Monkey   *see* **Ape**

Monster   *see* **Beast**

Moon   The moon is one of the "two great lights" that God made on the fourth day, according to Genesis 1.16, "the greater light to rule the day, and the lesser light to rule the night" (AV). Now known to be the only natural satellite of planet Earth, under the Ptolemaic cosmology it was thought to be the nearest or lowest of the seven planets that revolve around the earth on their transparent spheres: Moon, Mercury, Venus, Sun, Mars, Jupiter, and Saturn. In Latin and the Romance languages the seven days of the week are named after these planets, but in English and the other Germanic languages only the two great lights (and Saturn in English) have given their names to days. Monday, or Moon-day, corresponds to Latin *dies lunae*, "day of the moon," whence French *lundi*, Italian *lunedi*, and so on.

Because it reflects the sun's light from constantly varying angles to the earth, the moon passes through phases, one complete cycle taking one "moon" or "month" of about $29\frac{1}{2}$ days. Five distinct phases have names: new (when the moon is invisible or just the first sliver is visible), crescent, half, gibbous (from Latin *gibbus*, "hump"), and full. When the first thin crescent is visible, some call the dark remainder the old moon, which may appear "with swimming phantom light o'erspread" (Coleridge, "Dejection"). The crescent and gibbous phases are said to be waxing before the full moon and waning after it. The crescent phase is often called "horned": its "temples were marked with a small horn" (Claudian, *Rape of Proserpine* 2.54); it is likened sometimes to a boat, sometimes to an archer's bow. The nearer the apparent positions of sun and moon in the sky the less the moon is lit. Thus the full moon is always opposite the sun in the sky, rising when the sun sets and vice versa; only a full moon can be eclipsed by the shadow of the earth, and only a new moon can eclipse the sun. If the moon is at its meridian or high point at midnight, it must be full.

In Latin usage, the day when the moon is near the sun and thus invisible is the day of the "silent moon" (*silentis lunae*) or the "interlunar" day (*interlunii*) (Pliny, *Natural History* 16.190). When the Greeks return by stealth to Troy, according to Virgil, they come *tacitae per amica silentia lunae*, "by the friendly silence of the quiet moon" (*Aeneid* 2.255); that might mean they come in utter darkness. (Yeats borrows "Per Amica Silentia Lunae" as the title of an important essay.) Milton's phrase, "silent as the moon, / When she deserts the night / Hid in her vacant interlunar cave" (*Samson Agonistes* 87–89), is echoed by Wordsworth: "All light is mute amid the gloom, / The interlunar cavern of the tomb" (*Evening Walk* 267–68); and by Shelley: "the silent Moon / In her interlunar swoon" ("With a Guitar. To Jane" 23–24). Shelley also combines this terminology with the boat and with Coleridge's phantom light when he describes the earliest new phase: "I see a chariot like that thinnest boat / In which the Mother of the Months is borne / By ebbing light into her western cave / When she upsprings from interlunar dreams, / O'er which is curved an orblike canopy / Of gentle darkness" (*PU* 4.206–11). The synaesthesia lying behind this Latin usage is found also in Dante's description of hell as a place where "all light is mute" (*Inferno* 5.28).

Its regular phases make the moon a measurer of time. The word "moon" derives from an Indo-European root *me-, meaning "measure," which also appears in Latin *mensis*, "month," and *menstruus*, "monthly" (whence English "menstruate"), as well as in *mensura*, "measuring" (whence English "immense," "dimension," and "measure" itself).

In both Greek and Latin new terms for "moon" replaced forms based on the *me-* root: Greek *selene* ("blaze" or "flame") and Latin *luna* ("light"), both with feminine endings, as opposed to the masculine gender of the original words. (Homer twice uses a feminine form, *mene*, for "moon," which is based on masculine *men*, the usual word for "month." Old English *mona* was masculine, as is modern German *Mond*.) In the classical tradition, then, the moon is invariably feminine, and since Homer and Hesiod it has been associated with Greek and then Roman goddesses. Greek Artemis, protectress of virgins as well as mothers in childbirth, guardian of young animals and of the hunt (with bow and arrow), became a moon goddess; Roman Diana was identified with Artemis; both acquired the epithet "Cynthian" from Mt. Cynthus on Delos, where Artemis (and her brother Apollo) were born, and Cynthia became a name in its own right. Another epithet, "Phoebe," meaning "bright" in Greek, also became a name, like its masculine form "Phoebus" (Apollo). Horace calls Diana the *diva triformis*: her three forms are Luna in heaven, Diana on earth, and Hecate in the lower world (Shakespeare calls her "triple Hecate" at *MND* 5.1.370). All the Latin names enter English poetry singly or in combination as names of the moon or moon-goddess. She drives a chariot as the sun does, as we see as early as the Homeric Hymn to Selene and Pindar's third Olympian ode; for an English example see Spenser's Cynthia in *Mutabilitie Canto* 6.

Virginity or chastity is frequently attributed to the moon, partly through its connection with virgin goddesses and partly because its light is cold. Shakespeare calls it the "cold fruitless moon" (*MND* 1.1.73).

The moon's continually changing phases led to its association with mutability, metamorphosis, inconstancy, or fickleness. The "sublunary" realm, everything beneath the sphere of the moon, is governed mainly by change, chance, or fortune, as opposed to the divinely ordered spheres above it.

It has long been known to cause the tides; hence it is called "watery" or "liquid" and associated with water or the sea. Shelley called the sea "Slave to the mother of the months" (*Revolt of Islam* 1420). Dew was thought to come from the moon; in one version of her story, Herse (Dew) is the daughter of Zeus and Selene.

From its silvery light, alchemists associated the moon with silver, whereas gold belonged to the sun. In Spenser, Cynthia steeps things in silver dew (*FQ* 1.1.39); "silver moon" has been a formula in English poetry for centuries.

Moonlight was thought to cause madness or "lunacy"; lunatics have "moon-struck madness" (Milton, *PL* 11.486). A "lune" is a fit of lunacy: we must beware "These dangerous, unsafe lunes i' th' king" (Shakespeare, *WT* 2.2.28).

As the sun is the eye of day, the moon is the eye of night (e.g., Aeschylus, *Seven* 390; Euripides, *Phoenician Women* 543; Ronsard, *Odes* 3.25.51), or it has an eye (Pindar, *Olymp.* 3.19–20; Shakespeare, *AYLI* 3.2.3). Like the sun as well, the moon drives a chariot and team (Ovid, *Fasti* 5.16; Statius, *Thebaid* 8.160).

In Christian iconography, the Virgin Mary is sometimes shown with the moon under her feet (from Rev. 12.1). The church has been represented by the moon, shining benignly with the reflected light of Christ the sun. The date of Easter is set as the first Sunday after the first full moon after the vernal equinox.

Morning star   *see* **Star**

Moth   *see* **Butterfly**

Mould   *see* **Clay**

Mountain   Most cultures have considered mountains awesome, sacred, or dreadful. In the western tradition they are often the homes of gods, being near to heaven and dangerous to mortals. Jehovah dwells on Sinai or Horeb, the Greek gods hold Olympus, Apollo and the Muses live on Parnassus or Helicon, Dionysus and Artemis occupy Cithaeron, and so on. In the Tannhäuser legend Venus has a mountain, and there are demonic mountains, such as the Brocken, the resort of witches, where Goethe sets his "Walpurgis Night" scene in *Faust I*.

In the Bible mountains are the sites of revelation both natural and supernatural. Christ gives a "Sermon on the Mount," which is the counterpart or "antitype" of Moses bringing down the tablets from Mt. Sinai; revelation comes from on high. Christ's temptation in the wilderness takes place on "an exceeding high mountain" (Matt. 4.8).

From the top of Mt. Pisgah the Lord shows Moses the Promised Land; "I have caused thee to see it with thine eyes, but thou shalt not go over thither" (Deut. 34.4). "Pisgah" as a site for revelation is found in radical Protestant rhetoric from at least the seventeenth century. Browning appropriates it in a pair of poems called "Pisgah-Sights" – "and I see all of it, / Only, I'm dying!" Stephen Dedalus playfully titles one of his parables *A Pisgah Sight of Palestine* (Joyce, *Ulysses*, "Aeolus"). It reached its greatest expression in the sermons and speeches of Martin Luther King, Jr.: "I've been to the mountain top...I've seen the promised land. I may not get there with you" (sermon of 3 April 1968). God brings Ezekiel to the top of "a very high mountain" and shows him a vision of the Temple (40.2). Milton alludes to this verse when he has Michael lead Adam up the highest hill of Paradise from which the hemisphere of earth lay "to the amplest reach of prospect" (*PL* 11.380). Coleridge echoes the double sense of "prospect" when, after prophesying disaster if Britain continues in her ways, he climbs a hill and has "a burst of prospect" into the natural world, which softens his heart ("Fears in Solitude" 215).

Indeed a characteristic motif of Romantic literature, at least since Schiller's "Der Spaziergang," is the philosophical wanderer who feels moments of exaltation and profound insight on mountains. Byron's Manfred may be the archetype in English literature, perhaps Nietzsche's Zarathustra in German; Chateaubriand's René climbs mountains, as does Lamartine in "L'Isolement." The two most sublime "spots of time" or epiphanies in Wordsworth's *Prelude* come as he crosses the Alps (6.494–572) and as he climbs Mt. Snowdon (13.10–119, 1805 version). Thomas Mann fully exploits the philosophical mountain-view tradition in *The Magic Mountain*.

Before the eighteenth century few people seem to have found mountains attractive or sublime. Petrarch's climb to the top of Mt. Ventoux (in about 1336) just to see what he could see was probably unusual; to write about it was unprecedented ("The Ascent of Mt. Ventoux"). Mountains were thought of as dangerous obstacles and excrescences on the fair face of the earth, and early comments on the Alps were anything but favorable. Thomas Gray was one of the first poets to appreciate them: in a Latin ode he addresses the "Holy Spirit of this stern place," and claims "we behold God nearer to us, a living presence, amid pathless steeps, wild mountainous ridges and precipitous cliffs, and among roaring torrents" ("Grande Chartreuse among the Mountains of Dauphiné," trans. Starr and Hendrickson). Soon the Alps attracted tourists, and Mont Blanc in particular, the highest peak of Europe, "the monarch of mountains," inspired pious emotions in many of them. A short poem in German by Friederika Brun, called "Chamouny at Sunrise," asks the mountain several questions, such as "Who piled high into the ether's vault / Mighty and bold thy radiant face?" and answers, "Jehovah! Jehovah!" Coleridge more or less plagiarized this poem with his "Hymn before Sunrise, in the Vale of Chamouni": "Who bade the sun / Clothe you with rainbows? Who, with living flowers / Of loveliest blue, spread garlands at your feet? – / god! let the torrents, like a shout of nations / Answer! and let the ice-plains echo, god!" Tom Moore visited Mont Blanc (unlike Coleridge) and wrote several poems about the experience: "Alps on Alps in clusters swelling, / Mighty, and pure, and fit to make / The ramparts of a Godhead's dwelling!" (*Rhymes on the Road I*). With such poems as these in mind William Hazlitt wrote, "The Crossing of the Alps has, I believe, given some of our fashionables a shivering-fit of morality; as the sight of Mont Blanc convinced [Moore] of the Being of God" ("On Jealousy and Spleen of Party"). Hölderlin calls the Alps "the fortress of the heavenly ones / ... from where / in secret much is firmly / Handed down to men" ("The Rhine" 6–9). Victor Hugo exclaimed, "How trifling the monuments of man seem beside these marvelous edifices which a mighty hand raised on the surface of the earth, and in which there is for the soul almost a new revelation of God!" ("Fragment of a Journey to the Alps"). The atheist Shelley, however, probably goaded by Coleridge's poem, wrote the greatest of Mont Blanc poems, in which the mountain is the home of "Power" rather than the product of the Creator, and has a voice "to repeal / large codes of fraud and woe" rather than to hand them down ("Mont Blanc" 80–81).

Emerson's Monadnoc has a similar silent power: "We fool and prate; Thou art silent and sedate"; "Mute orator! well skilled to plead, / And send conviction without phrase, / Thou dost succor and remede / The shortness of our days" ("Monadnoc").

Because of their impassable homeland, mountain people have preserved their independence more effectively than people of the valleys or plains, or so it has seemed; the example of the redoubtable Swiss stood as a beacon and a reproach to those who yearned for liberty in the kingdoms of Europe. Milton's phrase, "The Mountain Nymph, sweet Liberty" ("L'Allegro" 36), has had many successors. Writing of Corsica, Barbauld claims "Liberty, / The mountain Goddess, loves to range at large / Amid such scenes" ("Corsica" 67–69). Of his Welsh hero, Southey tells that "Among the hills of Gwyneth and its wilds / And mountain glens, perforce he cherished still / The hope of mountain liberty" ("Madoc in Wales" 12.51–53). Growing up in the Lake District, Wordsworth acquired a "mountain liberty" (1805 *Prelude* 9.242); during the revolt of the Tyrol against Napoleon, Wordsworth begins a sonnet, "Advance – come forth from thy Tyrolean ground, / Dear Liberty! stern Nymph of soul untamed; / Sweet Nymph, O rightly of the mountains named!" Byron's Manfred, on the Jungfrau, feels "the liberal air" (*Manfred* 1.2.50). Musset has a character cry, "Elle est la sur les monts, la liberté sacrée!" (*La Coupe et les lèvres*, "Invocation" 48).

Yet nineteenth-century tourists to the Alps were often struck by the imbecility of those who lived there, and when Emerson went to Mt. Monadnoc, expecting "to find the patriots / In whom the stock of freedom roots; / To myself I oft recount / Tales of many a famous mount, – / Wales, Scotland, Uri, Hungary's dells: / Bards, Roys, Scanderbegs and Tells," he found a dull, hard-working stock instead ("Monadnoc"). More caustically he asks "Who dare praise the freedom-loving mountaineer? / I found by thee, O rushing Contoocook! / And in thy valleys, Agiochook! / The jackals of the negro-holder" ("Ode to Channing"). As if to endorse this deflation of the myth, T. S. Eliot has a rootless and timid countess claim, "In the mountains, there you feel free," but "I read, much of the night, and go south in the winter" (*The Waste Land* 17–18).

Music of the spheres

The Pythagoreans believed (according to Aristotle, *De Caelo* 290b12) that the stars make sounds as they move, and since their speeds are in the same ratios as musical concordances, the entire sound they produce is a harmony. We cannot hear it, for it is a constant background sound in our ears from birth. Plato presented a vision of eight cosmic "whorls" (Greek *sphondulos*), hollow and nested one inside the other; on each stood a Siren singing one note, and from all eight there came a single harmony (*Republic* 616d–17b). Plotinus (*Enneads* 2.3.9) and Cicero (*Dream of Scipio* 18), among others, elaborated this vision; in Cicero the spheres are those of the seven planets and the fixed stars, and we learn that the uppermost stars give out the highest pitch, the moon the lowest; on earth we are deaf to the music, but when raised into the heavens we will hear it. (There are some discrepancies in the texts as to the number of different notes.)

Another source of this idea is a passage from Job: "the morning stars sang together, and all the sons of God shouted for joy" (38.7).

Chaucer's Troilus, transported to heaven after his betrayal in love, saw "The erratik sterres [planets], herkenyng armonye / With sownes ful of hevenyssh melodie" (*TC* 5.1812–13) (see also *PF* 59–63). Shakespeare's Lorenzo tells Jessica, "There's not the smallest orb which thou behold'st / But in his motion like an angel sings; / Still quiring to the young-ey'd cherubins; / Such harmony is in immortal souls, / But whilst this muddy vesture of decay / Doth grossly close it in, we cannot hear it" (*MV* 5.1.60–65). Sir John Davies's poem about the cosmic dance, *Orchestra*, tells how "The turning vault of heaven formèd was, / Whose starry wheels he [Love] hath so made to pass, / As that their movings do a music frame, / And they themselves still dance unto the same" (130–33).

Milton calls on "ye Crystal spheres" to ring out "with your ninefold harmony" and accompany the angels singing in honor of Christ ("Nativity" 125–32) (see also "At a Solemn Music"). The opening lines of the "Prologue in Heaven" of Goethe's *Faust* allude to this music – "The sun intones as it has of old / in rival song with brother spheres" (243–44).

In the traditional scheme the earth, being motionless, made no sound, but Shelley transforms the tradition to suit the Copernican model. Panthea and Ione hear "the deep music of the rolling world," which is made of "Ten thousand orbs involving and involved" that "whirl / Over each other with a thousand motions," solemnly "Kindling with mingled sounds, and many tones, / Intelligible words and music wild" (*PU* 4.186, 241–51).

Myrrh   *see* **Frankincense and myrrh**

Myrtle   The myrtle plant was sacred to Aphrodite and to her Roman counterpart Venus, as it was to the Mesopotamian goddess Ishtar; hence it became the plant of love. There is little in Greek literature before Plutarch (*Marcellus* 22.4) connecting myrtle with Aphrodite, but apparently there were temples to Aphrodite where a sacred myrtle was cultivated. Aristophanes uses "myrtle" as a euphemism for the female genitalia (*Lysistrata* 1004).

According to Ovid, Venus crouched behind a myrtle bush to hide from the satyrs (*Fasti* 4.141–3, 869); another story has her emerge from the sea at birth covered with myrtle, which often grows by the shore. Venus' son Aeneas shades his temples with "maternal myrtle" (*materna myrto*) before the games (*Aeneid* 5.72), and later in the Underworld he sees a myrtle grove where those who died of love wander disconsolate (6.443). It soon became a common icon of Venus; e.g., Du Bellay's poem "To Venus" dedicates flowers to her and promises her myrtle if he is successful in love. Marlowe's description of Leander's "amorous habit [dress]" includes "Cupid's myrtle" (*Hero and Leander* 588–89).

Myrtle is an evergreen and thus suggestive of life's power against death; in Drayton's words, "*bay* and *myrtle*, which is ever new, / In spight of winter flourishing and green" (*Pastoral Eclogues* 6). Perhaps for this reason it was frequently used in garlands and crowns at festivals and to deck tombs. Early Greek lyric poets spoke of twining roses with myrtle. Horace praises the "simple myrtle" without embellishments: "myrtle suits you pouring, and me drinking" (1.38.5–7). Pliny reports that a Roman commander was crowned with the myrtle of Venus Victrix for a victory in which none was slain (*Natural History* 15.38).

Both its connection with festivals and its association with love, a common subject of song, may account for its use as a crown for poets, along with laurel, ivy, or oak, though each has distinctive connotations. Dante introduces the poet Statius as crowned with myrtle (*Purgatorio* 21.90). Garnier asks that the laurel grow green at Ronsard's tomb "with the ivy / and the amorous myrtle" ("Elegy on the Death of Ronsard"). Thomson imagines Sidney "with early Laurels crown'd, / The Lover's Myrtle, and the Poet's Bay" ("Summer" 1512–13).

A famous drinking song collected by Athenaeus tells of the two liberators of Athens: "In a myrtle bough will I carry the sword / Like Harmodius and Aristogiton / When they killed the tyrant / and brought equality to Athens" (*Deipnosophistae* 15.695). It is hard to see how myrtle branches could have concealed swords, but myrtle doubtless adorned the festival where the tyrant was killed (they actually killed Hipparchus, brother of the tyrant Hippias, in 514 BC), and the poetic point may lie in the contrast between the festive and friendly connotations of myrtle and the contrary sense of sword. Shelley, in any case, brilliantly recreates the image as he imagines earth and heaven united by beams "Like swords of azure fire, or golden spears / With tyrant-quelling myrtle overtwined," as if it is the myrtle of love that defeats tyranny and not the sword (*PU* 4.271–72).

See **Ivy, Laurel, Oak**.

N

Nature   "Nature" in Greek (*physis*) and Latin (*natura*) at first meant the nature *of* something, as in Lucretius' title "On the Nature of Things," but it came to stand alone, perhaps by means of phrases such as "the nature of everything," to mean the universe or the natural world. In this sense Ovid mentions "nature" as featureless before the creation (*Met.* 1.6). According to late ancient sources, the Orphics praised *Physis* as the mother of all, all-wise, all-ruling, and immortal; if so, that was the first instance of "Mother Nature," but the personification was not sustained. The more ancient myths about Gaia (Earth) must also have encouraged this personification; the Homeric "Hymn to the Mother of All" begins "I shall sing of well-founded Earth, mother of all, / Eldest of all, who nourishes all things living on land." In both Greek and Latin the words for "nature" and for "earth" (Greek *gaia, ge*, Latin *tellus, terra*) are all feminine in grammatical gender.

A later forerunner of Mother Nature is Lucretius' *alma Venus* ("nourishing Venus"), whom he invokes as the goddess of the generation of life and the muse of his poem (1.2); Spenser imitates his invocation in *FQ* 4.10.44–47. Statius makes Nature a "captain" (*dux*) (*Thebaid* 12.642); in Claudian, Nature is the "marriage-maker" (*pronuba*) (*Magnes* 38). She is a fully fledged allegorical figure in Bernard Sylvestris and Alanus de Insulis; the latter's "Complaint of Nature" influenced *The Romance of the Rose*, where Nature is the mistress of Venus' forge, making new generations of living things (15975ff.). She first appears in

English poetry as "this noble goddesse Nature" in Chaucer's *Parliament of Fowls* 303; Chaucer cites Alanus' "Pleynt of Kynde" as his authority. Gower has "Nature the goddesse" (*Confessio* 5.5961). Spenser also refers to "mother Nature" (*FQ* 2.6.16) and "great Dame Nature" with "fruitfull pap" that feeds the flowers (2.2.6). Amidst the manifold meanings of "nature" in Shakespeare, the "good goddess nature" persists (*WT* 2.3.104); "Nature hath fram'd strange fellows in her time" (*MV* 1.1.51). But when Edmund in his first speech announces "Thou, Nature, art my goddess; to thy law / My services are bound" (*Lear* 1.2.1–2), we are alerted that he will not be bound by traditional duty. Shakespeare himself, according to Gray, was "Nature's darling," for "To him the mighty Mother did unveil / Her awful face" ("Progress of Poetry" 84–87).

With the new feeling for nature in the literature of sensibility and romanticism, of course, richer and less allegorical accounts of nature prevail, but it often remains maternal, or at least feminine. Goethe's Faust asks, "Where do I seize you, unending Nature – / you breasts, where?" (455–56). Wordsworth constantly refers to nature as "she," and sometimes she is active in ministering to the growth of the poet's soul, the subject of *The Prelude*. Earth, too, has "something of a Mother's mind" in the "Intimations Ode" (79). Shelley invokes the "Mother of this unfathomable world" near the opening of "Alastor" (18). In his fallen state, according to Blake, Man perceives Nature as something apart from him, often as a domineering and faithless female whom he names Vala (punning on "veil"): "Vala, the Goddess Virgin-Mother. She is our Mother! Nature!" (*Jerusalem* 18.29–30). But the usual romantic view is that nature governs our most human feelings, our imaginations, our hearts. Dickens with typical sarcasm describes the utilitarian philosophers of self-interest as having deduced a "little code of laws" as "the main-springs of all Nature's deeds and actions: the said philosophers very wisely reducing the good lady's proceedings to matters of maxim and theory and, by a very neat and pretty compliment to her exalted wisdom and understanding, putting entirely out of sight and considerations of heart, or generous impulse and feeling" (*Oliver Twist* chap. 12).

Parallel to maternal nature is the widespread idea of the "virgin land," uncultivated territory that must be conquered and ploughed by men to make her a "motherland." One root of this notion is the biblical image of Israel or Jerusalem as the "married" land (Hebrew *beulah*): "Thou shalt no more be termed Forsaken; neither shall thy land any more be termed Desolate; but thou shalt be called Hephzibah, and thy land Beulah: for the Lord delighteth in thee, and thy land shall be married" (Isa. 62.4). Too often, however, Jerusalem plays the harlot and commits fornications with other countries (Ezek. 16 *passim*). Another source may be the plot of Virgil's *Aeneid*, where the hero leaves a wife behind in the flames of Troy and a mistress on a pyre in Carthage in order to conquer a destined land in Italy and confirm it by marrying Latinus' daughter Lavinia, "Miss Italy." The symbolism of ploughing enters into it, too; the word "colony" comes from the root in "cultivate" and "agriculture" (Latin *colere*, "to till" or "plough"), and early American colonies were often called "plantations". (*See* **Plow**.) Most national names in the European languages are feminine in gender and have feminine allegorical emblems: *la France* is symbolized by Marianne or by Joan of Arc, Britain by Britannia (derived from Minerva), America by Lady Liberty, and so on.

The very name "America" is the feminine form of "Americus," the Latin form of Amerigo (Vespucci); the noun *terra* may have been understood but it vanished quite early from the maps. "Virginia" is the perfect expression of this symbolism, though it was named for Queen Elizabeth; John Smith calls that colony the "blessed Virgin" and refers to "This Virgins sister (called New England)" (*New-England Trials* 1.243). According to Thomas Morton in 1632, New England herself was "Like a faire virgin, longing to be sped [made to prosper, or made pregnant], / And meete her lover in a Nuptiall bed" (*New English Canaan* Prologue 9–10). Blake's character Orc, who stands for the revolutionary American colonists who claim the land, seizes the womb of the nameless virgin who attends him and makes her pregnant (*America*, "Preludium").

Night   Milton describes Night as "eldest of things" (*PL* 2.962), though in Genesis it is coeval with day (1.5); it is "darkness" that precedes everything but the void or chaos itself. Spenser calls Night the "most auncient Grandmother of all" (*FQ* 1.5.22). Both authors hearken not only to Genesis but Hesiod's *Theogony*, where Night is the offspring of Chaos, though she seems to follow Earth, Tartarus, and Eros (116–23); she is the mother of Sky (*Aither*), Day, Heaven, the Hills, and Sea (124–32).

Like the sun, moon, and dawn, night is portrayed in classical literature (though not in Hesiod) as driving a chariot and team of horses. "The darkening chariot of Night / leans to its course," as Aeschylus has it in *Choephoroe* 660–61 (trans. Lattimore); Euripides writes, "black-robed Night, / Drawn by a pair, urged on her chariot" (*Ion* 1150–51, trans. Willets). Virgil has "And black Night borne upward in her chariot held the sky" (*Aeneid* 5.721). Ovid imagines a lover appealing for more time: "O slowly, slowly run, ye horses of night" (*Amores* 1.13.40), the Latin original of which Marlowe uses with great poignancy in Dr. Faustus's final terrified speech: "O lente, lente currite noctis equi" (5.2.152). Spenser's Night has an "yron wagon" with double team, two horses "blacke as pitch" and two brown (*FQ* 1.5.28); later she rides on a black palfrey (7.7.44). Milton has "Night-steeds" in his "Nativity" ode (236). Shakespeare several times has the night drawn by dragons (e.g., *MND* 3.2.379), perhaps a confusion with those of Ceres.

In the Greek and Roman poets there are standard features of night or nightfall: silence, loneliness, sleep, dreams; the star-filled sky, the bright moon; and occasionally festivities. A poem by Sappho or Alcaeus expresses the loneliness by understatement: "The moon has gone down / and the Pleiades; the middle / of the night, time goes by, / and I lie alone" (Sappho Campbell 168B). A brief description of night in Virgil's *Aeneid* makes a similar contrast to the sleepless Dido (4.80–81). Milton has a full description of night in Eden, with the silence (except for the nightingale), Hesperus, and the moon (*PL* 4.598–609). Goethe's "Wanderer's Night-Song" beautifully evokes the peace of night and the deeper peace to come.

Night is of course the time of unseen dangers, "night's black agents" (*Macbeth* 3.2.54), ghosts, magic, and moonstruck madness, as well as the pursuit of love or anything else restrained by daylight. We hardly need to give examples. Since the sun or light may stand for knowledge or insight, and "a great cause of the night is lack of the sun" (*AYLI* 3.2.26), night is also symbolic of spiritual error: Paul exhorts, "The night is far spent, the day is at hand: let us therefore cast off the works of darkness, and let us put on the armour of light" (Rom. 13.12); Dante is lost in the wood at night (*Inferno* 1); Spenser's Night is the mother of falsehood (*FQ* 1.5.27) and ignorance (*Teares of the Muses* 263). Night also stands for death: "I must work the works of him that sent me," Jesus says, "while it is day: the night cometh, when no man can work" (John 9.4). Racine's Olympe would be happy if her grief plunged her into "the night of the tomb" (*Thébaïde* 5.5.1478), while Phèdre wants to flee "into the infernal night" (*Phèdre* 4.6.1277). Shelley has "the night of death" (*Julian* 127), though he also has "the night of life" (*PU* 3.3.172), that is, "our night" (*Adonais* 352) in this life of misery and ignorance. Poe's raven seems to come from "the night's Plutonian shore" (47, 98).

Night is the traditional time for meditation and study, for "burning the midnight oil," and hence for melancholy. Milton's "Il Penseroso" (the pensive man) prefers the night: "let my Lamp at midnight hour, / Be seen in some high lonely Tow'r" (85–86). Night poetry was much in vogue in the eighteenth century as part of the literature of "sensibility," and particularly "graveyard" poetry; e.g., Young's *Night Thoughts*, Blair's *The Grave*, and Gray's "Elegy," which begins where the plowman "leaves the world to darkness and to me" (4). Goethe's Faust meditates at night (and practices magic), and so do Coleridge in "Frost at Midnight" and "Dejection," and Lamartine in his *Méditations*. Some Romantics revalued night as a place of imaginative revelation: Novalis's *Hymns to the Night*, and perhaps Keats's "Ode to a Nightingale."

See **Moon**.

Nightingale   The nightingale has had the most spectacular career of all literary birds. It has appeared in many thousands of poems from Homer to the twentieth century, and even in ancient times it acquired an almost formulaic meaning as the bird of spring, of night, and of mourning. Later, through its link to spring and night, it also became a bird of love.

The Greeks considered the nightingale, like the swallow and cuckoo, to be a notable harbinger of spring. A four-word fragment of Sappho sums it up: "spring's herald, lovely-voiced nightingale." Homer has it singing in the woods "when springtime has just begun" (*Odyssey* 19.519). In the late Latin *Vigil of Venus* the goddess of spring makes the bird sing a song of love (86–88). This tradition is repeated in Chaucer's *Parliament of Fowls*, where the nightingale is defined as the bird "That clepeth [calls] forth the grene leves newe" (351–52), and in Drayton's *Endimion and Phoebe*: "The Nightingale, woods Herauld of the Spring" (55).

Its melodious, liquid, and variable voice made the nightingale a popular housebird in ancient times. One of the two Greek names for it refers to its song: *aedon*, "singer"; the other, *philomela*, has been taken to mean "lover of music," but what *mela* means is uncertain (probably not "music").

The Greeks also heard in the nightingale's song something mournful, and imagined one of its "words" to be the name of a lost child; they also imagined, wrongly, that the female of the species does the singing. Its earliest literary appearance is in Penelope's simile for herself as Pandareos' daughter Aedon, wife of Zethos; Aedon in a mad fit killed her son Itylos and now, changed into a nightingale, pours out a mournful song (*Odyssey* 19.518–23).

It may be that the Greeks, listening to two prominent birds of early spring, were struck by the contrast between the tuneless chattering call of the swallow and the beautiful song of the nightingale, and so a different story arose about Procne, daughter of Pandion of Athens and wife of Tereus of Daulis (Thrace), and her younger sister Philomela. As Ovid tells it centuries later (*Met.* 6), Tereus rapes Philomela, tears out her tongue so she cannot speak, and confines her in a hidden cottage; she contrives to weave a message on her loom and send it to her sister, who rescues her. Together they take a horrible revenge on Tereus by killing his son by Procne, Itys, and serving him to his father for dinner. As the furious Tereus pursues the sisters, they both turn into birds, which Ovid does not name: one flies into the woods (presumably a nightingale), the other flies to the roof (presumably a swallow); Tereus becomes a hoopoe.

Ovid does not say which sister flew where, but presumably the tongueless one becomes the swallow. His vagueness may reflect a long-standing conflict in the myth, since *philomela*, if it is taken to mean "lover of music," is a poor name for the songless swallow, but if the nightingale's song sounds mournful then it should be she who has lost a son. There are variants where Tereus cuts out Procne's tongue, but it is always Procne's son who is killed, so Philomela would be singing a mournful song for her nephew. In any case, sometimes (as in Aristophanes) Procne is the nightingale.

This tale, in its Ovidian form, became very popular. In Medieval lyrics in several languages Philomela or Philomena replaces native words for nightingale. Chaucer tells part of the story in *The Legend of Good Women* and it recurs throughout Shakespeare's *Titus Andronicus*. T. S. Eliot makes use of it in *The Waste Land*. When Keats compares the silent Madeline to a "tongueless nightingale," however (*Eve of St. Agnes* 206), it is doubtful if we are to think of Philomela and her tragedy.

In Greek drama a simpler version prevailed. The chorus of Aeschylus' *Agamemnon* compares Cassandra's wild lament on the brink of her murder to the nightingale's clamor for Itys; Cassandra responds by saying she longs for the nightingale's fate, happier than her own (1140–49). The chorus of Sophocles' *Ajax* imagines the mother of Ajax grieving over her son more violently than the nightingale (621–31). The chorus of Euripides' *Helen* invokes the nightingale to sing mournfully with them over Helen's fate. (See also Sophocles, *Electra* 107–09, 147–49, 1077ff.) Seneca imitates Greek tragedy when his Octavia asks what nightingale could sing her song of sorrow (*Octavia* 914).

Perhaps because of the Athenian provenance of the Philomela myth, the nightingale came to be called the "Attic bird" (Propertius 2.20.5–6; Milton, *PR* 4.245–46; Gray, "Ode on the Spring" 5).

After three millennia of poetic nightingales Darío could claim "The same nightingales sing the same trills, / and in different tongues it is the same song" ("The Swans" 7–8), but a survey of human tongues gives a different impression. Aristophanes' comedy *The Birds* (737–52) gives the song as "tio tio tio tiotinx" and "totototototototototinx," which do not sound very mournful, but in a "tio" or "ito" Greeks heard the name Itys. Whether mournful or not, "tiotinx" is much more accurate than the conventional sound in English poetry since the Renaissance, "jug jug," which resembles the call of the nightjar. The medieval German poet Walther von der Vogelweide has the bird cheerfully sing "tandaradei!" (in "Under der linden"), but later German poets heard sadness in the sound, which they made into "zurück" ("back") or "zu spät" ("too late"). Provençal poets do not record its voice, but in Old French it is "oci" or "ochi," which sounds like the verb for "kill," whence its connection, in a few poems, with vengeance. According to Fitzgerald, Omar Khayyam imagines it saying "Wine! Wine! Wine! | Red Wine!" (22–23).

Nearly all brief allusions to the nightingale in Greek and Latin poetry mention its beautiful voice, its mournfulness, its presence in early spring, and/or its invisibility, hiding among thickets or leafy trees. Moschus in his "Lament for Bion" mentions "nightingales complaining in the thick foliage" (9); Catullus vows "I will always sing strains of mourning, as under the thick shadows of the branches sings the Daulian bird bewailing the fate of Itylus" (65.12–14). By describing a nightingale weeping all night long (*Georgics* 4.511–16), Virgil gave an impetus to the association of the nightingale, as its English name also implies, with night. (The "-gale" is from Old English *galan*, "sing." Its Latin name, *luscinia*, may mean "singer at twilight," though more likely "singer of grief," as Varro argued in *Latin* 5.76.)

The nightingale's nighttime provenance is well established in English poetry – it is stated, or overstated, by Christina Rossetti: "A hundred thousand birds salute the day: – | One solitary bird salutes the night" ("Later Life" 20). It is often paired with the lark as its opposite; the most famous of such pairings comes in *Romeo and Juliet* 3.5, which begins with a debate between the young lovers, the morning after their first night together, over whether it is the nightingale they have just heard or the lark.

Milton calls it the "wakeful Bird," which "Sings darkling, and in shadiest Covert hid | Tunes her nocturnal Note" (3.38–40), and "all night tun'd her soft lays" (7.436), among eight appearances in *Paradise Lost*. Perhaps because night is the time of lovers, Milton also stresses the amorous quality of the song: "She all night long her amorous descant sung" in Eden, while Adam and Eve "lull'd by Nightingales imbracing slept" (4.603, 771). His first sonnet, "O Nightingale," claims that its songs "Portend success in love," as opposed to the cuckoo, "the rude Bird of Hate." Combining love with the traditional mournfulness, Milton calls the bird "love-lorn" in *Comus* (234), as if it is her mate she has lost, not her child.

Any bird that sings might well become a metaphor for a poet (as the swan did), but the nightingale came to do so as early as Hesiod. In *Works and Days* (202–12) Hesiod tells a fable about a hawk who has a nightingale in his grasp; the hawk calls his prey an *aoidos*, the usual term for bard or minstrel in Hesiod and Homer; the implication is that Hesiod is himself a nightingale in a world of dangerous hawks (predatory lords). (See also Theognis 939.) Plato imagines the soul of the poet Thamyras choosing the life of a nightingale (*Republic* 620a). Theocritus calls Homer the "Chian nightingale" (7.47). It is a frequent conceit in Troubadour and Trouvère (Provençal and Old French) poetry that the poet is like a nightingale, which incites him to sing and reminds him of his unhappiness in love; the same is true among the German *Minnesänger*. One medieval tradition adds that they stop singing when love is fulfilled. The Troubadour tradition, incidentally, does not seem to draw much from the classical tradition: often the birds are male, and often they are happy.

In devotional literature the bird sometimes represents the soul, as it does in John Peacham's *Philomena*: "You should know that this bird is the figure / Of the soul who puts all its effort into loving God" (45–46, trans. Baird and Kane).

Milton, in the first passage quoted above (*PL* 3.38–40), compares himself to the nightingale, who like him sings in the dark. Keats alludes to this passage in his famous "Ode to a Nightingale," where he compares, or rather contrasts, himself with the invisible bird whose singing overwhelms him. In his *Defence of Poetry*, Shelley writes, "A Poet is a nightingale, who sits in darkness and sings to cheer its own solitude with sweet sounds; his auditors are as men entranced by the melody of an unseen musician, who feel that they are moved and softened, yet know not whence or why." "Of Philomela and the poet," Lamartine claims, "the sweetest songs are sighs" ("Adieux à la Poésie" 34–35). Mandelstam laments his incurable disease of poetry-writing: "there is no hope / For heart still flushed / with Nightingale Fever" ("Clock-Grasshopper's Song," trans. Hingley).

A secondary tradition has it that nightingales press a thorn against their breast to keep awake so they might lament all night. Shakespeare's Lucrece speaks to the bird: "against a thorn thy bear'st thy part / To keep thy sharp woes waking" (*Lucrece* 1135–36); according to Sidney she "Sings out her woes, a thorn her song-book making" ("The Nightingale" 4). Marvell seems to be alluding to this tradition in "Upon Appleton House" 513–20, and Oscar Wilde builds on it in his story "The Nightingale and the Rose."

The thorn motif goes back to sixteenth-century French poetry, which seems to have taken it from Arabic or Persian poetry, where the (male) nightingale or *bulbul* sings to the (female) rose until it blooms in the spring; he sometimes presses his breast against a rose thorn to ease his pain while singing. Fitzgerald in his version of Omar Khayyam indicates the Persian origin of the motif, the "divine / High piping Pehlevi [Persian]" in which "the Nightingale cries to the Rose" (21–23). In the early eighteenth century Mary Wortley Montagu introduced the "bulbul" to English readers with a translation of a Turkish love poem by Ibrahim Pasha, while Thomas Moore and Byron were among the first to put one in their poems: in *Lalla Rookh* (1.280) and in *The Bride of Abydos* (1.288 and 2.694; see also Byron's *The Giaour* 21–31). In the opening of *Epipsychidion* Shelley calls his beloved a nightingale and likens his poem to a rose: "soft and fragrant is the faded blossom, / And it has no thorn left to wound thy bosom" (11–12).

Ignoring the tradition that the bird sings a lament, some poets since the Middle Ages have made the nightingale an emblem of love. Ronsard has a nightingale court his beloved (*Odes* 4.22). Thomas Randolph imagines a nightingale singing in Elysium, where "The soules of happy Lovers crown'd with blisses, / Shall flock about thee, and keep time with kisses" ("On the Death of a Nightingale"). On a pair of young lovers, Byron comments, "there was no reason for their loves / More than for those of nightingales or doves" (*Don Juan* 4.151–52). "The nightingale," Hugo recalls, "sang like a poet and like a lover" ("La Fête chez Thérèse" 79–80). For the most part, however, melancholy remains the bird's dominant note, though the melancholy might be due, of course, to lost love.

Coleridge wrote a pair of nightingale poems that ought to have put an end to nightingale poems. In "To the Nightingale" he begins: "Sister of love-lorn

Poets, Philomel! / How many Bards . . . / . . . How many wretched Bards address thy name." He then quotes Milton's line about "Philomel" in *Il Penseroso*, "Most musical, most melancholy," as if to debunk it, but follows tradition himself in saying "Thou warblest sad thy pity-pleading strains." Three years later in "The Nightingale" he again quotes the Milton line and even quotes his own phrase "pity-pleading strains," but this time he refutes the idea that nightingales are melancholy. "In Nature there is nothing melancholy," and we owe to an anonymous unhappy "night-wandering man" the idle thought that nightingales are sad; "And many a poet echoes the conceit." This argument was not original with Coleridge. Socrates said that "no bird sings when it is hungry or cold or distressed in any other way – not even the nightingale or swallow or hoopoe, whose song is supposed to be a lament" (Plato, *Phaedo* 85a). Keats seems to be responding to Coleridge when he makes his nightingale happy, singing with no thought of death or other human woes, but he seems nonetheless to project such woes when near the end he imagines the bird singing a "requiem" or "plaintive anthem."

Despite Coleridge, more nightingale poems continued to get written, such as Matthew Arnold's "Philomela," Wilde's "The Burden of Itys," and Robert Bridges's "Nightingales." In France a notable example is Verlaine's "Le Rossignol," where the weeping nightingale's languishing voice evokes memories of his absent beloved.

See **Cuckoo, Lark**.

Noon   *see* **East and west**

Number   To the ancients, as well to many moderns of a mystical bent, numbers had meanings beyond their mathematical characteristics. The Pythagoreans developed a whole cosmology based on the interrelations of small numbers, in particular the ratios of string lengths underlying the musical intervals. Both the Hebrews and the Greeks used their alphabet as their written number system, with the result that words acquired numerical values. In Greek, for example, the letters in iesous (Jesus) sum to 888, a number notable not only for its repetition but because eight seemed significant in the life of Jesus (he was in Jerusalem eight days from Palm Sunday to Easter, for example), it can stand for the Eternal Sabbath after a seven-day week, and is the first perfect cube (2^3). Similarly 666, the famous "number of the beast" of Revelation 13.18, can be derived from the Hebrew spelling of nero caesar, though it is only fair to point out that different manuscripts of the text give 616 and 665. (666 is also the Pythagorean "triangle of the great tetractys," that is, the sum of all the numbers from 1 to 36 (or 6^2.) If 888 is a perfect number, then 666, appropriately enough, is an imperfect number, for it falls below the Hebrew measure of time just as 888 surpasses and "completes" it.

Seven, of course, is crucial in western number sense. As it is the number of days in the Hebrew week, it memorably structures the first chapter of Genesis as well as the whole of the Book of Revelation, the beginning and the end of the Christian Bible. There are seven visible "planets" in the original sense: the Moon, Mercury, Venus, the Sun, Mars, Jupiter, and Saturn. They give their names to the days of the week in the Romance languages and, converting five corresponding gods or goddesses, in the Germanic languages (e.g., Wodan was identified with Mercury, so Wodan's Day (Wednesday) is French *mercredi*). As for time, seventy is the traditional biblical lifespan, though it is sometimes stated in a way that disguises its "sevenness": "the days of our years are threescore and ten" (Ps. 90.10). The Greeks also found seven significant, and one of them, Hippocrates (or Pseudo-Hippocrates), wrote a treatise called "On the Sevens," in which he declared sevens to be everywhere: seven seasons, seven strata of the cosmos, and the like. Thomas Mann's *The Magic Mountain* is filled with sevens: seven chapters, seven main characters (one named Settembrini), seven years spent in the sanatorium from 1907 to 1914, and so on. So is Malcolm Lowry's *Under the Volcano*, which begins and ends at seven o'clock and rings changes on threes and fours, triangles and quadrangles, as well as on fateful sevens.

There is no space in this volume to discuss all the interesting symbolic numbers that appear in literature, such as the "pentangle" on the shield of Sir Gawain in *Sir Gawain and the Green Knight* (619ff.). Instead we shall mention a few cases of what has been called "numerical composition" or "numerological composition," the division of literary works into parts whose lengths correspond to significant numbers and ratios. The oldest and simplest case is the division of both the *Iliad* and the *Odyssey* into twenty-four books, corresponding to the number of letters in the Attic Greek alphabet after the fourth century BC; Virgil reduced the books to twelve in his *Aeneid*, and twelve books became standard for epics thereafter (e.g., *Paradise Lost*). Dante's *Divine Comedy* is structured almost obsessively on the number three: the three major divisions or *cantiche* each have thirty-three *canti* or cantos except the first, the *Inferno*, which has an additional introductory one, giving one hundred in all; each canto is made of a varying number of tercets or *terzine* of three lines; each line has eleven syllables, so each *terzina* has thirty-three; stitching the tercets together is a rhyme scheme called *terza rima*, where each rhyme except the first and last in the canto occurs three times. The entire work, then, foreshadows its culminating vision of the Trinity. A more ingenious example, not explicated until recently, is Spenser's *Epithalamion*, a poem about the day of his wedding; its twenty-four stanzas correspond to the hours, sixteen of them in daylight, eight in darkness (hence it is set at the summer solstice); its 365 long lines match the days of the year; and its sixty-eight short lines seem to be the sum of the four seasons, the twelve months, and the fifty-two weeks. Many other candidates for numerological structures have been offered by scholars, some of them plausible, others obscure or far-fetched.

O

Oak As the largest and strongest of common European trees, the oak (in several varieties) was originally "the tree" to the Greeks: their word for the oak, *drus*, originally meant "tree" before it was restricted to the oak (also called *phegos*). In fact *drus* is cognate with English "tree" and related to Greek *dendron*, "tree," and to *dryas*, "Dryad" – Dryads are wood nymphs, not just oak nymphs. There is evidence from Sanskrit, Celtic, Germanic, and Slavic cultures as well as

Greek and Latin that the Indo-Europeans worshiped the oak and connected it with a thunder or lightning god; "tree" and *drus* may also be cognate with "Druid," the Celtic priest to whom the oak was sacred. There has even been a study that shows that oaks are more likely to be struck by lightning than other trees of the same height.

Homer's epithets for the oak are "high-headed," "lofty-leaved," and the like. It was sacred to Zeus and to Roman Jupiter. The *Odyssey* tells of Zeus's holy grove of Dodona, where an oak (or several oaks) was consulted, perhaps by a priest or priestess who listened to the rustling of the leaves (14.327–28). Aeschylus refers to "talking oaks" (*Prometheus* 832), Sophocles to an "oak of many tongues" (*Trachiniae* 1168), at Dodona; the phrase from Aeschylus seems to have inspired Tennyson's "The Talking Oak." It is "Jove's spreading tree" in Ovid, *Metamorphoses* 1.106.

James Frazer's *Golden Bough*, an important source for twentieth-century poetry, turns on the idea that a sacred oak grove at Nemi near Rome was the scene of an annual sacrifice of a king or priest. His title refers to the branch Aeneas must carry to the Underworld (*Aeneid* 6.204–11), which is compared in a simile to mistletoe. Mistletoe is often associated with oaks (Sophocles calls the oak *ixophoros*, "mistletoe-bearing," in fragment 403), but Virgil does not name the tree.

As "Lord of the woods, the long-surviving oak" (Cowper, *Task* 1.313) has become a symbol of English rootedness and steadfastness; England's sons have "hearts of oak" in battle, though that phrase misquotes the song ("Heart of oak are our men"). (Similar traditions are found in Germany and throughout Europe.) Oaks were also the preferred timber for building beams. Chaucer calls it "byldere oak" (*Parliament of Fowls* 176) and Spenser echoes him: "The builder Oak, sole king of forrests all" (*FQ* 1.1.8). Older trees, however, had "knotty entrails" (*Tempest* 1.2.295) and were difficult to work with.

It is proverbial that "oaks may fall when reeds stand the storm," but oaks are also known to stand the storm, as a great simile at Virgil's *Aeneid* 4.441–49 suggests. Prehistoric associations between oaks and lightning (the weapon of Zeus/Jupiter) survive on such passages as this from Shakespeare: "Merciful heaven, / Thou rather with thy sharp and sulphurous bolt / Splits the unwedgeable and gnarled oak / Than the soft myrtle" (*MM* 2.2.114–17).

Occasionally the oak plays the part usually given to the elm as the support of the vine. Irving has an elaborate simile: "As the vine, which has long twined its graceful foliage about the oak and been lifted by it into sunshine, will, when the hardy plant is rifted by the thunderbolt, cling around it with caressing tendrils and bind up its shattered boughs, so is it beautifully ordered by Providence, that woman, who is the mere dependent and ornament of man in his happier hours, should be his stay and solace when smitten with sudden calamity, winding herself into the rugged recesses of his nature, tenderly supporting the drooping head, and binding up the broken heart" ("The Wife," in *The Sketch Book*).

In Republican Rome a crown of oak leaves was given to those who had saved the life of a citizen in battle; it was called the "civic oak" (*quercus civilis*). When Coriolanus "prov'd best man i'th'field, and for his meed / Was brow-bound with the oak" (*Cor.* 2.2.97–98), Shakespeare may have misunderstood his source in Plutarch, who goes on to speculate on the origin of the Roman custom.

After AD 86 the victor of the Capitoline poetry contest was also given an oak crown. Ovid says that the victor of the Pythian games was crowned with oak leaves before the laurel was introduced (*Met.* 1.448–50). Having crowned the poet Tasso with laurel, Alfonso promises to crown his ambassador Antonio with the civic crown of oak (Goethe, *Torquato Tasso* 1.4.681–85).

According to Lucretius (5.939, 1414), acorns were the original food of the human race (in Arcadia or elsewhere); Juvenal (10.80–81) says bread replaced acorns. Homer, however, considers acorns or mast to be the normal fodder of pigs (*Odyssey* 10.242).

See **Elm, Laurel, Mistletoe.**

Oat   *see* **Pipe**

Ocean   *see* **Sea**

Oil   In the ancient world most oil was pressed from olives, as even the English words suggest – going back through Latin *oleum* ("oil") and *oliva* ("olive") either to Greek *elaia* ("olive") or to a Mediterranean source for both the Greek and the Latin. Oil was used for food, cooking, medicine, sacrifice, lighting, and anointing the body after a bath or before gymnastics.

Among the Hebrews oil was used for anointing a king or priest. "Then Samuel took the horn of oil, and anointed him [David] in the midst of his brethren: and the spirit of the Lord came upon David from that day forward" (1 Sam. 16.13). "And Zadok the priest took an horn of oil out of the tabernacle, and anointed Solomon. And they blew the trumpet; and all the people said, God save king Solomon" (1 Kgs 1.39). Poured over the head, the oil symbolizes God's blessing, vitality, and power. The Hebrew word for "anointed," *mashiah*, becomes our "Messiah." When Simon Peter answers Jesus' question "But whom say ye that I am?" by saying, "Thou art the Christ, the Son of the living God" (Matt. 16.16, Mark 8.29), he calls him the Messiah, for Greek *christos* means "anointed." He is "thy [God's] holy child Jesus, whom thou hast anointed" (Acts 4.27). Milton calls him "Messiah king anointed" (*PL* 5.664) and "Anointed king Messiah" (12.359).

Since Charlemagne kings in Europe have usually been anointed. That Richard II is the anointed king is made a prominent theme in Shakespeare's play; twice Gaunt calls him "anointed" (1.2.38, 2.1.98), York once (2.3.96), Carlisle once (4.1.127), and once most poignantly Richard himself: "Not all the water in the rough rude sea / Can wash the balm [holy oil] off from an anointed king" (3.2.54–55).

When the oil spills or is used up, the lamp goes out. That fact became a metaphor for human life and death at least as early as Ecclesiastes, whose cryptic verse "Or ever the silver cord be loosed, or the golden bowl be broken" (12.6) seems to describe an oil lamp; it is in a series of images of death. Gaunt, again, near death, predicts "My oil-dried lamp and time-bewasted light / Shall be extinct with age and endless night" (1.3.221–22). In *All's Well* we hear of a man who said, "Let me not live … / After my flame lacks oil" (1.2.58–59). Cleopatra announces, "Our lamp is spent, it's out!" (*AC* 4.15.85).

"To burn the midnight oil" means to study late at night. The seed of this saying, which goes back to the seventeenth century in English, is in Juvenal:

"And is your labour more fruitful, writers / Of history? More time is wasted here, and more oil" (7.98–99).

See **Olive**.

Olive Olive trees grow very slowly. Virgil speaks of the "fruit of the slowly growing olive" (*Georgics* 2.3); Lope de Vega praises the "fruit so slow in maturing" ("O Fortune, pick me that olive"); Landor tersely follows with "slow olive" (*Gebir* 3.306). Olive trees were therefore planted only in times of peace or stability: a man planted a grove for his son. The chorus of Sophocles' *Oedipus at Colonus* sings of the sacred olive grove at Colonus; it uses the striking epithet "child-nurturing" (701) of the tree. Hence since classical times the olive has symbolized peace, though that meaning is clearer in Roman than in Greek literature. As Gibbon writes, "The olive, in the western world, followed the progress of peace, of which it was considered as the symbol" (*Decline and Fall* chap. 2). Greek suppliants carried olive branches (Orestes carries one in Aeschylus, *Eumenides* 43) and so did heralds. According to Virgil, the olive is *placitam Pacis*, "agreeable to Peace" (*Georgics* 2.425); when Aeneas encounters the Arcadians he extends "a branch of peaceful olive" (*Aeneid* 8.116). As Spenser later sums it up, "olives bene for peace" (*SC* "April" 124).

Where Peace is personified she is usually associated with the olive. As Shakespeare states it, when the rebellion in *2 Henry 4* comes to an end, "Peace puts forth her olive everywhere" (4.4.87). Milton imagines "meek-ey'd Peace" to be "crown'd with Olive green" and equipped with "Turtle wing" and "myrtle wand," attributes of Venus ("Nativity" 46–51); for Pope, "Peace descending bids her Olives spring, / And scatters Blessings from her Dove-like Wing" ("Windsor-Forest" 429–30).

The dove is borrowed not only from Aphrodite-Venus (*see* **Dove**) but from the story of Noah and the Flood. When the dove returns with an olive leaf in her mouth, Noah knows the waters have receded (Gen. 8.11). It is not clear if the olive connoted peace to the Hebrews, but dove and leaf together have come to do so, as in Milton: "in his Bill / An Olive leaf he brings, pacific sign" (*PL* 11.859–60).

Psalm 52.8 has "I am like a green olive tree in the house of God: I trust in the mercy of God for ever and ever," a passage that may have influenced later literary uses of the olive as a symbol of love and trust as well as of peace.

The olive was sacred to Athena (Roman Minerva), and a sacred olive tree grew on the acropolis of Athens. Herodotus tells of its miraculous rejuvenation after it was burned by the Persians (8.55); see Euripides *Ion* 1433ff. and *Trojan Women* 801ff. Virgil calls Minerva the "discoverer of the olive" (*oleae inventrix*) (*Georgics* 1.18–19); he is imitated by Petrarch in *Rime* 24. The association of the olive with Athens was already a well-worn theme when Horace invoked it in Ode 1.7.7.

Three times in Homer's *Odyssey* the olive seems to symbolize home, safety, or rest: when Odysseus is cast ashore on Scheria he makes a bed under two kinds of olive trees, ashore on Ithaca he sleeps while his belongings are placed under a sacred olive, and his bed in his palace is carved out of an olive. Athena, of course, is his protectress. She appears in his palace carrying a lamp, which burns oil (19.33); as she symbolizes wisdom or mental illumination we may have another reason for her connection with the olive.

Pindar in *Olympian* 3 tells the origin of the olive spray as the "crown of prowess" for victors at the games at Olympia, famous for its wild olives. See also Virgil, *Aeneid* 5.309.

The two kinds of olive are the wild olive (Greek *phylia*, Latin *oleaster*) and the cultivated olive (Greek *elaia*, Latin *oliva* or *olea*). The latter produces not only edible fruit but oil. The word "oil" is derived from the same source as "olive."

See **Oil**.

Ouroboros   *see* **Serpent**

Owl   The tradition that the owl is the bird of wisdom may owe something to the sharp glaring eyes and the nocturnal habits of most species (as if they were scholars studying late), but it may have more to do with the fact that the owl was the bird of Athena, Greek goddess of wisdom (Roman Minerva). That in turn was probably due to the large number of owls in Athens, Athena's citadel. "To bring owls to Athens" was to bring coals to Newcastle, that is, to bring something to a place already abundantly supplied with it; the phrase was already a commonplace in Aristophanes (*Birds* 301). Zeus wore an eagle on his head, Athena an owl on hers (*Birds* 514–16). Thus the owl became an official emblem of the city. The "Lauriotic" owls (*Birds* 1106) were the silver coins, made from silver from the mines of Laurion, which were stamped with an owl. In Pope's *Dunciad*, to "hunt th'Athenian fowl" means to seek money (b 4.361).

An owl (*skops*) is mentioned only once in Homer (*Odyssey* 5.66); none is mentioned in Hesiod. But an epithet from *glaux*, the generic term for "owl," is applied to Athena over ninety times in Homer and a dozen times in Hesiod: *glaukopis*. It may have meant "owl-eyed," but *glaux* itself comes from a root meaning "glare" or "gleam"; in Homer the adjective *glaukos* modifies "sea" and the verb *glaukiao* refers to the eyes of a lion. In Pindar *glaukopis* modifies "Athena" a few times but twice it modifies "serpent." So it may have meant "sharp-eyed" or "with gleaming eyes."

Since it is nocturnal and hard to see, the owl's most salient feature is its "shriek" or "screech" or "hoot." The word "owl" (like German *Eule*) comes from the same root as "howl"; one of the Latin names for "owl" is *ulula*, from the same root. Latin *ululare* (whence English "ululate") means "lament" or "howl in mourning"; the cry of the owl sounds mournful to most ears. The prophet Micah says, "I will make a...mourning as the owls" (1.8). To the Greeks the cry sounded like *kikkabau* (Aristophanes, *Birds* 261), similar to the Latin verb *cucubio*; we also find *tutu* in Latin (Plautus, *Menaechmi* 654). In English poetry the conventional cry is "Tu-who" or "Tu-whit, tu-who" (as in Shakespeare *LLL* 5.2.917–18; Coleridge, *Christabel* 3; R. Browning, *Flute-Music* 119). Another owl with onomatopoeic name is Greek *strinx* and Latin *strix*, the screech-owl.

To ancient and modern authors alike the owl's cry has sounded "ominous" or omen-filled, and especially prophetic of death. As Dido prepares to die, she seems to hear her dead husband's voice summoning her, and the owl (*bubo*) sings its "funereal song" (Virgil, *Aeneid* 4.462–63); in Dryden's translation, "Hourly 'tis heard, when with a boding note / The solitary screech-owl strains her throat, / And, on a chimney's top, or turret's height, / With songs obscene disturbs the silence of the night" ("obscene" here in the sense of Latin *obscenus,* "ill-omened"). Ovid tells how the boy Ascalaphus saw Proserpina eat the pomegranate and betrayed her so she must remain in the Underworld; for that he was transformed into "the slothful screech-owl [*ignavus bubo*] of evil omen to mortals" (*Met.* 5.550). Chaucer names the owl "that of deth the bode bryngeth" (*PF* 343). Spenser lists a group of "fatall birds" that includes the "ill-faste [ill-faced] Owle, deaths dreadfull messengere" (*FQ* 2.12.36; cf. 1.5.30); four times Spenser calls the owl "ghastly." The soldier Talbot is called an "ominous and fearful owl of death" by his enemy (Shakespeare, *1H6* 4.2.15), and King Henry tells Richard, "The owl shrieked at thy birth, an evil sign" (*3H6* 5.6.44). Gray uses an interesting adjective: "The moping owl does to the moon complain" ("Elegy" 10), perhaps echoing Ovid's *ignavus.*

The owl is the "bird of night," Ovid's *noctis avis* (*Met.* 2.564); indeed the Latin name for the most common of owls is *noctua.* (It is almost redundant to name one species the "night-owl.") Thus it is common in poetry to set the owl parallel to the raven (or night-raven) as birds of death. Chaucer has "revenes qualm [croak], or shrichyng of thise owles," as fearful auguries (*Troilus* 5.382); Spenser writes, "Owles and Night-ravens flew, / The hatefull messengers of heavy things, / Of death and dolor telling sad tidings" (*FQ* 2.7.23). It is also fairly common to set the owl in contrast to the lark, though more frequently the lark's counterpart is the nightingale. As Richard II yields to Bolingbroke, he laments, "For night-owls shriek where mounting larks should sing" (*R2* 3.3.183; cf. *Cym* 3.6.93). Sometimes, as in the final song of Shakespeare's *Love's Labour's Lost,* the owl is set against the cuckoo as symbols of winter and spring.

Latin *strix* could also mean "witch," and witches often transformed themselves into owls (Ovid, *Amores* 1.8.13–14; Apuleius, *Met.* 3.21).

Despite its glaring eyes, the owl proverbially has poor eyesight, at least by day. "Blind as an owl" was a commonplace by the seventeenth century. One of Herbert's proverbs is "The ignorant hath an Eagles wings, and an Owles eyes" (902). Tennyson writes, "thrice as blind as any noonday owl" (*Holy Grail* 866).

As the bird of wisdom that can only see at night, the owl can be invoked in a disparaging or humorous manner to refer to scholars or critics. Pope mocks those who, "in mild benighted days, / Mixed the Owl's ivy with the Poet's bays" (*see* **Ivy**) and the scholarly "Wits, who, like owls, see only in the dark" (1743 *Dunciad,* 53–54, 192).

P

Palm Palm trees are common in biblical lands, and the date palm in particular is highly prized for its many useful products, but they were not frequently found in ancient Greece or Rome. The Greek word for the palm, *phoinix,* points to a Phoenician homeland, while Virgil refers to *Idumaeas…palmas* (*Georgics* 3.12), as if they come from Edom.

Homer nonetheless has Odysseus refer to one in his courtly remarks to young Nausicaa: "Wonder takes me as I look on you. / Yet in Delos once I saw such a thing, by Apollo's altar. / I saw the stalk of a young palm shooting up" (*Odyssey* 6.161–63, trans. Lattimore). This might be the sacred palm of the

Delian Apollo, the one Euripides calls *protogonos* or "first-born" (*Hecuba* 458), except that Homer makes it "young" to suit Nausicaa. (The Homeric *Hymn to Apollo* 115–19 tells how Leto gave birth to Apollo while holding on to the tree.) Odysseus' comparison is a more discreet version of the simile in the Song of Solomon: "This thy stature is like to a palm tree, and thy breasts to clusters of grapes" (7.7). (The grapes are not in the Hebrew text; the clusters are surely of dates.) The Hebrew word for palm, *tamar*, was and remains a common girl's name.

The word "palm" (Latin *palma*) is the same as that for the palm of the hand: to the ancients the tree resembled the hand, the branches or fronds looking like fingers.

In Psalm 92.12 we are told that the righteous "shall flourish like the palm tree." Hamlet alludes to this verse as he rewrites the Danish message to England, hoping "love between them like the palm might flourish" (5.2.40), and a character in *Timon of Athens* invokes it when he says, "You shall see him a palm in Athens again, and flourish with the highest" (5.1.10–11).

Around 400 BC the palm leaf was introduced into Greece as a symbol of victory in athletic contests. An early reference is Aristotle's to "he who takes the palm" in a game (*Magna Moralia* 1196a36), but it is not much mentioned in Greek literature. According to Livy (10.47.3), it was introduced into Roman culture in 293 BC, and in Latin literature it soon became a commonplace. Horace begins his first ode by mentioning chariot races and their victors' palm (1.1.5), though he prefers the ivy of lyric poets. In their prologues both Terence and Plautus refer to the palm as a prize for winners of drama contests (*Phormio* 17, *Amphitryon* 69). Plutarch observes that the palm is an appropriate prize for athletes because, among other things, both tree and victorious athlete are resistant and resilient (*Moralia* 724e). It was soon a commonplace symbol. Apuleius tells of a man who fought many battles and won "many palms of victory" (*Met.* 10.25). In his list of trees Chaucer has "the victor palm" (*PF* 182). "To bear the palm" becomes synonymous for "be the victor," as it is twice in Shakespeare's Roman plays (*JC* 1.2.131, *Cor* 5.3.117), though it is for military conquest rather than a game. Horatio seems to coin a new word when he speaks of "the most high and palmy state of Rome" (*Hamlet* 1.1.113), suggesting both "triumphant" and "flourishing." Wilde refers to "the palmy days of the British Drama" (*Dorian Gray* chap. 4).

The New Testament reflects the classical symbolism of the palm. When Christ enters Jerusalem many people take palm branches and shout "Hosanna: Blessed is the King of Israel" (John 12.13), a ceremony reenacted in churches on Palm Sunday. According to John of Patmos, those who are "sealed" or saved will stand before the Lamb, "clothed with white robes, and palms in their hands" (Rev. 7.9). These are "those just Spirits that wear victorious Palms" in Milton's "At a Solemn Music" (14). The palm thus became "the palm of martirdom" (Chaucer, *Second Nun's Tale* 240), the symbol of the victory of the Christian believer over torture and death.

A pilgrim who went to Jerusalem was called a "palmer" for he brought back a palm from the Holy Land; then any pilgrim might be called a palmer: Chaucer so names those who go to Canterbury (*CT* Gen. Pro. 13). The Palmer, "a sage and sober sire," is a major character in Book Two of Spenser's *Faerie Queene* (introduced 2.1.7). At the Capulets' ball Romeo and Juliet make elegant puns on "palmer" as they dance: "saints have hands that pilgrims' hands do touch, / And palm to palm is holy palmers' kiss" (1.5.99–100).

Pansy "Pansy" is a common name for a kind of violet (*viola tricolor*), especially for the hybridized varieties in gardens. The name is from the French *pensée*, "thought"; in Spanish it is called *pensamiento*, in Italian *viola del pensiero*. Ophelia reflects its etymology when she says, "And there is pansies – that's for thoughts" (*Hamlet* 4.5.176). Pensiveness often entails remembering, of course, so Wordsworth chooses an appropriate flower, "The Pansy at my feet," to ask whither the visionary gleam is fled that attended him as a boy ("Ode: Intimations of Immortality" 54ff.). When Shelley advises the revolutionary Spanish to conquer not only their foes but their own desire for revenge, he tells them to bind their brows with violet, ivy, and pine but not with pansy: "Ye were injured, and that means memory" ("Ode: Arise" 35).

Lawrence offers "a bunch of pansies" in his book of poems called *Pansies*: "These poems are called *Pansies* because they are rather *Pensées* than anything else" ("Foreword").

The *viola tricolor* is often called, with rather different connotations, "heartsease" (heart's ease).

Panther *see* **Leopard**

Pard *see* **Leopard**

Path For as long as humans have walked they have made paths or followed natural ones. So fundamental is the experience of traveling on a path that many other basic human activities, even the whole of a human life, are described in cultures everywhere in such terms as "path," "way," or "course." In English "way" is used so often and in so many contexts that its metaphorical origin has long vanished: we speak of a "way" to do something or a "way of life" without thinking of a road or path. The same is true of words borrowed from other languages. Etymologically, if something is "viable" it has a "way" before it (from Latin *via*, "way"); if something is "obvious" it stands in our path; if something "deviates" it leaves the main road. "Routine" comes from "route" (French, from Latin *rupta* [*via*], "broken or beaten [way]"); "method" comes from Greek *hodos*, "path."

A similar metaphor is the frequent biblical use of "walk" (verb) as "behave" or "live." "Enoch walked with God" (Gen. 5.22); the Lord tests the people "whether they will walk in my law, or no" (Exod. 16.4); some "kept not the covenant of God, and refused to walk in his law" (Ps. 78.10); after the resurrection of Christ "we also should walk in newness of life" (Rom. 6.4) (Hebrew *halak*, Greek *peripateo*). From the verb comes the noun for "conduct of life": Scott names a righteous woman who has "an upright walk" (*Heart of Midlothian* 10); in a more general sense we use the phrase "in every walk of life." The Bible generally uses "path" for the noun corresponding to "walk": "Make me to go in the path of thy commandments," "Thy word is a lamp unto my feet, and a light unto my path" (Ps. 119.35, 105).

Life is a path or a journey on a path. Dante's *Divine Comedy* begins "*Nel mezzo del cammin di nostra vita*," "In the middle of the path of our life"; Bunyan's

Pilgrim's Progress begins, "As I walked through the wilderness of this world." We are all pilgrims, making our way on foot. Christ said, "I am the way" (John 14.6), he made the lame walk, and he washed the feet of his disciples. Bunyan explains in a note that when Christian the pilgrim is wounded by Apollyon in the foot, it is his "conversation" that is hurt – his conduct or capacity to "walk" properly. Tennyson writes, "I know that this was Life, – the track / Whereon with equal feet we fared" (*In Memoriam* 25.1–2). In "America the Beautiful" Katharine Lee Bates finds beautiful the "pilgrim feet, / Whose stern, impassioned stress / A thoroughfare for freedom beat / Across the wilderness!"

The path to salvation, or to any worthy destination, is steep, thorny, rugged, narrow. Matthew tells us, "strait is the gate, and narrow is the way, which leadeth unto life" (7.14). Dante tells us he lost the right path (*Inferno* 1.3, 11.9). Ophelia contrasts "the steep and thorny way to heaven" with "the primrose path of dalliance" (*Hamlet* 1.3.48–50; see *Macbeth* 2.3.18–19). Spenser's Knight and Una pass "forward by that painfull way … / Forth to an hill that was both steepe and hy, / On top whereof a sacred chappell was" (*FQ* 1.10.46). "Once meek," Blake writes, "and in a perilous path, / The just man kept his course along / The vale of death" (*Marriage of Heaven and Hell* 2.3–5).

The oldest classical statement of this metaphor is Hesiod's: the road to wickedness is short and smooth, but "the gods have put hard sweat between us and virtue. The road to it is long and uphill, and rough at first, though easier going at the summit, if you get there" (*Works and Days* 287–91). Theognis imagines himself at a crossroads, wondering whether to take a frugal or spendthrift path (911–12). Justice tells Parmenides he has chosen the right path, though "far indeed does it lie from the beaten track of man" (frag. 1.27). Persius refers to "the letter which separates the Samian branches" (*Satires* 3.56), i.e., "the upsilon of Pythagoras of Samos," which resembled a curved "y": the straight branch was the path of virtue, the crooked, of vice. "The Choice of Heracles" between Virtue and Pleasure, told by Xenophon (*Memorabilia* 2.1.22–34), is sometimes presented as a choice at a crossroads (*Hercules in bivio*). Another famous and fateful crossroads is the "triple road" where Oedipus kills his father Laius (Sophocles, *Oedipus* 716).

Paths and roads have had many other meanings in literature, of course, for they may be broad or narrow, crooked or straight, circular or irreversible; they may represent space or time, real things or ideal; they may unite some places but not others; and they may be literal or metaphorical or both. In America, to give one example, there has been almost a cult of the road, a belief in movement itself, notably in Whitman's "Song of the Open Road" and Jack Kerouac's *On the Road*.

There is a metaphor in Greek poetry, finally, that presents poetry itself as a path. The Homeric *Hymn to Hermes* speaks of the "bright path of song" (451), and Hesiod reports that the Muses "set his foot upon song" (*Works and Days* 659). Pindar was fond of the conceit: he has, for instance, "found the praiseworthy path of words" (*hodon logon*) in one ode (*Olymp.* 1.110); at the outset of another, "I have countless paths opening on every side" (*Isthm.* 4.1). Apollo bids Callimachus drive over "untrodden paths" (*Aetia* frag. 1.27–28). Lucretius explores "the trackless haunts of the Muses where no man's foot has trod" (1.926–27).

Peacock The peacock (Greek *taos*, Latin *pavo*) is striking for its large colorful tail that opens erect like a fan; as it struts about in full display the bird seems inordinately proud. It is not mentioned often in Greek literature (they were imported into the Mediterranean region from India), but in Latin literature the bird is sacred to Juno and a byword for beauty and pride: "the bird of Juno unfolds (*explicat*) its feathers" (Ovid, *Amores* 2.6.55). A list of superlatives in *Metamorphoses* includes "prouder than peacocks" (13.801). Chaucer presents a character: "as any pecok he was proud and gay" (*Reeve's Tale* 3926); Spenser describes an image with "More sondry colours than the proud Pavone / Beares in his boasted fan" (*FQ* 3.11.47). As doves or swans pull Venus' chariot, "Great Junoes golden chayre [is] . . . // Drawne of fayre Pecocks, that excell in pride, / And full of Argus eyes their tayles dispredden wide" (*FQ* 1.4.17). The story of Argus and how the peacock got its "eyes" is found in *Metamorphoses* 1.625–723.

The "paycock" in Sean O'Casey's well-known play *Juno and the Paycock* is the feckless, drunkard husband of "Juno" Boyle; he ought to be Jupiter, perhaps, but instead he goes "gallivantin' about all the day like a paycock" (Act 1) while she tries to keep her family together.

Pearl From their beauty, rarity, and great price pearls stand, not surprisingly, for beauty, rarity, or great price, as when we speak of pearls of wisdom or say that someone was a pearl, in these uses equivalent to "gem." Othello feels, at the end, that he "threw a pearl away" (5.2.347). Two biblical passages, however, have given "pearl" additional connotations.

The more important of these is Christ's brief parable: "the kingdom of heaven is like unto a merchant man, seeking goodly pearls: / Who, when he had found one pearl of great price, went and sold all that he had, and bought it" (Matt. 13.45–46). The anonymous medieval dream-poem *Pearl*, at one level about a girl lost to earthly life but flourishing in heaven, seems also to be about lost and restored faith. In "The Pearl," which cites the Matthew passage in the title, Herbert claims he "knows the ways" of learning, honor, and pleasure, has them in hand, knows their value as commodities, but gives them up and turns "to thee." Steinbeck's novella *The Pearl* is also based on the parable. Cowper several times calls truth a pearl, and once seems to rewrite the parable in asking "What pearl is it that rich men cannot buy, / That learning is too proud to gather up; / But which the poor, and the despis'd of all, / Seek and obtain, and often find unsought? / Tell me – and I will tell thee what is truth" (*Task* 3.285–89).

The second biblical passage is Christ's injunction not to "cast ye your pearls before swine, lest they trample them under their feet" (Matt. 7.6). Pearls here are usually taken to mean preaching (the kingdom) or wisdom, thus seconding the meaning of the parable. Shakespeare's absurd pedant Holofernes praises a saying by the lowly Costard as "pearl enough for a swine" (*LLL* 4.2.89). Milton felt that the barbarous noise that greeted his pamphlets was "got by casting Pearls to Hogs" (Sonnet 12).

That the pearl is the "treasure of an oyster" (Shakespeare, *AC* 1.5.44) allows the suggestion that it is hidden, or is found among base or ugly conditions. Touchstone says, "Rich honesty dwells like a miser, sir, in a poor house, as your pearl in your foul oyster" (*AYLI* 5.4.59–61). Shelley cleverly evokes the pearls-before-swine saying in describing his friend Hogg "a pearl within an oyster shell, / One of the richest of the deep" ("Letter to Gisborne" 231–32). Tennyson consoles himself over the loss of Hallam by vowing to wait until "Time hath sunder'd shell from pearl" (*In Memoriam* 52.16).

Pelican   The pelican is mentioned only briefly in Aristophanes (*Birds* 884), Aristotle, and a few other classical authors. The name (Greek *pelekan, pelekinos*) seems to be related to *pelekus*, "ax," because of the way the bird uses its bill. (The woodpecker is *pelekas*.)

In the Bible it is listed twice as unclean (Lev. 11.18, Deut. 14.17), and twice as one of the desert birds that will occupy the land after the Lord lays it waste (Isa. 34.11, Zeph. 2.14). (The AV renders the latter two as "cormorant," but Coverdale, Geneva, and Bishops' versions have "pelican.") The remaining biblical passage, however – "I am like a pelican of the wilderness" (Ps. 102.6) – had a fruitful history. Epiphanius and Augustine commented that the pelican there stands for Christ. In medieval legend the pelican was thought to revive its young with blood from its breast, and that act made the bird a symbol of Christ, who redeems us by his blood. Thomas Aquinas has the phrase *Pie pelicane Jesu Domine* in one of his hymns. In the Old French *Quest of the Holy Grail*, Sir Bors has a vision of the pelican and adopts it as his device. Dante's Beatrice identifies John the Apostle as "he who lay upon the breast / of our pelican" (*Paradiso* 25.112–13).

Without allusion to Christ, the image might stand for the self-sacrifice of a parent, as when Shakespeare's Laertes offers to open his arms to his friends and, "like the kind life-rend'ring pelican, / Repast them with my blood" (*Hamlet* 4.5.145–47); or for the ingratitude of children, as when Gaunt tells Richard that the blood of his father, "like the pelican, / Hast thou tapp'd out and drunkenly carous'd" (*R2* 2.1.126–27), or when Lear laments for "discarded fathers" with "pelican daughters" (3.4.72,75). The mother in Strindberg's *The Pelican* protests to her children that "I've nourished you with my life's blood" (scene 3) but it is a lie, as she has devoured them emotionally and nearly starved them physically.

Byron invokes the pelican "Whose beak unlocks her bosom's stream / To still her famish'd nestlings' scream, / Nor mourns a life to them transferr'd" (*Giaour* 952–54). It is probably this passage that inspired Musset's elaborate image of the pelican as a symbol of the poet, who offers his heart as nourishment for the young in a "divine sacrifice" ("The Night in May" 153–91). Musset's poem launched *pélicanisme* as the term for confessional poetry of the heart and its sorrows, though Goethe had already described his novel *The Sorrows of Young Werther* as having been nourished like the pelican with the blood of his heart (*Conversations with Eckermann* 2 January 1824).

Philomel   *see* **Nightingale**

Phlegm   *see* **Humor**

Phoenix   The earliest reference to a phoenix is found in a riddling fragment of Hesiod (frag. 304), from which we learn that it was already a byword for great longevity. Herodotus reports an Egyptian belief in a sacred bird, resembling a red and golden eagle, that comes from Arabia to Egypt once every five hundred years to bury the corpse of his father in the Temple of the Sun (2.73). He says it is very rare; later authors say it is unique – *unica semper avis*, according to Ovid (*Amores* 2.6.54). Philostratus says it comes from India, and adds that "the phoenix, while it is consumed in its nest, sings funeral hymns to itself" (*Life of Apollonius* 3.49). Ovid thinks it comes from Assyria, and describes it as the sole animal that regenerates itself. When it has lived five hundred years it builds a nest high on a lofty palm, covers it with spices, and dies among the odors (Ovid says nothing about fire). From the "father" phoenix a little phoenix is born, and when he grows sufficiently strong it carries the remains of its father to the Egyptian City of the Sun, Heliopolis (*Met.* 15.391–407).

Pliny, who thinks it might be fabulous, cites a report that it flew from Arabia to Egypt in AD 36; it has a gleam of gold around its neck, a purple body, a tail blue and rose; it lives 540 years, a period somehow correlated with the Great Year (*Natural History* 10.3–5). Tacitus dates its last visit at AD 34, cites the belief that it lives 1461 years (the Sothic or Canicular Period when the calendar year of 365 days realigns with the solar year of $365\frac{1}{4}$ days), and adds the detail that when it brings its father to the Altar of the Sun it consigns him to the flames (*Annals* 6.28).

Despite these variants, the phoenix became an emblem of rarity or uniqueness. Martial can make a typically extravagant claim that, compared to a certain lovely girl, the bird is *frequens*, "commonplace" (5.37.13). Shakespeare even speaks of "the sole Arabian tree" on which it nests ("Phoenix and Turtle" 2), or "that in Arabia / There is one tree, the phoenix' throne; one phoenix / At this hour reigning there" (*Tempest* 3.3.22–24). "There is but one Phoenix in the world," says Lyly (*Euphues and his England* 2.86). (See also Chaucer, *Duchess* 981–84; Milton, *PL* 5.272–74.) It is sometimes called "the Arabian bird" (e.g., Shakespeare, *Cym* 1.6.17).

The myth may be Egyptian in origin, as Herodotus reports, for a similar bird connected with Heliopolis is described in Egyptian texts, but it differs in several ways, and the name *phoinix* seems to means "Phoenician [bird]."

Clement of Rome cites the phoenix as proof that the Resurrection is possible (*First Epistle*). Its usual function in Christian writing, however, is emblematic. The rebirth of the soul is like that of the phoenix (*De Ave Phoenice*, ascribed to Lactantius). Samson's sudden display of strength after his seeming defeat Milton likens to the bird that "Revives, reflourishes, then vigorous most / When most unactive deem'd" (*Samson Agonistes* 1704–05). It can symbolize the death and resurrection of Christ or of a Christian soul. The Old English poem *The Phoenix* tells that the bird dwells in Eden, where he rises each dawn like a lark to sing to heaven; after a thousand years he flies west to his tree, builds a nest, is consumed in fire, is reborn in an apple but free of sin, and then flies back to Eden; the bird stands for the chosen servants of Christ. The fourteenth-century author of *Mandeville's Travels*, after describing the renewal of the bird from its ashes in three days, comments, "men may well liken that bird unto God because that there is no God but one, and also that Our Lord arose from death to life the third day" (chap. 7). So Skelton, in *Phyllyp Sparowe*, offers an elaborate conceit where the phoenix stands for the priest who celebrates the mass over the tomb, promising rebirth into eternal life (513–49).

Pig The pig, however unfairly, is a symbol of uncleanness, stupidity, sensuality, and/or greed; its wild variety also stands for anger or rage.

Until the nineteenth century "swine" was the most general term in English, and "pig" originally meant a young swine; "boar" is an adult male, "sow" an adult female, "barrow" a castrated boar, and "hog" any swine or a castrated boar; "farrow" once meant a young pig, then a litter of pigs.

To Jews (and Muslims) the pig is "unclean" and may not be eaten (Lev. 11.7, Deut. 14.8); the Lord shall punish the rebellious ones "which eat swine's flesh" (Isa. 65.4, 66.17). An old Greek taunt for stupidity is "Boeotian pig" (Pindar, *Olymp.* 6.90), Boeotia representing "the sticks" or backwoods. Another old phrase is "a pig contending with Athena" (as in Theocritus 5.23): a fool arguing with the goddess of wisdom or, as we might say, "teaching your grandmother." To "cast pearls before swine" is to give valuable things (such as pearls of wisdom) to those incapable of appreciating them (Matt 7.6). (*See* **Pearl**.)

The goddess and witch Circe turns men into pigs and other beasts, as Odysseus finds out (*Odyssey* 10). "Who knows not Circe / The daughter of the Sun?" Milton asks. "Whose charmed Cup / Whoever tasted, lost his upright shape, / And downward fell into a groveling Swine" (*Comus* 50–53). "Drunk as a pig" is a commonplace now; Gower has "drunk swine" (*Confessio* 5.6894), Shakespeare "swine-drunk" (*AWEW* 4.3.255). Virgil tells Dante that many sinners who are kings above "will dwell here like pigs in slime" (*Inferno* 8.50). It is perhaps symbolic that Odysseus, who has spent one year with Circe, arrives in Ithaca to find his faithful swineherd in charge of 360 swine, one of which he brings each day to the suitors, who are acting like pigs in his home (*Odyssey* 14.13–20).

The wild boar is ferocious and dangerous. Venus warns Adonis not to hunt the boars whose tusks have the force of lightning (Ovid, *Met.* 10.550); in Shakespeare's version Venus describes the horrors of "churlish swine" at length (*Venus and Adonis* 616–30) but in vain. The Calydonian Boar Hunt was another popular Greek tale (e.g., Ovid, *Met.* 8.260–444). The chorus of women in Aristophanes' *Lysistrata* warns, "I will set loose my sow" (683), meaning "I will vent my rage," "sow" being an appropriate change from the expected "boar." Shakespeare makes much of the fact that the badge of Richard III was a white boar. He is known simply as "the boar" (e.g., 3.2.11), and his many enemies call him such things as "elvish-marked, abortive, rooting hog" (1.3.227) and "The wretched, bloody, and usurping boar, / That spoiled your summer fields and fruitful vines, / Swills your warm blood like wash, and makes his trough / In your emboweled bosoms" (5.2.7–10).

In Orwell's political allegory *Animal Farm* it is the pigs who commandeer the animals' revolution against man, and in the end "The creatures outside looked from pig to man, and from man to pig, and from pig to man again; but already it was impossible to say which was which."

Pigeon *see* **Dove**

Pipe, Flute, Reed, Oat The Greeks and Romans had many kinds of wind instruments, made of many different materials, and played on many different occasions. The Greek *aulos*, for instance, usually but wrongly translated "flute" (it was really an oboe), could accompany marches, dances, and choral songs; Plato and Aristotle thought it could send listeners into a religious frenzy, though others praised its calming, meditative effect. (Pipes in the Bible are used for both mourning and rejoicing.) In literature wind instruments appear on a similar variety of occasions, as when the troubled Agamemnon gazes at the plain filled with Trojan campfires and hears oboes and panpipes (*syrinx*) (*Iliad* 10.13), or when oboes and lyres play at a wedding (18.495), or when the pipe (*lotos*) accompanies the ecstatic dances of the Maenads (Euripides, *Bacchae* 160).

The *syrinx* was invented by Hermes, according to the Homeric *Hymn to Hermes* 512. In Ovid, Mercury charms Argus with his pipes and tells him how the pipes were invented: the girl Syrinx, fleeing Pan, is changed into marsh reeds, which then make a plaintive sound when Pan sighs in dismay, whereupon he constructs the first panpipes (*Met.* 1.677–712; see Lucretius 5.1382–83). The panpipes are the most distinctive rustic or pastoral instrument, but by the time of Theocritus at least all the pipes became assimilated into one another in the pastoral world. The reed (Greek *kalamos*, Latin *calamus, harundo*) the oat (Latin *avena*), the tube (Latin *fistula*) and other terms all became more or less synonymous: the pipe that shepherds play, the *rustica...fistula...avenis* ("rustic pipe of reeds," *Met.* 8.191–92).

In the English pastoral tradition we find the "oaten pype" (Spenser *SC* "January" 72), "shepherds pipe on oaten straws" (Shakespeare *LLL* 5.2.911), "Arcadian pipe, the pastoral reed / Of Hermes" (Milton, *PL* 11.132–33), "my Oat" (*Lycidas* 88), "a pipe of straw" (Wordsworth, "Ruth" 7), and "The natural music of the mountain reed" (Byron, *Manfred* 1.2.48), to mention a few. In an obvious synecdoche the pipe could stand for pastoral poetry itself: Spenser announces he must "chaunge mine Oaten reeds" for the trumpet of epic (*FQ* 1 Pro. 1). In his sonnet on Torquato Tasso, Marino names pipe, lyre, and trumpet as the three genres of Tasso's poetry.

In the "Introduction" to Blake's pastoral *Songs of Innocence*, the piper "pluck'd a hollow reed," the material of his pipe, but "made a rural pen" out of it to write his happy songs.

Planet A planet is a "wandering star" (Greek *aster planetes*). In the pre-Copernican view of the cosmos, established mainly by Aristotle and Ptolemy, there are seven of them, seven heavenly bodies that seem to move against the backdrop of the fixed stars. According to their distance from the earth, the center of the cosmos, they are the Moon, Mercury, Venus, the Sun, Mars, Jupiter, and Saturn. Each is fastened to a solid translucent sphere, or perhaps a sphere upon a sphere (to account for such complications as the retrogression of Mars), all of which revolve at various speeds around the earth. The eighth sphere is that of the fixed stars, and the ninth the *primum mobile* or "first movable," the sphere that communicates its motion to all the others.

Each planet has an "influence" on terrestrial life, usually in complex synergy with stars and other planets, and each is associated with a metal on earth, a day of the week, a human temperament, and so on. Thus Saturn's influence produces lead on earth, melancholy in people, and disastrous events in history; Mars makes iron, a warlike temperament, and wars. In English six of the planets, or the gods they embody, yield psychological terms still in use: lunacy and lunatic (Latin *luna*, moon), mercurial, venereal, martial, jovial

(Jove = Jupiter), and saturnine. Three English day-names, Sunday, Monday, and Saturday, come directly from the planets, and the other four are based on equivalent Germanic gods. The Romance languages preserve more of the Latin names: Italian *lunedi* is Monday, *martedi* is Tuesday, and so on.

If a planet has a malign influence it is said to "strike." At Christmas-time, according to Shakespeare's Marcellus, "no planets strike" (*Hamlet* 1.1.162). The great warrior Coriolanus "struck / Corioles like a planet" (*Cor* 2.2.114). A character in Jonson's *Every Man in his Humour* says, "sure I was struck with a planet thence, for I had no power to touch my weapon" (4.7.121–22). As Sin and Death spread their bane in Milton's *Paradise Lost*, "the blasted stars looked wan, / And planets, planet-strook, real eclipse / Then suffered" (10.412–14).

Traditional astrology takes the sky as a mirror of events on earth. Thus a comet, for instance, spells a drastic change in regime or empire (*see* **Comet**), and planets, though more orderly in their movements, create intricate patterns from which astrologers prognosticate, and poets allegorize. We cannot examine astrology here, but we will give two examples of *ad hoc* planetary allegorizing. A mysterious passage in Blake's *America* claims that Mars "once inclos'd the terrible wandering comets in its sphere. / Then Mars thou wast our center, & the planets three flew round / Thy crimson disk; so e'er the Sun was rent from thy red sphere" (5.3–5). This is absurd as astronomy or astrology, but as political allegory it makes sense: Mars, the planet of war, is imperial England; the three planet-comets are Ireland, Scotland, and Wales, threatening to leave its empire; the sun is America, now free of England's "sphere of influence" and attracting the three wanderers. In an autobiographical passage of *Epipsychidion*, Shelley makes the women of his life into planets or comets: the "cold chaste Moon" seems to be Mary, the "Planet of that hour" is Harriet, the "Comet beautiful and fierce" is Claire, and the "Incarnation of the Sun" is "Emily," his latest ideal love.

See **Moon, Star, Sun**.

Plow   The plow (or plough) is almost as old as agriculture itself, and all the civilizations of the ancient world relied on it. The plowman behind his ox or horse was the typical laborer until quite recent times; indeed in some languages plowing is the generic form of labor. French *labourer* means "to plow," and in Milton among others we find such phrases as "labouring the soil" (*PL* 12.18). Greek *erga*, "work," usually meant agricultural work unless otherwise spelled out; Hesiod's poem *Works and Days* is a georgic, a poem about farming.

So fundamental to life was tilling the earth that the plow acquired sacred and symbolic connotations as early as we have record. The Romans used the plow to mark out the territory of new towns; see Virgil's *Aeneid* 5.755, where Aeneas delineates town borders. Ancient peoples used to raze conquered cities with the plow, as if to return them to farmland; that was the actual fate of Carthage in 146 BC and the legendary fate of Troy – Aeschylus presents Agamemnon as the man who "dug up Troy with the pick-axe of Zeus" (*Agamemnon* 525–26). Micah prophesied that "Zion shall be plowed like a field" (Jer. 26.18). Horace blames uncontrolled rage as the reason that city walls have been "imprinted with the insolent enemy plow" (*Odes* 1.16.17–21); as Shakespeare's outcast Coriolanus turns against his city he says, "Let the

Volsces / Plough Rome and harrow Italy" (*Cor* 5.3.33–34). Byron's General Suwarrow vows "that shortly plough or harrow / Shall pass o'er what was Ismail" (*Don Juan* 7.502–03).

According to Plutarch, Athens held several rites of plowing at different seasons. After the passage where he describes them he gives one of the most widespread of plowing metaphors. "The Athenians observe three sacred plowings … But most sacred of all is the marital sowing and plowing for procreation of children" (*Moralia* 2.144a–b). The figure is obvious and irresistible. The earth is female, our nurturing mother; rain from father sky fertilizes the earth; men with plows enter the earth and plant seeds in her. In Greek *aro* meant "to plow" and "to beget [a child]," *aroter* meant "plowman" and (in poetry) "father," while *aroura* meant "tilled field" and (again in poetry) "woman receiving seed." According to Euripides, Priam was the plowman (*aroter*) of fifty sons (*Trojan Women* 135). Theognis speaks of a lustful man who wants to plow another man's field (582). All three tragedians used the field metaphor in the story of Oedipus' incest with his mother: Aeschylus has him "sowing the sacred field of his mother" (*Seven Against Thebes* 753–54); Sophocles has Oedipus say, when he learns the truth, "Bring me a sword, I say, / To find this wife no wife, this mother's womb, / this field of double sowing whence I sprang / and where I sowed my children" (*Oedipus Tyrannus* 1255–57, trans. Grene); and Euripides has Jocasta tell how Laius was warned not to "sow the furrows of fateful sons" (*Phoenician Women* 18). A late Greek version of the cycle of myths tells that "Cronus cut off his father's male plowshare (*arotron*)" and sowed the sea with his seed (Nonnus, *Dionysiaca* 12.46).

The metaphor was less often used in Latin literature. It is found in Lucretius, who frowns upon the sensuous movements of a harlot because she thereby "diverts the furrow out of the direct path and place of the plow, and turns away the impact of the seed from its plot" (4.1272–73; cf. 1107).

Jean de Meun revives it when he denounces at great length those who will not plow (preferring celibacy), or who deliberately overturn the plow, or who plow in sterile fields, and so on (*Romance of the Rose* 19513–722). Shakespeare uses it, most succinctly in *Antony and Cleopatra*: "He ploughed her, and she cropped" (2.2.228). Less bluntly, he asks, "For where is she so fair whose uneared [unplowed] womb / Disdains the tillage of thy husbandry?" (*Sonnets* 3), and Lucio in *Measure for Measure* announces that "her plenteous womb / Expresseth his full tilth and husbandry" (1.4.43–44).

A similar metaphor is implicit in our words "culture" and "cultivate." Latin *cultura* originally meant "tilling" or "agriculture" and later "education" or "cultivation of the mind." Cowper brings this dead metaphor to life: "Their mind a wilderness through want of care, / The plough of wisdom never entering there" (*Hope* 234–35).

A minor tradition links plowing with poetry or with writing. Pindar calls poets "plowmen of the Muses" (*Nem.* 6.32), and a poet who won contests "gave the Muses a field for their tilling" (gave them work to do) (*Nem.* 10.26). Latin *aro* and *exaro* ("plow up") were occasionally used to mean "write"; so Ovid: "to her brother she plows [*exarat*] written letters" (*Ex Ponto* 3.2.90); and Atta: "Let us turn the plowshare on the wax and plow with the point of bone" (quoted in Isidore, *Etymologiae* 6.9.2). Greek *grapho*, Latin *scribo*, English "write" all go back to roots meaning "cut" or "scratch," and the similarity to plowing must have been noted as soon as literacy arrived. One form of Greek writing, where the lines go left-to-right and right-to-left alternately, was called *boustrophedon*, "turning like an ox" (plowing). Latin *versus*, "turn," meant a plowed furrow as well as a line of verse. Spenser likens his narrative line to a furrow where, late in *The Faerie Queene*, he remembers some unfinished labor: "Now turne againe my teme, thou jolly swayne, / Backe to the furrow which I lately left. / I lately left a furrow, one or twayne, / Unplough'd, the which my coulter hath not cleft" (6.9.1). Blake elaborates a complex symbolism of plow, harrow, and mill to express three types of artistic labor, and when he says "Follow with me my Plow" he may be evoking his use of the engraving tool or burin (*Milton* 8.20).

The plow, and especially the plowshare, resembled a sword, and the two tools began to stand for the two ways of life, peace and war. The most famous instance of this contrast is the prophecy of Isaiah, "and they shall beat their swords into plowshares, and their spears into pruning hooks: nation shall not lift up sword against nation, neither shall they learn war any more" (Isa. 2.4, also Mic. 4.3), but note the less famous reversal, "Beat your plowshares into swords, and your pruning hooks into spears" (Joel 3.10). It is interesting that the passage from *Oedipus Tyrannus* quoted above includes a sword, and so does the full speech from *Antony and Cleopatra*: "Royal wench! / She made great Caesar lay his sword to bed; / He ploughed her, and she cropped" (2.2.226–28).

In the Christian tradition the plowman became an emblem of virtue, especially of grace or charity, or of laboring in one's calling, especially the calling of the priest or preacher. The source is Christ's saying, "No man, having put his hand to the plow, and looking back, is fit for the kingdom of God" (Luke 9.62), and it was richly elaborated in the Middle Ages. Some church allegorists identified the plowman with the preacher of the word, and St. Gregory used the phrase "plowshare of the tongue" (*vomer linguae*) as the means by which the heart or mind of the Christian is opened to receive the word. (Christ's Parable of the Sower lies behind this idea as well.) Langland's *Piers Plowman* makes extensive use of this tradition. After a spiritual crisis Piers vows "Of preyers and of penaunce my plow shall be hereafter" (b 7.119), and another character explains that priests should go about the world "To tulien [till] the erthe with tonge, and teche men to lovye [love]" (c 11.199). Chaucer describes his Plowman as "A trewe swynkere [laborer] and a good was he, / Lyvynge in pees and parfit charitee" (*CT*, Gen. Pro. 531–2), though he does not preach.

It is interesting, again, that the "sword of Christ" ("I came not to send peace, but a sword," in Matthew 10.34), was also interpreted to mean the Word or the Gospel and assimilated to the sword that comes out of the mouth of Christ in the Book of Revelation (1.16, 19.15). So sword and plowshare could both serve the idea of preaching the word of God.

The plow finally, has been an emblem of Cincinnatus, the legendary Roman general who was called from his plow to become dictator during a dangerous war; he defeated the enemy and immediately resigned his powers and returned to his farm. When George Washington surrendered his sword to Congress and returned to his farm at Mt. Vernon, he earned the title of the new Cincinnatus.

Several metaphorical extensions of plowing have been common in literature since Homer. In the *Odyssey* ships often "cut" across the water (e.g., 3.174–75); more explicitly, Arion has ships "cutting furrows in Nereus' plain" (quoted in Aelian 12.45). Since flying with wings resembles rowing with oars, as in Aeschylus' *Agamemnon* 52, and chariots leave tracks that resemble furrows, flying can be described as cutting or cleaving the air, especially flying in a chariot (*Hymn to Demeter* 383; Euripides, *Phoenissae* 1–3).

See **Seed**.

Pole star   *see* **Star**

Poplar   The white poplar is mentioned only in passing in the *Iliad* (e.g., 13.389), but Homer's word for it (*acherois*) suggested a connection with the underworld, through which the River Acheron flows. So Servius, commenting on Virgil, tells how Pluto carried off Leuce (from Greek *leuke*, meaning "white [poplar]") to the underworld and when she died caused poplars to grow by the Acheron. When Virgil says that the oarsmen in the racing boats in the funeral games are crowned with poplar leaves (*Aeneid* 5.134) he relies on another tradition as well: that the poplar is the plant of Hercules, patron of athletes. He makes that explicit later in describing King Evander: "two-colored poplar leaves were placed on his hair, / like those which shaded Hercules" (8.276–77). Theocritus' phrase, "the poplar, Heracles' sacred plant" (2.121), may have been the source for Virgil, who also mentions it in the *Eclogues* ("poplar dearest to Alcides" 7.61) and *Georgics* ("the shady tree of Hercules' crown" 2.66). A commentator on Theocritus says that Heracles made a crown for himself after bringing Cerberus up from the underworld. Servius ties this tale to the abduction of Leuce, and explains the two colors as the dark of the underworld and the silvery white bleached by Hercules' sweat.

The poplar is the tree described by Spenser as "the stately tree / That dedicated is t'Olympick Jove, / And to his sonne Alcides, whenas hee / In Nemus gayned goodly victory" (*FQ* 2.5.31) – referring to a different labor, the killing of the Nemean lion. A character named "Prays-desire" (love of honor) holds a poplar branch (2.9.37, 9).

A famous and seemingly symbolic poplar is the one Tennyson's Mariana looks upon in her desolation: "All silver-green with gnarlèd bark: / For leagues no other tree did mark / The level waste, the rounding gray." When the moon is low "The shadow of the poplar fell / Upon her bed, across her brow"; "and the sound / Which to the wooing wind aloof / The poplar made, did all confound / Her sense" ("Mariana" 42–44, 55–56, 74–77). The tree seems to stand for Mariana herself, for the lover who has abandoned her, and for something like the slow hand of a clock. A possible source for it is the poplar whom Oenone addresses in Ovid, *Heroides* 5.23–24; her lover Paris has carved in its bark a promise never to desert her.

Poppy   In several varieties and in several colors, the poppy is a common plant in the Mediterranean and northern Europe, often found growing amid grainfields. The Greeks and Romans raised it in gardens and ate its seeds, usually mixed with honey; from some kinds of poppy they extracted opium. Where it appears in classical literature the poppy is usually the *papaver somniferum*, the "sleep-bearing" or garden poppy (Greek *mekon*), the source of the narcotic.

The poppy, or rather its capsule or head (Greek *kodeia*), was associated with the goddess Demeter (Latin Ceres), probably because it often flowers at harvest time. Theocritus ends his Seventh Idyll with an evocation of Demeter of the Threshing Floor "with wheatsheaves and poppies in either hand." Perhaps the poppy head, filled with seeds, represents fertility; perhaps it stands for the beginning of the growing season as the wheatsheaves stand for the end; or perhaps it alludes to the grief of Demeter in her search for Persephone (Latin Proserpina): the opiate poppy would assuage her sorrow. Ceres, according to Ovid, gave a child poppies in warm milk to make him sleep (*Fasti* 4.547–48). In the Cave of Sleep, where Lethe flows, poppies bloom (*Met.* 11.605–07). Virgil calls it the *Cereale papaver*, "the poppy of Ceres," in *Georgics* 1.212 and *soporiferum papaver*, "soporific poppy," in *Aeneid* 4.486; the poppy is "perfused with Lethean sleep" in *Georgics* 1.78.

Spenser's Garden of Proserpina has various herbs and fruits "fitt to adorne the dead," including the "Dead sleeping Poppy" (*FQ* 2.7.52). Shakespeare mentions it only once: it is one of the "drowsy syrups" that induce sleep, like mandragora (*Othello* 3.3.330); Jonson also links it to mandrake (and hemlock) in *Sejanus* 3.596. Among English poets Keats seems most fascinated with the poppy. His Endymion is put to sleep by a breeze blowing through poppies (*Endymion* 1.555, 566) and has a "soft poppy dream" (4.786). Even where there is no literal poppy he speaks of "the poppied warmth of sleep" ("Eve of St. Agnes" 237); Sleep is "Wreather of Poppy buds" and wears a "poppy coronet" ("Sleep and Poetry" 14, 348). In "To Autumn," the goddess of Autumn is "Drows'd with the fume of poppies" in the midst of reaping, much like Theocritus' Demeter. Tennyson, in "The Lotos-Eaters," describes a scene where "poppies hang in sleep" (Choric Song 11). See also Francis Thompson, "The Poppy."

With this tradition of sleep, peaceful death, and oblivion so firm, it is surprising that today, at least in Britain and the Commonwealth, the poppy symbolizes remembrance of the fallen soldiers of World War I. Crimson poppies were plentiful on the battlefields of France and Belgium, as they grow easily on disturbed soil. Blood-colored – the French poet Jammes had called the poppy "that drop of blood" (*Géorgiques* [1911] p. 54) – they were assimilated into the tradition in which purple flowers symbolize the death of a young man or god. "Poppies, whose roots are in man's veins, / Drop, and are ever dropping," as the war poet Isaac Rosenberg writes ("Break of Day in the Trenches"). In late Victorian and Edwardian England, poppies had gained an erotic (and homoerotic) significance in the writings of Wilde, Douglas, and others: Wilde's Dorian says, "I must sow poppies in my garden" and Lord Henry replies, "Life has always poppies in her hands" (*Picture of Dorian Gray* chap. 8); this connotation may have fed into the war poetry. John McCrae's immensely popular poem "In Flanders Fields" established the poppy's new significance: "In Flanders fields the poppies blow / Between the crosses, row on row / That mark our place."

But there are classical sources for the connection between the poppy and a fallen soldier. In the *Iliad*, a warrior, hit in the chest, "droops his head to one side, as a garden poppy bends beneath the weight of its fruit and the spring rains" (8.306) (see also 14.499). Drawing also from Catullus 11.22–24, Virgil imitates this beautiful simile in the *Aeneid*: Euryalus dies, and "his neck / Collapsing let his head fall on his shoulder – / As a purple flower (*purpureus…flos*) cut by a passing plow / Will droop and wither slowly, or a poppy / Bow its head upon its tired stalk / When overborne by a passing rain" (9.434–37; after Fitzgerald).

    See **Mandrake, Purple flower**.

Purple   It seems that the Greek word *porphureos*, from which our word "purple" derives, did not originally name a color or hue but a sheen or iridescence, a mixture of light or dark on the surface, like the deep, rich brightness of a cloth dyed with an extract from the shell of the murex or purpura (Greek *porphura*), a snail found in the Mediterranean Sea. In Homer, *porphureos* can modify not only "cloth" but also "sea," "blood," "cloud," "rainbow," and "serpent." It also occurs three times as a formulaic epithet of "death." The glittering movement of the sea may be the primary sense, as the verb *porphuro* means "heave" or "swell." "And at the cutwater / A *porphureon* wave rose and shouted loudly as the ship went onward" (*Iliad* 1.481–82). The term must often be translated as "bright," "sparkling," "lustrous," "shining," or the like, rather than "purple."

    Latin *purpureus* often referred to the hue, but Latin poetry borrowed from Homer and other Greek writers its application to certain things that are not purple. Horace writes of "purple swans" whose color is surely white (*Odes* 4.1.10); Ben Jonson makes them "bright swans" in his translation. Virgil has Venus breathe the "purple light of youth" onto her son Aeneas (1.590); Dryden blurs the sense with his translation, "breath'd a youthful vigor on his face," but modern translators do better with "the glow of a young man" (Mandelbaum) or "bloom of youth" (Fitzgerald). See also *Aeneid* 6.641. Occasionally in Ovid love (Amor) is *purpureus* (e.g., *Amores* 2.1.38), and it may be at Ovid's hint that Milton gives Love "purple wings" (*PL* 4.764) and Gray writes "The bloom of young desire and purple light of love" ("Progress of Poesy" 41).

    Another Greek word, *phoinikeos* (from *Phoinikia*, Phoenicia, where the dye originates), was usually applied more narrowly to purple (or dark red) colors. The same is true of the Latin derivative *puniceus*. In verse each is sometimes used synonymously with *porphureos/purpureus*, as in successive lines (28–29) of Bion's "Lament for Adonis," describing blood.

    Homer's purple sea continues in Catullus' waves "glittering with purple light" (64.275) and much more recently in Shelley's "Ocean's purple waves" (*PU* 1.109) and Yeats's "glimmering purple sea" (*Oisin* 384).

    Another striking usage is Virgil's "purple spring" (*ver purpureum*) in *Eclogues* 9.40; it may mean "brilliant" but perhaps also evokes the color of spring flowers. Here Dryden keeps "purple" in his translation, while Pope in "Spring" 28 varies it to "purple year" (i.e., the phase of the year). The influential fourth-century Latin poem *Vigil of Venus* has Venus painting the "purpling year" (*purpurantem…annum*) with flowery gems (13). In his once-famous opening of "Ode on the Spring," Gray follows the *Vigil* and Pope: "Lo! where the rosy-bosomed Hours, / Fair Venus' train, appear, / Disclose the long-expecting flowers, / And wake the purple year!" When Milton imitates the somewhat rare Latin usage of "purple" as a verb in *Lycidas* 141 – "purple all the ground with vernal flowers" – he is not claiming that all spring flowers in England are purple in color. Indeed they may be white, as in Thomson's startling phrase, "one white-empurpled Shower / Of mingled Blossoms" ("Spring" 110–11).

Latin poetry occasionally uses *purpureus* of the sun or its light, perhaps with the sense "radiant" but perhaps to suggest the color of dawn or sunset. Shakespeare opens *Venus and Adonis* with "the sun with purple-colour'd face." Wordsworth's phrase, "fields invested with purpureal gleams" ("Laodamia" 106), and Yeats's "noon a purple glow" ("Lake Isle of Innisfree") both have a classical aura – or a visionary one.

In *The Eve of St. Agnes* Keats presents his lover-hero Porphyro as a bringer of bright color to the pale cold world of Madeline; in an echo of the Homeric context of both blood and heaving seas, Porphyro's thought of stealing into her bedroom "in his pained heart / Made purple riot" (137–38).

A colorful or florid passage in an otherwise decorous and dignified poem is called a "purple patch" (*purpureus pannus*), from Horace's *Art of Poetry* 15.

Because of both the striking effect and great cost of the murex dye, often called "Tyrian purple" (from the city of Tyre in Phoenicia), its use was restricted largely to kings, emperors, and aristocrats (hence "royal purple"). In one of the most spectacular scenes of Greek drama, Clytemnestra insists that Agamemnon walk upon a path of garments dyed in "the juice of *porphura*, worth its weight in silver," as he enters his palace (Aeschylus, *Agamemnon* 959–60). Roman consuls wore purple togas, and senators and knights had a purple strip on their tunics. Dryden's Antony gained "purple greatness" (*All for Love* 1.1.298). A purple pall was used to cover the coffin of a person of high rank.

In a mocking use of the royal purple, the soldiers of Pilate took Jesus and "clothed him with purple, and platted a crown of thorns, and put it about his head, / And began to salute him, Hail, King of the Jews!" (Mark 15.17–18).

Blood and gore are typically purple in English poetry as they are in classical poetry. Shakespeare has "purple blood" (*3H6* 2.5.99), "the purple testament of bleeding war" (*R2* 3.3.94), "purple fountains issuing from your veins" (*RJ* 1.1.85), and so on. Blood is purple in Spenser's *Faerie Queene* half a dozen times, and so is gore; we also find "a purple lake / Of bloudy gore" (6.1.37). Among many other examples, see "purple gore" (Marvell, *Britannia* 40), and "purple Vengeance bath'd in Gore" (Pope, *Windsor-Forest* 417). Milton connects the two most common meanings in *Eikonoklastes*: "covering the ignominious and horrid purple robe of innocent blood that sat so close about him with the glorious purple of royalty and supreme rule" (sec. 28).

Whether from the sign of rank or the color of blood, Horace refers to "purple tyrants" (*Odes* 1.35.12); Gray repeats it in "Ode on Adversity" 7, Blake in "The Grey Monk" 34; and in fact "purple" is often associated with tyrants in eighteenth-century English poetry; e.g., "the purple tyranny of Rome" (Thomson, *Summer* 758), "the blood-purpled robes of royalty" (Southey, *Wat Tyler* 2.1).

A Catholic priest is "raised to the purple" when he becomes a cardinal. Purple is also the ecclesiastical color of Advent and Lent, and of the spirit of penitence and mourning. Dante uses "purple" (*porpora*) only once in *The Divine Comedy*, as the color of the robes of the four personified moral virtues, but scholars disagree over its significance: it might mean that these virtues are as nothing without love, whose color is red (*rossa*) a few lines earlier; or that, as the four "cardinal" virtues, they are not only pivotal but raised to the purple like the clerical office; or that, as the four classical virtues, they wear the color of empire (*Purgatorio* 29.131).

See **Blood, Dawn**.

Purple flower   In one of the earliest pastoral elegies, the "Lament for Adonis," Bion imagines flowers growing red with grief: purple blood from Adonis' fatal wound turns into a rose, tears from Aphrodite turn into an anemone; then his corpse lies wreathed in flowers. Moschus begins his "Lament for Bion" by calling on roses, anemones, and hyacinths to join him in mourning. Thus began the literary existence of purple (or red) flowers as signs of mourning and as regular features of the pastoral elegy.

Ovid tells the story of two of these flowers in the *Metamorphoses*. The anemone grows from the blood of Adonis (10.731–39), while the hyacinth grows from the blood of the youth Hyacinthus, beloved of Apollo, who then inscribes on its petals the word "ai," the cry of mourning (10.214–16; also in Moschus 6). In his version of the former story, *Venus and Adonis*, Shakespeare is vague as to Adonis' flower, saying only that "A purple flower sprung up, checker'd with white" (1168). Milton in his pastoral elegy *Lycidas* describes the hyacinth as "that sanguine flower inscrib'd with woe" (106); its color decorates the robe of a mourner, but the flowers strewn on the hearse of Lycidas, though the valley is asked to "purple" the ground with them (141), come in many colors. Ovid also tells how the blood of Pyramus turns the berries of the mulberry tree purple (4.121–27), and how the violet springs from the blood of Attis (*Fasti* 4.283ff., 5.226).

Perhaps decisive for this tradition is the *Aeneid*, where purple flowers (*purpureos flores*), not further identified, are cast on tombs on two occasions (5.79, 6.884).

In his pastoral elegy *Astrophel*, Spenser tells how the two lovers are transformed "Into one flowre that is both red and blew" (184). The dead Adonais, in Shelley's elegy of that name, lies with his head "bound with pansies overblown, / And faded violets, white, and pied, and blue" (289–90). Walt Whitman's elegy on the death of Lincoln begins "When lilacs last in the dooryard bloomed." John McCrae's poem "In Flanders Field" established the poppy as the symbol of memory for the dead of World War I.

See **Pansy, Poppy, Violet**.

Pyramid   The great pyramids of Egypt, still imposing after five thousand years, have nonetheless entered literature as bywords for impermanence or for the futile vainglory of kings. Already to the Romans Egypt's day seemed to have passed. Horace opens his famous ode "Exegi monumentum" with what sounds like a proverbial expression: "I have achieved a monument more lasting / than bronze, and loftier than the pyramids of kings, / which neither gnawing rain nor blustering wind / may destroy" (3.30.1–4, trans. Shepherd). His poetry will keep him famous as long as Rome survives (longer, as it has turned out). Propertius tells his girl she is lucky to be named in his poems, for while the pyramids and other great monuments will be destroyed by wind, rain, and time, the name achieved by wit shall be immortal (3.2.18ff.). Milton hearkens to both these poets in his "On Shakespeare," which begins, "What needs my Shakespeare for his honored bones / The labor of an age in piled stones, / Or that his hallowed relics should be hid / Under a star-ypointing pyramid?" He lives on instead in our "wonder and astonishment." Shelley often relished the thought that the monuments tyrants built to guarantee their immortality will crumble into dust: "Beside the eternal Nile, / The Pyramids have risen. / Nile shall pursue his changeless way: / Those pyramids shall fall" (*Queen Mab* 2.126–29).

The origin of the word "pyramid" is unknown, but to the Greeks it suggested *pyr* ("fire"). Plato thought that since the pyramid, or tetrahedron, was the most mobile, the smallest, and the sharpest of the perfect (Platonic) solids, it was "the element and seed of fire" (*Timaeus* 56b). It was also thought to resemble a flame. Milton's Satan "Springs upward like a pyramid of fire" (*PL* 2.1013). The Pyramid of Cestius in Rome, in Shelley's words, "doth stand / Like flame transformed to marble" ("Adonais" 446–47).

R

Rain Of the many symbolic aspects of rain we shall describe two, both obvious developments of rain's real effects: rain as suffering or bad luck and rain as fertilizing force from above.

Rain often stands as a synecdoche for all bad weather and thus a symbol of life's unhappy moments. We save for a "rainy day"; into every life some rain must fall. The Lord's mysterious ways include bringing sun and rain on the just and unjust alike (Matt. 5.45). Feste's song about the unpleasant events of each phase of life (at the end of Shakespeare's *Twelfth Night*) has the refrain, "For the rain it raineth every day." Lear on the heath finds wind and rain responding to his inner fury and pain.

In the oldest Greek texts the subject of the verb "rains" is often "Zeus" (e.g., Homer, *Iliad* 12.25; Hesiod, *Works and Days* 488); later the subject is omitted, as it always is in Latin *pluit*; in English and other modern languages a place-holding "it" governs "rains" (cf. French *il pleut*). Zeus is "high-thundering," "cloud-gathering," "rejoicing in the thunderbolt," while a common epithet of Jupiter is *Pluvius*. In Latin poetry it is sometimes Sky that sends rain, and it is the seed that fertilizes mother Earth. "Father Sky / pours it down into the lap of Mother Earth," says Lucretius (1.250–51); "And so we all arise from sky-born seed. / There is one father for all. When the fostering earth, / Our mother, takes within her his moist droplets, / Grown big, she bears the glossy corn" (2.991–94 trans. Esolen). According to Virgil, "in spring, the country swells / Clamouring for the fertilizing seeds. / Then the almighty father Heaven descends / Into the lap of his rejoicing bride / With fecund showers" (*Georgics* 2.324–26 trans. Wilkinson). Claudian uses similar sexual imagery for dew, not always distinguished from rain: "[Zephyrus] shook his wings wet with fresh nectar and played the bridegroom's part to the soil with fertile dew" (*Rape of Proserpine* 2.88–89, trans. Gruzelier). In Spenser's variant, "angry Jove an hideous storme of raine / Did poure into his Lemans [Lover's] lap" (*FQ* 1.1.6).

In Christian terms, of course, it is God who sends what Shakespeare's Portia calls "the gentle rain from heaven," which she invokes as a simile for mercy (*MV* 4.1.184). Rain is the cure for spiritual dryness or thirst, for the waste land of "accidie" (torpor) or despair. So Eliot's *The Waste Land* begins with a flight from the cruel rain of spring, the surprising rain of summer, and ends with the "dry sterile thunder without rain" that announces what the soul must learn to do.

See **Cloud, Dew, Lightning, Rainbow, Wind**.

Rainbow The seminal text for the symbolism of the rainbow is Genesis 9.8–17, where God makes a covenant with Noah: there shall be no more floods, and "I do set my bow in the cloud, and it shall be for a token of a covenant between me and the earth" (13). It is a "natural symbol" for a bond between earth and heaven, as it is a product of the sun (heaven) and rain (falling from heaven to earth), while its arc reaches from earth to heaven and back to earth. Milton, who calls it the "humid bow" and "showery arch" (*PL* 4.151, 6.759), retells the story: Noah "over his head beholds / A dewy cloud, and in the cloud a bow / Conspicuous with three listed [banded] colours gay, / Betokening peace from God, and Covenant new" (11.864–67).

In classical literature the rainbow is also a divine token, though not so benign. Marked on clouds by Zeus, rainbows are portents to mortals; Zeus sends a rainbow as a sign of war or storm (*Iliad* 11.27–28, 17.548–49). It is personified as Iris, the messenger of the gods, but her rainbow-like qualities are not brought out in Homer or Hesiod. In Virgil's *Aeneid*, where she often does Juno's bidding, she descends "on the path of a thousand-colored arc" and ascends by "cutting an arc under the clouds" (5.606, 9.15). Ovid's Iris, "clad in various colors," also traces a rainbow path on her missions (*Met.* 1.270, 11.585). The rainbow was thought to drink up moisture, which then falls as rain (Plautus, *Curculio* 131a; Virgil, *Georgics* 1.380; Ovid, *Met.* 1.271).

For the most part Renaissance literature repeats classical and biblical usage, but Shakespeare may be evoking a recent sense of "iris" as the circular colored membrane of the eye when the Countess asks Helena why she weeps: "What's the matter, / That this distempered messenger of wet, / The many colored Iris, rounds thine eye?" (*AWEW* 1.3.150–52).

For the Romantics rainbows retain their numinous character but they are symbols of a covenant less with God than with nature. Wordsworth's heart leaps up at the sight of one in a surge of "natural piety" ("My heart leaps up"). Goethe's Faust turns his back on the sun at the opening of *Part II*, as if to say he will cease trying to grasp Truth or the Absolute directly, and instead turns to the rainbow, the *Wechseldauer* ("change-permanence") of transient waterdrops in eternal pattern, which symbolizes human life, lived in colored reflections of the light (4715–27).

Newton's theory of optics caused a stir among poets mainly for its explanation of the spectrum, and hence the rainbow. Thomson uses such optical terms as "refracted" and "prism" to describe "the grand etherial bow," which looks one way to the "sage-instructed eye" (instructed by "awful Newton") and another to the "swain" filled with wonder and amazement as he "runs / To catch the falling glory" (*Spring* 203–17). At a famous dinner with Wordsworth, Lamb, Haydon, and others Keats lamented that Newton had "destroyed all the poetry of the rainbow, by reducing it to the prismatic colours" (Haydon's account). Drawing on the metaphor of weaving, which since Milton at least was a commonplace in rainbow descriptions (see "Iris' Woof," *Comus* 83), Keats in *Lamia* states, "There was an awful rainbow once in heaven: / We know her woof, her texture; she is given / In the dull catalogue of common things" (2.231–33). The rainbow thus became the main exhibit in the contest of science and poetry.

Raven   The raven and the crow are not consistently distinguished in biblical or classical literature, and in English literature they are both sometimes grouped among such similar birds as the chough, daw (or jackdaw), and rook. The primary associations of these black carrion birds, not surprisingly, are negative, but there are some interesting favorable associations.

The first raven in the Bible (Hebrew *'oreb*, which can refer to the crow as well) is the first of four birds Noah sent forth to learn if land had appeared; the raven "went forth to and fro, until the waters were dried up from off the earth" (Gen. 8.7). As a carrion-eater the raven presumably found something edible floating on the flood, so it did not return to the ark: a good sign. Elsewhere in the Old Testament ravens are scavengers, and hence "unclean" (Lev. 11.15), but once, rather mysteriously, they bring bread and meat to Elijah in the desert (1 Kgs 17.6). (Milton retells this story in *Paradise Regained* 2.266–69). One of the many rhetorical questions the Lord puts to the humbled Job is "Who provideth for the raven his food?" (Job 38.41), a question answered at Psalm 147.9 – "He giveth to the beast his food, and to the young ravens which cry" – and elaborated by Luke (12.24). God will provide. Shakespeare's Adam invokes these texts when he offers his life's savings to Orlando in *As You Like It* (2.3.43).

In the Song of Songs the lover's locks are "black as a raven" (5.11), a phrase that must be commonplace wherever ravens are found. It is very often hair that provokes comparison with them, as in Chaucer's description of the hair of King Lygurge: "As any ravenes fethere it shoon for blak" (*Knight's Tale* 2144). "Raven" has become an adjective meaning "black," with little or no additional connotation. Alluding perhaps to the Song of Songs Byron praises "the nameless grace / Which waves in every raven tress" of a beautiful woman ("She Walks in Beauty"). In Greek and Latin "white raven" was proverbial for something extremely rare or unheard-of, like "black swan."

The raven was occasionally said to be the companion or messenger of Apollo; it is "Phoebus' bird" in Ovid, *Met.* 2.545 (see 5.329), and "the dark attendant of Apollo's tripod" in Statius, *Thebaid* 3.506.

It is mainly as an eater of carrion, including human carrion, that the raven is known in classical literature. The raven (Greek *korax*) does not appear in Homer, though it is a major theme in the *Iliad* that corpses may be devoured by birds. Theognis complains that everything has "gone to the ravens" (833), perhaps better translated as "to the crows," the equivalent of "to the dogs" in English. Several characters in plays by Aristophanes have a habit of saying *es korakas!* – "to the ravens!" or "Go and be hanged!" (*Wasps* 852, 982; *Birds* 27; etc.). In a memorable simile the chorus of Aeschylus' *Agamemnon* depicts Clytemnestra after she murders Agamemnon: "standing on his body like a loathsome raven she hoarsely sings her hymn of triumph" (1472–74).

The raven (and the crow) prosper when men slaughter one another, and so they are associated with battlefields and gallows and more generally with imminent death. Horace sardonically assures a servant, *non pasces in cruce corvos*, "You won't hang on a cross to feed ravens" (*Epistles* 1.16.48), while Petronius records an insult: "a gallow's tidbit, ravens' food" (58).

The raven is one of the three beasts of battle (the others being the wolf and the eagle/vulture) that occur as a formula or commonplace a dozen times in Old English poetry. In *Brunanburh*, "The host of corpses behind them they left / to the black raven (*sweartan hraefn*), the beak-faced one, / the dark-clothed one, and to the dun eagle, / the white-tailed erne, hungry war-bird, / and to the greedy wolf, grey beast of the woods, / to devour and relish" (60–65, trans. Malone). On the eve of the great battle in *Elene*, the wolf howls a war-song and the eagle shrieks (27–31); as the battle looms "over their heads the raven cried, dark, thirsty for slaughter" (52); and then as the battle begins, raven, eagle, and wolf rejoice. There is an interesting variation near the end of *Beowulf*, where "the dark raven, / eager for the dying, will have much to say, / to tell the eagle how it thrived at the feast, / while with the wolf he spoiled the corpses" (3024–27).

The raven, like the wolf, belonged to Odin, the Norse war god, sometimes called Hrafnagud, "Ravengod." An epithet of "raven" in the Old English *Exodus* (164) is *wealceasig*, "chooser of the slain" or "carrion-picker," cognate with Valkyrie (or Walkyrie), the terrible Norse goddesses of battle who work out the fate of warriors. An early Old Norse poem, *Hrafnsmal*, is a dialogue between one of the Valkyrie and a raven. Celtic traditions are similar. In the Irish *Tain Bo Cuailnge*, the war goddess Badb Catha is called "Raven of Battle." The medieval ballad "The Twa Corbies" begins with a plan by the ravens to breakfast off a slain knight. Joel Barlow gives sarcastic "Advice to a Raven in Russia" who has been following Napoleon in 1812: the corpses will be too frozen to eat – "With beak and claw you cannot pluck an eye" – so fly south, fly anywhere, for there are plenty of men slain in Napoleon's ubiquitous battles.

It was proverbial that ravens peck out the eyes of the slain: see Proverbs 30.17 and Aristophanes' *Birds* 582. Catullus wishes a miserable end to an enemy: "your eyes torn out and swallowed by the raven's black throat" (108.5). Villon's "Ballade of the Hanged" announces that "Magpies and ravens [*corbeaulx*] have caved our eyes / And plucked out our beards and eyebrows" (23–24). Milton denounces bishops as "ravens … that would peck out the eyes of all knowing Christians" (*Animadversions* sec. 13).

In Latin literature the raven (*corvus*) or crow (*cornix*) was thought to foretell a rainstorm (Virgil, *Georgics* 1.382; Horace, *Odes* 3.27.10–11) and in both Greek and Roman culture these birds, among many others, were used in augury or bird-prophecy generally. Combined with its habit of eating corpses, this association led to the widespread view that the raven (in particular) is a bird of ill omen, usually foretelling death. The owls' shriek and "revenes qualm [croak]" both foretell evil in Chaucer's *Troilus and Cressida* 5.382. The crow has a "vois of care" in Chaucer's *Parliament of Fowls* 363. "The ominous raven with a dismal cheer, / Through his hoarse beak of following horror tells" (Drayton, *Barons' Wars* 5.42). Marlowe's Barabas opens the second act of *The Jew of Malta* with a fine simile: "Thus like the sad presaging raven that tolls / The sick man's passport in her hollow beak, / And in the shadow of the silent night / Doth shake contagion from her sable wings." Lady Macbeth says, "The raven himself is hoarse, / That croaks the fatal entrance of Duncan / Under my battlements" (*Macbeth* 1.5.38–40). And Othello cries, "O, it comes o'er my memory, / As doth the raven o'er the infected house, / Boding to all" (*Othello* 4.1.20–22). The most famous raven of the foreboding sort is Edgar Allen Poe's.

Aristophanes records the belief that the raven or crow lives five human generations (*Birds* 609), while Ovid gives the crow (*cornix*) a life-span of nine (*Met.* 7.274). The longevity of the bird was so well established that Martial could write of an old woman, "Plutia, having outlived all crows…" (10.67.5). Shakespeare calls the crow "treble-dated" ("Phoenix and Turtle" 17); Tennyson calls it "many-winter'd" ("Locksley Hall" 68).

The two ravens of Odin were named Huginn and Muninn, Thought and Memory, faculties of the mind that quickly fly over space and time. This Norse tradition may have combined with the classical notions of the birds' longevity and prophetic powers, and perhaps with Noah's sending of the raven as scout, to produce the idea that ravens know everything. In his catalog of birds, Chaucer lists "the raven wys [wise]" (*PF* 363). This idea, seconded by the Elijah story, may have led to the tradition of good and helpful ravens, as in these lines by Shakespeare: "Some say that ravens foster forlorn children / The whilst their own birds famish in their nests" (*Titus* 2.3.154–55).

Red Red in literature is the color of fire, gold, and roses; it is the color of faces when they show embarrassment, anger, or the flush of health or passion. It is also the color of blood, of course, but less often than one might think, purple being its traditional literary color.

In Renaissance poetry red and white are often paired as the colors of beauty or love. Spring, according to Petrarch, is *candida et vermiglia*, "white and vermilion" (*Rime* 310). Shakespeare's Venus tells Adonis he is "More white and red than doves or roses are" (10); when Adonis alternately blushes for shame and turns pale with anger, she is pleased with both his red and white (76–77). Viola says, "'Tis beauty truly blent, whose red and white / Nature's own sweet and cunning hand laid on" (*12N* 1.5.239–40). Red and pale make another contrast frequent in Shakespeare; it means cheerful and sad. "Looked he red or pale," asks Adriana, "or sad or merrily?" (*CE* 4.2.4); Hamlet asks Horatio the same question about the ghost (1.2.232); Autolycus jokes, "the red blood reigns in the winter's pale" (*WT* 4.3.4). In Milton even angels blush red with love, "Celestial rosy red, love's proper hue" (*PL* 8.619).

Red is sometimes the color of the devil, in a tradition that goes back to Esau, who was "red, all over like a hairy garment" (Gen. 25.25). Mann invokes this tradition with his eerie red-haired figures in *Death in Venice* and *Doctor Faustus*.

The red cross of St. George is the old emblem of England; Spenser adopts it for his Red Cross Knight in *Faerie Queene* book 1. The red planet is Mars; it indeed looks pink, and it stands for the god of bloody war: "Ye shal be deed

[dead]," a character in Chaucer vows, "by myghty Mars the rede!" (*Knight's Tale* 1747).

See **Purple, Rose, Scarlet**.

Reed *see* **Pipe**

Right *see* **Left and right**

Ring The ring is a sign of a pledge. In Terence's *Eunuch* the phrase "made pledges" is literally "gave rings" (541). In *Beowulf* and other Germanic epics rings are the most prominent bonds between lord and vassal: Hygelac dispenses rings (1970), Beowulf is called "ring prince" (2345), castles have a "ring hall" (2010, 2840), and so on. In modern literature the ring is more often a pledge between a man and woman, either of betrothal or marriage. Shakespeare makes good use of improper pledging and parting with rings in several of his comedies, such as *All's Well that Ends Well*, where Diana extracts a ring from Bertram, who intends to break his vows to Helena, who passes *her* ring to Diana, etc. In *Merchant of Venice* rings circulate like ideal money (real money being the major source of conflict in the play): given away impulsively they end up on the right fingers and bind their wearers more tightly together.

There are many magic rings in literature. To name a few: the ring that makes Gyges invisible (Plato, *Republic* 359–60); *The Ring of the Nibelung* (the title of Wagner's opera cycle), which gives absolute power to its owner; the ring of Canace in Chaucer's *Squire's Tale*, which lets her understand birds; the ring of Tolkien's *Lord of the Rings*, which gives power but also corrupts.

River As rivers mark territorial boundaries, crossing them is often symbolically important. The literal crossing of the Jordan into the Promised Land by the Israelites has served as the vehicle for many Christian and Jewish spiritual concepts; Christian meanings are seconded by the baptism of Christ in the Jordan by John the Baptist. In classical myths the shades of the dead had to cross the river Acheron into Hades, ferried by Charon. When Dante drinks of Lethe and Eunoe at the top of the mount of Purgatory he is ready to ascend into heaven.

To "cross the Rubicon" has been proverbial since the seventeenth century for an irrevocable step; the Rubicon marked the border between Italy and Cisalpine Gaul, and when Julius Caesar crossed it with his army in 49 BC he became an invader (see Lucan 1.183ff.). It is equivalent to "the die is cast," which Caesar said as he crossed the stream (Suetonius, *Julius* 32). When young Jane Eyre is punished by the hypocritical Mr. Brocklehurst, she began "to feel that the Rubicon was passed" (C. Brontë, *Jane Eyre*, chap. 7).

Traveling up or down rivers might also mark changes in symbolic states. Drifting down the Mississippi on a raft into slave territory, Huckleberry Finn and Jim seem to give themselves to fate. In general, as George Eliot observes, "So our lives glide on: the river ends we don't know where, and the sea begins, and then there is no more jumping ashore" (*Felix Holt* chap. 27). As Conrad's Marlow steams up the Congo in search of Kurtz, he goes deeper into something primitive and horrible, though whether it is Africa itself or the character of the Europeans is left ambiguous (*Heart of Darkness*).

In classical literature a country, region, or city was often named after its rivers. Dionysus announces at the beginning of Euripides' *Bacchae*, "I have come to Dirce's stream and Ismenus' water," that is, to Thebes, known as the "two-river city." Dante reports that "I was born and grew up / Above the lovely river Arno in the great city [i.e., Florence]" (*Inferno* 23.94–95). A poet might then be identified as "the poet of River X," as we occasionally call Shakespeare the Bard of Avon. This habit combined with the symbol of the swan, the singing river-bird, to produce Horace's phrase for the Theban Pindar, "the swan of Dirce" (4.2.25–27), imitated in "Swan of Avon," and the like. (*See* **Swan**.) A similar formula identifies inhabitants of a country by naming the river that they drink. Homer reports a group of Trojan allies as those who "drink the black water of Aisepos" (*Iliad* 2.825). Horace refers to those who "drink the Don" (the Scythians) and those who "drink the deep Danube" (the Dacians) (3.10.1, 4.15.21).

In the 1840s hundreds of poems and songs about the Rhine were published in Germany as part of a surge in nationalist sentiment. "Father Rhine," suffused with memories of the Nibelungen and the Lorelei, was taken as the source and essence of the German spirit.

The river has been pressed into many metaphorical uses. A poet in the *Greek Anthology* praises Stesichorus for channeling "the Homeric stream" into his own verses (9.184). In one of his odes Horace praises another Greek poet for his eloquence: "As a river swollen by the rains above its usual / banks rushes down from the mountain, / so does Pindar surge and his deep / voice rushes on" (4.2.5–8; trans. Shepherd). Cicero and Quintilian in their treatises on rhetoric stress the importance of "fluency," the *flumen orationis* or *flumen verborum*, "river of speech" or "stream of words." When Dante meets Virgil in the opening of the *Inferno*, he asks, "Are you that Virgil, then, and that fountain / Which pours out so broad a river (*fiume*) of speech?" (1.79–80). After describing the river Thames, Denham addresses it: "O could I flow like thee, and make thy stream / My great example, as it is my theme! / Though deep, yet clear, though gentle, yet not dull, / Strong without rage, without ore-flowing full" ("Cooper's Hill" 189–92). Pope, in his imitation of Horace, *Epistle* 2.2, writes, "Pour the full Tide of Eloquence along" (171). Thomson distinguishes two sorts of eloquence among many: "In thy full language, speaking mighty things, / Like a clear torrent close, or else diffused / A broad majestic stream, and rolling on / Through all the winding harmony of sound" (*Liberty* 2.257–60). Poetic genius is compared to the Nile by Lebrun-Pindare: it rises in the rocks "without glory or name," sometimes "buries itself amid unknown gulfs," and then suddenly comes into the light and is worshipped by all Egypt ("Ode on Enthusiasm" 93–100). Shelley refers to "Poesy's unfailing River, / Which through Albion winds forever" ("Euganean Hills" 184–85). Mangan begins a poem by addressing it: "Roll forth, my song, like the rushing river / That sweeps along to the mighty sea" ("The Nameless One").

A tributary of this tradition traces the river of poetry back to Mount Helicon, sacred to the Muses, on the slopes of which were Hesiod's village of Ascra and two springs, Aganippe, which produced the stream Olmeius, and Hippocrene, which gave rise to the Permessus; the water of either of these would inspire the poet who drank. Petrarch complains that "he is pointed to as a strange thing / who wishes to make a river flow from Helicon" (*Rime* 7).

"From Helicon's harmonious springs," Gray writes, "A thousand rills their mazy progress take"; they grow into a "rich stream of music" ("Progress of Poetry" 3–4, 7).

The inverse of the river of speech is the speech of the river. In English "babbling brook" is a cliché, and in literature every variety of speech has been heard in rivers: they babble, brawl, murmur, prattle, rave, shout, sing, and so on. Not surprisingly poets have found rivers companions, counterparts, exemplars, and teachers. Near the opening of *The Prelude*, for instance, Wordsworth remembers the river Derwent that flowed past his boyhood home: "one, the fairest of all rivers, loved / To blend his murmurs with my nurse's song, / And .../... sent a voice / That flowed along my dreams" (1805 version 1.272–76).

If speech or poetry flows like a river, so does the mind. We commonly speak of the "stream of consciousness" and the Freudian theory of the unconscious is filled with hydraulic metaphors. Dante speaks of "the stream of mind" (or "memory": *de la mente il fiume*, *Purgatorio* 13.90). Wordsworth, finding the sources of his mind unsearchable, asks who could say "This portion of the river of my mind / Comes from yon fountain"? (1805 *Prelude* 2.214–15). Shelley speaks several times of "the stream of thought" (e.g., *Alastor* 644), and his poem "Mont Blanc" begins with a complex simile likening the Ravine of Arve before him with the "everlasting universe of things" that "Flows through the mind," while "from secret springs / The source of human thought its tribute brings / Of waters" (punning on "tributary") (1–6).

It is common to speak of the phases of a river from its source to its mouth as ages in a human life. So Thomson describes the Nile: rising from two springs he "rolls his infant stream," then "he sports away / His playful youth amid the fragrant isles"; "Ambitious thence the manly river breaks" and "Winds in progressive majesty along" (*Summer* 806–15). The metaphor is implicit in the description of "Alph the sacred river" in Coleridge's "Kubla Khan," which rises from a fountain that seems to be in labor, meanders for a while, and then sinks into the "lifeless ocean." In *The Excursion* Wordsworth offers an elaborate simile: "The tenour / Which my life holds, he readily may conceive / Whoe'er hath stood to watch a mountain brook / In some still passage of its course .../... Such a stream / Is human Life" (3.967–87). "O stream!" the Poet in Shelley's *Alastor* asks, "Whose source is inaccessibly profound, / Whither do thy mysterious waters tend? / Thou imagest my life" (502–05).

In Wordsworth again, that great poet of rivers, we find real rivers and many of their possible symbolic meanings (speech, poetry, life) flowing together. To give one more example from *The Prelude* (1805), book 9 opens with a retrospect on the poem so far: "As oftentimes a river, it might seem, / Yielding in part to old remembrances, / Part swayed by fear to tread an onward road / That leads direct to the devouring sea, / Turns and will measure back his course – far back, / Towards the very regions which he crossed / In his first outset – so have we long time / Made motions retrograde."

Hölderlin was as interested in rivers as Wordsworth, and in several of his *Hymns*, such as "The Rhine" and "The Migration," he has a great river stand for the life or spiritual history of a nation.

Informing most of these meanings is the river as an image of time itself. According to Plato (*Cratylus* 402a), Heraclitus said that "all things are in process and nothing stays still, and likening existing things to the stream of a river he says that into the same river you could not step twice."

Ovid has a catalogue of rivers in *Met.* 2.239–59. Spenser gives a short catalogue of great rivers, from the Nile to the Amazon (*FQ* 4.11.20–21), followed by a long one of English rivers (4.11.29–47).

See **Fountain, Sea**.

Rook   *see* **Raven**

Rose   There were several varieties of rose in the ancient world, as there are hundreds in the modern, but the rose in poetry has always been red (or "rose") in color, unless otherwise described. "Red as a rose" is the prime poetic cliché, and poets have used every other term for red to describe it, such as Shakespeare's "deep vermilion" (*Sonnets* 98) or the "crimson joy" of Blake's "Sick Rose". The rose blooms in the spring, and does not bloom long; the contrast is striking between its youth in the bud and its full-blown maturity, and again between both these phases and its final scattering of petals on the ground, all in the course of a week or two. It is rich in perfume, which seems to emanate from its dense and delicate folds of petals. It is vulnerable to the cankerworm. And it grows on a plant with thorns. All these features have entered into its range of symbolic uses.

The rose is "the graceful plant of the Muses," according to the Anacreontic Ode 55; indeed Sappho had called the Muses themselves "the roses of Pieria" (frag. 55). So it is only right that the rose has been the favorite flower of poets since antiquity. The most beautiful poems, in fact, were compared to the flower, as when Meleager praises some of Sappho's as roses (in "The Garland"), a metaphor in keeping with the meaning of the word "anthology," which is a gathering of poetic flowers. (See **Flower**.)

Homer does not mention the rose (Greek *rhodon*), but his favorite epithet for Dawn is "rosy-fingered" (*rhododaktylos*). (Sappho also liked "rose" compounds, calling the moon "rosy-fingered" and both Dawn and the Graces "rosy-armed.") The Greek tragedians do not mention the rose, either. But thereafter the rose comes into its own: it is the flower of flowers, their glory, their queen, their quintessence. In Achilles Tatius' novel (2.1), Leucippe sings a song in praise of the rose: "If Zeus had wished to give the flowers a king, he would have named the rose, for it is the ornament of the world, the glory of plants, the eye of flowers, the blush of the meadow…the agent of Aphrodite." Another Anacreontic poem (no. 44) goes on in the same vein: "rose, best of flowers, / rose, darling of the spring, / rose, delight of the gods," and so on. Goethe theorized that the rose was the highest form of flower. Cowper wrote: "Flow'rs by that name promiscuously we call, / But one, the rose, the regent of them all" ("Retirement" 723–24).

Almost any flower can represent a girl, but the rose has always stood for the most beautiful, the most beloved – in many languages "Rose" remains a popular given name – and often for one who is notably young, vulnerable, and virginal. Shakespeare's Laertes, when he sees his sister Ophelia in her madness, cries "O Rose of May!" (*Hamlet* 4.5.158), bringing out not only her uniqueness but the blighting of her brief life. Othello, on the verge of killing Desdemona, thinks of her as a rose which he is about to pluck (*Othello* 5.2.13–16); Orsino tells Viola, "women are as roses, whose fair flower | Being once display'd, doth fall that very hour" (*12N* 2.4.38–39). The French poet Baïf vows, "I will not force the Rose | Who hides in the bosom | Of a tightly closed bud | The beauty of her flower" ("La Rose," in *Livre des Passetems II*).

Ronsard writes, "such a flower only lasts | From morning until evening" (*Odes* 1.17, "A sa maistresse"); Quevedo asks, "What good does it do you, | rosebush, to presume on your good looks, | when no sooner are you born | than you begin to die?" ("Letrilla lirica" 4–7); but its brevity has made it the more cherished. "Loveliest of things are they | On earth that soonest pass away. | The rose that lives its little hour | Is prized beyond the sculptured flower," according to Bryant ("Scene on the Banks of the Hudson"). Lamenting the passing of great Persian kings, Omar Khayyam, in Fitzgerald's famous version, says, "Each Morn a thousand Roses brings, you say; | Yes, but where leaves the Rose of Yesterday? | And this first Summer month that brings the Rose | Shall take Jamshyd and Kaikobad away" (33–36).

A sexual connotation of Greek *rhodon*, the hymen or female genitalia (as in the modern French phrase, "to lose her rose"), was combined with the brevity of the rose-bloom to embody the common ancient theme of *carpe diem* ("seize the day," from Horace 1.11): make the most of your brief time on earth, or your even briefer youth. In another ode Horace urges us to bring wine and perfume and "the too brief blooms of the lovely rose" (2.3.13–14). Anacreon uses rose imagery in his odes on this theme, but it was Ausonius who explicitly equated the brevity of our life with that of the rose. His influential poem *De Rosis Nascentibus* has the much-translated line *Collige, virgo, rosas, dum flos novus et nova pubes* ("Pluck roses, girl, while flower and youth are new" 48); it is interesting that he addresses a virgin, not a boy or man who might pluck her, a displacement not unlike the girl-gathered-while-gathering-flowers motif common in classical poetry. (*See* **Flower**.) Ausonius' symbol is repeated in the bird song in Tasso's *Gerusalemme Liberata* (16.15) – "So in the passing of a day, passes | The flower and the youth [or "green"] of one's mortal life…Gather the rose of Love" – which in turn inspired the song meant to tempt Guyon into the Bower of Bliss in Spenser's *Faerie Queene*: "Ah! see the Virgin Rose, how sweetly shee | Doth first peepe forth with bashfull modestee…Lo! see soone after how she fades and falls away. || So passeth, in the passing of a day, | Of mortall life the leafe, the bud, the flowre;…Gather therefore the Rose whilest yet is prime, | For soone comes age that will her pride deflowre" (2.12.74–75). Ronsard has "Gather from this day the roses of life" (*Second Sonnets for Hélène* 43). The best-known example in English is Herrick's stanza "Gather ye Rose-buds while ye may, | Old Time is still a flying: | And this same flower that smiles today, | To morrow will be dying" ("To the Virgins, to Make Much of Time"). In a poem addressed to a lady, *Perswasions to Love*, Carew offers a variant where the rose is a rose-tree: "The faded Rose each spring, receives | A fresh red tincture on her leaves: | But if your beauties once decay, | You never know a second May" (75–78). In another famous example, Milton's Comus fails to persuade the Lady despite his rosy simile: "If you let slip time, like a neglected rose | It withers on the stalk with languish't head" (*Comus* 743–44).

Lamartine revives the motif in his "Elégie": "Let us gather the rose in the morning of life." And so it goes into at least Victorian times, as we see in William Henley's "O, gather me the rose, the rose, / While yet in flower we find it, / For summer smiles, but summer goes, / And winter waits behind it!"

There have been attempts to Christianize the *carpe diem* theme, whereby time is to be put to good spiritual uses, but many devout Christians have scorned it, taking the rose to be an emblem of the false and fleeting pleasures of this world, especially those of lust. Herbert, however, in "The Rose," offers the flower as an antidote to worldly joys, and in doing so implicitly appeals to the medieval tradition that Christ is the Mystic Rose. In another tradition it is the Virgin Mary who is the Mystic Rose, sometimes a white rose, a rose without thorns. Both associations are derived in part from the "Rose of Sharon" in the Song of Solomon 2.1. The Hebrew word *habasselet*, which is found only there and at Isaiah 35.1 ("the desert shall rejoice, and blossom as the rose" in the AV), is an uncertain flower, probably not a rose, more likely a crocus or daffodil; but the rose was established early as the official translation. Thanks in part to St. Bernard of Clairvaux, the rose (alongside the lily) became Mary's symbolic flower. Mary is "the rose in which the divine word became flesh," as Dante puts it in *Paradiso* 23.73–74. In the fifteenth-century English carol "There is no rose of swich vertu" presses the image: "For in this rose conteined was / Hevene and erthe in litel space."

If red and white roses are distinguished, the red stands for charity or Christian love, the white for virginity. The red rose can also represent Christian martyrdom, red for the love martyrs showed and for the blood they shed. Shelley, writing of atheist martyrs to Christian bigotry, nonetheless preserves the image: "earth has seen / Love's brightest roses on the scaffold bloom" (*Queen Mab* 9.176–77).

The rose had been the flower of Aphrodite (Venus) and Dionysus (Bacchus). The Anacreontic Ode 44 begins, "Let us mix the rose of the Loves [plural of *Eros*] with Dionysus [wine]," and a connection between wine and roses was established that has lasted in common phrases to this day. Horace describes rose petals scattered about in a scene of love-making (1.5.1), and Propertius writes, "I am glad that plenteous Bacchus enchains my mind, / And that I always keep my head in vernal roses" (3.5.21–22). The statue of Venus in Chaucer's *Knight's Tale* wore "A rose gerland, fressh and wel smellynge" on her head (1961). The rose garden, or "bed of roses," is the traditional place of love, as in the medieval French allegorical *Romance of the Rose* (where the lover's goal is to pluck the rosebud), in Walther von der Vogelweide's medieval German poem "Under der Linden," or in Tennyson's *Maud* 1.22. So the transformation of the rose into a symbol of Christian charity or chastity is a good example of the cultural expropriation of pagan culture by the church. As Spenser tells it, God planted the rose in Paradise and then replanted it in earthly stock so women may wear it as a symbol "Of chastity and vertue virginall" (*FQ* 3.5.52–53; cf. "fresh flowring Maidenhead" in the next stanza). While Adam and Eve slept (before the Fall), according to Milton, "the flow'ry roof / Show'r'd Roses, which the Morn repair'd" (*PL* 4.772–73).

The penultimate vision of Dante's *Paradiso* is the gathering of all the redeemed souls into a formation like an "eternal rose" (30.124), white with the light of God's love (31.1).

A familiar proverb, repeated in many poems, is "Roses have thorns" (Shakespeare, *Sonnets* 35) or "ne'er the rose without the thorn" (Herrick, "The Rose"). If you go about plucking roses, gentlemen, you may get pricked. In his famous "Heidenröslein," Goethe presents a dialogue between a boy and a rose: "The boy said, 'I shall pick you, / Little rose on the heath.' / The little rose said, 'I shall prick you / So you'll always think of me.'" Ovid combines the *carpe diem* theme with a reminder of thorns: "While it flowers, use your life; / the thorn is scorned when the rose has fallen" (*Fasti* 5.353–54). Shakespeare's Diana alters the image nicely when she tells Bertram, "when you have our roses, / You barely leave our thorns to prick ourselves" (*AWEW* 4.2.17–18). Blake's "My Pretty Rose Tree" tells how he foreswears a beautiful flower to remain loyal to his rose tree, but nonetheless "my Rose turnd away with jealousy: / And her thorns were my only delight." Thomas Moore's "The Pretty Rose-Tree" is also about promised faithfulness, for "the thorns of thy stem / Are not like them / With which men wound each other." In the Christian transfiguration of the rose, of course, the thorns were omitted: Mary, according to St. Ambrose, is a rose without thorns, as Herrick's "The Rose" tells us. In Paradise, according to Milton, was every sort of flower "and without Thorn the Rose" (*PL* 4.256).

The rose is also renowned for its perfume – "And the rose herself has got / Perfume which on earth is not," as Keats says ("Bards of Passion") – which lingers on after the flower has blown and fallen; perhaps that underlies its use as a symbol of martyrdom. As Shakespeare puts it in Sonnet 54, which is an extended rose simile, "Sweet roses do not so [die to themselves]; / Of their sweet deaths are sweetest odours made." Another form of rose immortality is oil or attar of rose, known to the Greeks and Persians and probably earlier.

The rose has two traditional enemies, both of which are common in poetry: worms and winds. Shakespeare's Sonnet 95 begins, "How sweet and lovely dost thou make the shame / Which, like a canker in the fragrant rose, / Dost spot the beauty of thy budding name!" ("Canker" means "cankerworm"; see also Sonnets 35 and 70.) The loss of Lycidas, Milton writes, is "As killing as Canker to the Rose" (*Lycidas* 45). Herbert likens the Church to a rose, made red by the blood of Christ, and disputes within the Church to a worm ("Church-Rents and Schisms"). Perhaps the most resonant use of the canker image is Blake's "The Sick Rose": "O Rose thou art sick. / The invisible worm, / That flies through the night / In the howling storm: // Has found out thy bed / Of crimson joy: / And his dark secret love / Does thy life destroy." As for howling storms, Keats writes, "love doth scathe / The gentle heart, as northern blasts do roses" (*Endymion* 1.734–35).

In the late nineteenth century was founded the mystical cult of Rosicrucianism, whose central symbols were the rose of perfection or eternity and the cross of time; we may gain the "inconsolable rose," in Villiers de l'Isle-Adam's phrase (in *Axel*), through suffering and renunciation in this world. Yeats adopts this symbolism in the poems in *The Rose* and the stories in *The Secret Rose*: the first poem is addressed "To the Rose upon the Rood [Cross] of Time."

The rose is often associated with the lily, both to express a contrast in colors and to symbolize two usually complementary virtues, love and purity (or virginity): both flowers, of course, are emblems of the Virgin Mary. Tennyson has "My rose of love for ever gone, / My lily of truth and trust" ("The Ancient

Sage" 159–60). Roses and violets are often joined as two flowers of love, both rich in aroma; Keats strikingly assigns the rose to Madeline and the violet to her lover Porphyro (whose name means "purple"): "Into her dream he melted, as the rose / Blendeth its odour with the violet" (*Eve of St. Agnes* 320–21).

The phrase "under the rose," more often used in the Latin *sub rosa*, means "in secret" or "silently." It was supposed to be a practice in ancient Greece and Rome to swear a council to secrecy by placing a rose overhead during its deliberations. Many council chambers in Europe for that reason have roses sculpted into their ceilings.

The Wars of the Roses (1455–85) were fought between the Houses of Lancaster and York. Shakespeare presents Henry VI (of Lancaster) putting on a red rose (*1H6* 4.1.152) and Richard Duke of York announcing he will "raise aloft the milk-white rose" (*2H6* 1.1.252).

S

Sable   *see* **Black**

Saffron   Saffron, made from the dried stigmas of the crocus, has been used since ancient times as a dye, flavoring, perfume, and medicine. It is mentioned once in the Bible (Hebrew *karkôm*) as one of the condiments and incenses of the garden of the beloved in Song of Solomon 4:14. The related Greek word *krokos* referred not only to the flower but to saffron and, more often in classical poetry, to the yellow or orange-yellow color of the dye. It was expensive, like Tyrian purple, and like purple it connoted majesty and rank; it also connoted purity, and was often worn by girls in sacred rituals.

It was particularly associated with Artemis, the protectress of virgins and hunted animals. Because Agamemnon offended her, Artemis demanded the sacrifice of his virgin daughter Iphigenia, who wore a "saffron-dyed robe" at her death (Aeschylus, *Agamemnon* 238). It is also sometimes the color of Bacchus and his (usually female) followers.

In Homer and Virgil, Dawn is saffron-robed (*krokopeplos* in Homer) and saffron-haired, her chariot-wheels are saffron, and so is the bed of Tithonus. (*See* **Dawn**.)

Perhaps because brides often wore it, saffron became the color of the robe of Hymen, god of weddings, as in Ovid, *Met.* 10.1. The chief association of saffron in English poetry is with Hymen: "Hymen, the god of marriage, in a saffron coloured robe" (Jonson, *Hymenaei*, 42–43); "There let Hymen oft appear / In Saffron robe" (Milton, *L'Allegro* 125–26).

Salamander   This small amphibian, according to Pliny, could live inside fire because it was too cold-blooded to be burned (*Natural History* 10.86). A notion also arose that the salamander could extinguish fire as well. Thus it was almost inevitable that it would be recruited into the fire imagery of passionate love. After being both nourished and set afire by glances at his beloved's face, Petrarch reports, "I feed on my death and live in flames, / strange food and wondrous salamander!" (*Rime* 207.38–41). The French King Francis I adopted the salamander surrounded by flames as his emblem, with the motto *Nutrisco et extinguo* ("I feed [on fire] and extinguish it"). After citing this "royal serpent," Scève addresses his mistress: "O would that you were by your cold nature / The Salamander dwelling in my fire! / You would find delicious pasture there / And extinguish my burning passion" ("Sans lésion le Serpent Royal vit"). Robert Browning refers to the king's "Salamander-sign– / Flame-fed creature: flame benign / To itself or, if malign, // Only to the meddling curious," in "Cristina and Monaldeschi" 14–17.

Pope enjoys imagining that when fair ladies die their souls return to their "first elements"; some become earth, some water, some air, while "The Sprights [spirits] of fiery Termagants in Flame / Mount up, and take a *Salamander*'s Name" (*Rape of the Lock* 1.59–60). Keats calls one of his four elemental fairies Salamander in "Song of Four Fairies."

Of the sunken ship *Titanic* Hardy envisages her "Steel chambers, late the pyres / Of her salamandrine fires" ("Convergence of the Twain"). See **Fire**.

Scarlet   As an expensive cloth, and a color derived from costly dyes, scarlet in the Bible is associated with wealth and luxury. David reminds the daughters of Israel that Saul clothed them in scarlet (2 Sam. 1.24), Jeremiah laments that those "brought up in scarlet" now "embrace dunghills" (Lam. 4.5), and Belshazzar announces that whoever interprets the mysterious writing "shall be clothed with scarlet, and have a chain of gold about his neck" (Dan. 5.7). So Chaucer's Wife of Bath's "hosen [stockings] weren of fyn scarlet reed" (*CT* Pro. 456), and Spenser describes some "costly scarlot of great name" (*FQ* 1.12.13).

Its conspicuous brightness makes it appropriate for Isaiah to say, "though your sins be as scarlet, they shall be as white as snow" (Isa. 1.18), and scarlet has become the common color of sin. Shakespeare's Surrey calls Wolsey's ambition "thou scarlet sin" (*H8* 3.2.255); before Wilde's Dorian Gray, "Out of the black cave of Time, terrible and swathed in scarlet, rose the image of his sin" (chap. 18).

The Isaiah passage may have seconded scarlet's aura of luxury in John of Patmos's vision of the woman on a scarlet beast, herself arrayed in purple and scarlet, who is Mystery, Babylon, the Mother of Harlots (Rev. 17.3–5). The "scarlet whore" became the standard term for whatever rich and powerful enemy a Christian wanted to denounce; in English Protestant usage it usually meant the Roman Catholic Church. The "faithlesse Sarazin" (Sans Foy) of Spenser has a woman companion "clad in scarlot red" (1.2.13), who turns out to be the "scarlot whore," Duessa (1.8.29). Scarlet then became associated with real as well as allegorical whores. Hawthorne's Hester Prynne is made to wear a letter A (for "adultery") embroidered in scarlet on her dress (*The Scarlet Letter*).

Scorpion   When Gilgamesh begins his journey to bring back his dead friend Enkidu (in the Babylonian epic of Gilgamesh), he encounters the terrible Scorpion People, who live on the mountain that guards the coming and going of Shamash the sun; they allow him to enter and follow the path of Shamash. Little symbolism survives about these monsters beyond this connection with the sun.

Scorpions are mentioned several times in the Bible as dangerous creatures of the wilderness (e.g., Deut. 8.15, Ezek. 2.6). The plague of locusts prophesied in Revelation will be made worse when they are given the power of scorpions; those men who are not sealed by God will be tormented by them for five months (9.3–5).

Simply because its sting is in its tail, the scorpion became an emblem of fraud or deception. Geryon, the monster that guards the circle of fraud in Dante's *Inferno*, has a tail like a scorpion's (17.27). Following Vincent of Beauvais, Chaucer likens unstable Fortune to "the scorpion so deceyvable, / That flaterest with thyn heed [head] whan thou wolt stynge; / Thy tayl is deeth, thurgh thyn envenymynge" (*Merchant's Tale* 2058–60) (see also *Book of the Duchess* 636–41). Feeling deceived by his son Samson's defeat, Manoa asks why God gave him a son, if the gift should "draw a Scorpion's tail behind?" (Milton, *Samson Agonistes* 360).

Perhaps inspired by Macbeth's cry, "O! full of scorpions is my mind, dear wife!" (3.2.36), some later English poets took scorpions as emblems of remorse. Dryden has Ventidius tell Antony he is "too conscious of your failings; / And, like a scorpion, whipt by others first / To fury, sting yourself in mad revenge" (*All for Love* 1.313–15). "Remorse," according to Cowper, "proves a raging scorpion in his breast" (*Progress of Error* 239–42). Coleridge says "vain regret" has "scorpion stings" (sonnet: "To Rev. Bowles," 1st version, 10). It seems implicit in Shelley: "the sting / Which retributive memory implants / In the hard bosom of the selfish man" (*Queen Mab* 1.173–75).

The legend that when surrounded by fire scorpions commit suicide by stinging themselves is not ancient; it is first reported by Paracelsus. Shelley makes frequent use of it: he predicts, for instance, that the truths that virtuous people speak "Shall bind the scorpion falsehood with a wreath / Of ever-living flame, / Until the monster sting itself to death" (*Queen Mab* 6.36–38). E. B. Browning's heroine remembers a period in her life as "A weary, wormy darkness, spurred i'the flank / With flame, that it should eat and end itself / Like some tormented scorpion" (*Aurora Leigh* 1.220–22). Byron adds this idea to the scorpion as remorse: "The Mind, that broods o'er guilty woes, / Is like the Scorpion girt by fire, / ... / One sad and sole relief she knows, / The sting she nourish'd for her foes" (*Giaour* 422–29).

Sea We are at home on the land. The sea has always been alien and dangerous, and those who have made it a second home have learned special skills and habits. For that very reason the literature of the sea is ancient and vast: from the *Odyssey*, the *Argonautica*, and the story of Jonah through Melville's *Moby-Dick*, London's *The Sea-Wolf*, several novels of Conrad's, Hemingway's *The Old Man and the Sea*, and Patrick O'Brian's recent *Master and Commander* and its sequels. Science fiction is largely derivative of sea stories (Jules Verne providing a link), as the word "spaceship" and "astronaut" (from Greek *nautes*, "sailor") remind us; planets are islands in the sea of space. Among many other things, the sea has symbolized chaos and the bridge among orderly lands, life and death, time and timelessness, menace and lure, boredom and the sublime. Out of this welter of contrary symbols we shall select a few prominent ones.

In Middle Eastern mythology the sea is the primordial element. The Babylonian creation myth *Enuma Elish* posits the male Apsu and the female Tiamat as the parents of the gods; they are "sweet water" (or fresh water) and "bitter water" (salt water), and their union begets the world. Later Marduk slays Tiamat and divides her body, placing half of it in the sky. The creation in Genesis begins with a formless earth covered with water; the "deep" (1.2) is *tehom* in Hebrew, cognate with "Tiamat," and like her it is divided by a "firmament" into two waters (6–8); then comes the emergence of land from the gathering of the lower waters (9–10). The Greek creation story as Hesiod tells it begins with *Chaos* but it is not water; Earth emerges first (*Theogony* 116–17), and later generates Sea (*Pontos*) by herself and Ocean (*Okeanos*) by lying with Heaven (131–33). Ocean is a "perfect river" (242) that surrounds the world. There are two passages in Homer, however, that suggest Ocean is the source of all things: it is called the "begetter" or "origin (*genesis*) of the gods" and the "begetter of all things" (*Iliad* 14.201, 14.246). Plato quotes the former passage twice; he takes Homer to be saying that all things are the offspring of flux and motion (*Theaetetus* 152e). In the first *Iliad* passage Homer includes "Mother Tethys" in parallel to (father) Ocean; in Hesiod she mates with Ocean to produce the rivers and water nymphs (337–70), but here she seems simply a female equivalent of Ocean.

With Tiamat and Tethys, then, we have a "mother sea," a rich mythological element half suppressed by the biblical creation story where a male sky god does everything. This idea also had to contend with the obvious facts that sea water is not drinkable – it is not "living water," in the Hebrew phrase for fresh water (Gen. 26.19; cf. John 4.10) – and that, of course, the sea has claimed countless lives through drowning. An epithet for sea in both Hesiod and Homer is "sterile" or "barren" (though there is some debate about the word). The biblical Flood destroys all life not in the ark, and there is the "Dead Sea" in Palestine. Salvation through Christ is often imagined as rescue from drowning: Christ walks on water, he makes Peter a fisher of men, baptism by immersion is a death and rebirth, and the church is the "antitype" of Noah's ark; when the new heaven and earth come, there will be "no more sea" (Rev. 21.1). Dante, having narrowly escaped the dark wood of sin, likens his state to that of one who "with laboring breath / has just escaped from sea to shore" (*Inferno* 1.22–23). Milton mourns Lycidas, who drowned, but "Sunk though he be beneath the wat'ry floor," he is "mounted high, / Through the dear might of him that walk'd the waves" (167, 172–73). Ancient cosmologies and philosophies and their modern descendants often posited this life as watery, indeed as underwater; the Naasene gnostics considered this mortal world of generation to be a sea into which the divine spark has sunk, while Blake imagines "the sea of Time & Space," beneath which fallen man is "a Human polypus of Death" (*Four Zoas* 56.13,16).

Modern theories of the origin of life restored the sea as its source, but in literature birth is often not far from death. Goethe stages a debate between Thales the "Neptunist" and Anaxagoras the "Vulcanist" (*Faust, II* 7851ff.); Thales wins, and the fiery Homunculus plunges into the Aegean, filled with sea goddesses, to be reborn and evolve. Faust will go on, however, to combat the sea, which "unfruitful itself, pours out unfruitfulness" in floods on the land, by building dikes and channels (10198ff.). Swinburne announces "I will go back to the great sweet mother, / Mother and lover of men, the sea," but it is to lose himself and forget his grief: "Save me and hide me with all thy waves, / Find me one grave of thy thousand graves" ("Triumph of Time" 257–58, 269–70).

A parallel to this pattern is the water cycle: evaporation from the sea creates clouds, which pour down rain, which collects in rivers, which flow into the sea. The older symbolism generally had rivers rising from springs, representing birth, through the widening and slowing course of life, into the sea of death. (*See* **River**.)

The deadliness of the sea sometimes seems the worse for its not being a god, for its blind heedlessness. "Alas! poor boy!" Shelley has a character say, "A wreck-devoted seaman thus might pray / To the deaf sea" (*Cenci* 5.4.41–43). Yeats has the great phrase "the murderous innocence of the sea" ("Prayer for my Daughter" 16).

Writers have nonetheless given the sea a voice, just like babbling or murmuring rivers, usually as heard from shore. Homer's epithet for the sea can scarcely be bettered: *polyphloisbos*, "much-roaring," (e.g., *Iliad* 1.34), which Fitzgerald forgivably overtranslates as "the tumbling clamorous whispering sea." Seas can roar, rage, bellow, pound, and "chide" (Emerson, "Seashore" 1). But even on calm days the repeating sound of waves on the shore may seem to have a message. "Listen!" Arnold enjoins, "you hear the grating roar / Of pebbles which the waves draw back, and fling, / At their return, up the high strand, / Begin, and cease, and then again begin, / With tremulous cadence slow, and bring / The eternal note of sadness in" ("Dover Beach" 9–14). When Tennyson listens to the waves he feels akin to it in his inarticulateness: "Break, break, break, / On thy cold gray stones, O Sea! / And I would that my tongue could utter / The thoughts that arise in me" ("Break, Break, Break"). In different moods Woolf's Mrs. Ramsay finds the sea a mother and a destroyer: "the monotonous fall of the waves on the beach...for the most part beat a measured and soothing tattoo to her thoughts and seemed consolingly to repeat over and over again as she sat with the children the words of some old cradle song, murmured by nature, 'I am guarding you – I am your support,' but at other times...[it] made one think of the destruction of the island and its engulfment in the sea, and warned her whose day had slipped past in one quick doing after another that it was all as ephemeral as a rainbow" (*To the Lighthouse* 1.3).

As the sea has so much to say, it has sometimes stood for great poets. Homer, likened in ancient times to a fountain and a river, was compared to the ocean by Quintilian (*Institutes* 10.1.46). Dante describes Virgil as "the sea of all sense" (*Inferno* 8.7). Byron playfully compares himself to Homer as a war reporter, but concedes, "To vie with thee would be about as vain / As for a brook to cope with ocean's flood" (*Don Juan* 7.638–39). Keats likens his discovery of Chapman's version of Homer to Cortez's discovery of the Pacific ("On First Looking into Chapman's Homer"). (*See* **Fountain, River**.)

The waves are a measure of time. "Like as the waves make toward the pebbled shore, / So do our minutes hasten to their end" (Shakespeare, *Sonnets* 60). "Unfathomable Sea! whose waves are years, / Ocean of time" (Shelley, "Time"). Emily Brontë speaks of "Time's all-severing wave" ("Remembrance" 4). "Consider the sea's listless chime: / Time's self it is, made audible" (D. G.

Rossetti, "Sea-Limits"). So are the tides; indeed "tide" originally meant "time." "The little waves, with their soft, white hands, / Efface the footprints in the sands, / And the tide rises, the tide falls" (Longfellow, "Tide Rises"). But the endless repetitiveness of both of them, and the sheer enormousness of the sea, has made the sea an emblem of infinity and eternity, and as such it both dwarfs our human doings, as Mrs. Ramsay feels, and also lures us as if to a peaceful sleep or death. Tennyson imagines one day putting out to sea on "such a tide as moving seems asleep, / Too full for sound and foam, / When that which drew from out the boundless deep / Turns again home" ("Crossing the Bar"). Mann has Aschenbach sit on the shore gazing out to the Adriatic sea from the Lido as he yields to an infinite longing and dies (*Death in Venice*). Even on an inland hill, thoughts about eternity may summon a metaphorical sea, as Leopardi writes: "So in this / immensity my thoughts are drowned: / and shipwreck is sweet to me in this sea" ("L'Infinito").

A "sea" of something can mean a vast quantity of it, as when Spenser speaks of a "sea of deadly daungers" (*FQ* 1.12.17) or Byron of a "sea of slaughter" (*Don Juan* 7.399). When Hamlet ponders whether "to take arms against a sea of troubles" (3.1.59) he is using "sea" in a similar sense but also evoking an ancient metaphor. Psalm 69 begins, "Save me, O God; for the waters are come into my soul. / I sink in deep mire, where there is no standing; I am come into deep waters, where the floods overflow me." A variant is the sea of stormy passion, which goes back at least to Horace, who pities a boy in love with the experienced Pyrrha; she will overwhelm him with "black winds" as she did Horace, who now stays ashore, having "hung / My dank and dripping weeds / To the stern God of Sea" (1.5., trans. John Milton). Less wise, Petrarch is aboard ship in a storm of sighs, hopes, and desires (*Rime* 189). Sitting on shore, watching the surf, Spenser's Britomart, separated from her knight, complains to the "Huge sea of sorrow, and tempestuous griefe, / Wherein my feeble bark is tossed long, / Far from the hoped haven of relief" (*FQ* 3.4.8). (*See* **Ship**.)

Seasons   "Symbols," Dylan Thomas says, "are selected from the years' / Slow rounding of four seasons' coasts" ("Here in this Spring"). Many of the meanings of the trees and flowers, beasts and birds found in this dictionary depend on their comings and goings at certain seasons of the year. And of course the seasons themselves have long been applied metaphorically to human lives, as we see in this conventional passage from James Thomson's "Winter": "See here thy pictur'd Life; pass some few Years, / Thy flowering Spring, thy Summer's ardent Strength, / Thy sober Autumn passing into Age, / And pale concluding Winter comes at last, / And shuts the Scene" (1029–33).

The ancients did not at first distinguish four seasons. There is some evidence that the oldest Indo-European division was into two, winter and summer, traces of which we find in the English phrases "midwinter" and "midsummer," which refer to the winter solstice (or Christmas) and summer solstice, and the absence of such terms for spring and autumn. We find evidence as well in the use of "winter" and "summer" as synonyms for "year." Juvenal writes of an old man, "Thus many winters and his eightieth solstice he saw" (4.92–93). In the oldest English poetry "winter" is often used in this way: Beowulf held the land "fifty winters" (*Beowulf* 2209); "no man may become wise before he endure / His share of winters in the world" ("The

Wanderer" 64–65). Counting by winters continues into the twentieth century; for example, Yeats advises us "from the fortieth winter" to look on everything in the light of death ("Vacillation" 29). Seemingly absent from Old English, but fairly common later, is "summer" in the same sense; so Shakespeare: "Five summers have I spent in farthest Greece" (CE 1.1.132) and "Till twice five summers have enriched our fields" (R2 1.3.141); and Milton: "Summers three times eight save one / She had told" ("Epitaph on the Marchioness of Winchester" 7–8). "Spring" and "autumn" or "fall" are seldom so used, and then usually in an elaboration of the figure with "winter" or "summer"; e.g., "Four lagging winters and four wanton springs" (R2 1.3.214; see Sonnets 104). Ovid does have Tiresias spend "seven autumns" as a woman (Met. 3.326–27), and "five autumns" pass before Procne visits her sister (6.439).

Homer and Hesiod generally recognize three seasons, spring, summer, and winter. In the Homeric Hymn to Demeter, Demeter tells her daughter Persephone she must "go to the depths of the earth, / to dwell there a third part of the seasons every year, / but two of them with me and the other immortals" (398–400). In the Odyssey, however, Homer distinguishes "summer" from the latter part of it (e.g., 12.76). Alcman was the first to list the four seasons, but the passage where he does so (quoted by Athenaeus) reflects the older tripartite division: "and he created three seasons, summer and winter and autumn the third, and the fourth the spring, when things grow but there is not enough to eat." Four became the norm, though three remained common. Shelley, a good classicist, can write in Epipsychidion of "the seasons three," though it is a little surprising that he names them as spring, autumn, and winter (364–66). Ovid names the four seasons and applies them, like Thomson many centuries later, to the ages of human life (Met. 15.199–213). Though the Athenian or Attic year began with summer, as the Alcman passage suggests, the Roman year (originally) began with spring in March, a sequence that lends itself better to the phases of human life. In England the year officially began in March until 1753: "the month in which the world bigan, / That highte March, whan God first maked man" (Chaucer, Nun's Priest's Tale 3187–88).

The Greek word for season, hora, borrowed by Latin and passed through French into English as "hour," was personified in various ways. In Homer the Horai guard the gates of the sky (e.g., Iliad 5.749–51); in Hesiod they are the daughters of Zeus and Themis (Theogony 901); in both Hesiod and the Homeric Hymns they are associated with the three Graces, though they are not themselves enumerated. Hora in both Greek and Latin had a broader range of meaning than "season": it could also mean a year, a day, or a time of day ("hour"). In Attic cult two Horai were named Thallo and Karpo, not summer and winter but spring ("I bloom") and autumn or late summer ("I bear fruit"). Ovid mentions the Horae but distinguishes them from the four seasons (Met. 2.26).

In Hellenistic times the description of the seasons or times (ekphrasis chronon) became a set theme in poetry and rhetoric. In ancient paintings and in literature at least as old as Ovid we find Spring holding flowers, usually as a young woman and often identified as Flora or Venus; Summer with a sickle and ears or sheaf of grain, often taken as Ceres; Autumn with grapes and vine leaves, taken as Bacchus; and Winter shivering and thickly clothed, often an old man, sometimes Boreas or Vulcan. The most frequently personified season is Spring; Ovid explains that the Greek maiden Chloris, raped and married by Zephyrus (the west wind), is the same as Roman Flora (*Fasti* 5.197ff.). In the *Metamorphoses* Ovid offers four brief personifications (2.27–30), Lucretius describes them at slightly greater length at 5.737–47, while Horace portrays their march through the year as a reminder that death awaits us (*Odes* 4.7).

Among many poetic descriptions of the seasons in English one of the best known is Spenser's, who gives a stanza each to "lusty Spring, all dight in leaves of flowres," "jolly Sommer, being dight / In a thin silken cassock coloured greene," "Autumne all in yellow clad," and "Winter cloathed all in frize" (*FQ* 7.7.28–31), and then twelve more to the months, starting with March (32–43), one to day and night, one to the Hours, and one to Life and Death (44–46). Thomson's *The Seasons* is perhaps the culmination of this descriptive genre in English. The four seasons were an equally popular theme in painting, sculpture, and music (e.g., Vivaldi's *The Seasons*).

In English the terms for summer and winter have remained constant, but those for spring and autumn have varied a good deal. Beginning with Old English (and setting aside spelling differences), for spring we find "lencten" (or "lenten"), "new time," "prime time," "first summer," "springing time," "spring of the year," "springtime," and "springtide"; for autumn or fall we find "harvest" and "fall of the leaf."

See **April, Autumn, Spring, Summer, Winter**.

Seed   "Seed" (Hebrew *zera*) is the standard biblical term for "offspring" or "progeny." "Unto thy seed will I give this land," the Lord promises Abraham (Gen. 12.7; cf. 13.15, 15.18, etc.). The phrases "seed of Abraham" or "Abraham and his seed" occur four times in the Old Testament and nine times in the New. "Fear not: for I am with thee: I will bring thy seed from the east, and gather thee from the west" (Isa. 43.5). On the "seed of Abraham" formula, Paul makes the hair-splitting comment, "Now to Abraham and his seed [Greek *sperma*] were the promises made. He saith not, And to seeds, as of many; but as of one, And to thy seed, which is Christ" (Gal. 3.16). The Authorized Version rightly does not substitute "offspring" or "children" for the many instances of "seed," for sometimes the seed is literally semen (from Latin *semen*, "seed"), as when Onan spills his seed on the ground: "And Onan knew that the seed should not be his [it would be his brother's, whose widow Onan was expected to marry]; and it came to pass, when he went in unto his brother's wife, that he spilled it on the ground, lest that he should give seed to his brother" (Gen. 38.9). The concreteness of "seed" is never far from its other meaning, as indeed God's promise of "land" for Abraham's seed suggests; we may also have here the reason for the rite of circumcision, the identifying mark of Abraham's seed on the organ that produces it.

In classical literature "seed" could also mean "offspring" but it more often had the slightly different sense of "race" or "lineage." Oedipus says he would like to see his seed (ancestry) (Sophocles, *Oedipus Tyrannus* 1077); the chorus asks him what seed he comes from on his father's side (*Oedipus at Colonus* 214). Agamemnon's father Atreus is "he who sowed you" (*Ajax* 1293). Cicero uses the phrase *Romani generis et seminis*, "of the race and seed of the Romans" (*Philippics*

4.13). Lucretius and Virgil both use "seed" for the "brood" of a lion (3.741–42, *Georgics* 2.151–52). Rejected by women he desired, Villon decides "I must plant in other fields" (*The Legacy* 31).

Spenser is fond of such phrases as "sonnes of mortall seed," i.e., ordinary mortal men (*FQ* 1.7.8), and "thy race and royall sead" (3.2.33). The term continues into recent times, mainly in religious contexts, as in R. Browning's line, "Adam's sin made peccable his seed" (*Ring and Book* 8.1425).

In classical literature also "seed" could mean "germ," "spark," or "element." The only instance of *sperma* in Homer's epics is the "seed of fire" (a burning log buried in ashes for the next day) in a simile for the way the naked Odysseus buries himself in leaves (*Odyssey* 5.490); Pindar also has "seed of flame" (*Olymp.* 7.48). Lucan has the line, "Quickly let him [Caesar] carry off the evil seeds of cursed war" (3.150). Anaxagoras uses *sperma* for the basic elements or ingredients of all things, and it comes to mean "element" in the Epicurean system as well (e.g., Lucretius 1.501).

In his conversation with Phaedrus, Socrates plants a fruitful metaphor, comparing the dispensing of knowledge with the planting of seeds by a careful farmer. The unserious man will write in ink, "sowing words through his pen," but the serious man will select a soul of the right type and "plant and sow words of knowledge" by conversation, words which contain a seed of new words (Plato, *Phaedrus* 276b–77a). The most famous version of this metaphor is Jesus' Parable of the Sower, in which a man casts seeds on various grounds; some seeds grow and some do not; Jesus explains that the seed is the word of the kingdom and the grounds are different sorts of hearers (Matt. 13.3–23). A related parable is that of the Mustard Seed (Matt. 13.31–32). Partial precedents may be found in the Old Testament, e.g., speech is like dew or rain (Deut. 32.2), or like rain or snow that will make the earth bring forth and "give seed to the sower" (Isa. 55.10–11).

Augustine develops the image when he speaks dismissively of his father's attempt to have him "cultured," "though his 'culture' really meant a lack of cultivation from you, God, the one true and good landlord and farmer of this field of yours, my heart" (*Confessions* 2.3, trans. Warner). Our words "seminar" and "seminary" denote places where a student's mind is implanted with seeds of knowledge (Latin *seminarium*, "plantation," from *semen*); we say knowledge is "disseminated," and we "conceive" an idea. Novalis titles his Romantic manifesto *Bluthenstaub* ("Pollen"), and in the epigraph writes, "Friends, the soil is poor, we must richly scatter / Seeds to produce even a modest harvest" (trans. O'Brien). Wordsworth is grateful that "Fair seed-time had my soul, and I grew up / Fostered alike by beauty and by fear" (1805 *Prelude* 1.305–06). Emerson imagines the spring as renovating the earth, "Planting seeds of knowledge pure, / Through earth to ripen, through heaven endure" ("May-Day" 467–68).

The Greek myth of Persephone (Latin Proserpina) seems to have something to do with seed, as Cicero among others claimed (*Nature of the Gods* 2.66): she must spend a third of the year with Hades, and returns in the spring. A modern personification of seed is Burns's "John Barleycorn," which takes him through burial, resurrection, harvest, soaking, threshing, roasting, milling, and distilling into whiskey.

See **Plow.**

Serpent   All cultures that know them have found serpents fascinating. Indeed serpents are said to "fascinate" their prey, cast a spell on them with a look; human cultures seem to have fallen under their sway. Snakes can be extremely dangerous, being both venomous and "subtle" or sneaky; they strike without warning from grass or coverts; they can look beautiful in their glittering multi-colored skin; they creep on their bellies but can rear up; they shed their skin and seem rejuvenated; they sidle or meander; and in legend at least some can fly, some swallow their own tails, and some have a head at each end. The symbolic possibilities are rich and often ambiguous.

The most important serpent for western literature, of course, is the one in the garden of Eden, who persuaded Eve to eat of the tree of knowledge of good and evil and thus brought about the expulsion of Adam and Eve from the garden and the advent of death. He was "more subtil than any beast of the field" and simple Eve was no match for him (Gen. 3.1–7). St. Paul worries that "as the serpent beguiled Eve through his subtilty," the minds of Christians might be "corrupted from the simplicity that is in Christ" (2 Cor. 11.3). The serpent was thus connected with knowledge or wisdom, though a false or even fatal knowledge, and with human mortality. Behind these connections may lie the notion that serpents are themselves immortal because they shed their skins; their wisdom might be due to their great age or to their intimate relation with the earth (they even look wise). In the Sumerian/Babylonian Gilgamesh epic, a snake denies Gilgamesh the plant of immortality by snatching it, eating it, and then shedding its skin; a structuralist would call this a variant of the Eden story. As for wisdom, despite the serpent's evil connotations, Christ calls on his followers to be "wise as serpents" (Matt. 10.16).

In the Christian scheme the serpent of Eden became "the great dragon," "that old serpent, called the Devil, and Satan, which deceiveth the whole world" (Rev. 12.9); "Oure firste foo, the serpent Sathanas," in Chaucer's phrase (*Prioress's Tale* 1748); "The infernal Serpent" of Milton (*PL* 1.34). Goethe's devil Mephistopheles invokes "my aunt, the famous snake" (*Faust I* 335). The "dreadful Dragon" that Spenser's Redcrosse Knight vanquishes after a terrible battle (*FQ* 1.11.4–55) is the dragon of Revelation, and the Knight reenacts the victory of Michael and the angels (Rev. 12.7).

The older belief that serpents are wise, and not just subtle or cunning, was revived in the gnostic sects of snake-worshippers, known as the Naasenes (from Hebrew *nahas*, "serpent") and Ophites (from Greek *ophis*, "serpent"). They seem to have believed that the serpent in the garden was trying to bring true wisdom and divinity to Adam and Eve, who were trapped in the fallen world by a wicked creator god; as the embodiment of *gnosis* or wisdom the serpent descends again as Christ. Something of this inversion of Christian symbols may be found in Shelley, who stages an elaborate allegorical contest between "An Eagle and a Serpent wreathed in flight": the Serpent, "the great Spirit of Good did creep among / The nations of mankind, and every tongue / Cursed and blasphemed him as he passed; for none / Knew good from evil" (*Laon and Cythna* 193, 373–76). Keats's poem *Lamia* might be taken as another swerve from orthodoxy, for the lovely serpent-woman whom Lycius loves is defeated by a cold skeptical philosopher; the wisdom of this serpent is imagination and love.

Another biblical serpent is the one Moses made out of brass at God's command, the sight of which cured the Israelites of snakebite (Num. 21.8–9). Much later this piece of magical homeopathy did not sit well with Hezekiah, who destroyed it (2 Kgs 18.4). Nonetheless John cites it as a type of Christ crucified, faith in whom cures us of all ills (John 3.14–15).

"Serpent" comes from Latin *serpens, serpent-*, from a root meaning "crawl" or "creep." A meandering river could be called "a serpent river" (Jonson, "To Robert Wroth" 18) without evoking Satan. The river in London's Hyde Park is called The Serpentine, as several Greek rivers were called Ophis or Drakon. When Milton describes the early rivers of creation "With serpent error wandering" (*PL* 7.302), however, it is hard to rule out suggestions of the Fall. If to sin is to wander in error (Latin *errare* means "wander"), a snake's sidling, meandering motion seconds its evil associations.

In Homer snakes are often omens. The Greeks recall a "great sign": a snake (*drakon*) devours eight sparrow nestlings and their mother, and the seer interprets it to mean that nine years must pass before they sack Troy (*Iliad* 2.301–30); it is as if the snake symbolizes time, or eternity, which swallows the bird-years. Another omen is the appearance of the eagle with a serpent in its talons; the serpent stings the bird, who lets it drop; the Trojan seer takes the portent to mean they will not drive the Greeks away (12.200–29).

A similar image grips Orestes in Aeschylus' *Choephoroe*. He sees himself and his sister as fledglings of eagle-Agamemnon, who was killed by a deadly viper (*echidna*), Clytemnestra (246–59). The imagery continues in the play: the viper stands for underhand domestic treachery, as it does in Sophocles' *Antigone*, where Creon denounces Ismene as "a viper lurking in the house" (531). Close to this sense of betrayal is Aesop's fable of "The Snake and the Rustic": the peasant rescues a frozen snake by placing it in his bosom, but when it thaws out it bites him. "You are nourishing a viper in your bosom" (Petronius, *Satyricon* 77) became proverbial: "O familier foo,...// Lyk to the naddre [adder] in bosom sly untrewe" (Chaucer, *Merchant's Tale* 1784–86); "O villains, vipers,...// Snakes, in my heart-blood warmed, that sting my heart!" (Shakespeare, *R2* 3.2.129–31). Racine's Oreste warns Pyrrhus against raising the son of Hector in his home "lest this serpent reared in your bosom / Punish you one day for having saved him" (*Andromaque* 1.2.167–68). Dryden's Antony accuses Cleopatra and Dolabella of being "serpents / Whom I have in my kindly bosom warmed, / Till I am stung to death" (*All for Love* 4.1.464–66). This snake thus becomes the emblem of ingratitude. "How sharper than a serpent's tooth it is," Lear cries, "To have a thankless child" (1.4.288–89).

The snake in the bosom grew more internal and metaphorical until it could represent an entirely mental pain or poison. In Envy's bosom, according to Spenser, "secretly there lay / An hatefull Snake" (*FQ* 1.4.31), while Malbecco, followed by jealousy and scorn, was "So shamefully forlorne of womankynd, / That, as a Snake, still lurked in his wounded mynd" (3.10.55). Cowper seems to echo Milton on rivers as he begins his "Progress of Error" by asking the Muse to sing how "The serpent error twines round human hearts" (4). "Every mortal," says Chénier, "hides in his heart, even from his own eyes, / Ambition, the insidious serpent" ("Le Jeu de Paume" st. 15).

The most common snake in the mind or heart since the Romantics, at least, is remorse or guilt. Coleridge addresses a dissolute man who gaily laughs during nightly orgies "while thy remembered Home / Gnaws like a viper at thy secret heart!" ("Religious Musings" 285–86); later he dismisses his own "viper thoughts" of remorse in "Dejection" (94). Wordsworth writes of a man suffering from "the stings of viperous remorse" (1850 *Prelude* 9.576). Shelley imagines a bloated vice-ridden king trying to sleep, but "conscience, that undying serpent, calls / Her venomous brood to their nocturnal task" (*Queen Mab* 3.61–62). Pushkin's Eugene Onegin is "gnawed by the snake of memory and repentance" (1.46); Pushkin himself, in the darkness, feels "the bite of all the burning serpents of remorse" ("Remembrance"). (*See* **Worm**.)

Homer compares Paris' sudden fear at the sight of Menelaus to that of a man who comes upon a snake and suddenly steps back "and the shivers come over his body, / and he draws back and away, cheeks seized with green pallor" (*Iliad* 3.33–35, trans. Lattimore; see Virgil, *Aeneid* 2.379–81). Half a line of Virgil's, "a cold snake lurks in the grass" (*Eclogues* 3.93), has led to a proverbial phrase. Fortuna, according to Dante's Virgil (who quotes himself), shifts the world's goods about according to her judgment, "which is hidden like a snake in grass" (*Inferno* 7.84). Spenser's Despair comes "creeping close, as Snake in hidden weedes" (1.9.28). This image merges with the biblical account of the subtle serpent in the garden, and with the traitor cherished in one's home, to yield the symbolism of King Hamlet's murder. The Ghost tells his son "'Tis given out that, sleeping in my orchard, / A serpent stung me" (1.5.35–36); young Hamlet has already felt that the world is "an unweeded garden / That grows to seed; things rank and gross in nature / Possess it merely" (1.2.135–37); the serpent turns out to be the king's brother. (*See* **Garden**.)

The Greek word for the slough or skin of a snake, which it casts in the spring, was *geras*, which also meant "old age." When Pyrrhus the son of Achilles leads the final assault on Troy, "he is like a snake that, fed on poisonous plants / and swollen underground all winter, now / his slough cast off, made new and bright with youth, / uncoils his slippery body to the light" (*Aeneid* 2.471–74, trans. Mandelbaum); he is his father reborn. Spenser imitates this passage in his account of a knight who fights with newborn strength after being wounded, "Like as a Snake, whom wearie winters teene [affliction] / Hath worne to nought, now feeling summers might, / Casts off his ragged skin and freshly doth him dight" (4.3.23). Shelley concludes *Hellas* with a chorus singing of hope for a new world: "The world's great age begins anew, / The golden years return, / The earth doth like a snake renew / Her winter weeds outworn" (1060–63). Saying "Farewell to Florida" as he sails for his New England home, Stevens urges his ship on: "Go on, high ship, since now, upon the shore, / The snake has left its skin upon the floor. // . . . and the past is dead."

Stories of the foundation of a settlement or city sometimes include the slaying of a monstrous serpent or dragon. Cadmus slays one at the site of Thebes and sows his men with its seeds (told by Ovid, *Met.* 3.28–130); later he is himself tranformed into a snake (Euripides, *Bacchae* 1330; *Met.* 4.563–614). The cliché of the damsel in distress from a dragon rescued by a knight goes back at least to the story of Perseus and Andromeda (*Met.* 4.614–803). Every hero has to slay a dragon, it seems: Heracles (the Lernaean Hydra), St. George, Siegfried, Beowulf, Orlando (in Ariosto's *Orlando Furioso*), and the Redcross Knight, to name a few.

There are other snaky creatures in classical legend, such as the Medusa, one of the Gorgons, who had hair made of snakes. The Furies were similar ladies: as Orestes describes the "Eumenides" (Furies) who come to avenge his mother, "they come like gorgons, they / wear robes of black, and they are wreathed in a tangle / of snakes" (*Choephoroe* 1048–50, trans. Lattimore). The best-known Fury is Allecto, whom Juno summons to start a war between the Latins and Aeneas' Trojans. She casts a serpent into Queen Amata's breast and then inflames Turnus by throwing a torch into his (*Aeneid* 7.349–56, 445–57). She becomes a stock figure of terror and vengeance, as we hear from the lips of Shakespeare's Pistol: "Rouse up revenge from ebon den with fell Alecto's snake, / For Doll is in [prison]" (*2H4* 5.5.37–38).

The infant Heracles strangled two serpents in his cradle (see Theocritus, *Idyll* 24). Virgil's brief reference to this tale in the *Aeneid* (8.288–89) is assimilated into a larger pattern of snake pairs: the two serpents who strangle Laocoon (representing the two Atreidae, who will sack Troy), the two snakes who stand out on Allecto's head as she incites Turnus, and Cleopatra's two asps. The French revolutionary republic adopted Hercules, the people's hero, as its emblem; Wordsworth recounts the defeat of the Austrian and Prussian troops in France: "the invaders fared as they deserved: / The herculean Commonwealth had put forth her arms, / And throttled with an infant godhead's might / The snakes about her cradle" (1805 *Prelude* 10.361–64).

Perhaps because they seem to renew themselves, serpents were sometimes held to have the power to heal. Apollo the healer god was associated with serpents, and so was Asclepius/Aesculapius; the staff of the latter, with a serpent around it, is the symbol adopted by the modern medical profession. A similar staff, with two snakes twined around it, is the caduceus of Hermes/Mercury, with which he tames Furies and conducts the shades of the dead to the underworld. Tennyson puts it metonymically: Persephone's eyes "oft had seen the serpent-wanded power / Draw downward into Hades with his drift / Of flickering spectres" ("Demeter and Persephone" 25–27).

The amphisbaena is an interesting snake. Its first appearance comes in a speech of Cassandra's in the *Agamemnon*; she calls Clytemnestra an "amphisbaena" with perhaps only the sense of treacherous "viper" (1233). But it was thought to have a head at both ends, making it duplicitous or at least unpredictable. Lucan includes it among many other serpents as "dangerous Amphisbaena, which moves towards both its heads" (9.719). The Spirit of the Hour in Shelley's *Prometheus* tells how his steeds will cease from toil (time will stop) but a sculpture will remain of his chariot and horses "Yoked to it by an amphisbaenic snake," the snake without a direction (like time), and thus a symbol of timelessness (3.4.119).

An old symbol of eternity, apparently going back to Egypt, is the ouroboros (or uroboros), the snake with its tail in its mouth. It appears on the coffin of Clarissa Harlowe: "The principal device...is a crowned Serpent, with its tail in its mouth, forming a ring, the emblem of Eternity" (Richardson, *Clarissa*, 3rd edn., vol. 7 letter 82). Shelley evokes it as the "vast snake Eternity" (*Daemon of the World* 100). Frost's character Job speaks of "The serpent's tail stuck down the serpent's throat, / Which is the symbol of eternity / And also of the way all things come round" ("A Masque of Reason" 340–42). In Yeats's eternity: "There all the serpent-tails are bit" ("There," in "Supernatural Songs").

Seven

Lucan gives a catalog of horrible snakes in Libya (9.700–33), which is echoed and outdone by Dante (*Inferno* 24.82–90, 25.94ff.).

Seven *see* **Number**

Sewing and quilting "The works of women are symbolical," Elizabeth Barrett Browning writes. "We sew, sew, prick our fingers, dull our sight, / Producing what? A pair of slippers, sir…" (*Aurora Leigh* 1.456–58). In countless works of literature, as in life, women's distinctive labor is stitching, darning, knitting, embroidering, etc., if it is not the more fundamental labor of spinning and weaving. Where it rises to thematic importance, it is often seen as emblematic of the confinement, if not the enslavement, of women to endless tedious tasks, as it is for Aurora Leigh, who escapes it first by taking walks and then by writing poetry. It may be used as an expression or metonym of the difference between two female characters, as for instance Maggie Tulliver in George Eliot's *The Mill on the Floss* has learned only plain hemming while Lucy Deane can do pretty embroidery. But it may turn into an inward escape from confinement or source of self-esteem, as it does for Hawthorne's Hester Prynne, whose needlework gains her respect in town (*The Scarlet Letter*), or for Celie in Walker's *The Color Purple*, who sews clothing and curtains for others and gains economic independence through her skill.

Quilting may be emblematic of social integration, both because it creates a large and often beautiful object out of many little fragments and because they are sometimes made collectively by women at quilting bees. In Steinbeck's *Grapes of Wrath* the communal spirit of quilt-making contrasts with the isolation of the individual. Aunt Mehetabel, the mouselike old maid who does much of the drudgery of the family in Canfield Fisher's story "The Bedquilt," slowly grows in importance and esteem as her genius for quilting becomes manifest and she wins first prize for her quilt at the county fair. Not only quilting but any needlework might connote social unifying; Woolf's Mrs. Dalloway takes a little time from her busy day planning her party to mend her dress: she collects the folds together with needle and thread as she gathers her friends at the party.

Any of this needlework may become a metaphor for telling stories or writing poems, as both spinning and weaving have done. Dickinson's poem "Don't put up my Thread and Needle" (#617) seems to be an implicit vehicle for the subtle craft, even perfection, of poetry. Aunt Mehetabel felt "the supreme content of an artist who has realized his ideal." The drab quilt with two "wild" orange patches in Morrison's *Beloved* may at first symbolize life in the household but by the end it seems to suggest the nonlinear plot of the novel itself with its gathering of fragments. Though women writers have recently enriched this symbolic pattern, it may be traced back to the Greek word *rhapsodos*, the "rhapsode" or reciter of poetry, which is a compound of *rhapt-* "stitch" and *ode*, "ode" or "song"; a rhapsode stitches together words to make a song. Pindar has "bards stitching words" (*Nem.* 2.2). Our word "rhapsody" has entirely lost its link to sewing or weaving or labor of any sort.

See **Weaving and Spinning.**

Sheep   For thousands of years sheep-raising was the primary industry of the hilly regions of the Mediterranean lands, so it is not surprising that imagery of sheep and shepherds permeates biblical and classical literature. It was only slightly less important in several western European regions; as late as 1750 woollen goods made up half the value of all British exports. Many current English phrases and proverbs, some of biblical or classical origin, testify to the continuing presence of the world of sheep in our culture: we count sheep to fall asleep, we may be fleeced of our possessions, we beware of a wolf in sheep's clothing, someone is a black sheep in the family, babies are innocent lambs, and so on.

"Sheep" is the generic term in English. The male is a ram, the female a ewe, the young a lamb. A ram, especially if castrated, may be called a wether (as in "bell-wether"). A new-born lamb was until recently called a yeanling or eanling, from the verb "yean" or "ean," which is related to "ewe"; see Shakespeare, *MV* 1.3.79, 87, for "eanling" and "eaning time." A newly weaned lamb is called a weanling. Sheep are herded in a flock, and sometimes kept in a sheepfold, sheepcote, or sheeppen. To fold is to shut sheep in the fold; to unfold is to lead them out. "And sheep unfolded with the rising sun / Heard the swains shout and felt their freedom won," writes John Clare ("The Mores" 27–28). "The Star that bids the Shepherd fold" (Milton, *Comus* 93) is the evening star (Vesper or Hesperus), called the "folding star" in Collins's "Ode to "Evening" 21 and Wordsworth's *Evening Walk* 280, while "th'unfolding star" that "calls up the shepherd" (Shakespeare, *MM* 4.2.203) is the morning star (Lucifer or Phosphorus). (*See* **Star**.)

The Old Testament is filled with sheep metaphors. "I saw all Israel scattered upon the hills, as sheep that have not a shepherd" (1 Kgs 22.17). "All we like sheep have gone astray" (Isa. 53.6). "My people hath been lost sheep: their shepherds have caused them to go astray" (Jer. 50.6). But the 23rd Psalm reminds us that "The Lord is my shepherd; I shall not want. / He maketh me to lie down in green pastures" (1–2), while the 80th begins, "Give ear, O Shepherd of Israel, thou that leadest Joseph like a flock."

The New Testament makes Jesus Christ the shepherd of Israel. "I am the good shepherd: the good shepherd giveth his life for the sheep," unlike the "hireling" who flees at the sight of a wolf (John 10.11–16); "My sheep hear my voice, and I know them, and they follow me" (10.27). Christ is particularly sent "unto the lost sheep of the house of Israel" (Matt. 15.24), and tells a parable of the shepherd who leaves his ninety-nine sheep to find the one in a hundred that is lost (Luke 15.4–7). In one of his appearances after the resurrection, Jesus tells his disciples to "Feed my sheep" (John 21.15–17): they are to become the shepherds of the endangered flock of Christians.

This metaphor remains in Christian churches today. Christians are a flock or congregation (from Latin *grex*, "flock" or "herd"), their minister may be called a pastor (Latin for "shepherd"; cf. English "pasture"), and if they have a bishop he may carry a shepherd's crook or crosier. "Perhaps the use of this particular convention," Northrop Frye writes (*Anatomy of Criticism* 143), "is due to the fact that, being stupid, affectionate, gregarious, and easily stampeded, the societies formed by sheep are most like human ones." But Dante has a profounder meditation on the sheeplike character of the true Christian in a wonderful simile: "Even as sheep that move, first one, then two, / then three, out of the fold – the others also / stand, eyes and muzzles lowered, timidly; / and what the first sheep does, the others do, / and if it halts, they huddle close behind, / simple and quiet and not knowing why: / so, then, I saw those spirits in the front / of that flock favored by good fortune move – / their looks were modest; seemly, slow, their walk" (*Purgatorio* 3.79–87, trans. Mandelbaum). He calls both the Baptistry of San Giovanni (St. John) and the city of Florence a "sheepfold" (*ovile*) (*Paradiso* 16.25, 25.5–6).

Christ's denunciation of "hireling" shepherds also continues in Dante: he calls Clement V a "lawless shepherd" (*Inferno* 19.83), for example, and in a variant of the wolf in sheep's clothing he denounces "rapacious wolves / clothed in the cloaks of shepherds" (*Paradiso* 27.55–56; cf. 9.132). Milton in *Lycidas* has St. Peter denounce the false shepherds that "for their bellies' sake, / Creep and intrude and climb into the fold"; they are "Blind mouths! that scarce themselves know how to hold / A Sheep-hook," and they leave their sheep hungry, infected by disease, and prey to the wolf (113–29).

Kings have been called "shepherd of the people" in many cultures since ancient Egypt. In the Babylonian epic of *Gilgamesh*, Gilgamesh the king is the "Shepherd of Uruk." "Shepherd of the people" is a frequent epithet of Agamemnon in Homer's *Iliad*. Also in the *Iliad* is a strangely effective simile that likens the Trojan army clamoring for battle to a flock of milk-swollen ewes bleating incessantly when they hear their lambs (4.333–35). In *Beowulf* the word *hyrde* ("herd," i.e., "shepherd") is a synonym for *cyning* ("king").

The classical tradition of pastoral poetry, hinted at in Homer but generally taken to date from Theocritus in the third century BC, is based on an idealized and simplified version of the life of shepherds and goatherds. Pastoral literature is no longer popular, but for over two thousand years the greatest poets, playwrights, and even novelists used the pastoral mode for elegy, comedy, tragedy, romance, and satire. Two of Shakespeare's plays, for example, are pastoral: *As You Like It* and *The Winter's Tale*. This classical tradition could combine with the Christian, as it does in the passage just quoted from *Lycidas*, Milton's pastoral elegy.

Another metaphor in the New Testament combines uneasily with that of the shepherd: Jesus as the Lamb. In Exodus 12 God institutes the ceremony of Passover (Hebrew *pesach*), which requires each household to sacrifice a lamb: "your lamb shall be without blemish, a male of the first year" (5). The Last Supper was the meal (*seder*) of the first night of Passover, and the Crucifixion then seemed a sacrifice of a human lamb for the salvation of his household. John the Baptist anticipates the events of Easter when he greets Jesus by saying, "Behold the Lamb of God [Greek *ho amnos tou theou*, Latin *agnus dei*], which taketh away the sin of the world" (John 1.29). John of Patmos constantly calls Christ the Lamb (Greek *to arnion*) in his vision of the Second Coming. The faithful "have washed their robes, and made them white in the blood of the Lamb" (Rev. 7.14) and they are invited to "the marriage supper of the Lamb" (19.9). "Lamb" in Revelation becomes a name or title that loses its connection to real lambs: John even speaks, absurdly, of "the wrath of the Lamb" (6.16).

Sheep were regularly sacrificed in Greek and Latin culture as well. The ram was particularly offered to Aphrodite. Lambs are sacrificed several times in Homer's two epics.

The traditional enemy of sheep, and especially lambs, is the wolf. "Till the wolf and the lamb be united" seems to have been a Greek equivalent to "never" (Aristophanes, *Peace* 1076). But Isaiah memorably imagines a time when the land is restored to the Lord's favor: "The wolf shall also dwell with the lamb, and the leopard shall lie down with the kid; and the calf and the young lion and the fatling together; and a little child shall lead them" (11.6). To leave someone behind "as a sheep among wolves" was also proverbial in Greek (e.g., Herodotus 4.149). "Baneful to folds is the wolf," is Virgil's succinct if obvious comment (*Eclogues* 3.80). Shakespeare's Cassius comments on Julius Caesar's tyranny: "I know he would not be a wolf / But that he sees the Romans are but sheep" (1.3.104–05). Jesus' use of the metaphor to his disciples, "Behold, I send you forth as sheep in the midst of wolves" (Matt. 10.16), has had a long influence, notably in Silone's novel *Bread and Wine*. (*See* **Wolf**.) So also has Jesus' prophecy of Judgment Day, when the Son of Man shall separate the nations "as a shepherd divideth his sheep from the goats: / And he shall set the sheep on his right hand, but the goats on the left"; the sheep shall be saved and the goats damned (Matt. 25.32–33).

In English poetry adjectives such as "harmless," "humble," and "simple" got attached to "sheep" and "lambs" – e.g., "harmless sheep" in Shakespeare's *3H6* 5.6.8 and "harmless Race" in Thomson's "Summer" 388 – but one adjective whose meaning has since changed was once the distinctive epithet: "silly." Sometimes found in the form "seely," its oldest sense is "blissful" and "blessed" (cf. modern German *selig*, "blessed") and by extension "innocent," "harmless," and "simple," then "pitiable" and "helpless." It is the perfect epithet of Christians, and hence of sheep. Spenser has "silly/seely sheep/lamb" about ten times, and "silly/seely shepherd" twice. In Shakespeare we hear of "shepherds looking on their silly sheep" (*3H6* 2.5.43) and "silly lamb(s)" (*Venus* 1098, *Lucrece* 167). The phrase was so well established by Shakespeare's day that his comic characters can play on it in their badinage: "A silly answer, and fitting well a sheep" *2GV* 1.1.81). Milton imagines the unsuspecting shepherds on the first Christmas: "Perhaps their loves, or else their sheep, / Was all that did their silly thoughts so busy keep" ("Nativity" 91–92). The term remained in use through the nineteenth century, though with an archaic ring, as in Matthew Arnold's pastoral elegy "Thyrsis" (45).

Shell   *see* **Harp**

Shield   *see* **Armor**

Ship   A fragment of the early Greek lyric poet Alcaeus describes a ship struggling through a fierce storm at sea: "one wave rolls in from this side, another from that … bilge-water covers the mast-hold; all the sail lets the light through now … " (frag. 208, trans. Campbell). There is nothing in what survives to suggest that this is anything other than what it seems, but Heraclitus of Helicarnassus tells us that it is an allegory for political strife; Archilochus, he says, another poet, used the same symbolism (*Homeric Allegories*). If Heraclitus is right, these are the earliest examples of the ship-of-state metaphor, whereby the king or tyrant is the captain or helmsman, the citizens are the crew, the weather is all political, and the goal is safe harbor. It is found in a poem attributed to Theognis, where he complains of a mutinous crew that has deposed the pilot and refused to bail (667 – 82). It is found throughout Aeschylus' *Seven Against Thebes* (1–3, 62–64, 208–10, 652), and in Sophocles' *Antigone* (163, 189); in both cases it is Thebes that is rocked by waves or set straight again. It is explicitly developed in Plato's *Republic* 488a–89b.

The Alcaeus poem probably inspired a similar allegory by Horace (*Odes* 1.14). It begins: "Oh Ship! New billows sweep thee out / Seaward. What wilt thou? Hold the port, be stout"; this translation is by W. E. Gladstone, who captained the British ship of state for many years. Dante denounces Florence as "a ship without a helmsman in a great storm" (*Purgatorio* 6.77). The metaphor is concealed in the words "govern" and "government," which descend from Latin *guberno*, from Greek *kuberno*, "steer (a ship)." It has informed many modern literary works, more or less by implication in Shakespeare's *Tempest* and Melville's *Moby-Dick*, and explicitly in the anonymous fifteenth-century poem "The Ship of State" (where the mast is Prince Edward, the stern is the Duke of Somerset, etc.); Longfellow's "The Building of the Ship"; Whitman's lament for Lincoln, "O Captain! my Captain! our fearful trip is done"; and Auden's "The Ship." The whole of humankind might be thought of as launched upon a sea, an idea encapsulated in the recent catch-phrase "Spaceship Earth."

A partly parallel symbolism lies in the identification of the Christian church as a ship, which derives largely from the typological mode of reading the Old Testament. Noah's ark is the "type" of the church, outside of which there is no salvation. So the long central room of a Gothic church is called the nave, from Latin *navis*, "ship." The mast is inevitably likened to the cross.

Thousands of literary works, of course, including many central to the western tradition, are based on voyages across perilous seas, through narrow straits, past whirlpools and sea-monsters, against divine or magical forces, with stops at islands friendly or hostile, and so on; Homer's *Odyssey*, Apollonius' *Argonautica*, Virgil's *Aeneid*, Camoens' *The Lusiads*, Coleridge's *Rime of the Ancient Mariner*, and Melville's *Moby-Dick* are a few examples. W. H. Auden has observed (in *The Enchafed Flood*) that for most of human history no one went to sea unless one had to, in literature as in life, whereas in the Romantic era a shift took place: now the sea beckoned for its own sake, and life ashore seemed tame and unworthy. So Byron: "Once more upon the waters! yet once more! / And the waves bound beneath me as a steed / That knows its rider. Welcome to their roar! / Swift be their guidance, wheresoe'er it lead!" (*Childe Harold's Pilgrimage* 3.10–13); Baudelaire: "But true travellers are those, and those alone, who set out / Just to set out; light hearts, like balloons, / They never swerve from their destiny, / And, without knowing why, always say: Onward!" ("Le Voyage" 17–20); or John Masefield's "Sea Fever." Sometimes the voyage stands for one's progress through "the sea of life," as Arnold calls it in "Human Life" (27). (*See* **Path**.)

In classical myth a small boat piloted by Charon takes the dead to Hades, as if to show that death is on "the other shore" (as we still sometimes say) opposite this life. This boat is itself symbolized, for example, by the Venetian gondola, painted "coffin-black," that ferries Gustav Aschenbach to his destination in Mann's *Death in Venice*.

Pindar likens the composition of a work to a nautical voyage (*Nem.* 3.27) and asks the Muse to send the "wind of song" (*Pyth.* 4.3) or "wind of words" (*Nem.*

6.28). In his poem about farming Virgil invites his patron Maecenas to "Set sail with me on this my enterprise," while later in the same work he furls his sail and points prow to land (*Georgics* 2.41, 4.117). The final ode of Horace's four books begins, "For wishing to speak of battles and conquered cities Phoebus rebukes me with his lyre, lest I set my little sail on the great Tyrrhenian Sea" (4.15.1–4). Propertius elaborates this conceit in the same context: Apollo warns him away from writing epics, for "Your talent's skiff is not to be overladen. | Let one oar scour the water, the other sand, | And you'll be safe: at sea, the tumult's vast" (3.3.22–24, trans. Shepherd). Dante's *Purgatorio* begins with the same trope: "To course across more kindly waters now | my talent's little vessel lifts her sails, | leaving behind herself a sea so cruel" (1.1–3, trans. Mandelbaum); a greatly elaborated version comes early in the *Paradiso* (2.1–15). Chaucer imitates: "Owt of thise blake wawes [waves] for to saylle, | O wynd, o wynd, the weder gynneth clere; | For in this see the boot hath swych travaylle, | Of my connyng [skill], that unneth [hardly] I it steere" (*Troilus* 2.1–4). Camoens makes the same comparison, and adds that he is on a real voyage even as he writes (*Lusiads* 7.78). As Spenser launches the final canto of book 1 of *The Faerie Queene* (1.12.1) he calls his poem "my feeble barke"; he concludes the canto by declaring the poem must land some passengers and repair her tackles before setting out again (1.12.42; see 6.12.1). After saying he has left out a long tale of two tragic lovers, Wordsworth adds, "But our little bark | On a strong river boldly hath been launched; | And from the driving current should we turn | To loiter wilfully within creek, | Howe'er attractive, Fellow voyager! | Would'st thou not chide?" (1850 *Prelude* 9.559–64). Keats promises to "steer | My little boat, for many quiet hours, | With streams that deepen freshly into bowers" (*Endymion* 1.46–48). After five cantos of *Don Juan*, Byron takes stock: "Thus far our chronicle, and now we pause, | Though not for want of matter; but 'tis time, | According to the ancient epic laws, | To slacken sail and anchor with our rhyme" (5.1265–68; see 10.23–32). As Pushkin nears the end of *Eugene Onegin* he turns to his reader for the last time: "Let us congratulate | each other on attaining land" (8.48.12–13, trans. Nabokov).

Siege   The main metaphorical use of a military siege of a city or fortress is the wooing or seduction of a woman, especially a maiden. This metaphor is probably prehistoric, for many ancient citadels were identified with a virgin goddess, notably Athena, protectress of the Acropolis of Athens and several other Greek cities. Only after Odysseus and Diomedes stole Troy's sacred statue of Athena, the Palladion, did the city fall to its besiegers. Possibly in two passages of Homer the city is likened to a woman pursued: Achilles wishes that he and Patroclus could alone "loosen Troy's sacred girdle," though *kredemna* might mean "veil" or "head-bindings" (*Iliad* 16.100; cf. *Odyssey* 13.388). More important, the two epics that inaugurate western literature, however much they differ, begin in a curiously similar situation. In the *Iliad* Greeks besiege a city in order to rescue a woman who has been abducted from another citadel, while in the *Odyssey* a woman is the object of a host of unwelcome suitors. The rescuer of Penelope is the same who devised the sack of Troy for Helen's sake, in both cases by devious means; in both epics he is the favorite of Athena.

In English an unconquered city is a "maiden" city. Venice, writes Wordsworth, "was a maiden City, bright and free; / No guile seduced, no force could violate" ("On the Extinction of the Venetian Republic"). We say a fortress is "impregnable," as if to say it cannot be raped, though that word respells a different root from the one in "pregnant."

Perhaps the greatest elaboration of this metaphor is found in de Lorris and de Meun's *Romance of the Rose*, where a woman is a besieged tower, defended by Rebuff, Evil Tongue, Jealousy, and the like, coaxed open by Fair Welcome, assaulted by an army of Love, and so on. When Sidney's Stella is asleep Astrophel decides, "Now will I invade the fort" to steal a kiss, but he retreats ("Stella Sleeping"). Spenser's Sansloy first tries to seduce Una with words – "her to persuade that stubborne fort to yilde [yield]" – and then, when his flattery fails, "with greedy force he gan the fort assayle, / ... / And win rich spoils of ransackt chastitee" (*FQ* 1.6.3,5; see 1.2.25). Tennyson combines literal with figurative in his account of fair Lyonors, in her castle, and a knight who "so besieges her / To break her will, and make her wed with him" ("Gareth and Lynette" 601–02).

It is not only a woman or a woman's honor that may be thought of as a fortress under attack. "What warre so cruel, or what siege so sore," Spenser asks, "As that which strong affections doe apply / Against the forte of reason...?" He goes on to paint an elaborate allegorical scene of the siege, where enemy batteries, for example, assail five bulwarks representing the five senses. A "noble Virgin," of course, is the "Ladie of the Place," Alma, the soul (*FQ* 2.11.1–16). Sidney reverses the standard trope and portrays his heart as conquered by Stella and "Whole armies of thy beauties entered in" ("Astrophel and Stella" 36). Hamlet tells how one's innate vice might grow, "Oft breaking down the pales and forts of reason" (1.4.28), a metaphor with large resonance in a play set in a fort under threat by an external enemy but already taken by internal subterfuge.

Silver Silver is "the second metal," in Saint-Amant's phrase ("Winter in the Alps"), following gold. "Gold and silver" or "silver and gold" are commonplaces in classical literature, and they occur in the same or successive verses scores of times in the Bible; often there is no distinction in meaning. Both "gold" and "silver" are synonyms for money in Greek, Latin, Hebrew, and many modern languages (cf. French *argent*). But wherever there is a ranking, silver comes second, as the monetary value of the metal is always less than that of gold.

The silver race was the second of the five races described by Hesiod, and it was much inferior to the golden (*see* **Metal**); "It was the silver age that saw the first adulterers," according to Juvenal (6.24). In literary history the distinction between a golden and silver age of Roman literature has been current since the seventeenth century. "With Ovid," Dryden says, "ended the golden age of the Roman tongue" ("Preface" to the *Fables*); the silver age was the period from the death of Augustus to that of Hadrian. A witty essay by Peacock called "The Four Ages of Poetry" traces two cycles from iron through gold and silver to brass, the second brass age being the contemporary one; it was this scornful survey that prompted Shelley's "A Defence of Poetry." A well-known anthology by Gerald Bullet, *Silver Poets of the Sixteenth Century* (London, 1947), defines a set of "minor" English poets (Wyatt, Surrey, Sidney, Raleigh, Davies), while C. S Lewis defines a "Golden Age" of English poetry, that of the Elizabethans (Spenser, Sidney, Marlowe), as "innocent or ingenuous" (*English Literature in the Sixteenth Century* [London, 1954] 64).

As a bright, precious metal silver belongs to the classical gods only less insistently than gold. Apollo is particularly associated with a silver bow; "silverbow" is a title of his in the *Iliad* (1.37); Pindar refers to "the silver bow of Phoebus" (*Olymp.* 9.32–33). The Homeric *Hymn to Artemis* gives Apollo's sister a golden bow (5), as does Ovid (*Met.* 1.697), but later Artemis (or Diana) seems to have acquired a silver one, probably to align her better with the moon, of which she is regent. So "the moon, like to a silver bow / New bent in heaven," suggests the reign of Diana the huntress in *A Midsummer Night's Dream* (1.1.9–10); Pericles refers to Diana's "silver livery" (*Per* 5.3.7); while in Milton's *Comus* Diana is the "Fair silver-shafted Queen forever chaste" (442). For the moon is always silver. "Silver moon" and various more decorative phrases such as "faire Phebe with her silver face" recur in Spenser (*FQ* 2.2.44), Shakespeare, Wordsworth, Keats, Shelley, and many other poets. The sun, however, is always golden. In parallel couplets Spenser has "Phoebus golden face" and "silver Cynthia" (1.7.34), and after centuries of this pairing Stevens states as a dull fact "The sun is gold, the moon is silver" ("Mandolin and Liqueurs"). (For more examples, *see* **Gold**.)

"Silver-eddying" is an epithet of rivers in Homer, and it has been attached to rivers and other forms of water ever since. In a persistent display of the power of poetry over fact, the Thames has been silver for centuries: "the christall *Thamis* wont to slide / In silver channell" (Spenser, "Ruins of time" 134–35); "silver Thames" (Jonson, *Forest* 6.15); "silver Thames" (twice in Wordsworth); but in a novel, a more realistic touch: "A lodging...which looked out upon the silver Thames (for the Thames was silver then)" (Kingsley, *Westward Ho!* 12).

A beautiful voice or other sound is frequently silver. When Spenser's Belphoebe speaks one hears "A silver sound, that heavenly musicke seemd to make" (*FQ* 2.3.24); hearing Juliet say his name, Romeo notes "How silver-sweet sound lovers' tongues by night" (2.2.166); evoking silver rivers as well as music Shelley's Asia feels "My soul is an enchanted Boat / Which, like a sleeping swan, doth float / Upon the silver waves of thy sweet singing" (*PU* 2.5.72–74); Keats imagines Spenser blowing a "silver trumpet" ("Ode to Apollo" 30); Emerson mourns the loss of his boy with his "silver warble wild" ("Threnody" 12). It was already such a cliché by Shakespeare's day that a servant in *Romeo and Juliet* can ask why a song has the phrase "music with her silver sound"; none of the musicians knows the answer, so they resort to quips: "I say 'silver sound' because musicians sound for silver" (4.5.128–41).

See **Metal, Moon**.

Sirius   *see* **Dog star, under Star**

Skylark   *see* **Lark**

Sleep   *see* **Dream, Night**

Snake   *see* **Serpent**

Sowing   *see* **Seed**

Sparrow   Sparrows occur once in Homer as the helpless birds swallowed by a snake in an omen forecasting the length of the war (*Iliad* 2.308–30); the eight fledglings and their mother stand for the nine years already devoured by time.

There are three more distinctive ancient associations of sparrows. It is one of the birds of Aphrodite, for it is sparrows not doves that pull her chariot in Sappho's "Ode to Aphrodite," probably because they seemed the most lustful of common birds. An ancient commentator on the *Iliad* passage states the sparrow is sacred to the goddess. Sparrows escort Venus' dove-driven chariot in Apuleius (*Met.* 6.6). *Strouthos* ("sparrow") in Greek could mean a "lewd fellow" or "lecher," as did *passer* in Latin (Juvenal 9.54); the latter could also be a term of endearment between lovers. Chaucer's Summoner was "As hoot...and lecherous as a sparwe" (*CT* Gen. Pro. 626). In his list of distinctive bird features Sidney has "Sparrow's letchery" (*First Eclogues* 10.79). Shakespeare's Lucio complains of the puritanical Angelo that "Sparrows must not build in his house-eaves because they are lecherous" (*MM* 3.2.175–76). There are no Latin examples of the sparrows of Venus, but in his bird catalog Chaucer lists "The sparwe, Venus sone" (*Parliament of Fowls* 351), Sidney sees "a chariot faire by doves and sparrowes guided" that carries Venus and Diana (*Fourth Eclogues* 73.59), and Marlowe's Hero tells Leander that "I play / With Venus' swans and sparrows all the day" (351–52). Robert Browning writes "spring bade the sparrows pair" ("Youth and Art" 33).

The most famous individual sparrow is Lesbia's pet, celebrated in two poems by Catullus (2 and 3). The first is addressed to the bird and describes the way his girl plays with it, the second is a lament over its death. So well known were these poems that Martial refers to the bird half a dozen times, once claiming that his Stella's pet dove surpasses Catullus' sparrow (1.7.1–3); see also Juvenal 6.8. (There is some question whether the bird, *passer*, is really a sparrow and not a thrush or goldfinch.) Skelton's long poem *Phyllyp Sparowe*, an elegy for a woman's pet bird killed by a cat, seems inspired by Catullus. Byron translated Catullus' lament into English.

The third ancient use of the sparrow is Jesus' example of God's providence: "Are not two sparrows sold for a farthing? and one of them shall not fall on the ground without your Father"; "Fear ye not therefore, ye are of more value than many sparrows" (Matt. 10.29,31). It marks the final turn in Hamlet's readiness that he cites Matthew: "We defy augury. There is a special providence in the fall of a sparrow" (5.2.215–16). According to Pope, God sees "with equal eye... / A hero perish, or a sparrow fall" (*Essay on Man* 1.87–88).

A charming poem that tries to see sparrows with fresh eyes, without literary connotations, is W. C. Williams's "The Sparrow."

Spider   Most of the spider's literary appearances have to do with spinning and weaving. The Greek tale of the girl Arachne (Greek for "spider") and her weaving contest with Athena is memorably told by Ovid (*Met.* 6.1–145). The word "spider," from Old English *spithra*, is from the same root as "spin"; the German word for "spider" is *Spinne*. (The source of Greek *arachne* and Latin *araneus* is unknown.)

Spider webs are of course a sign of neglect or decay (as in Catullus 68.49), but an interesting use of them in Homer with that sense – where Telemachus wonders whether his mother has remarried and the bed of Odysseus lies empty "holding evil spider webs" (*Odyssey* 16.35) – resonates with the only other appearance of the word, in a simile for the net Hephaestus contrives to catch his unfaithful wife Aphrodite in bed with Ares (8.280). With a similar set of associations, the image is used by the chorus of Aeschylus' *Agamemnon*, who bewail the dead Agamemnon, "lying in this web of the spider," his faithless wife Clytemnestra (1492). We are reminded that spiders weave webs to catch unwary insects.

Spider webs are used as examples of fineness or delicacy, as in Hephaestus' skillful net or the hair of a girl Ovid describes (*Amores* 1.14.7–8). Spenser has Clotho the Fate show "thrids so thin as spiders frame" (*FQ* 4.2.50).

The fact that spiders produce their threads out of their own abdomen, to weave what Shakespeare calls a "self-drawing web" (*H8* 1.1.63), has suggested a symbolic contrast to the bee, which gathers its materials from many sources. Swift's *Battle of the Books* centers on a debate between the "modern" spider, who spins books out of his own entrails ("the guts of modern brains"), and the "ancient" bee, who ranges over nature and collects knowledge with great labor; the one produces dirt and poison, the other honey and wax. (*See* **Bee**.) The modern Walt Whitman, by contrast, compares the human soul to "A noiseless patient spider" (the title of a poem); the spider launches forth filaments into the vast space around it, as the soul must, "Till the gossamer thread you fling catch somewhere, O my soul."

Jonathan Edwards famously adduces a spider dangling over a fire as a type or symbol of the human sinner ("Sinners in the Hands of an Angry God"). Robert Frost finds a white spider on a white flower holding a dead white moth as something like another type, perhaps an instance of the "design of darkness to appall" ("Design").

After Emma Bovary's marriage, "boredom, like a silent spider, was weaving its web in the shadows, in every corner of her heart" (Flaubert, *Madame Bovary*, chap. 7).

Spleen   *see* **Bile**

Spring   Spring is the most celebrated of seasons. Poets since antiquity have delighted in spring's return and relished its many distinctive features. Certain conventions were established early that have influenced poetry up to the present.

The Greeks and Romans considered spring the beginning of the year, whence the Latin phrase *primum tempus*, "first season," which yields French *printemps* and the Middle English translation "prymetyme." In English "prime" by itself could mean "spring" as well as the first hour of the day; so Shakespeare: "The lovely April of her prime" and "The teeming autumn, big with rich increase, / Bearing the wanton burden of the prime" (*Sonnets* 3.10, 97.6–7). The main Latin word for spring, *ver* (whence English "vernal"), was combined with *prima* to give the Italian and Spanish *primavera*. Latin *ver* is cognate with Greek *ear*; the season of spring (*hore earos*) is one of the three seasons (*horai*) distinguished by Hesiod. In Homer *hore* alone occasionally means "spring," as if it were *the* season.

The Old English word for "spring" was "lencten" or "lenten" (probably akin to "length," for it is the time when days noticeably lengthen), shortened to "lent" and now restricted to the church season before Easter; German *Lenz* preserves the original meaning. A Middle English lyric begins: "Lenten ys come with love to toune." The word "spring," as its other meanings today imply, meant a rise or leap of something, hence a first onset; the phrase "springing time" was used in the fourteenth century, and "spring of the year" and "spring of the leaf" were once common. As a verb it was often found in poems: "When the nightingale sings the woods waxen green, / Leaf and grass and blossom springs in April" (MS Harley 2253). Shakespeare has "springing things" (young growths) and "tender spring" (young shoot or bud) (*Venus* 417, 656). The King James Bible has "spring of the day" (1 Sam. 9.26) and "dayspring" (Job 38.12, Luke 1.78) for dawn. "Springtide" adds "tide," meaning "time." Shakespeare also has "spring of time" (*R2* 5.2.50), and, most striking, "middle summer's spring" (*MND* 2.1.82). German *Fruhling* and (less common) *Fruhjahr* are from *fruh*, "early."

Latin poetry has several descriptions of spring that set the conventions: winter thaws and relaxes its grip, Venus or love pervades the land, the Graces and Nymphs dance, swallows or cuckoos and then nightingales sing, birds and then beasts seek their mates, showers descend as heaven impregnates the earth, the west wind (Zephyrus or Favonius) gently blows, the land turns green and then bright or purple with buds and blossoms, Flora strews flowers, dew falls on them, boys and girls seek each other, and so on. See Lucretius 1.10–20, 250–61, 2.991–98, 5.737–47; Horace, *Odes* 1.4, 4.7, 4.12; Virgil, *Georgics* 2.323–35. These conventions were crystallized in medieval Latin poetry, such as the *Carmina Burana*, and in Provençal and Old French songs; a common type of dance song in Old French, for example, was the *reverdie* or "regreening." The best-known brief description of spring in Middle English is the opening of Chaucer's *Canterbury Tales*. (*See* **West wind**.)

A common theme in medieval poetry was the "debate" or *conflictus* between Winter and Spring. *The Owl and the Nightingale* (*c.* 1200) is such a poem, where the owl represents winter and the nightingale, of course, spring. An echo of this theme is found in the concluding song of Shakespeare's *Love's Labour's Lost*.

Another great influence on post-classical poetry of spring is this passage from the Song of Solomon: "For, lo, the winter is past, the rain is over and gone; / The flowers appear on the earth; the time of the singing of birds is come, and the voice of the turtle [dove] is heard in our land; / The fig tree putteth forth her green figs, and the vines with the tender grape give a good smell. Arise, my love, my fair one, and come away" (2.11–13).

Spring is the season of love, "For love is crowned with the prime, / In spring-time" (Shakespeare, *AYLI* 5.3.32–33). A nearly formulaic epithet for spring in medieval and Renaissance poetry is "lusty." The most often quoted English line on the subject is probably Tennyson's: "In the spring a young man's fancy lightly turns to thoughts of love" ("Locksley Hall" 20).

The biblical Paradise and the classical Golden Age (as found in Ovid, *Metamorphoses* 1.107–10) were thought of as places of perpetual spring. The orchard of Alcinous in Homer's *Odyssey* is the classical prototype: it always has some trees with ripe fruit, for "always Zephyrus blowing on the fruits brings some to ripeness while he starts others" (7.112–21). Virgil speculates in the *Georgics* that spring was the season at the dawn of the infant world (2.337–43). Genesis 1.11 was read as suggesting that seed and fruit were once simultaneous, but the classical sources were sufficient to prompt descriptions of the Garden of Eden as the site of "Eternal Spring" where there are "goodliest Trees loaden with fairest Fruit, / Blossoms and Fruits at once," as Milton puts it (*PL* 4.268, 147–48); "spring and autumn here / Danced hand in hand" (5.394–95). Spenser's account of the Garden of Adonis elaborates the tradition: "There is continuall Spring, and harvest there / Continuall, both meeting at one tyme; / For both the boughes doe laughing blossoms beare, / And with fresh colours decke the wanton Pryme, / And eke attonce the heavy trees they clyme, / Which seeme to labour under their fruites lode" (*FQ* 3.6.42). In the masque of *The Tempest*, Ceres blesses the lovers with the wish that "Spring come to you at the farthest / In the very end of harvest" (4.1.114–15). "Great Spring, before [the Deluge], / Green'd all the Year," according to Thomson ("Spring" 320). And Shelley's vision of the renovated world in *Queen Mab* is a garden with "ever verdant trees" where "fruits are ever ripe, flowers ever fair, / And autumn proudly bears her matron grace, / Kindling a flush on the fair cheek of spring" (8.118–21).

Spring, of course, is metaphorical of youth. The "prime of youth" used to refer to one's twenties, and phrases such as "springtime of life" are commonplaces (French *printemps de la vie*, German *Lenz des Lebens*).

See **Autumn, Seasons, Summer, Winter.**

Spring (Wellspring)   *see* **Fountain**

Staff   *see* **Bread**

Stage   *see* **Theatre**

Star   Among their many meanings, stars have stood for numerousness, glory, prophecy, times of night or year, and fate or "influence"; many particular stars, of course, have had particular senses.

In biblical and classical literature "star" can refer to any of the heavenly bodies, including (occasionally) to the sun and the moon. What we call a planet was a "wandering star" (Greek *aster planetes*), what we call a comet was a "hairy star" (*aster kometes*); today we still call a meteor a "shooting star" or "falling star," though we know it is not a star in the strict sense. Ovid once uses *sidus* ("star") for the sun (*Met.* 1.424); Virgil likens an advancing army to a storm-cloud "cutting off the star" (*abrupto sidere*), where the star must be the sun (*Aeneid* 12.451). Seneca calls the moon the "star of the night" (*Medea* 750).

After their awe-inspiring beauty and distance, perhaps the most striking fact about stars is the sheer number of them, indeed a numberless number. Stars in the Bible are a commonplace for numerousness or innumerability. The Lord promises Abram: "Look now toward heaven, and tell the stars, if thou be able to number them: and he said unto him, so shall thy seed be" (Gen. 15.5; see 26.4). Stars are sometimes coupled with sand for the same purpose: "I will multiply thy seed as the stars of the heaven, and as the sand which is upon the sea shore" (22.17; see Hebr. 11.12). Thus a dramatic way of expressing the mightiness of God is to say "He telleth the number of the stars; he calleth them all by their names" (Ps. 147.4).

In the *Iliad* there is a striking simile that, in typical Homeric fashion, elaborates a scene beyond its point, which is simply numerousness: "As when in the sky the stars about the moon's shining / are seen in all their glory, when the air has fallen to stillness, / And all the high places of the hills are clear, and the shoulders out-jutting, / and the deep ravines, as endless bright air spills from the heavens / and all the stars are seen, to make glad the heart of the shepherd; / such in their numbers blazed the watchfires the Trojans were burning " (8.555–60, trans. Lattimore).

Catullus tells Lesbia he wants as many kisses as the sand in Libya and the stars at night (7.3–7). After a long list of Nereids, Spenser relies on that commonplace to express their countlessness: it would be easier "To tell the sands, or count the starres on hye" (FQ 4.11.53). Milton's Satan leads "an host, / Innumerable as the stars of night, / Or stars of morning" (PL 5.744–46). "But who can count the Stars of Heaven?" Thomson asks ("Winter" 528), forgetting, perhaps, that the Psalmist had already answered that question.

Stars in the Bible sometimes stand for glory, human or otherwise. Daniel concludes his prophecy by claiming "they that be wise shall shine as the brightness of the firmament; and they that turn many to righteousness as the stars for ever and ever" (12.3). At the resurrection, Paul writes, we shall have incorruptible heavenly bodies with a "glory" (Greek *doxa*) like those of the sun, moon, and stars (1 Cor. 15.41).

Several times in Homer the fame (*kleos*) of a person or thing "goes up to heaven" (e.g., *Iliad* 10.212, *Odyssey* 9.20). Homer does not make the next step explicit by likening the famous to stars, though he does compare the appearance of Achilles in armor to a star. He also names a few constellations – the Bear (or Wagon), the Pleiades, Orion, Bootes – behind some of which lie stories about the translation of heroes or objects from earth to heaven. Euripides takes the next step when he has a chorus call Hippolytus "the brightest star of Athens" (*Hippolytus* 1121). Virgil has Aeneas boast that his fame goes *above* the sky (*Aeneid* 1.378–89), Dido hope her former fame was going up to the stars (4.322), and a voice tell Latinus that strangers' blood "will carry our name to the stars" (7.99); but Virgil like most Hellenistic and Roman poets reserves the stars themselves for deified heroes and emperors. He imagines the zodiac, for instance, making room for the new star of Octavian, not yet dead (*Georgics* 1.32). Chaucer alludes to this process of "catasterism" or transformation into a star in, appropriately, *The House of Fame* 599. Shakespeare's Bedford invokes the ghost of Henry V, asking it to "Combat with adverse planets in the heavens! / A far more glorious star thy soul will make / Than Julius Caesar" (1H6 1.1.54–56). Shelley hopes his fame will become "A star among the stars of mortal night" (*Revolt of Islam* 6). In this ancient and traditional use we have the origin of "movie star" and "superstar," the metaphorical force of which is now spent.

Because he or she stands out among all others, one's beloved is often called a star. Since Plato's epigrams to a young man whom he calls Aster, "star" has become a conventional name: Martial writes of Stella, Sidney (who dubs himself "Astrophil" or "Star-Lover") has a Stella, Swift also has a Stella, and Dickens's Pip loves Estella in *Great Expectations*.

Several stars in the Bible are prophetic or symbolic. Balaam prophesies, "there shall come a Star out of Jacob, and a Sceptre shall rise out of Israel," who shall smite the enemy (Num. 24.17); Christians have taken this as referring to Christ. At Jesus' birth there was the star of the Magi, or star of Bethlehem, that appeared in the east (Matt. 2.2ff.); the Magi were astrologers, so they particularly recognized the significance of this *stella nova* or new star as the sign of a new reign, and new kind of reign, on earth. Milton insists on its newness whenever he mentions it: "A Star, not seen before in Heaven appearing / ...thy Star new-grav'n in Heaven" (PR 1.249–53; see PL 12.360). That, surely, is the main point, a point completely effaced by well-meaning modern attempts to "explain" the star by finding a conjunction of planets at about 4 BC, the sort of thing astrologers would not find unusual in the least.

In a nice example of the internalization of Jewish and pagan symbols, Peter refers to "a more sure word of prophecy; whereunto ye do well that ye take heed, as unto a light that shineth in a dark place, until the day dawn, and the day star arise in your hearts" (2 Pet. 1.19); the "day star" in the Authorized Version is *phosphoros*, the morning star, Venus. When Jesus in the Book of Revelation says, "I will give him [the faithful] the morning star" (2.28) he seems to be promising salvation, the entrance into a new day in heaven, but near the end of the book he announces that he himself is "the bright and morning star" (22.16). The morning star has been taken as prophetic generally ever since; to give one modern example, Hugo's "Stella" is a dream vision in which the morning star announces "I am fiery Poetry" sent ahead as herald by Liberty and Light.

The acknowledgment by the Wise Men that Jesus is the new king may be taken as the defeat of Magian star-worship. Though Joseph dreamt of symbolic stars and Daniel was a star-reader, there are a number of passages of the Bible that denounce the star cults widespread in the Middle East. Moses warns his followers "lest thou lift up thine eyes unto heaven, and when thou seest the sun, and the moon, and the stars, even all the host of heaven, shouldest be driven to worship them, and serve them" (Deut. 4.19). Isaiah sarcastically offers: "Let now the astrologers, the stargazers, the monthly prognosticators, stand up, and save thee from these things that shall come upon thee. / Behold, they shall be as stubble; the fire shall burn them" (47.13–14). In other passages, however, astrology of some sort seems to be assumed. In Judges we are told that "the stars in their courses fought against Sisera" (5.20), and Jesus himself tells us that during the time when "Nation shall rise against nation," "there shall be signs in the sun, and in the moon, and in the stars" (Luke 21.10, 25).

Early interpreters of the Bible, if not its authors, took stars sometimes to mean angels. A chief passage justifying that meaning is from Job: "When the morning stars sang together, and all the sons of God shouted for joy" on the day the foundations of the earth were laid (38.7). Isaiah's cryptic verse (in the AV), "How art thou fallen from heaven, O Lucifer, son of the morning!" (14.12), refers to two star-deities in Hebrew, Helel and Shahar, but in various translations the passage has been enormously influential on later stories of fallen angels. The "great star" that falls from heaven and is given a key to the bottomless pit (Rev. 9.1) must be an angel of some kind, and perhaps the "Lucifer" of Isaiah. John of Patmos makes explicit that the seven stars in the right hand of Christ (Rev. 1.16) are the angels of the seven churches he addresses (1.20). The dragon's tail "drew the third part of the stars of heaven, and did cast them to the earth" (12.4). Milton compares Lucifer to "the morning star that guides / The starry flock, allured them, and with lies/ Drew after him the third part of heaven's host" (*PL* 5.708–10). To take stars as angels may help clarify many mysterious passages in William Blake, such as the one about the stars throwing down their spears in "The Tyger."

Stars of course tell direction and time of year. Hesiod's *Works and Days* and Virgil's *Georgics* are filled with precise information about risings and settings of various stars. Navigating by stars must have been widely practiced for centuries, though only one instance of it is found in Homer (*Odyssey* 5.272ff.). Certain constellations show up frequently in literature. On Achilles' shield Hephaestus puts the sun and moon and "all the constellations that festoon the heavens, / the Pleiades and the Hyades and the strength of Orion / and the Bear, whom men give also the name of the Wagon, / who turns about in a fixed place and looks at Orion / and she alone is never plunged in the wash of the Ocean" (*Iliad* 18.485–89, trans. Lattimore; repeated with Bootes for Hyades at *Odyssey* 5.272–75). Pleiades, Hyades, and Bear are together in *Georgics* 1.138, Bootes and Pleiades in Propertius 3.5.35, Orion and Bear in Ovid's *Art of Love* 2.53. "The Bear," Greek *Arktos*, is the Great Bear, *Ursa Major*; the Greek word gives us "arctic" and "antarctic." Today it is often called the Big Dipper, but the older term is still used, the Wain (wagon) or Charles' Wain. It is the most prominent of the north circumpolar constellations, and in ancient times, at Greek latitudes, it never set, never bathed in Ocean's stream (no longer true, thanks to the precession of the equinoxes). The heliacal rising of the Pleiades marked the beginning of summer (mid-May), that of Arcturus, the brightest star of Bootes, the beginning of winter (mid-September), and so on.

The twelve signs or constellations of the zodiac, the band of the sky through which the sun, moon, and planets pass, have been widely cited in literature at least since Statius as ways of indicating the season. The most famous English example comes in the "General Prologue" of Chaucer's *Canterbury Tales*: it is April, when "the yonge sonne / Hath in the Ram his halve cours yronne" (7–8); the sun is young because it is early in the year, which began in March, and it is now emerging from the constellation Aries, the Ram, the first sign of the zodiac.

Despite the strictures against it in the Bible and some of the church fathers, astrology remained a rich source of literary imagery. The common meanings of "influence" today have their origin in the belief that the stars sent an etherial fluid down to earth. A "sphere of influence" in the geopolitical sense draws twice from celestial notions, for the pre-Copernican model of the heavens posited solid transparent spheres surrounding the earth. A "disaster" is etymologically a "bad star" or unfavorable aspect of a star or planet; Shakespeare's Horatio speaks of "disasters in the sun" (*Hamlet* 1.1.118). To "consider" was originally to consult the stars (Latin *sidera*).

Many people read the horoscope today for amusement, but many others still believe in "natal stars" or planets that were dominant or prominent at the time of their birth or at other crucial moments. Chaucer likens the heavens to a large book written with stars; at one's birth one can determine one's death, "For in the sterres, clerer than is glas, / Is writen, God woot [knows], whoso koude it rede, / The deeth of every man, withouten drede [doubt]" (*Man of Law's Tale* 194–96). A lady in Spenser asks her lord, "what evill starre / On you hath frownd, and poord his influence bad" (*FQ* 1.8.42), while another hails a knight as "borne under happie starre" (1.1.27); in Spenser stars can also be "cruel," "unhappy," or "luckless." Many characters in Shakespeare feel predetermined by "favourable," "auspicious," "inauspicious," "thwarting," "angry," or "malignant and ill-boding" stars; Romeo and Juliet are "A pair of star-crossed lovers" (Prologue 6); Malvolio thanks his stars he is happy (*12N* 2.5.170–71); and so on. But the contrary view is also frequent. Cassius argues that "Men at some time are masters of their fates. / The fault, dear Brutus, is not in our stars, / But in ourselves, that we are underlings" (*JC* 1.2.139–41), though heavenly portents at Caesar's murder suggest Cassius is wrong. The wicked Edmund dismisses his father's belief in "heavenly compulsion," "spherical predominance," and "planetary influence" as fopperies (*King Lear* 1.2.118–33). More convincing is Helena in *All's Well*: she grants she is born under "baser stars" or "homely stars" (1.1.183, 2.5.75), that is, of humble parents, but she acts on the knowledge that "the fatal sky / Gives us free scope" (1.1.216–18); by contrast Polonius tells Ophelia that "Lord Hamlet is a prince out of thy star" or sphere (*Hamlet* 2.2.141). Helena's view is expressed by Basilio in Calderón's *Life is a Dream*, where he states that "the most impious planet" can "only incline the free will, not force it" (1.6.789–91); events bear him out. Or, as Southey states it, "for though all other things / Were subject to the starry influencings, / . . . / The virtuous heart and resolute mind are free" (*Curse of Kehama* 18.10.129–32).

Particular stars are not uncommonly recruited for symbolic meanings. Melville's Billy Budd, for instance, always aloft in the foretop of the ship, is associated with the constellation Taurus and its brightest star Aldebaran, which are high above the celestial equator, while Claggart is likened to Scorpio, which lies far below it.

The "day star" has sometimes meant the morning star, but in poetry it is usually the sun. In Milton's *Lycidas* the "day-star" is almost certainly the sun, for it sinks in the ocean and yet soon "Flames in the forehead of the morning sky" (168–71), whereas Venus cannot be both evening and morning star in the same season. It is the "diurnal star" of *PL* 10.1069, and the "star of noon" of Young's *Night Thoughts* 9.1683. Wordsworth sees the day-star sinking in the west in his *Evening Walk* 190–91. Carew calls the sun "the Planet of the day" ("Boldness in Love" 5).

The "dog star" (Latin *Canicula*, "little dog") is Sirius, the brightest fixed star in the sky, found in the constellation Canis Major, the "Great Dog," which Homer calls Orion's Dog (*Iliad* 22.29). Sirius rises just before the sun (its "heliacal rising") in mid-July, or rather it did so in ancient times; hence it is a sign of the dangerous heat of high summer. Sirius "parches head and knees," as Hesiod puts it (*Works and Days* 587), as if it is the star itself that sends the feverish heat. The name "Sirius" seems to be an adjective, Greek *seirios*, meaning "burning" or "sparkling": Hesiod once has *seirios aster*, which might be translated either "blazing star" or "Sirian star" (*Works* 417), and Aeschylus writes of foliage providing shade against the *seiriou kunos* or "Sirian dog"

(*Agamemnon* 966–67). Ibycus once uses it in the plural for stars generally (314).

It appears twice in similes in the *Iliad*, first for the shining of Diomedes' shield (5.5–6), and then, in an elaboration that rests not only on its brightness but on its balefulness, for Achilles himself, who looks "like that star / which comes on the autumn and whose conspicuous brightness / far outshines the stars that are numbered in the night's darkening, / the star they give the name of Orion's Dog, which is brightest / among the stars, and yet is wrought as a sign of evil / and brings on the great fever for unfortunate mortals" (22.26–31; trans. Lattimore). Apollonius tells the story behind the sacrifices to Sirius by the priests of Keos – to keep it from ever again burning the islands with its fire from heaven (2.516–27); he also likens Jason's impression on Medea to that of Sirius, for he is both brilliant and the bringer of the hot disease of love (3.956–61). In the *Aeneid* "Sirius burns the sterile fields" while men die of pestilence (3.141); it also appears in a simile for the shining helmet of Aeneas (10.273–75), a reworking of the *Iliad* similes. In the *Georgics* Virgil calls Sirius *canis aestifer*, "dog the summer-bearer" (2.353). The Greeks and Romans designated the hottest weeks of summer the "dog days" (*hemerai kunades, dies caniculares*), a phrase still used in English. Spenser imagines the July sun hunting the lion (the constellation Leo) "with Dogge of noysome breath, / Whose balefull barking bringes in hast / pyne, plagues, and dreery death" (*SC* "July" 22–24); like Aeschylus he calls it "the hot Syrian Dog" (*Mother Hubberd* 5).

Milton calls Sirius the "swart Star" in *Lycidas* 138, "swart" meaning "black" or "dark." Unusually for Milton no classical precedent for this epithet has turned up: it may mean "evil," or perhaps it is a transference from the vegetation scorched black by the star.

The "evening star," called *hesperos* in Greek and *vesper* in Latin, both meaning "evening" (and cognate with "west"), is the planet Venus, which is never far from the sun, sometimes rising before it ("morning star") and sometimes setting after it ("evening star"). It is named once in Homer: "as a star moves among stars in the night's darkening, / Hesper, who is the fairest star who stands in the sky, such / was the shining from the pointed spear Achilleus was shaking / in his right hand" (*Iliad* 22.317–20, trans. Lattimore). In the tradition of the epithalamium or wedding song, the appearance of the evening star, with its link to the goddess of love, is the signal to light the bridal lamp and lead the bride to the bridegroom. Catullus' epithalamium (62) begins by announcing, "Vesper is here, young men, stand up." Milton evokes this tradition when Adam describes his nuptial evening with Eve (*PL* 8.519).

The "morning star," called *phosphoros* in Greek and *lucifer* in Latin, both meaning "light-bringer," is also the planet Venus. In Homer once it is called *Heosphoros*, "Dawn-bringer" (*Iliad* 23), and once it is described as "that brightest star, which beyond others / comes with announcement of the light of the young Dawn goddess" (*Odyssey* 13.93–94, trans. Lattimore). The epigram of Plato's mentioned earlier reads: "Aster, once you shone as the Dawn Star among the living; now you shine as the Evening Star among the dead." Shelley uses this as an epigraph to his elegy on the death of Keats, *Adonais*, which is filled with star imagery. Milton relies on the traditional name of the unfallen Satan, Lucifer, in likening him to the morning star.

The "pole star" or "polar star" is Polaris, the North Star, the brightest star in Ursa Minor, the Lesser Bear or Wain (or Little Dipper), and in recent centuries very near the north celestial pole. It is "the stedfast starre" (Spenser, *FQ* 1.2.1) around which all the other stars revolve. In a circumlocution for "night" Tennyson describes the time "when the lesser wain / Is twisting round the polar star" (*In Memoriam* 101.11–12).

The "fixed stars" are what we call stars today. They do not move relative to each other, but revolve together once a day around the pole. According to the Aristotelian-Ptolemaic system they are affixed to the eighth sphere from the earth.

The "wandering stars" are the planets (Greek *aster planetes*, "wandering star"); Chaucer calls them the "erratik sterres" (*TC* 5.1812). They move relative to the fixed stars in complex patterns, moving at varying rates through the zodiac night after night, some of them even retreating for a time before resuming their progress. There were seven of them: the moon, Mercury, Venus, the sun, Mars, Jupiter, and Saturn, in order of distance from the earth, each affixed to its own sphere, which rotated according to its own rules. Dante's "planet that leads men straight on every road" is the sun (*Inferno* 1.17–18). (*See* **Planet**.)

The "star of the sea" (Latin *stella maris*) is a title given to the Virgin Mary in the Middle Ages, apparently in the belief that "Mary" (or Hebrew "Miriam") was the same as the Latin word for "sea." She is the Hope of Sailors, or as Joyce puts it, "a beacon ever to the storm-tossed heart of man, Mary, star of the sea" (*Ulysses*, "Nausicaa" para. 1).

The "watery star" is the moon. "Nine changes of the watery star" (Shakespeare, *WT* 1.2.1) means nine months. It is associated with water because it is "the governess of floods" or tides (*MND* 2.1.103). Shakespeare also calls it "the moist star, / Upon whose influence Neptune's empire stands" (*Hamlet* 1.1.121–22).

The "lode star" or "load star" is the guiding star ("load" is related to "lead"), that is, the north star.

For the "folding star" and "unfolding star," see under **Sheep**.

Stork   The stork is mentioned occasionally in the Bible with no particular symbolic meaning, but the Hebrew word for it, *hasidah*, means "pious." That suggests that the Hebrews shared the Greek view that the stork (*pelargos*) is notable for its parental and especially filial piety. In Aristophanes' *The Birds* a character cites an ancient law in the tablets of the storks: "When the old stork has brought his storklings up, / And all are fully fledged for flight, then they / Must in their turn maintain the stork their father" (1355–57, trans. Rogers). (Aristophanes also wrote a play called *The Storks*, but it is lost.) Sophocles may be referring to storks in *Electra* 1058ff.: "We see above our heads the birds, / true in their wisdom, / caring for the livelihood / of those that gave them life and sustenance" (trans. Grene). Socrates alludes to storkling piety at the end of his first dialogue with Alcibiades: "So my love will be just like a stork; for after hatching a winged love in you it is to be cherished in return by its nestling" (Plato, *Alcibiades* 1.135e).

Pliny believes that storks nourish their parents in old age (*Natural History* 10.31). Dryden expands on a hint in Juvenal's first *Satire*: "the Stork on high / Seems to salute her Infant Progeny: / Presaging Pious Love with her Auspicious Cry" (173–75). Drayton describes the "carefull Storke" who "his ag'd Parents naturally doth feed, / In filiall duty" (*Noahs Flood* 1395–98). Dante makes use of this tradition in a simile for his relation to the image of the Eagle of Justice in Heaven: "Just as, above the nest, the stork (*cicogna*) will circle / When she has fed her fledglings, and as he / whom she has fed looks up at her, so did / the blessed image do, and so did I, / The fledgling, while the Eagle moved its wings" (*Paradiso* 19.91–95, trans. Mandelbaum).

The ancients seem to have extended the notion of filial and parental devotion to constancy in marriage. Aelian, for example, tells a story of a stork that struck out the eyes of a servant who committed adultery with his master's wife (*De Natura Animalium* 8.20), and it was believed that the male stork destroys or abandons a female he finds unfaithful. That idea must lie behind Chaucer's sole reference to the stork as "the wrekere of avouterye" ("the avenger of adultery") (*Parliament of Fowls* 361), and this by Skelton: "The storke also, / That maketh his nest / In chymneyes to rest; / Within these walles / No broken galles [open sores?] / May there abyde / Of cokoldry syde" (*Phyllyp Sparowe* 469–75). "Constancy is like unto the stork," Lyly writes, "who wheresoever she fly cometh into no nest but her own" (*Euphues and his England*).

Occasionally the stork has a negative meaning, as in Spenser's *Epithalamion* 345–52, where he wishes that the screech owl, the stork, the raven, ghosts, vultures, and frogs all kept silent during the night; some of these creatures are listed together in Deuteronomy 14.12–19 as unclean (not to be eaten).

Storm   *see* **Wind**

Summer   Summer and winter were once probably the only seasons distinctly named, and both have long been used to indicate a year, especially when several of them are counted. Dido calls on Aeneas to tell his tale, for "now the seventh summer carries thee / a wanderer over every land and sea" (Virgil, *Aeneid* 1.755–56). Shakespeare's Egeon has spent "five summers" in Greece (*CE* 1.1.132). Wordsworth begins "Tintern Abbey" by counting the years: "Five years have passed; five summers, with the length / Of five long winters!" On other occasions Wordsworth remembers "twice five summers" (1850 *Prelude* 1.560) and "two-and-twenty summers" (8.349). (For more examples, *see* **Seasons**.)

Summer is the most pleasant season, at least in the temperate zone, not only for its warmth but its long days. "As fressh as is the brighte someres day" (Chaucer, *Merchant's Tale* 1896) became something of a commonplace. Shakespeare can evoke it, if only to find fault with it (it can be too hot or too windy), in comparison with his beloved (*Sonnets* 18). Spenser calls him "jolly Sommer" and describes him clothed in green, and sweating (*FQ* 7.7.29).

If one's life is figured as a year, summer is maturity, the full flowering of a man's powers, "Summer's ardent strength," in Thomson's phrase ("Winter" 1030). Wordsworth imagines Coleridge "with the soul / Which Nature gives to poets, now by thought / Matured, and in the summer of its strength" (1805 *Prelude* 10.998–1000). With women, however, summer is already a bit late; as

Byron puts it, "Some said her years were getting nigh their summer" (*Don Juan* 6.277).

See **Autumn, Seasons, Spring, Winter**.

Sun   The sun is so overwhelming a phenomenon and so fundamental to earthly life that its meanings in mythology and literature are too numerous to count. The sun is not only the most striking thing to be seen but the very condition of sight; light and seeing, some have argued, lie at the root of all symbolism. What follows, then, must be a highly selective discussion.

For the Greeks, to be alive was to see the sun. When a child was born he was brought "into the light, and he saw the sun's rays," according to Homer, while during one's life one sees the light and when one dies one "must leave the light of the sun" (*Iliad* 16.188, 18.61, 18.11). The realm of Hades is never illuminated by the sun (*Odyssey* 11.15–19); it is located in the far west, where the sun sets. Wordsworth succinctly states the Greek view when he laments that so many friends have passed "From sunshine to the sunless land" ("Extempore Effusion" 24). Leopardi borrows the ancient idea in his phrase "give to the sun" (*dare al sole*) for "give birth" ("Canto notturno" 52).

Plutarch wrote that "sunlight is the symbol of birth" (*Aetia Romana* 2). Shelley was to echo this idea frequently, as in his phrase "birth's orient portal" (*Hellas* 202). To live on earth is to live "under the sun and starry sky" (*Iliad* 4.44). A similar idea is found in Hebrew thought. "Under the sun" is the formulaic expression of Ecclesiastes for "in this life": "there is no new thing under the sun" (1.9), and "I saw vanity under the sun" (4.7). In Latin literature, *lux* ("light") can mean "life": Virgil has *invisam . . . lucem* ("hateful life"; *Aeneid* 4.631). Similarly "day" can mean "life" in several languages. Death "shuts up the day of life" (Shakespeare, *RJ* 4.1.101). When one dies, as Gray puts it, one leaves "the warm precincts of the cheerful day" ("Elegy" 87). At the end of it, our life can seem no longer than a day; we are "ephemeral" beings (from Greek *epi* "on" and *hemera* "day"). The comparison of human life in its brevity to a day is indeed ancient. Mimnermus says one's youth is "short as the sunlight spreads on the earth" (2.8). Catullus urges his Lesbia to give thousands of kisses, for time is short: "suns can set and rise again; / For us, once our brief light has set, / There's one unending night for sleeping" (5.4–6, trans. Lee). It became a commonplace, but variously evoked. After urging his "Coy Mistress" to hold out no longer but "sport us while we may," Marvell concludes, "Thus, though we cannot make our sun / Stand still, yet we will make him run" (45–46). Hopkins concludes a sonnet, "all / Life death does end and each day dies with sleep" ("No worst, there is none").

Sophocles wrote that "everyone worships the turning wheel of the sun" (frag. 672). In Homer Helios the sun is invoked as a god who sees everything and hears everything (*Iliad* 3.277, *Odyssey* 11.109, etc.); for that reason he is the god of oaths (like the Mesopotamian sun-god Shamash), the ever-present witness. Aeschylus' Prometheus calls on the "all-seeing circle of the sun" to witness his sufferings (*Prometheus* 91). (The phrase "circle of the sun" or "wheel of the sun" is a common Indo-European expression: cognate forms are found in Sanskrit and Old English poetry.) Sol sees all things in Ovid, *Metamorphoses* 2.32, 4.227–28, and 14.375. In Shakespeare, the "all-seeing sun" (*RJ* 1.2.92) has a "burning eye" (*RJ* 2.3.5), a "precious eye" (*KJ* 3.1.79), a "sovereign eye" (*Sonnets*

33.2); "The sun with one eye vieweth all the world" (1H6 1.4.84). If to be alive is to see the sun, it is also to be seen by it, as in Bryant's "Thanatopsis": "Yet a few days, and thee / The all-beholding sun shall see no more / In all his course" (17–19).

Rather than have an eye, the sun may be an eye itself. It is the "eye of day" in Sophocles' *Antigone* 104. The Hebrew phrase translated in the Authorized Version as "the dawning of the day" (Job 3.9) probably means "the eyelids of the morning" (as in the NEB). Ovid calls the sun the *mundi oculus* or "eye of the world" (*Met.* 4.228), Ronsard "the eye of the gods" and "the eye of God" (*Odes* 3.10.60, *Stances* 4.137), Spenser "the great eye of heaven" (FQ 1.3.4), Shakespeare "the eye of heaven" (*Sonnets* 18.5), Byron "the bright eye of the universe" (*Manfred* 1.2.10). Cicero, Pliny, and other Latin writers call the sun the mind or soul of the world. Milton combines these metaphors: "Thou sun, of this great world both eye and soul" (PL 5.171); Shelley in his *Hymn of Apollo* has Apollo call himself "the eye with which the universe / Beholds itself and knows itself divine."

The conventional attributes of Helios or Sol are well known. Brother of the Moon and Dawn, he drives his chariot of four (or seven) horses up from the eastern sea, across the sky, and down into the western sea, whereupon he somehow travels under or around the world, usually in a golden boat or cup on the river Ocean, back to the east. The Homeric *Hymn to Helios* and second *Hymn to Athena* mention the horses and chariot; Euripides describes sunset thus: "Helios drove his horses / Toward his final flame" (*Ion* 1148–49); it is these that Phaethon borrows in the disastrous tale told by Ovid in *Metamorphoses* 2. Homer sometimes calls the sun Hyperion, while Hesiod makes Hyperion his father; his mother is Theia. Later Apollo became associated with the sun, or with its brightness or clarity.

The sun's celestial team became a commonplace in Medieval and Renaissance poetry. Spenser, for example, has "Phoebus fiery carre" (FQ 1.2.1); Shakespeare speaks of "The hour before the heavenly-harness'd team / Begins his golden progress in the east" (1H4 3.1.214–15); and Milton describes the same hour as "Now while the Heav'n by the Sun's team untrod, / Hath took no print of the approaching light" ("Nativity" 19–20).

It became a persistent image that the sun's horses breathed fire. Pindar sings of "the lord [sun] of fire-breathing horses" (*Olymp.* 7.71. Virgil, in Dryden's expansive translation, has "Th'ethereal coursers, bounding from the sea, / From out their flaming nostrils breath'd the day" (*Aeneid* 12.115; see *Georgics* 1.250). Marlowe writes, "The horse that guide the golden eye of heaven, / And blow the morning from their nostrils" (2 *Tamburlaine* 4.4.7–8). In discussing Phaethon Spenser twice mentions the "flaming mouthes of steedes" (FQ 1.4.9) or "the firie-mouthed steedes" (5.8.40). Horses need not be divine to breathe fire, according to Lucretius, who refers to "the fire-snorting horses of Thracian Diomedes" (5.30 trans. Esolen); Virgil describes a thoroughbred whose "nostrils churn the pent-up fire within" (*Georgics* 3.85, trans. Wilkinson). In Blake's *Book of Thel*, the lily's perfume "tames the fire-breathing steed" (2.10).

Milton alludes to the myth that the sun is "the lusty Paramour" or lover of the Earth ("Nativity" 36). It goes back at least to Lucretius, who explains the fertility of Mother Earth as due to the casting of rain in her lap by Father Sky

(1.250–51); Virgil writes of the sexual intercourse between her and Father Aether (= Heaven) (*Georgics* 2.325–27). Sidney's *New Arcadia* begins: "It was in the time that the earth begins to put on her new apparel against the approach of her lover." (*See* **Rain**.)

Sun worship in Hellenistic and Roman times left its mark on Christianity. Christ was crucified on the 14th day of Nisan (on the full moon of the first month) in the Jewish lunar calendar, on the eve of the Sabbath, and rose from the dead two days later, which happened to be *dies Solis* or "Sunday" in the Greco-Roman solar calendar. At Jesus' death, according to Luke 23.45, "the sun was darkened." The last chapter of the Hebrew Bible seemed to prophesy a "Sun of righteousness" (Malachi 4.2). All this and the doctrine of the Logos as light in the Gospel of John made the equation inevitable: Christ is the new and greater sun. "As the sun returns from the west to the east," Athanasius wrote, "so the Lord arose out of the depths of Hades to the Heaven of Heavens" (*Expositio in Psalmen* 67.34).

After much debate, the church in the west adopted the Roman calendar and set Easter as the first Sunday after the first full moon after the vernal equinox: the time of ascendancy of both sunlight and moonlight. Christmas was eventually set at the winter solstice, the "birth" of the sun out of darkness. To quote Milton's "Nativity" ode once more, on the morning of Christ's nativity "The Sun himself withheld his wonted speed, / And hid his head for shame, / As his inferior flame, / The new-enlight'n'd world no more should need; / He saw a greater Sun appear / Than his bright Throne, or burning Axletree could bear" (79–84).

The sun rises in the east – due east on the two equinoxes, north of east during spring and summer, south of east during fall and winter – moves upward and southward until noon, and moves downward and northward until it sets in the west. In Europe and all areas north of the Tropic of Cancer its highest point or meridian is south of the zenith. The south was often considered the quarter of the sun; the word "south," in fact, is derived from "sun."

The day and the year are natural units of time determined by the sun, as the month is determined originally by the moon. Seasons are more arbitrary divisions, and not all cultures have four.

The annual movement north and south of the sun's daily track, which causes the changing seasons, is due to the tilt of the earth's axis, but from an earthly viewpoint it appears that the annual path of the sun against the sky (the ecliptic) is tilted at an angle of 23° to the path of the midpoint between the celestial poles (the celestial equator). The moon and planets also follow paths along the ecliptic, which Dante calls "the oblique circle that carries the planets" (*Paradiso* 10.14), though two planets, Mercury and Venus, are never very far from the sun.

A belt along this path, called the zodiac, contains a great many constellations, twelve of which were singled out in ancient times to mark twelve "houses" or stations in the yearly migration of the sun through them. This migration we know is due to the annual revolution of the earth around the sun, the sun appearing against a constantly changing backdrop of fixed stars, but it looks as if the sun is wandering through them. Hence the sun was considered in the Ptolemaic system (and earlier) as a planet (from Greek *planetes*, "wanderer"), the fourth in distance from the earth; it is in Dante's words "the planet / which leads men straight through all paths" (*Inferno* 1.17–18), and the "fayrest Planet," according to Spenser (*Epithalamion* 282). The twelve constellations form the basis for astrology and the daily horoscope in newspapers today. (*See* **Planet, Star**.)

The sun is no longer in Aries (the Ram) during the first month of spring, however, as it was when the Babylonians established the system about four thousand years ago. When Chaucer says in the opening of his *Canterbury Tales* that "the yonge sonne / Hath in the Ram his halve cours yronne" he is specifying April but he using the conventional and badly out-of-date sign for it. Because of the precession of the equinoxes or backward slippage of the ecliptic–equator intersection points (precession is a phenomenon of rotating bodies), spring began in Pisces (the Fish) around the time of Christ and is now entering Aquarius. In one lifetime the slippage is about one degree, and the entire cycle takes about 26,000 years to return to the starting point, an interval known to the ancients as the *magnus annus* or "great year" (or "Platonic Year"). It may underlie the symbolism of Virgil's "Fourth Eclogue," an enormously influential poem because it seemed to prophesy the coming of Christ; a phrase from this eclogue has been altered to *novus ordo seclorum* ("new order of the ages") and adopted for the great seal of the United States (found on the back of the one-dollar bill). See also the first of Yeats's "Two Songs from a Play": "And then did all the Muses sing / Of Magnus Annus at the spring, / As though God's death were but a play."

Another cycle that the Greeks understood is the nineteen-year Metonic cycle, the period when the phases of the moon begin on the same date of the year. This cycle may be the basis for the pervasive solar symbolism of the *Odyssey*, the hero of which returns home after nineteen years.

See **Black sun, East and west, Gold, Moon**.

Sunflower   Ovid tells the tale of a nymph, Clytie, who pined away for the love of Helios, the Sun, until she was transformed into a flower whose face always turns to follow her love through the sky (*Met.* 4.256–70). This heliotrope was probably not what we call the sunflower, which is named for its appearance rather than its behavior, but the sunflower has long been linked to the unrequited devotion of a lover, or to the longing of the earthbound soul for its heavenly home.

A sonnet attributed to Dante laments the disdain of his mistress: "Nor did she who turns to see the sun / and changed, preserves her unchanged love, / ever have as bitter fate as I" ("Nulla mi parve," trans. Galassi). Blake's evocative little poem "Ah! Sun-flower" takes the flower, "weary of time, / Who countest the steps of the Sun," as an emblem of "the Youth pined away with desire" and "the pale Virgin shrouded with snow," who arise from their graves. Blake may have been prompted by an account of the neo-Platonic philosopher Proclus, who cites the heliotrope as a symbol of souls who long for spiritual illumination. The same source seems to have led Bronson Alcott to choose the name *The Dial* (i.e., sundial) for the journal of the Transcendentalists.

Byron's Julia, confined to a nunnery after her affair with the young Don Juan, writes her lover one last letter on gilt-edged paper, "The seal a sunflower; *Elle vous suit partout* ["She follows you everywhere"], / The motto"

(*Don Juan* 1.198). Robert Browning's Rudel tells his lady that he will "choose for my device / A sunflower outspread like a sacrifice / Before its idol" ("Rudel to the Lady of Tripoli" 24–26). Carolina Coronado addresses a sunflower as a kindred spirit who has suffered the neglect of "the beautiful sun you adored," whose "eyes won't even stop to see / that you were consumed by the love of his fire" ("Sunflower 48–52," trans. Myles). Montale demands, "Bring me the sunflower crazed with light" in an early poem ("Portami il girasole"), and the flower remains a symbol throughout his poetry, sometimes associated with a woman named Clizia (Clytie).

Swallow   In ancient Greece as in modern times the return of the swallow was a sign that spring has returned as well. The Greeks held ceremonies at the beginning of the season in which children would dress as swallows and go from house to house begging for treats. A song from Rhodes sung on such occasions, the *Chelidonismos* (from Greek *chelidon*, "swallow"), begins, "The swallow has come, bringing lovely seasons and lovely years." In *Works and Days* Hesiod tells us that sixty days after the winter solstice "the swallow appears to men when spring is just beginning" (564–69). This is the common understanding behind the cautionary proverb quoted by Aristotle, "A single swallow doesn't make a spring."

The bird is often linked in poetry to the spring zephyr, the west wind (Virgil, *Georgics* 4.304–07; Horace, *Epistles*, 1.7.13). The Greeks sometimes called the spring west wind *chelidonias* because it brought the swallows.

It is also associated with the sun, whose warmth and light revive with the spring. In "The Spring," Carew writes, the warm sun "gives a sacred birth / To the dead Swallow." That passage may allude to the belief that swallows do not migrate but nest throughout the winter; in March, according to Spenser, "The Swallow peepes out of her nest" (*SC* "March" 11).

It was considered a good omen if a swallow nested under the eaves of one's house. In the midst of Odysseus' slaughter of the suitors in the *Odyssey* (22.240), his protectress Athena turns into a swallow and perches on a beam. (In *Macbeth* 1.6.3–10, the "temple-haunting martlet" seems to be the martin, a kind of swallow.)

The final line of Keats's "To Autumn" – "And gathering swallows twitter in the skies" – poignantly evokes their association with a spring that now seems long past. At the end of *The Waste Land* T. S. Eliot invokes the swallow in two quotations as a possible harbinger of spring and redemption from the "arid plain." The first is from a late Latin poem, *The Vigil of Venus*: "When is my spring coming? When shall I be as the swallow, that I may cease to be voiceless?" The second is from a love song about a migrating swallow in Tennyson's *The Princess* (4.75–98).

The tuneless, chattering sound of the swallow, also noted in the Bible (Isa. 38.14), may have prompted the tale of Philomela and Procne (told in full by Ovid in the *Metamorphoses* but without naming the birds), where Philomela, with her tongue cut out, is transformed into a swallow. So Dante has a swallow (*rondinella*) singing sad songs near dawn (*Purgatorio* 9.14). (In other versions of the myth Procne becomes the swallow and Philomela the nightingale.) Swinburne's "Itylus" is a song sung by the nightingale to her sister the swallow. (*See* **Nightingale**.)

Swallows are proverbially swift in flight. In Spenser a speedy ship glides "More swift then swallow sheres the liquid skye" (*FQ* 2.6.5). "True hope is swift and flies with swallow's wings" (Shakespeare, *R3* 5.2.23). Perhaps for this reason they were sometimes identified with swifts in ancient times. Blake has a rather awkward simile, "swift as the swallow or swift" (*Milton* 15.48).

Swan The swan (Greek *kyknos*, Latin *cycnus* or *cygnus*, or *olor*) has long been one of the most popular birds in poetry, not least because of the association of swans with poets themselves. The trumpet-like call of some swans apparently sounded beautiful to ancient ears; Virgil in *Eclogues* 9.29 refers to the famous singing swans of his city, Mantua, and Lucretius compares the song of the swan with the art of the lyre (2.503). We learn in Aristophanes' *Birds* that the swan is the bird of Apollo, god of poetry (869); see Martial 13.77. In Latin poetry it is also sometimes the bird of Venus, who is borne by a chariot of swans in Ovid (*Met.* 10.717) and Horace (3.28.13–15).

It became a commonplace of modesty to contrast one's own song (or poem) to another poet's as a goose's (or swallow's) song beside a swan's: see *Eclogues* 8.55, 9.36, Lucretius 3.6–7; Shelley playfully repeats the gesture by comparing his poem to an ephemeral fly that cannot climb to the heights where the swan sings (*Witch of Atlas* 9–12). Theocritus, in *Idyll* 5.136, has a goatherd boast of his singing prowess by using the comparison in reverse. Horace elaborates a conceit in which he is transmogrified into a swan and flies over many nations, that is, he shall gain great fame as a poet (*Odes* 2.20). Pope, in "On the Candidates for the Laurel," deploys the comparison with his usual wit. Unable to endorse any of the candidates for the office of poet laureate, he seizes on Stephen Duck, a poet of very minor talent: "Let's rather wait one year for better luck; / One year may make a singing swan of *Duck*."

In describing Pindar as the "swan of Dirce" (one of the rivers of Thebes), Horace (4.2.25–27) began a tradition that continued into modern times, e.g., Homer is the Swan of Meander, Shakespeare is the "Sweet Swan of Avon" (from Jonson's memorial poem), Vaughan is the Swan of Usk, and so on. This convention depends, of course, on the fact that, as Ovid puts it, "swans love the streams" (*Metamorphoses* 2.539). (*See* **River**.) Or the poet's city is named, as when Cowper calls Virgil "the Mantuan swan" (*Table Talk* 557), or the nation, as when Garnier addresses Ronsard "O Swan of the French" ("Elegy on the Death of Ronsard" 50).

As swans are migratory, and are frequently seen alone, they can be imagined as exiles from their homelands. So Shelley, referring to Byron's emigration to Italy, writes, "a tempest-cleaving Swan / Of the songs of Albion, / Driven from his ancestral streams / By the might of evil dreams, / Found a nest in thee [Venice]" ("Euganean Hills" 174–78). Baudelaire in "Le Cygne" describes a swan escaped from a menagerie, crying for water and dreaming of his native lake. Mallarmé's best-known sonnet, *Le vierge, le vivace et le bel aujourd'hui*, likens the new "today" to a swan caught in the ice of a lake of past failures to fly: it might tear itself free but it remains fast in useless exile. See also Edmund Gosse's "The Swan." Yeats in "1919" writes, "Some moralist or mythological poet / Compares the solitary soul to a swan"; he is probably alluding to Shelley's *Alastor* 275–90, where the wandering poet contrasts his own homelessness with the flight of a swan to his nest and mate.

It was also thought that swans sang at their deaths. Clytemnestra in Aeschylus' *Agamemnon* 1444–45 gloats that Cassandra cried out at her death like a swan. Plato has Socrates disparage this belief as a human projection (*Phaedo* 85a), but Socrates' opinion did not much affect the poets. It was so commonplace a belief that Seneca can allude to the sweetness of a swan's last song (*Phaedra* 301). Chaucer names "The jelous swan, ayens his deth that syngeth" (*PF* 342). When Ronsard declares he is weary of life, he sings his passing "the way a swan does, / Who sings its death on the banks of the Meander" (sonnet: "Il faut laisser maisons"). Shakespeare has: "And now this pale swan in her wat'ry nest / Begins the sad dirge of her certain ending" (*Lucrece* 1611–12). The phrase "swan song" often refers to the last work of a poet or musician. Ovid declares the final book of his *Tristia* to be the sorrowful song of a swan (5.1.11–14), probably the passage Darío invokes when he writes, "I salute you [swans] now as in Latin verses / Publius Ovidius Naso once saluted you" ("Los Cisnes" 5–6). Yeats in "The Tower" beautifully describes "the hour / When the swan must fix his eye / Upon a fading gleam, / Float out upon a long / Last reach of glittering stream / And there sing his last song." The image is implicit in Tennyson's "The Lady of Shalott," where the Lady, whose magic web and mirror are destroyed when she looks down to Camelot, lies down, "robed in snowy white" (136), in a boat and sings her last song as she floats downstream.

An ancient myth tells how Zeus in the form of a swan raped Leda, who then gave birth to Helen and Clytemnestra from one egg and Castor and Pollux from another. It was a popular subject in ancient art, and several of the Renaissance masters painted it (e.g., Michaelangelo, Leonardo, Raphael). See also Darío's "Leda" and Yeats's "Leda and the Swan."

Tennyson knew some of the legends about swan-maidens and swan-princes that were common in the Middle Ages; the best-known of these is the tale of Lohengrin. After Wagner's opera *Lohengrin* mysterious swans swim through Symbolist poems, notably in many by Darío, who celebrates a new "Wagnerian swan," which will grasp beauty (Leda) and/or conceive a greater ideal beauty (Helen) ("The Swan"); it is "the poet of perfect verses" ("Blazon").

Swine   *see* **Pig**

Sword   *see* **Armor**

T

Tempest   *see* **Wind**

Tercel   *see* **Hawk**

Theatre   "The world hath been often compared to the theatre," writes Fielding, "and many grave writers as well as the poets have considered human life as a great drama, resembling in almost every particular those scenical representations which Thespis is first reported to have invented" (*Tom Jones* 7.1). The comparison most often quoted is Shakespeare's: "All the world's a stage, / And all the men and women merely players; / They have their exits and their entrances, / And one man in his time plays many parts" (*AYLI* 2.7.139–42). It is an old metaphor, going back at least to Plato, not long after the rise of Greek drama. He speculates: "We may imagine that each of us living creatures is a puppet made by the gods, possibly as a plaything, possibly with some more serious purpose" (*Laws* 644d–e, trans. Taylor); in another dialogue Socrates considers "the whole tragedy and comedy of life" (*Philebus* 50b). Indeed Plato's influential Cave is a kind of shadow-theatre with people as spectators rather than actors (*see* **Cave**). Like Plato, Horace thinks of man as a puppet (*Satires* 2.7.82), and other Latin writers, pagan and Christian, followed suit.

By and large the image of puppet or actor implies that people are under the control of puppeteers or playwrights, that is, the gods, or God, or fate. Its germ may be found in the *Iliad*, where the gods watch the war, comment on it (as the nobles do during the mechanicals' play in *A Midsummer Night's Dream*), and sometimes intervene in it, though fate seems in overall control. From the spectator's viewpoint, which is really that of an actor stepping back from his or her role, the metaphor tends to bring out a sense of life's unreality, as when Prospero likens the globe to the "insubstantial pageant" he has just put on (*Tempest* 4.1.155), or life's brevity and meaninglessness, as when Macbeth sums up: "Life's but a walking shadow; a poor player, / That struts and frets his hour upon the stage, / And then is heard no more" (5.5.24–26).

Spenser complains that his beloved is like a spectator who remains unmoved while "beholding me that all the pageants play, / disguysing diversly my troubled wits" (*Amoretti* 54). Cervantes' Don Quixote stresses the superficiality of dramatic roles as he explains to Sancho that "some play emperors, others popes, and in short, all the parts that can be brought into a play; but when it is over, that is to say, when life ends, death strips them all of the robes that distinguished one from the other, and all are equal in the grave" (2.12, trans. Starkie). Several of Caldéron's plays depend on the notion of "the theatre of the world," with God as director or playwright. While Wilhelm Meister is expatiating on the ignorance, vanity, and selfishness of actors, a friend breaks in: "don't you realize that you have been describing the whole world, not just the theatre?" (Goethe, *Wilhelm Meister's Apprenticeship* 7.3). Poe restates Don Quixote's lesson in lurid terms in "The Conqueror Worm": angels watch a "motley drama" put on by "mere puppets" with "horror the soul of the plot" until death puts out the lights on the tragedy called "Man," of which the hero is "the Conqueror Worm." Yeats developed a complex theory of masks to account for human character, and in many of his own plays he returned to ancient Greek or Japanese styles of masked acting to bring out the essential role of artifice in life. "It was the mask engaged your mind," one lover says to another, "And after set your heart to beat, / Not what's behind" ("The Mask"); in a late poem Yeats admits, "Players and painted stage took all my love / And not those things that they were emblems of" ("Circus Animals' Desertion" 31–32). Literary critics often use "persona" (Latin for "mask") to refer to the speaker or narrator of a work (as opposed to the author); the "dramatic monologue," perfected by R. Browning, is spoken in character, not *in propria persona*, "in the author's own voice." Ezra Pound, speaking ventriloquistically through many voices and styles, titled an early collection *Personae*.

Thread   *see* **Weaving and spinning**

Three   *see* **Number**

Thyme   *see* **Bee**

Tiger   Not found in the Mediterranean area, tigers go unmentioned in the Bible and in Greek poetry and drama. In Latin literature it is sometimes the beast of Bacchus: in Virgil's *Aeneid* the god drives his tigers down the slopes of Nysa (6.805; see also *Eclogues* 5.29), while Horace (3.3.14–15) and Martial (8.26.8) have him drawn by a pair of tigers. Dionysus wears a tiger skin in Claudian (*Rape of Proserpine* 1.17–18). The point here is surely that Bacchus/Dionysus represents the power to tame what is wild or fierce. For even more than the lion, with which it is often paired, the tiger represents cruelty or ferocity. Dido accuses Aeneas of being suckled by a tigress (4.367); if she fails to help Jason, Medea tells herself, "I'll surely own / I am a child of a tigress" (Ovid, *Met.* 7.32). Over a pathetic scene in Chaucer "ther nys tigre, ne noon so crueel beest," that would not weep (*Squire's Tale* 419); "cruel" occurs as the epithet several times in Chaucer and Spenser. In *The Faerie Queene* the wicked Maleger rides on one (2.11.20). When Shakespeare's Albany turns on Goneril for her cruel treatment of her father, he says, "What have you done? / Tigers, not daughters" (*Lear* 4.2.39–40).

In his *Ars Poetica* Horace gives as an example of artistic incongruity the linking of wild with tame, "of pairing snakes with birds or lambs with tigers" (13). Byron's version of this is "Birds breed not vipers, tigers nurse not lambs" ("Hints from Horace" 20).

The most famous tiger in literature is the mysterious creature in Blake's "The Tyger." The poem is a series of unanswered and unanswerable questions addressed to the beast and his creator, climaxing in "Did he who made the Lamb make thee?"

During the joyous cosmic celebration that concludes Shelley's *Prometheus Unbound*, the moon likens herself to a Maenad, worshipper of Dionysus, in her rapture, while the earth responds that the moon's rays charm "the tyger joy" that fills her (4.501). An even more striking image is T. S. Eliot's "Christ the tiger" in "Gerontion." If "April is the cruelest month" (*The Waste Land*) to a man in spiritual despair, then he would also think "In the juvescence of the year / Came Christ the tiger" (19–20); "The tiger springs in the new year. Us he devours" (48).

Note: Tigers in classical literature generally come from Hyrcania, on the southeast shore of the Caspian (Virgil, *Aeneid* 4.367; Claudian, *Rape of Proserpine* 3.263), or from Armenia (Propertius 1.9.19; Virgil, *Eclogues* 5.29). Macbeth names "th'Hyrcan tiger" (3.4.100).

See **Lion**.

Time   Seldom a symbol of something else, time is itself often symbolized, like dawn, death, and the seasons, in images no less interesting for being conventional.

"Time's scythe," or his "bending sickle," is his most salient prop (Shakespeare, *Sonnets* 12 and 116); with it "wicked Tyme ... | Does mow the flowring herbes and goodly things | And all their glory to the ground downe flings" (Spenser, *FQ* 3.6.39). Resembling the harvest, and death the Grim Reaper, time's scything or mowing would seem an obvious trope, but it probably owes something to the Greek god Kronos, an agricultural god who was imagined as carrying a sickle, and whose name was confused with *khronos*, "time" (Latinized as *chronus*, whence "chronic," "chronology," etc.); Plutarch mentions that some Greeks identify the two (*De Iside et Osiride* 363d) (and see Cicero, *De Natura Deorum* 2.25).

Ovid calls time *edax rerum*, "gluttonous of things" (*Met.* 15.234); Shakespeare addresses him as "Devouring Time" (*Sonnets* 19), "eater of youth" (*Lucrece* 927), and "cormorant devouring Time" (*LLL* 1.1.4). Ronsard says, "Time the glutton (*Le temps mangeard*) consumes all things, | Cities, Castles, Empires: indeed man" (*Discours de l'altération et change des choses humaines* 49–50). Milton defies him to "glut thyself with what thy womb devours" ("On Time"). That metaphor too may go back to Kronos, who swallowed his children as they were born: so time consumes what it creates. "Thou nursest all, and murder'st all that are" (*Lucrece* 929).

In variants of these images Shakespeare and many other poets call time a thief, a "bloody tyrant" (*Sonnets* 16), a waster; envious, injurious, inexorable, fatal. Sometimes he drives a chariot or coach. Marvell hears "Time's winged chariot hurrying near" and it threatens to turn him and his coy mistress to dust ("Coy Mistress" 22). Goethe's "An Schwager Kronos" ("To Coachman Chronus") imagines the coach rolling briskly downhill into life, then laboriously uphill to a splendid view, pausing for a drink with a maiden, and then careering toward a sinking sun through the gate of hell.

As opposed to eternity, one seldom finds a favorable account of time, but he has his virtues. He heals wounds, and Truth is his daughter – he can "unmask falsehood and bring truth to light" – and he has the power to redress wrongs and reward diligence (*Lucrece* 936–59). This latter idea goes back at least to Pindar, who wrote "for just men Time is the best savior" (frag. 159). Sophocles' Ajax learns that "Vast and measureless time makes all | hidden things grow and hides what appears" (*Ajax* 646–47). Jesus said, "there is nothing covered, that shall not be revealed; and hid, that shall not be known" (Matt. 10.26). In a sinister context Racine writes, "There are no secrets that times does not reveal" (*Britannicus* 4.4.1404). Time may also be disparaged as a "ceaseless lackey to eternity" (*Lucrece* 967), for he will consume himself in the end and "long Eternity" will prevail (Milton, "On Time"); but Blake says "time is the mercy of Eternity" (*Milton* 24.72) and "Eternity is in love with the productions of time" (*Marriage of Heaven and Hell* 7).

Marvell's chariot and Goethe's coach remind us that time is unidirectional and fast. By contrast the motion of eternity is circular, stately, and dancelike. During the eternal spring of unfallen Eden, according to Milton, the Hours danced (*PL* 4.267). Shelley's fateful Hour rose in a chariot to dethrone Demogorgon, but after the death of Time there are no more chariots; "Once the hungry Hours were hounds | Which chased the Day" but now they dance in "mystic measure" (*PU* 4.73–78). At the "still point" of eternity, according to Eliot, "there is only the dance" ("Burnt Norton" sec. 2).

Times of day   *see* **Day, Dawn, East and west, Sun**

Toad   *see* **Frog and toad**

Tortoise   *see* **Harp**

Tower   As its most striking feature at a distance, a tower often stands as a synecdoche for a great city, as in Marlowe's "topless towers of Ilium" (*Doctor Faustus B* 5.1.94). As a human structure striving towards heaven, and as a dwelling for noble lords, a tower might mean pride or hubris, marked for destruction, like the Tower of Babel; see also Milton's phrase "proud towers" (*PL* 5.907). It can symbolize a woman besieged, as in *The Romance of the Rose* (8566), or a woman sequestered, as in the tale of Rapunzel or Tennyson's "The Lady of Shalott." (*see* **Siege**.)

A tower may also be a refuge of solitude for sage or poet. "Or let my lamp at midnight hour / Be seen in some high lonely tower," Milton writes in "Il Penseroso" (85–86). Having moved into a house with an "ancient tower," Yeats saw the chamber at the top of a winding stair as like that of Milton's contemplative, and where he could meditate on history and rise above it ("My House").

Though "tower of ivory" is a simile for the neck of the beloved in the Song of Solomon (7.4), the common phrase "ivory tower," referring to a retreat or shelter from the real world, such as a university, seems to derive from a poem by Sainte-Beuve ("Pensées d'Août") where he contrasts the embattled Victor Hugo with the aloof Alfred de Vigny, who withdraws to his *tour d'ivoire*. Why ivory? Perhaps Sainte-Beuve alludes to Vigny's own *cor d'ivoire*, the ivory horn in "Le Cor" sounded by the dying knight at Roncevaux – surely an emblem of the poet – and perhaps to the gate of ivory in Homer and Virgil, the gate of false dreams, dreams or revery being the Romantic refuge from this sordid world. Flaubert wrote to Turgenev, "I have always tried to live in an ivory tower, but a sea of shit is beating against its walls" (13 November 1872). *The Ivory Tower* is the title of Henry James's last, unfinished, novel.

Tree   Most symbolic trees are specified, for the symbolism of individual trees is usually highly specific. But anything that can grow, "flourish," bear "fruit," and die might be likened to a tree: a person, a family, a nation, a cultural tradition. In the Bible a tree often stands for a person, usually to distinguish the godly from the ungodly. Thus in Psalm 1 the godly man "shall be like a tree planted by the rivers of water, that bringeth forth his fruit in his season; his leaf shall not wither" (1.3; cf. Jer. 17.8), whereas Jude warns against false Christians, who are "trees whose fruit withereth, without fruit, twice dead, plucked up by the roots" (1.12). Job contrasts a man to a tree, which might grow again after being cut down (14.7–10). Daniel interprets Nebuchadnezzar's dream of a tree that grew to heaven only to be ordered cut down by an angel as really about Nebuchadnezzar himself (Dan. 4.8–27). Paul calls a new member of the church a "neophyte" (Authorized Version "novice"), i.e., "newly planted" (1 Tim. 3.6). Isaiah extends the image: "as the days of a tree are the days of my people" (65.22; cf. 56.3); Ezekiel's riddling parable in chapter 17 establishes Jerusalem as a tree. The now common notion of a "family tree" is found in the tree of Jesse: "And there shall come forth a rod out of the stem of Jesse, and a Branch shall grow out of his roots" (Isa. 11.1, quoted by Paul in Rom. 15.12). It is implicit in Homer's *Iliad*, where the generations of men are likened to leaves on a tree (6.145–50; *see* **Leaf**).

The two most important trees in the Bible, of course, are "the tree of life" and "the tree of knowledge of good and evil" (Gen. 2.9). Though what they symbolize is more or less expressed in their names, why the book's author chose trees as the vehicle is less clear: perhaps to make the link between knowing and tasting, of the sort that Milton makes as he exploits the original sense of "sapience" (from the root of Latin *sapere*, "to taste of") (*PL* 9.797, 1018), and perhaps to establish the first of a series of dietary taboos that define the Hebrew people. The notion of two trees, variously named, has entered into western religious traditions, such as the Kabbalah, and literature. Byron's Manfred has learned that "Sorrow is knowledge: they who know the most / Must mourn the deepest o'er the fatal truth, / The Tree of Knowledge is not that of Life" (*Manfred* 1.1.10–12). Yeats's "Two Trees" are an inner one that grows in one's heart with "great ignorant leafy ways" (16) and an outer one reflected in a glass where "ravens of unresting thought" fly through broken branches (34). In the pageant that Dante sees atop Mt. Purgatory, one tree, the tree Adam ate from, loses all its leaves and fruit, but after the chariot of the church is tied to it the tree is renewed, as if to say that Christ reconciles our fallen nature to God (*Purgatorio* 32.37–60). Mephistopheles tells a student, "All theory is gray, dear friend, / And green is the golden tree of life" (*Faust* 2038–39).

The bleeding tree is an interesting topos or motif traceable from Virgil's *Aeneid* 3.22–68, where Aeneas, after breaking a branch off a bush, sees blood dripping from it, and learns that it is his friend Polydorus. Dante (at Virgil's urging) breaks a branch of a tree in the wood of suicides and hears the sinner's story (*Inferno* 13.28–108). Ariosto in book 6 of *Orlando Furioso* and Tasso in *Jerusalem Liberated* 13.41 have similar tales; Spenser imitates these in his story of Fradubio, enchanted by Duessa (*FQ* 1.2.30ff.).

Ovid's tale of Orpheus includes a tree-list or small catalogue of trees (and other plants) that came crowding around him when he sat down to sing: poplar, oak, beech, maple, fir, willow, pine, and so on (*Met.* 10.90–105). Other tree-lists after Ovid are found in Seneca's *Oedipus* 566–75, Statius' *Thebaid* 6.98–106, the *Roman de la Rose* 1338–68, Boccaccio's *Teseide* 11.22–24, Chaucer's *Parliament of Fowls* 176–82, and both Spenser's *Faerie Queene* 1.1.8–9 and his *Virgil's Gnat* 190–224. Sidney gives a catalogue with symbolic meanings attached in *First Eclogues* 13.113–54. See also Shelley, "Orpheus" 105–14.

Tree entries in this dictionary: **Almond, Apple, Ash, Beech, Cedar, Cypress, Elm, Holly, Laurel, Linden, Oak, Olive, Palm, Poplar, Willow, Yew.** See also **Forest, Leaf, Seed.**

Trumpet   "Trumpet" in English translates several types of ancient horns, whether the curved ram's horn of the Hebrews (usually *shopar*) or the straight bronze horn of the Greeks (*salpinx*) and Romans (*tuba*). In the Bible and classical literature its main uses are similar – to send signals, to summon an assembly, and especially to prepare for battle – but its extended senses are interestingly different.

The Book of Numbers explains that trumpets are to be used to call assemblies, announce a war, and sound over sacrifices (10.1–10). Already Jehovah had summoned the Israelites to go up to Mt. Sinai with a long loud trumpet sound (Exod. 19.13,16,19). Leviticus ordains a "trumpet of jubile" after forty-nine years (25.9). In Joshua seven priests blow seven trumpets for seven days as part of the campaign to destroy Jericho (6.4–20).

The prophets serve as trumpets of the Lord. "Cry aloud, spare not," Isaiah is told, "lift up thy voice like a trumpet" (58.1). "Blow ye the trumpet...for the day of the Lord cometh" (Joel 2.1). That day, according to Zephaniah, is a "day of the trumpet" (1.16), while according to Zechariah "the Lord God shall blow the trumpet" (9.14). Shelley evokes these prophets when he asks the west wind to be through his lips "The trumpet of a prophecy" ("West Wind" 69).

The Christian meaning of the "last trump" (1 Cor. 15.52) subsumes the Jewish uses – gathering the exiled Israelites, preparing for the Messiah's war – and adds the resurrection of the dead. To John of Patmos the voice of Christ is as great as a trumpet's (1.10); then John sees seven angels, each with a trumpet that produces a revelation of the last days (8.1ff.).

In the Sermon on the Mount, Christ enjoins his followers to give alms in secret: "do not sound a trumpet before thee, as the hypocrites do in the synagogues and in the streets, that they may have the glory of men" (Matt. 6.2). We still speak of "trumpeting" one's virtues or doing something "with a flourish of trumpets."

Homer's warriors do not use trumpets, but a trumpet appears once in a simile for Achilles' piercing cry (Iliad 18.219). Though it had other uses in Greece, it became almost synonymous with war and war's alarms. Bacchylides' trumpet "shrieks out the song of war" (18.3). Greeks attack boldly, says Aeschylus, inspired by blaring trumpets (Persians 395). When peace is established, a trumpet-maker has a useless and expensive trumpet on his hands (Aristophanes, Peace 1240).

Quite a few trumpets appear in the Aeneid and other Roman epics, though it is not always the tuba; sometimes it is the curved horn called the bucina, or just a "horn" (cornu) that summons men to arms (e.g., Aeneid 6.165). In the Golden Age, according to Ovid, one heard "no trumpet straight, no horn of bent brass" (Met. 1.98). In literature ever since, trumps or trumpets, with such epithets as "thundering" (Chaucer), "dreadful," "doleful" (Spenser), "braying," "angry," "hideous" (Shakespeare), and "warlike" (Milton), have sounded whenever battles are described. Even Milton's angels form ranks when "to arms / The matin trumpet sung" (PL 6.525–26).

Antipater of Sidon called Pindar "the Pierian trumpet" (Greek Anthology 7.34). Traditional (Renaissance) portraits of Clio, the muse of history, give her a trumpet. Spenser has Clio say "I, that doo all noble feates professe / To register, and sound in trump of gold" (Tears of the Muses 97–98). Fame, a poor cousin of Clio, also has a "trompe of gold" in Chaucer (House of Fame 3) and Spenser (FQ 3.3.3). Since history is mainly a tale of wars and famous deeds of warriors, the trumpet became a synecdoche for epic poetry. When Alexander came to Achilles' tomb, according to Petrarch, he called him fortunate to have found "so clear a trumpet," i.e., Homer (Rime 187). Spenser, improving on the supposed preamble to the Aeneid, announces he is forced "For trumpets sterne to change mine Oaten reeds," that is, to give up pastoral poetry and take up

"Fierce warres and faithful loves" (*FQ* 1 Pro. 1; see 1.11.6). Alfieri notes that Tasso made the ancient trumpet sound in modern tones ("On Tasso's Tomb"). Wordsworth, however, claims that it was the sonnet that, in Milton's hands, "became a trumpet; whence he blew | Soul-animating strains" ("Scorn not the sonnet").

Turtle-dove   *see* **Dove**

U

Urn   In classical literature literal urns have three functions: to hold liquids (the Greek word for "urn" is *hydria*, from *hydor*, "water"), to hold ballots or lots, and to hold the ashes of the dead. From the first use comes the image of the urn as the source of a river. Virgil pictures Father Inachus pouring his stream from an urn (*Aeneid* 7.792), while Statius has Ismenus drop his urn in despair (*Thebaid* 9.410). Imitating these river-gods, Dryden writes, of the great fire of London, "Old Father Thames raised up his reverend head, | But feared the fate of Simois would return" – the Trojan river that fought the fire of Hephaestus; "Deep in his ooze he sought his sedgy bed, | And shrunk his waters back into his urn" (*Annus Mirabilis* 925–28). Thomson's eye roves "To where the Nile from Ethiopian clouds, | His never drained ethereal urn, descends" (*Liberty* 3.252–53). Schiller laments the time when "Out of urns the lovely Naiads carried | Leapt the rivers' silver foam" ("Gods of Greece" (1800) 23–24), while Shelley imagines a northern clime where Liberty teaches "every Naiad's ice-cold urn" to speak of her ("Ode to Liberty" 111).

The urn's occasional use as the source of fate derives from another passage of the *Aeneid* that names the urn full of lots for choosing which seven young Athenian men must be sacrificed to the Minotaur (6.22). In Seneca's *Troades* we learn that the captive Trojan women have been assigned to their captors by lots from a spinning urn (974). Behind this tradition lies the two jars (*pithoi*) of Zeus, one containing griefs, the other good things, to be distributed to mortals below (*Iliad* 24.527ff.).

Propertius warns his friend Postumus that he may be sent back from the wars in an urn (3.12.13). "Urn" became a general term for tomb or grave in poetry. Donne's lovers will forgo a long chronicle for a sonnet or two, for "As well a well wrought urn becomes | The greatest ashes, as half-acre tombs" ("The Canonization" 33–34). Admonishing us to remember the vanity of fame, Gray asks, "Can storied urn or animated bust | Back to its mansion call the fleeting breath?" ("Elegy" 41–42). Byron describes Athens under the Ottomans as "a nation's sepulchre" and a "defenceless urn" (*Childe Harold* 2.20–21).

Keats does not tell us what he thinks was the original function of his Grecian urn, but since it is "storied" like Gray's, it is plausible to think of it as a cinerary urn, once holding the ashes of the dead. That use may give it another means to "tease us out of thought | As doth eternity" (44–45).

V

Valley Valleys are low places, where villagers dwell, as opposed to mountains, where the lordly might have their fortresses or castles; thus the social ranks of high and low often correspond to the terrain. But when the Lord comes, according to Isaiah, the ranks will be reversed: "Every valley shall be exalted, and every mountain and hill shall be made low" (40.4). This revolutionary prophecy lent its imagery to militant Christians for millennia, as we see in a sermon of John Bunyan: "If you would understand the Scriptures, you shall read it calleth rich men wicked Mountains, and poor believing men Valleys" ("The Right Devil Discovered"). *See* **Mountain**.

In a less militant mode, many poets accepted the valley as the right place for a humble Christian. Young wishes to "steal / Along the vale / Of humble life, secure from foes" (*Ocean* st. 61). Of his unchronicled villagers Gray writes, "Along the cool sequestered vale of life / They kept the noiseless tenor of their way" ("Elegy" 75–76).

The Latin hymn *Salve, Regina* (11–12C) entreats the Virgin to pity those *in hac lacrimarum valle*, "in this valley of tears." "Vale of tears" is the Bishops' Bible version (1568) of Psalm 84.6, rendered by the AV as "valley of Baca" (an unknown name); recent versions give it as "valley of thirst." "Vale of tears" has become a commonplace for this life; Shelley names "our state" as "This dim vast vale of tears" ("Hymn to Intellectual Beauty" 16–17). A verse of the most famous Psalm gives a similar image: "Yea, though I walk through the valley of the shadow of death, I will fear no evil" (23.4). With or without tears, then, many writers have taken this life to mean a difficult and often frightening passage through a valley. Dante has been walking through a valley "that had harassed my heart with so much fear" when he reaches the foot of a sunlit hill (*Inferno* 1.15, trans. Mandelbaum). "Yet whilest I," Spenser writes, "in this wretched vale doo stay, / My wearie feete shall ever wandring be" ("Daphnaida" 456–57). Blake imagines the "just man" following his path along the "vale of death" (*Marriage of Heaven and Hell* 2.3–5).

Almost as an echo of "vale of tears," Shakespeare has Othello say "I am declin'd / Into the vale of years" (3.3.269–70), into old age (see also Gray, "Eton" 81).

Veil In the ancient world veils were worn by brides (e.g., Gen. 24.65), sometimes by prostitutes (Gen. 38.14–19), and by women in mourning (*Iliad* 24.93). Since medieval times most orders of nuns have worn veils; "to take the veil" is to become a nun.

The most important biblical veil is the cloth in the Tabernacle, and later the Temple, that separates the inner sanctuary or Holy of Holies from the outer room. "The holy place within the vail" was to be entered only on the annual Day of Atonement by the high priest (Lev. 16). When Jesus died, "behold, the vail of the temple was rent in twain from the top to the bottom" (Matt. 27.51), an event that the Epistle to the Hebrews interprets as Jesus' becoming the new high priest (6.19–20) who lets us all enter the holy place "By a new and living way, which he hath consecrated for us, through the veil, that is to say, his flesh" (10.20).

This allegorical use of the veil leads us to the veil as a symbol of allegory itself. When Moses came down from Mt. Sinai with the tablets, his face shone with the glory of the Lord, frightening the Israelites, so "he put a vail on his face" while he spoke with them (Exod. 34.33). Paul interprets the veil as veiled speech, concealing the transience of his law, in contrast to the plain speech of Christians, and adds an allegory about reading allegorically: the children of Israel are blinded, "for until this day remaineth the same vail untaken away in the reading of the old testament; which vail is done away in Christ," but when their heart turns to Christ "the vail shall be taken away" and we shall behold "with open face" the glory of the Lord (2 Cor. 3.12–18). Spenser invokes this passage in his allegorical *Faerie Queene*: he asks the Queen to "pardon me thus to enfold / In covert vele, and wrap in shadowes light, / That feeble eyes your glory may behold" (2 Pro. 5; see also Dedicatory Sonnet 3).

The Book of Revelation or Apocalypse means literally "unveiling" or "lifting up the veil" (there is nothing in the word *apocalypsis* itself that implies the end of the world). Writers committed to revealing the truth often resort to veil imagery. Blake's writings are filled with veils, symbolizing not only our lack of vision but the entire fallen world; he has a female character named Vala (with a veil) who among other things stands for nature. The veil is a favorite image of Shelley's: he has a "veil of life and death" ("Mont Blanc" 54), a "veil of space and time" ("Ode to Liberty" 86), and "Time's eternal veil" (*Queen Mab* 8.12). These will all be rent when we behold the truth in this life or the next, but sometimes he cautions, "Lift not the painted veil which those who live / Call Life" (sonnet: "Lift not . . .").

Another influential ancient veil is the one that covered the statue of Isis at Sais (Egypt). According to Plutarch, an inscription on the statue read: "I am all, past, present, and future, and my robe no mortal has unveiled" (*De Iside et Osiride* 354c). Schiller's poem "The Veiled Image at Sais" tells of an over-eager novice who unveils the statue to learn the "Truth" and is smitten by sorrow, while Novalis's unfinished story tells that he who lifts the veil sees only himself (*The Novices of Sais*). Tennyson's despairing lines – "What hope of answer, or redress? / Behind the veil, behind the veil" (*In Memoriam* 56.27–28) – may derive from the Isis legend as well as from Shelley's cosmic veils. Elsewhere Tennyson writes, "For the drift of the Maker is dark, an Isis hid by the veil" (*Maud* 1.144).

Vintage   *see* **Wine**

Violet   In classical literature the "violet" (Greek *ion*, Latin *viola*) referred to several kinds of flowers, such as the pansy (*viola tricolor*), so it is not always clear whether to translate it as "violet" or not. Its earliest appearance, a unique usage in Homer (*Odyssey* 5.72), was questioned in ancient times as a scribal error, but Homer also uses the compound word *ioeides*, "violet-colored," as an epithet of the sea, and that usage suggests that Homer thought of the *ion* as the purple flower we call the violet, the *viola odorata* or *purpurea*, the "sweet violet." (It was used, like the murex, to make dye. *See* **Purple**.) Our violet, in any case, is the usual and most distinctive reference of both ancient words.

The flower had various associations in classical culture. Along with several other flowers it belonged to Persephone (Latin Proserpina): see the first

Homeric *Hymn to Demeter* 2.6, Bacchylides' *Epinician* 3.2, and Ovid, *Metamorphoses* 5.392. It also belonged to Attis the dying god: Ovid tells how it sprang from his blood in *Fasti* 4.283ff. and 5.226. It thus had strong associations with the dead. Again in *Fasti* Ovid recommends that we honor our dead ancestors with such simple things as grain, salt, bread, and loose violets (2.539); Martial (10.32.1) states that violets and roses may be placed by a portrait of the dead; and Juvenal (12.90) has "violets of every color" (here perhaps pansies) offered to the paternal Lares or gods of the hearth. On 22 March, at the beginning of spring, the Romans celebrated the *dies violaris*, the day on which violets were put on graves, probably to betoken the renewal of life here or hereafter. The violet's appearance in early spring, its brief life, and its dark blood-like color lent it naturally to the cult of the dead.

The violet also belonged to Aphrodite (Venus), along with the rose. Homer calls her "violet-crowned" in his second *Hymn to Aphrodite* 6.18 and Solon repeats the epithet in one of his elegies (19.4). At the spring Dionysia in Athens, violet garlands were worn by celebrants. Thus the two gods of eros and ecstasy both blessed the violet, giving the flower associations with love that long remained in western poetry. Along with its flourishing in early spring, the natural basis for this symbolism probably lay in its rich, sweet odor. At least three Greek poets, Theognis (250), Simonides (frag. 150), and Bacchylides (*Epinician* 5.34), called the Muses "violet-crowned," and a famous fragment by Pindar (frag. 76) attached the epithet to the city of Athens, perhaps because of the spring Dionysia, one of the most important civic rites (Aristophanes quotes Pindar at *Knights* 1323, 1329, and *Acharnians* 637).

The violet's association with both love and death may account for the striking use of it in Shakespeare's *Hamlet*. Laertes warns Ophelia not to trust Hamlet's professions of love but to consider it "A violet in the youth of primy nature, / Forward, not permanent, sweet, not lasting, / The perfume and suppliance of minute, / No more" (1.3.7–10). (The violet is also "forward" or early-blooming in *Sonnets* 99.) In her mad scene, Ophelia hands out several kinds of flowers, and ends by saying (perhaps to the King), "I would give you some violets, but they withered all when my father died" (4.5.184–85), thus linking the loss of her love for Hamlet with her father's death at his hands. At her funeral, Laertes tells the priest, "Lay her i'th' earth, / And from her fair and unpolluted flesh / May violets spring" (5.1.238–40). This last passage echoes Persius' lines, "Will not violets now spring up from the tomb and its blessed ashes?" (*Satires* 1.39–40); both passages underlie Tennyson's wish, "From his ashes may be made / The violet of his native land" (*In Memoriam* 18.3–4).

The mourner at Keats's funeral in Shelley's *Adonais* had his head "bound with pansies overblown, / And faded violets, white, and pied, and blue" (289–90), evoking not only the decorum of the dead but the transience or brevity of Keats's life, as well as the fact that he died in late February, when violets (in Italy) might begin blooming, and that Shelley wrote the elegy in April and May, when the violets will have faded. Keats himself wrote of "fast fading violets cover'd up in leaves" in his *Ode to a Nightingale* 47. A "violet past prime" is one of Shakespeare's examples of beauty wasted by Time (*Sonnets* 12).

Laertes' use of "unpolluted" reminds us of another association of the violet, that of faithfulness in love, not particularly what we might expect from Aphrodite or Dionysus. Perhaps because of its "retiring" nature, its preference for out-of-the-way shady places, the violet acquired a reputation for modesty and "perfect chastity" (see Lydgate, *Troy Book* 3.4380). Meredith combines the sweet perfume of the violet with virginity: "She breathed the violet breath of maidenhood" (*Modern Love* 40).

In post-classical European poetry, the timidity, humility, and neglect of the violet came to the forefront of its symbolic meanings. Goethe, thinking of young maidens, writes of a *Veilchen* (violet) "bowed in itself and unknown" and of another that he treasures because "it is so shy." *Humble* and *timide* are frequent epithets of the violet in French poetry. In English, Thomson calls it "lowly" (*Spring* 448), and Wordsworth several times refers to its secrecy, most notably in his simile for Lucy, in "She dwelt among th'untrodden ways": "A Violet by a mossy stone / Half-hidden from the Eye!" It is probably the violet Wordsworth means in the final line of *Miscellaneous Sonnets* 2.9: "The flower of sweetest smell is shy and lowly." Keats writes of "that Queen / Of secrecy, the violet" ("Blue!" 11–12), and Hood calls them "Those veiled nuns, meek violets" ("Plea of the Midsummer Fairies" 318). We still use the phrase "shrinking violets" of shy girls, but Moore seems to be evoking the fragility and transience of the shade-loving plant in his simile, "Shrinking as violets do in summer's ray" (*Lalla Rookh* 2.294).

A common epithet of "violet" is "sweet" (twice, for example, in Spenser's *Shepherd's Calendar*); common also are other terms evoking its rich odor ("fragrant," for example, in *FQ* 3.1.36). Perhaps because of its similarly strong aroma or its common association with Aphrodite, the rose is frequently coupled with the violet; the ancients twined the two flowers together into spring garlands. The Romans had a festival in early summer much like the one in March, called the *Rosalia* or *Rosaria*, when one placed roses on the graves. Our trite Valentine's Day jingle "Roses are red, violets are blue," goes back centuries; Spenser names "roses red, and violets blew," as among the "sweetest flowres" (*FQ* 3.6.6). Milton's Zephyr mates with Aurora "on Beds of Violets blue, / And fresh-blown Roses washt in dew" (*L'Allegro* 21–22). At the erotic climax of Keats's *Eve of St. Agnes* the lover melts into his beloved's dream, "as the rose / Blendeth its odour with the violet, – / Solution sweet" (320–22).

See **Pansy, Purple flower**.

Viper   *see* **Serpent**

Volcano   The Greeks did not have a word for volcanoes, nor did the Romans ("volcano" is Italian, from Latin *Vulcanus* the god), but they were both very familiar with them. In Greek myth volcanoes and earthquakes are caused by the belching of a subterranean giant or by his efforts to turn over or rise up. Hesiod tells how the enormous, hundred-headed, fire-flashing monster Typhoeus (elsewhere Typhon) challenged Zeus after his defeat of the Titans; after a vast struggle Zeus hurled Typhoeus, still flaming, into the gulf of Tartarus (*Theogony* 820–68). Pindar says that the monster is buried under Mt. Etna (Greek *Aitna*) in Sicily, and "Thence erupt pure founts of unapproachable fire / from the secret places within .... / The monster hurls aloft such spouts / of weird flame; a portent and a wonder to behold" (*Pyth.* 1.15–28, trans. Lattimore). Ovid imagines him supine: "Etna weighs down his head, / Where, face upturned, his fierce throat vomits forth / Cinder and flames" (*Met.* 5.351–53). Virgil memorably describes an eruption of Etna and then refers to the legend that the giant Enceladus is buried under it: "ponderous Etna piled upon him / breathes forth flame from its bursting furnaces" (*Aeneid* 3.579–80; see also Statius, *Thebaid* 3.594–96). Virgil also says that the Cyclopes have their workshop in a cave under Etna (*Georgics* 4.169–73) or near it on an island off Sicily called Vulcania (still called Vulcano today) (*Aeneid* 8.416–23); they work for Vulcan the smith god. The Cyclopes may be "the sons of Vulcan" who "vomit smoke" in Milton's *Comus* 655.

New theories of volcanic action in the eighteenth century and new eruptions of Etna, Vesuvius, and Hecla brought new literary interest in volcanoes; by late in the century the volcano came to symbolize three explosive processes central to Romantic concerns, revolution, passion, and poetry. The first is really implicit in the classical stories; indeed some have argued that they were originally allegories, the hundred-headed monster standing for the mob or masses and Zeus/Jupiter for monarchy. Spenser's simile for Arthur's surge of strength uses the figure of an emprisoned nobleman: "Like as a fire, the which in hollow cave / Hath long bene underkept and down supprest, / With murmurous disdayne doth inly rave, / And grudge in such streight prison to be prest, / At last breakes forth with furious unrest, / And strives to mount unto his native seat" (*FQ* 2.11.32). Blake's character Orc, who represents revolutionary energy, is figured as a volcano: "The Cave of Orc stood to the South a furnace of dire flames / Quenchless unceasing" (*Four Zoas* 74.14–15); his other name is Luvah, which is possibly a pun on "lava." The narrator of Shelley's *Revolt of Islam* vows, "I will arise and waken / The multitude, and like a sulphurous hill, / Which on a sudden from its snows has shaken / The swoon of ages, it shall burst and fill / The world with cleansing fire" (784–88). In Italy Shelley wrote, "We are surrounded here in Pisa by revolutionary volcanos…the lava has not yet reached Tuscany" (letter to Peacock, 21 March 1821). His character Demogorgon, who overthrows the tyrant Jupiter, resembles the hot magma under a volcano (*PU*, Act 2). A remark by the Count de Salvandy just before the Naples revolution of 1830 is often quoted by German and French writers: "We are dancing on a volcano." Concerning the build-up to the July Revolution in France (also 1830), Hugo writes, "Thinkers were meditating…turning over social questions, peacefully, but profoundly: impassive miners, who were quietly digging their galleries into the depths of a volcano, scarcely disturbed by the muffled commotions and the half-seen glow of lava" (*Les Misérables* 4.1.4).

A passionate personality is tempestuous, fiery, volcanic. So Dryden's Antony is described by Dolabella: "He heaved for vent, and burst like bellowing Aetna" (*All for Love* 4.1.162). Chateaubriand's René would sometimes blush suddenly and feel "streams of burning lava (*lave ardente*)" roll in his heart (*René*, Prologue). Gazing into the depths of the active crater of Vesuvius, de Staël's Lord Nelvil reveals to Corinne the depths of his soul, and wonders if he is looking at hell (*Corinne* 11.4, 13.1). Byron's Byronic character Christian "stood / Like an extinct volcano in his mood; / Silent, and sad, and savage, – with the trace / Of passion reeking from his clouded face" (*The Island* 3.139–42). Elsewhere Byron treats the volcano image itself as extinct: "But Adeline was not indifferent: for / (*Now* for a common-place!) beneath the snow, / As a volcano holds the lava more / Within – *et caetera*. Shall I go on? – No / I hate to hunt down a tired metaphor, / So let the often-used volcano go. / Poor thing!" (*Don Juan* 13.281–87). Yet it lived on, for example in Charlotte Brontë's *Jane Eyre*, where both Jane and Rochester are described in volcanic terms; e.g., "To live, for me, Jane, is to stand on a crater crust which may crack and spue fire any day" (chap. 20).

The active Mexican volcano Popocatepetl, with its snow-capped peak and plumes of smoke, is the major symbol of Lowry's novel *Under the Volcano*. As he dies of gunshot wounds the Consul, the protagonist, whose life has been one of passionate self-destruction, imagines he is climbing it and then falling into its erupting abyss. At the same time it represents the world, poised, in 1938, on the brink of World War II.

If poetry is the spontaneous overflow of powerful feelings, as Wordsworth famously says, then it is only a step from eruptions of passion to explosions of verse. Perhaps the earliest instance of the volcanic poet is found in Cazotte's *Le Diable amoureux* (1772): "my imagination is a volcano" (p. 355). Lamartine writes, "the lava of my genius / overflows in torrents of harmony, / And consumes me as it escapes" ("L'Enthousiasme" 28–30). Byron defines poetry as "the lava of the imagination whose eruption prevents an earth-quake" (letter to Annabella Millbanke, 29 November 1813). E. B. Browning's poet-heroine Aurora Leigh speaks of the "burning lava of a song" (5.214). Emily Dickinson might be speaking of emotion or of poetry when she writes, "On my volcano grows the Grass / A meditative spot – / … / How red the Fire rocks below – / How insecure the sod / Did I disclose / Would populate with awe my solitude" (no. 1677). Matthew Arnold's Empedocles, on the edge of Etna's crater that still brims with life, feels dead to hope and joy: "Oh, that I could glow like this mountain!" he cries; then with a last glowing of his soul he leaps into the crater (*Empedocles on Etna* 2.323, 412).

See **Cave, Fire.**

W

Wasp Wasps in literature are mainly what they are in life, unpleasant stinging insects that swarm and attack as bees do but, unlike bees, produce nothing useful.

"The Myrmidons came streaming out like wasps at the wayside," says Homer, "when little boys have got into the habit of making them angry / by always teasing them as they live in their house by the roadside" (*Iliad* 16.259–61, trans. Lattimore). The waspish behavior of the Athenian jurors who make up the chorus of Aristophanes' *Wasps* shows itself in their furious punishment of those who anger them; a character remarks, "What stings they have!" (420).

A character in Sidney's *Third Eclogues* compares a wife to a wasp. He would choose one if it had no sting; "The Waspe seemes gay, but is a combrous [troublesome] thing" (67.21). Spenser's "Displeasure" and "Pleasance" are symbolized by an "angry Waspe" and a "hony-laden Bee" (*FQ* 3.12.18). In a similar contrast, Tennyson's Ida dismisses barbarian invaders as "wasps in our good hive" (*Princess* 4.514).

See **Bee**.

Watery star (moon)	*see* **Moon, Star**
Wave	*see* **Sea**
Wax	*see* **Bee**
Weather	*see* **Cloud, Comet, Dew, Rain, Rainbow, Seasons, Wind**
Weaving and spinning	

In classical literature, weaving and spinning are the chief female occupations, as they no doubt were in life. The most prominent women in Homer, both mortal and divine, are engaged in one or the other. Helen weaves a great purple web with scenes of the war fought for her sake (*Iliad* 3.125–28), Andromache is weaving when she learns of Hector's death (22.440–47), the goddesses Calypso and Circe weave (*Odyssey* 5.61–62 and 10.220–23), and, most famously, Penelope weaves (and unweaves) her shroud for Odysseus' father as a ruse to fend off the suitors (2.93–110, 19.137–56, 24.128–46). That trick has a folk-tale quality like so many of Odysseus' adventures and may be very old; the name Penelope may be derived from *pene* "thread" and the root of *lope* "robe."

When Helen is back home in Sparta with Menelaus, she is seen spinning, not weaving (*Odyssey* 4.121–35); Queen Arete of ideal Phaeacia spins (6.52–53); and Penelope takes up spinning when Telemachus returns ready to take matters in hand and when Odysseus comes to the palace in disguise (17.96–97, 18.315–16). Homer may be suggesting that weaving expresses insecurity, particularly the absence of a husband or fear for him, or fear of losing a mortal consort in the case of the goddesses, while spinning expresses security and the renewal of the thread or continuity of life.

A more clearly metaphorical use of weaving is the use of the Greek verb *hyphainein* ("to weave") to govern "words," "counsel," "stratagem," or "wile." Menelaus and Odysseus weave their speech and counsels (*Iliad* 3.212), Odysseus wonders which of the mortals is weaving deception against him (*Odyssey* 5.356), and so on. It is almost as if Penelope's wile with real weaving is a literal embodiment of the common metaphor. Most modern European languages use "weave" or "spin" to govern "plot" or "deception." Old English *webbian* could mean "contrive." Two lines of Scott's *Marmion* are often quoted: "O what a tangled web we weave, / When first we practise to deceive!" (6.17).

When Penelope tells the disguised stranger that she "carries out wiles" (19.137), the verb she uses (*tolupeuo*) is everywhere else in Homer used to govern "war," as if to say she is conducting her own domestic war on behalf of her husband, but an older sense of the verb may be "spin carded wool into a ball of thread"; hence when the men fight they "spin out the thread of war." Consonant with this usage is the Old Norse kenning (riddling formula) *vef darrathar*, "web of the dart," which means "battle," and perhaps the Old English phrase *wig-speda gewiofu*, "webs of battle-speed" (*Beowulf* 697).

Circe and Calypso each sing while weaving, and the connection between singing and weaving, though not made explicit by Homer, was noted by later poets, perhaps first by Sappho, who calls Eros *mythoplokos*, "weaver of stories" (frag. 188) (she also calls Aphrodite *doloploke*, "weaver of wiles," in the "Ode to Aphrodite"), and then by Pindar, who tells his lyre to "weave out (*exuphaine*) this song" (*Nem.* 4.44) and who "weaves a many-colored song for fighting men" (*Olymp.* 6.86–87). A description of a statue of Sappho, from the *Greek Anthology*, imagines her "weaving a lovely melody" (2.70). Greek looms even looked like lyres, and the shuttles looked like the spoon-shaped plectra or picks. The root of *hyphainein* was felt to be related to *hymnos*, "hymn" or "song," as Bacchylides suggests when he refers to his work as a "woven hymn" (*hyphanas hymnon*) (*Victory Odes* 5.8–14).

The Old English poet Cynewulf ends his poem *Elene* on a proud personal note: "Thus I, wise and willing, ... | Wordcraft wove (*wordcraeft waef*) and wondrously gathered" (1236–37). There are a number of examples of weaving song in the modern languages. Spenser asks one of his patrons to accept his "Rude rymes, the which a rustick Muse did weave | In savadge soyle, far from Parnasso Mount, | And roughly wrought in an unlearned Loome" (Dedicatory Sonnets to *Faerie Queene*). Shelley's "To Wordsworth" is a well-known case: "In honoured poverty thy voice did weave | Songs consecrate to truth and liberty" (11–12); and in *Laon and Cythna* Shelley has "Hymns which my soul had woven to Freedom" (915) (weaving imagery pervades this epic poem). Campbell has "Then weave in rapid verse the deeds they tell" (*The Pleasures of Hope* 1.165). Heine writes: "the poet | sat on the weaving stool of thought, | day and night, and busily wove | the giant tapestry of his song" ("The Poet Firdusi" 1.21–24). Edna St. Vincent Millay imagines a harp on which a mother weaves clothing for her child in "The Ballad of the Harp-Weaver." Close in meaning is the metaphor of weaving or spinning a story. Shakespeare's Holofernes remarks of Nathaniel, "He draweth out the thread of his verbosity finer than the staple [fibre] of his argument" (*LLL* 5.1.16–17). Cowper complains that "sedentary weavers of long tales | Give me the fidgets, and my patience fails" (*Conversation* 207–08). We speak of losing the thread of a story or strand of an argument, or spinning a tale out at too great length. "To spin a yarn" is nautical slang, first recorded about 1800.

In his *Poetics*, which set terms for drama criticism still in use, Aristotle uses *desis* for the "complication" of a plot; *desis* might be translated as a "tying" or "knotting," and once he uses *ploke* ("weaving" or "web") as a synonym. For his word *lusis*, the "solution" or "untying" of the plot, we use "dénouement" today, borrowed from French, from *nouer*, "to tie a knot."

Two Latin word-families for weaving have developed in interesting ways, somewhat parallel to what we have already seen. The verb *texere* meant "weave" or "form by plaiting," and then "construct with elaborate care" or "compose." Thus Cicero claims that his familiar letters are "woven/composed in everyday words" (*quotidianis verbis texere*) (*Epistulae ad Familiares* 9.21.1). From the past participle comes *textum*, "cloth" or "fabric," whence English "textile" and "texture"; and also *textus*, a "weave" or "pattern of weaving" or "method of constructing," and hence occasionally the "body" of a passage of words joined together (Quintilian, *Institutio* 9.4.13). From the latter sense we get our word "text": a text is originally something woven. Milton, a good Latinist, writes "A book was writ ... | And wov'n close, both matter, form and style"

(Sonnet 11). It may also be relevant that papyrus was described by Pliny the Elder as woven out of strips (*Natural History* 13.23.77).

The oldest sense of Latin *ordo* is "thread on a loom," hence "line of things," "row," "rank," "sequence" or "order of succession or priority," "pattern," and "regularity"; it is of course the source of English "order." The verb *ordior* means "to lay the warp of a web" and then "to begin," especially "to begin speaking"; it is the source of French *ourdir*, "to weave." More common was *exordior*, with virtually the same meanings, from which comes the noun *exordium*, "warp set on a loom before weaving begins," and hence any "beginning" or "introduction." The English word "exordium" preserves this latter sense as the entrance or prologue of a speech or essay. To a friend who has begun a philosophical discourse, Cicero says, *Pertexe...quod exorsus es*, "Weave out the warp you have begun" (*De Oratore* 2.145). As Virgil begins the second half of the *Aeneid* he promises "I will recall the prelude (*exordia*) of the first strife" (7.40). The phrase *exordia fati*, perhaps "the undertakings of fate," appears twice in Statius' *Thebaid* (1.503, 3.636).

As for fate, the greatest spinners in classical literature, of course, are the Fates. Alcinous says of Odysseus, "there in the future / he shall endure all that his destiny and the heavy Spinners / spun for him with the thread at his birth, when his mother bore him" (*Odyssey* 7.196–98; trans. Lattimore). The word for "Spinners" is *Klothes* (*klotho* is one of the Homeric verbs for "spin") but they are not named individually in Homer. Once in the *Iliad* the Fates (*Moirai*) appear in the plural (24.49); sometimes it is "the gods" who spin an event (e.g., *Odyssey* 1.17) and sometimes a single Fate: "Let us weep for Hector, and the way at the first strong Destiny (*Moira*) spun with his life line when he was born" (*Iliad* 24.209–10). *Moira* is from a root meaning "lot, portion, division." It is Hesiod who first names them in the *Theogony* (218, 905): Klotho (spinner), Lachesis (disposer of lots), and Atropos (one who cannot be averted). They have been variously imagined, sometimes all three as spinners, sometimes with a division of labor: Klotho at the spinning wheel or distaff, Lachesis measuring out the "span" (related to "spin") of one's life, and Atropos with the shears cutting off the thread or lifeline – in Milton's lines, "Comes the blind Fury with th'abhorred shears, / And slits the thin-spun life" ("Lycidas" 75–76). See Plato, *Republic* 10.617c. Byron writes of "life's thin thread" (*Don Juan* 13.319). The English word "stamina" reflects this concept: it is the plural of Latin *stamen*, "thread of a warp."

In Latin they are called the *Parcae*, perhaps from the root in *pario*, "bring forth, bear"; before they were assimilated into the Greek *Moirai* they may have been goddesses of childbirth; their names, obscure in meaning, are Nona, Decuma, and Morta (the last certainly sounds like "Death"). Virgil's lines in the "Fourth Eclogue", "'Speed on those centuries,' said the Parcae to their spindles, / 'Concordant with the steadfast nod of Destiny'" (46–47, trans. Lee), suggests that the Fates bow to a higher Fate, but elsewhere the Fates seem to *be* Fate, which even the gods must obey. Horace calls them "the three sisters" (2.3.15), Ovid "the ancient sisters" (*Met.* 15.781). Chaucer calls them the "fatal sisters": "O fatal sustren, which, er any cloth / Me shapen was, my destine me sponne," alluding to the idea that a child's fate is spun before any clothing is made for it (*Troilus* 3.733–34), an idea that combines metaphorical spinning with literal weaving. A visitor to "the three fatall sisters" in Spenser's *Faerie Queene* finds them "all sitting round about, / The direfull distaffe standing in the mid, / And with unwearied fingers drawing out / The lines of life, from living knowledge hid. / Sad Clotho held the rocke [distaff], the whiles the thrid / By griesly Lachesis was spun with paine, / That cruel Atropos eftsoones undid, / With cursed knife cutting the twist in twaine" (4.2.48). Herrick imagines a more cheering possibility: "Let bounteous Fate your spindles full / Fill, and wind up with whitest wool" ("Epithalamie"). But usually fate is grim, "fateful" and "fatal" are near synonyms, and their web is a net. "For in the time we know not of," Swinburne writes, "Did fate begin / Weaving the web of days that wove / Your doom, Faustine" ("Faustine" 93–96). For Hardy, Fate is "the Spinner of the Years" ("Convergence of the Twain" 31).

The thirteenth-century Icelandic *Prose Edda* by Snorri Sturluson describes three sister Fates called Norns; their names are Urthr, Verthandi, and Skuld, which seem to mean "past," "present," and "future." Classical influence is possible here, but it seems less likely in a few phrases of Old English poetry. Guthlac, who lived around 700, uses the phrase *wefen wyrdstafun*, "weave the decree of fate" (*Guthlac B* 1351 in *The Exeter Book*); *wyrd* is related to Icelandic *Urthr* and is the source of our word "weird": the three witches in *Macbeth*, who play a role much like the Fates (though they are not spinners), are called "the Weird Sisters." The "Riming Poem" in *The Exeter Book* has *Me thaet wyrd gewaef*, "that fate wove (for) me" (70). The Old Norse kenning quoted above is elaborated in a battle scene in the thirteenth-century *Njals Saga*, which Thomas Gray rendered in "The Fatal Sisters." Twelve gigantic women are gathered around a loom, singing as they work: "Glittering lances are the loom, / Where the dusky warp we strain, / Weaving many a soldier's doom, / Orkney's woe, and Randver's bane. / See the grisly texture grow, / ('Tis of human entrails made,) / And the weights that play below, / Each a gasping warrier's head" (5–12).

See **Sewing and quilting**, **Spider**.

Wellspring   *see* **Fountain**

West   *see* **East and west**

West wind   In literature the west wind is usually the wind of springtime, *Zephyrus* or *Favonius*. In spring, says Virgil, "warmed by breezes / Of Zephyrus the fields unloose their bosoms" (*Georgics* 2.330–31); the plants do not fear a southern gale or northern rainstorm; and in the springtime of the world there were no wintry blasts from the east (2.334–39). "Sharp winter thaws for spring and Favonius," writes Horace (1.4.1); "frosts melt for Zephyrus" (4.7.9). Wind and breath were more than metaphorically linked, as the words *pneuema*, *psyche*, and *spiritus* all suggest (*see* **Wind**), and the west wind in particular was personified and given lungs. Virgil refers to the sound of Zephyrus breathing (*spirare*) (*Aeneid* 4.562). In Chaucer's famous description of April, "Zephirus eek with his sweete breeth / Inspired hath in every holt and heeth / The tendre croppes" (*CT* Gen. Pro. 5–7), "inspired" probably meaning "breathed in/on." Spenser has "sweete breathing Zephyrus" (*Prothalamion* 2); Milton considers ways to pass the winter "till Favonius re-inspire / The frozen earth" (Sonnet

20), and describes Zephyr as "The frolic Wind that breathes the Spring" ("L'Allegro" 18). This breath seems to echo the "breath of life" that God breathed into the nostrils of Adam (Gen. 2.7).

The Greek word *zephyros* is related to *zophos*, "gloom" or "darkness," hence the "dark region" or west. Latin *favonius* may be kin to *faveo*, "favor" or "be favorable to." "Zephyr" in English is often in the plural: Pope has "the tepid Zephyrs of the spring" (*Dunciad* 4.422), in Shelley "vernal zephyrs breathe in evening's ear" (*Queen Mab* 4.2).

The evocative Middle English lyric "Westron wind, when will thou blow?" may be pleading for spring to come, when his love will be in his arms, but the speaker might be out at sea with no favorable wind toward land.

The west wind also blows in the fall. "And nowe the Westerne wind bloweth sore," Hobbinol tells us in "September" of Spenser's *Shepheardes Calender* (49), while elsewhere Spenser calls the wind "wroth" (*FQ* 2.11.19). Shelley's "Ode to the West Wind" addresses the "breath of Autumn's being," a wild and powerful spirit, as opposed to "Thine azure sister of the Spring" (1, 9); he asks it to lift him from his fallen state and give his words the power usually attributed to the spring wind, "to quicken a new birth" in "unawakened earth" (64, 68).

Whale   A convenient list of literary references to whales may be found at the opening of Melville's *Moby-Dick, or The Whale*. The first five extracts on the list, all from the Old Testament, illustrate the difficulty of establishing the whale's ancient symbolic associations. "And God created great whales" (Gen. 1.21 AV) is a mistranslation, or at best too narrow a translation, for the Hebrew word (*tannin*) can mean "sea-monster." That is more or less the meaning of "leviathan" in three of Melville's passages (Job 41.32, Ps. 104.26, Isa. 27.1). The third is plausibly a whale – "Now the Lord had prepared a great fish to swallow up Jonah" (Jonah 1.17) – but is not called a whale. The word in Greek (*ketos*) and Latin (*cetus*) that came to mean "whale," and is used in modern scientific nomenclature, originally was vague: in Homer's *Odyssey* it means "sea-monster" and in one context (4.443ff.) it refers to the seal.

"Leviathan" has come to mean "whale" in modern languages, including modern Hebrew, but in the Old Testament it is serpentine and connected with rivers; it symbolizes the enemies of Israel. "In that day the Lord with his sore and great and strong sword shall punish leviathan the piercing serpent, even leviathan that crooked serpent; and he shall slay the dragon that is in the sea" (Isa. 27.1); it may refer to Babylon (land of two rivers, one of them crooked) or Egypt (land of the Nile with its crocodiles). Ezekiel calls the Pharaoh "the great dragon [*leviathan*] that lieth in the midst of his rivers" (29.3); but, saith the Lord, "I will put hooks in thy jaws, . . . and I will bring thee up out of the midst of thy rivers . . . / And I will leave thee thrown into the wilderness" (4–5). Until that day, however, the Israelites will have lived mainly in Egyptian or Babylonian captivity, as if inside the monster. That idea is seconded by the tale of Jonah, who spends three days and nights in the great fish before his redemption.

According to Jesus, Jonah is a type of Jesus himself: "For as Jonas was three days and three nights in the whale's belly [Greek *ketos*]; so shall the Son of man be three days and three nights in the heart of the earth" (Matt. 12.40). "In the belly of the whale" has come to mean "inside the land of oppression":

Orwell warns in *Inside the Whale* that "The autonomous individual is going to be stamped out of existence" and literature "must suffer at least a temporary death."

Milton names the Leviathan twice. At the creation "leviathan / Hugest of creatures, on the deep / Stretched like a promontory sleeps or swims, / And seems a moving land" (*PL* 7.412–15); Satan, afloat on the fiery sea of hell, resembles "that sea-beast / Leviathan" (1.200–01) which sailors mistake for an island. This simile has older Christian sources: the whale stands for Satan in his deceptiveness; do not cast your anchor near him. As the swallower of Jonah (and, typologically, Jesus) the whale is hell (which Christ harrows during his time in the tomb); the "jaws of hell" are sometimes thought of as a whale's.

As for Moby-Dick, Melville lists the many things whiteness may represent (*see* **White**) and concludes, "Of all these things the Albino whale was the symbol. Wonder ye then at the fiery hunt?" (chap. 42). But that may make the whale too vague to be a symbol at all. Lawrence writes, "Of course he is a symbol. Of what? I doubt if even Melville knew exactly. That's the best of it" (*Studies in Classic American Literature* chap. 11); but he cannot resist offering his own theory: "He is the deepest blood-being of the white race" – no worse than many other claims, such as God, Satan, innocence, nature, death, the id, the super-ego, America, the ideal, or nothingness.

White   One could hardly do better than read the tenth chapter of book 1 of Rabelais's *Gargantua*, called "Concerning the significance of the colors white and blue." There he asserts that white stands for joy, solace, and gladness, because its opposite, black, stands for grief, and because white dazzles the sight as exceeding joy dazzles the heart. Rabelais points out that the ancients used white stones to mark fortunate days and that when the Romans celebrated a triumph the victor rode in a chariot drawn by white horses; sunlight and the light of Christian revelations are also white.

To these examples we may add Plato's claim that in picturing the gods white is the most appropriate color (*Laws* 956a), and that Roman "candidates" for office wore white – as a sign, presumably, of "candor" or sincerity. (Latin *candidus* meant "bright white," in contrast to *albus*, "pale white"; it also meant meant "sincere" and even "spotless" or "faithful," as in Ovid's *candida Penelope* in *Amores* 2.18.29.)

The best literary source after Rabelais is chapter 42 of Melville's *Moby-Dick*, "The Whiteness of the Whale." There Ishmael tells us "It was the whiteness of the whale that above all thing appalled me," nicely bringing out the buried meaning of "appalled" as "made pale." He concedes, however, that "various nations have in some way recognized a certain royal pre-eminence in this hue"; that it is the emblem of "the innocence of brides, the benignity of age"; that priests wear a tunic called an alb (from *alba*); and that in "the Romish faith, white is specially employed in the celebration of the Passion of our Lord." But he goes on to mention ghastlier associations, as in the polar bear, the white shark, albino men, the pallor of death, or leprosy, and then speculates that "by its indefiniteness [white] shadows forth the heartless voids and immensities of the universe" or it is "the visible absence of color" – "a colorless, all-color of atheism from which we shrink." Something of this heartlessness appears in Frost's "Design," where the white spider holding a white moth on a white flower seems the "design of darkness to appall."

See **Black, Light.**

Willow   The willow tree, commonly found near rivers, as Virgil reminds us in *Georgics* 2.110–111, seems by its very shape to suggest mournfulness. Its appearance in the well-known Psalm 137 may be due simply to its presence by rivers, but the theme of the psalm lent it mournful associations: "By the rivers of Babylon, there we sat down, yea, we wept, when we remembered Zion. We hanged our harps upon the willows in the midst thereof" (1–2).

The willow has long had a more specific connotation, however, in the classical tradition. Homer describes a grove that includes "fruit-destroying willows" (*itea olesikarpoi*) at the entrance to Hades (*Odyssey* 10.510). This mysterious epithet may be based on the fact that willows cast their blossoms early, before the fruit grows; the blossoms were mistaken for the fruit itself, and the idea arose that willows were sterile. They came to symbolize chastity and the fate of a maiden dying without a lover or children. Goethe repeats the Homeric phrase ("unfruchtbaren Weiden") in *Faust II* 9977. Spenser names "The Willow, worne of forlorne Paramours" (*FQ* 1.1.9). So the report of Ophelia's drowning in Shakespeare's *Hamlet* 4.7.165–82 begins with a willow, and Desdemona sings of a willow before she is murdered by Othello (4.3.40–56); see also *MV* 5.1.10, *12N* 2.1.268, and *3H6* 3.3.227–28. Robert Herrick's "To the Willow-Tree" describes its role as a crown for "young men and maids distressed": "When once the lover's rose is dead, / Or laid aside forlorn; / Then willow-garlands, 'bout the head, / Bedewed with tears, are worn." A traditional Irish ballad, "The Willow Tree," has these lines: "She hears me not, she cares not, nor will she list to me, / While here I lie, alone to die, beneath the willow tree."

A phrase recorded in 1825, "she is in her willows," means "she is mourning her husband (or betrothed)." The Gilbert and Sullivan song "Willow, Tit-willow" is about "blighted affection." In eighteenth-century British literature, however, the association with forlorn lovers begins to yield to the idea of mourning for anyone dead. It may not be a coincidence that the "weeping" willow was imported from China in the eighteenth century, and its more dramatically mournful shape may have replaced the casting of blossoms as its most distinctive feature.

The osier and the sallow are both kinds of willow. The long willow twig is called a withe or withy, and is noted for its strength: Virgil speaks of the "tough willow" (*Eclogues* 3.83, 5.16).

Wind   The phrase "four winds" occurs in both testaments of the Bible (e.g., Ezek. 37.9, Matt. 24.31) to refer to every quarter of the sky or earth, but they are not named or described. Only the east wind is distinguished; it is generally a baleful force sent by God to "blast" the corn (Gen. 41.6) or bring locusts (Exod. 10.13) or wither the vine (Ezek. 17.10).

Homer names the four winds as Poseidon sets them loose upon Odysseus: "Eurus and Notus clashed together, and Zephyrus the hard-blown / and Boreas the begetter of clear sky" (*Odyssey* 5.295–96). Hesiod names three of them as the offspring of Astraeus and Eos (Dawn): "bright Zephyrus, Boreas swift in its path, / and Notus" (*Theogony* 379–80); he names them again (870) as godsent blessings, as opposed to "other" unnamed winds, dangerous ones sent by Typhoeus.

Eurus (also Eurus in Latin) is the east wind, Notos (Latin Auster) the south wind, Zephyrus (Favonius) the west wind, usually seen as gentle or favorable, and Boreas (Aquilo) the north wind, also called "bright" (*clarus*) by Virgil (*Georgics* 1.460) but usually seen as bringing storms and winter. In Ovid's tale of Boreas and Orithyia the wind boasts, "By force I drive / The weeping clouds, by force I whip the sea, / Send gnarled oaks crashing, pack the drifts of snow, / And hurl the hailstones down upon the lands" (*Met.* 6.680–83, trans. Melville), while Lucan mentions "ships wrecked by Aquilo" (4.457). Zephyrus/Favonius is most often the spring wind that revives the land. (*See* **West wind**.) Virgil says, however, that Boreas, Zephyrus, and Eurus can all bring thunderstorms (*Georgics* 1.370–71).

Milton gives a more elaborate catalog, mixing classical names with English and Italian: Boreas, Caecias, Argestes, Thrascias, Notus, Afer, Levant, Eurus, Zephir, Sirocco, and Libecchio (*PL* 10.699–706).

The similarity between wind and breath is inscribed deep in both the symbolism and the common vocabulary of Hebrew and western literature. The first wind of the Bible, in the second verse of Genesis, is the "Spirit of God" that "moved upon the face of the waters." The Hebrew word is *ruach*, which can mean "breath" and "wind" as well as, more abstractly, "spirit." "Spirit," in fact, comes from Latin *spiritus*, which means "breath" and "breeze" as well as what we mean by "spirit"; *spiro*, "I breathe," is the basis of "respiration," "expire," "conspire," "inspire," and so on: when a poet is inspired he breathes in the spirit. Latin *anima* had a similar range, from "wind" (like the cognate Greek *anemos*) and "breath" to "life" and "soul"; *animus* meant "soul," "heart," and "mind." Greek *psyche* is from a root meaning "breath"; *pneuma* meant "breath," "wind," and "spirit," including the "Holy Spirit" of the New Testament.

This interconnection of meanings underlies the association of winds, whirlwinds, and storms with the highest gods or God: Zeus the Cloudgatherer, who throws a thunderbolt, Jupiter Pluvius, and Jehovah who sends winds, breathes life, speaks to Job out of the whirlwind (38.1), and is seen "upon the wings of the wind" (2 Sam. 22.11, Ps. 18.10). So the "ungodly" are "like the chaff which the wind driveth away" (Ps. 1.4), "as stubble before the wind, and as chaff that the storm carrieth away" (Job 21.18).

On the other hand, wind is empty and evanescent. Words and speeches are wind (Job 6.26), and one's life is wind (7.7); Isaiah says, "Behold, they are all vanity; their works are nothing: their molten images are wind and confusion" (41.29). "For he their words as wind esteemed light," Spenser says (*FQ* 4.5.27). Preachers who display idle learning to the faithful leave them empty, says Dante, "so that the wretched sheep, in ignorance, / return from pasture, having fed on wind" (*Paradiso* 29.106–07, trans. Mandelbaum). Milton uses the same image for the false shepherds who sing their "lean and flashy songs": "The hungry Sheep look up, and are not fed, / But swoln with wind, and the rank mist they draw, / Rot inwardly" ("Lycidas" 123–27).

Winds are fickle, they snatch things away, they clear the air or darken it, they change the weather. Homer's Euryalus makes amends to Odysseus for his insult and asks that any improper word be carried off by the stormwinds (*Odyssey* 8.408–09). When Turnus chases a phantom Aeneas, he does not see that "the winds carry away his victory" (Virgil, *Aeneid* 10.652). Catullus has the abandoned Ariadne complain to Theseus that all his promises and all her expectations "the airy winds have tattered into nothing" (64.142, trans. Lee). This commonplace might be said to culminate in the title of Margaret Mitchell's novel *Gone with the Wind*.

Strong winds or storms have long been a metaphor for passionate or tumultuous emotion. "For love is yet the mooste stormy life," Chaucer writes (*Troilus* 2.778). When Spenser's cruel mistress summons him, heaven sends superfluous tempests: "Enough it is for one man to sustaine / the stormes, which she alone on me doth raine" (*Amoretti* 46). Racine's Hermione laments, "He thinks he'll see this storm dissolve in tears" (*Andromaque* 5.1.1410).

Though it is first a plot device, it is tempting to take the fateful storm that drives Aeneas and Dido into the same cave as also symbolic of the passion they yield to (4.160–68); that lightnings and Sky "witness the wedlock" certainly gives it cosmic significance. The storm over Lear on the heath (3.2) seems matched by Lear's ventings of his fury at his daughters. The literature of sensibility and romanticism often assumes a sympathetic connection between nature and subjective feelings, so that all weather may be symbolic. The storm in Chateaubriand's *Atala* accompanies the stormy emotions of the lovers; storms propel the plot in Emily Brontë's *Wuthering Heights* and are especially connected with Heathcliff; and it is a storm that finally brings Dorothea and Will to embrace in Eliot's *Middlemarch* (chap. 83).

Poets in the Romantic era have a particular affinity for winds, for the inspiration of the spirit of nature. In Goethe's "Wanderer's Storm-Song" the poet defies Jupiter Pluvius because his "Genius" is with him; he defies Apollo the sun god, too, with his inner, creative warmth. Wordsworth's epic autobiography *The Prelude* opens with a "gentle breeze" that brings joy – "I breathe again" – "For I, methought, while the sweet breath of heaven / Was blowing on my body, felt within / A corresponding mild creative breeze" (1805 version, 1.1.19, 41–43). Coleridge wishes "that even now the gust were swelling, / And the slant night-shower driving loud and fast! / Those sounds which oft have raised me, whilst they awed, / And sent my soul abroad" ("Dejection" 15–18). Byron's Childe Harold finds an Alpine storm an expression of night's "delight" and the hills' "glee," but it also brings "desolation"; he asks the tempests, "Are ye like those within the human breast?" (3.871, 875, 903). The most passionate Romantic identification with a wind is Shelley's "Ode to the West Wind."

See **Aeolian harp, West wind**.

Wine   Wine is "heart-gladdening," according to Homer (*Iliad* 3.246), and the Book of Proverbs tells us to "Give...wine unto those that be of heavy hearts" (31.6). "Now drive away cares with wine," advises Horace (*Odes* 1.7.31); "Bacchus dissipates gnawing cares" (2.11.17). Too much wine, of course, is a danger and a curse, as the Cyclops found out in the *Odyssey*, and the Centaurs at Pirithous' wedding (Ovid, *Met.* 12.189–535); Horace, though a wine-drinker, devotes an ode to moderation (1.18).

It is one of the two gifts of God: He gives "plenty of corn and wine" (Gen. 27.28). "Bread and wine" is the standard biblical fare (e.g., Judges 19.19, Neh. 5.15), no doubt often literally as well as metonymically. Tiresias lectures Pentheus on the two blessings of humankind, that of Demeter (grain) and that of Dionysus (wine); the latter brings sleep, oblivion, and medicine for grief (Euripides, *Bacchae* 274–85).

In the same play we are told that wine brings love: "without wine there is no Cypris [Aphrodite]" (773). Ovid puns, "Venus in wine [*Venus in vinis*] was fire in fire!" (*Art of Love* 1.244). Chaucer's much-married Wife of Bath confesses, "after wyn on Venus most I thynke" ("Wife of Bath's Prologue" 464).

The famous saying, *In vino veritas*, "In wine is truth," has two senses, depending on whether one is drinking it or watching someone else do so. For Theognis, "Wine is the test to show the mind of man; / Even a wise man, clever up to now, / When he gets drunk, brings shame upon himself" (500–02, trans. Wender). Plato quotes the proverb "Drunkards and children tell the truth" (*Symposium* 217e). Theocritus begins a frank poem by quoting the saying "Truth in our cups" (29.1). Rabelais's Panurge is made to sing an old Greek drinking song: "Bacchus... / Holds all truth, for truth's in wine. / And in wine no deceit or wrong / Can live, no fraud and no prevarication" (5.45, trans. Cohen). Dickens sums up: "Wine in truth out" (*Nicholas Nickleby* chap. 27). Addressing his glass of wine, Baratynsky says, "fertile, noble, spring eternal, / you have power to bring to birth / visions straight from realms infernal, / or send dreams from heav'n to earth" ("The Wineglass" 37–40, trans. Myers). Emerson imagines a higher wine, a "wine of wine," drinking which he will know what birds and roses say; "I thank the joyful juice / For all I know" ("Bacchus").

Emerson's transcendent wine culminates a long association of poets with wine, at least as old as Horace's frequent praise of it. "For Bacchus fruite is frend to Phoebus wise [Apollo, god of poetry], / And when with Wine the braine begins to sweate, / The nombers flowe as fast as spring doth ryse" (Spenser, *Shepheardes Calendar*, "October" 106–08). Poets, says Hölderlin, are "like the holy priests of the wine god, / who went from country to country in holy night" ("Bread and Wine" sec. 7).

Wine may represent the blood of Dionysus/Bacchus, and it was poured in honor of many other gods as well. In Genesis wine is called "the blood of grapes" (49.11), and in Christian symbolism it stands for the blood of Christ. At the Last Supper Jesus takes bread and says, "this is my body," and takes the cup of wine and says, "this is my blood of the new testament, which is shed for many for the remission of sins" (Matt. 26.26–28). Bread and wine are served at the Christian sacrament of the Eucharist or Communion; they are sometimes called the Eucharist themselves. Hölderlin conjures a new testament himself in his poem "Bread and Wine," as does Silone in his novel with the same title; both ponder the roots of the Christian symbols.

Wine in a cup is sometimes a symbol of God's wrath. So the Lord tells Jeremiah: "Take the wine cup of this fury at my hand, and cause all the nations, to whom I send thee, to drink it" (25.15). (*See* **Cup**.) In one of Isaiah's parables Israel is a vineyard that brings forth wild grapes [the unrighteous], unsuitable for wine, so the Lord promises to lay it waste (5.1–7). Later Isaiah prophesies a conqueror from Edom, red from the wine vat, who announces,

"I have trodden the winepress alone; and of the people there was none with me: for I will tread them in mine anger, and trample them in my fury" (63.1–3). These passages underlie the vintage imagery of Revelation, where the angel harvests grapes (people) and casts them into "the great winepress of the wrath of God. | And the winepress was trodden without the city, and blood came out of the winepress" (14.19–20). As blood was flowing in the American civil war, Howe wrote "He is trampling out the vintage where the grapes of wrath are stored" ("Battle-Hymn of the Republic"). Blake's "Wine-press of Los" is "War on Earth" where the "Human grapes" suffer, but it is also spiritual war, conducted by the "Printing-Press | of Los" (*Milton* 27.1–30).

See **Bread**.

Winter   In classical as in Old English poetry there were conventions for describing winter: winter, ice, or snow binds or locks the earth, ice makes bridges across rivers, darkness prevails, the north wind blows, and so on. The earliest description is Hesiod's, where he dwells on the effects of cruel Boreas (*Works and Days* 504–63). There are brief descriptions in Virgil: don't try to plant "when Boreas is blowing; | then winter (*hiems*) locks the land with frost" (*Georgics* 2.316–17); he has a fuller account of a Scythian winter where rivers now bear heavy wagons (3.356–71). Old English poetry is poor in descriptions of spring or summer but has several grimly vivid pictures of winter, e.g., "The Wanderer" and "The Seafarer." In *Beowulf*, "the sea boiled with storms, | warred against the wind, winter locked up the wave | with ice-bond" (1132–33). Descriptions of the seasons were popular in the Middle Ages and the Renaissance, and reached a kind of culmination in Thomson's *The Seasons*, the "Winter" section of which gives hundreds of lines to describing winter's gloom, rain, winds, snow, ice, and their deadly consequences.

When Winter is personified he is often an old man. Tasso describes him as "cold and white-haired, | His face wrinkled, his hair filled with snow" (*La mutabilità del tempo* 12–13). "Lastly, came Winter cloathed all in frize [rough cloth]," writes Spenser, "Chattering his teeth for cold that did him chill; | ... | For he was faint with cold, and weak with eld [age]" (*FQ* 7.7.31); Shakespeare calls him "limping" (*Romeo* 1.2.28); Milton calls him "decrepit" (*PL* 10.655). But he is also strong, even violent. Chaucer refers to "the swerd of wynter, keene and coold" (*Squire's Tale* 57); Blake thinks of him as a king in a chariot, as well as a "direful monster" who "withers all in silence, and his hand | Unclothes the earth, and freezes up frail life" ("To Winter"). Wordsworth notes that "Humanity, delighting to behold | A fond reflection of her own decay, | Hath painted Winter like a traveller old, | Propped on a staff," but it was "mighty Winter," "dread Winter!" who destroyed Napoleon's grand army ("French Army in Russia"). Standard epithets for winter in Spenser and Shakespeare are "stern," "sad," "breme" ("cold" or "harsh" in Spenser), "angry," "churlish," "furious," and "barren."

"Winter" is occasionally used in Latin poetry for "year" (cf. Horace 1.11.4, 1.15.35), but it is quite frequent in Old English poetry; it is as if it is only winters that age one. In the translation of Genesis, Methuselah lives 969 winters. The dragon of *Beowulf* held his hoard variously three hundred or a thousand winters (2278, 3050). And so in later English literature: "I trowe a thritty wynter he was oold" (Chaucer, *Shipman's Tale* 26); "I have followed thee in faith this five and forty winters" (Langland, *Piers Plowman* b 12.3; spelling modernized); "When forty winters shall besiege thy brow" (Shakespeare, *Sonnets* 2); "I number three-score winters past" (Cowper, "Yardley Oak" 3); "that shape / With sixty or more winters on its head" (Yeats, "Among School Children" 37–38).

If winter is portrayed as old, old age is described as wintry; it is the last of the four seasons of human life. (*See* **Seasons**.) "Age and Winter accord full nie," according to Spenser (*Shepheardes Calendar*, "February" 27); "wintry age" is found in Spenser, Cowper, Wordsworth, and other poets. Old Egeon's face is "hid / In sap-consuming winter's drizzled snow" (*CE* 5.1.312–13). "Life's autumn past, I stand on winter's verge" (Wordsworth, *Excursion* 4.611). Sir Bedivere is "no more than a voice / In the white winter of his age" (Tennyson, "Passing of Arthur" 3–4).

Thomson thinks the clouds and storms of winter "exalt the soul to solemn thought / And heavenly musing," when one sees through the "lying vanities of life" while sitting by a fire to "hold high converse with the mighty dead" ("Winter" 3–4, 209, 432). Pushkin celebrates the short days, the long nights by the fire when "I forget the world" and "poetry wakes in me" ("Autumn" 73–75). Mallarmé on the other hand thinks "Winter belongs to prose. With the burst of autumn verse ceases" (*Crayonné au Théâtre*, "Notes" 4). Stevens seems to agree with Mallarmé when he describes "the antipodes of poetry, dark winter," but he goes on to say that in winter "The first word" might arrive, "The immaculate disclosure of the secret no more obscured" ("A Discovery of Thought"); winter sweeps away romantic clutter and returns us to "The vivid thing in the air": "Only this evening I saw it again, / At the beginning of winter" ("Martial Cadenza").

See **Autumn, Spring, Summer**.

Wolf   The wolf seems to be the most feared and despised mammal in literature; a good wolf is extremely rare until recent times. As early as Homer wolves are ferocious and warlike: the Myrmidons, for example, swarm "as wolves / who tear flesh raw, in whose hearts the battle fury is tireless, / who have brought down a great horned stag in the mountains, and then feed / on him, till the jowls of every wolf run blood" (*Iliad* 16.156–59, trans. Lattimore). In fact one of Homer's terms for "battle fury" (*lussa*) is derived from the root of "wolf" (*lukos*); it is a rabid, wolfish rage, like that of the Norse *berserkr*; it later came to mean "madness" and then "rabies."

Aeschylus calls wolves "hollow-bellied" (*Seven* 1036–37), and they have been hungry ever since. Spenser and Shakespeare, for instance, routinely give them the epithets "greedy" and "ravenous"; Shakespeare also calls them "hunger-starved" (*3H6* 1.4.5). In Ulysses' great "degree" speech, "appetite" is called "an universal wolf" (*TC* 1.3.121). As an emblem of famine it lingers in our phrase "to keep the wolf from the door," and when we devour our food we "wolf it down."

Aesop has thirty-seven fables in which the wolf is the chief actor, such as "The Shepherd and the Wolf," where a naïve shepherd trusts a wolf, which then devours the flock. Not surprisingly indeed in the literature of pastoral societies, the characteristic prey of wolves are sheep, especially lambs. In the *Iliad* wolves attack sheep when they are not attacking stags (16.352–55). "As wolf to lamb" was a proverb when Plato used it (*Phaedrus* 241d), as was "To trust the wolf with the sheep" when Terence used it (*The Eunuch* 832). Shakespeare's Menenius asks, "who does the wolf love?" Sicinius replies, "The lamb." Menenius: "Ay, to devour him" (*Cor* 2.1.8–10).

It was inevitable that Jewish and especially Christian writers, for whom the symbolism of sheep, shepherds, and sacrificial lambs was central, would extend it to wolves. As the Christian faithful are the "flock," Paul warns that "after my departing shall grievous wolves enter in among you, not sparing the flock" (Acts 20.29). These seem to be the same surreptitious wolves as those in the more famous passage from the Sermon on the Mount: "Beware of false prophets, which come to you in sheep's clothing, but inwardly they are ravening wolves" (Matt. 7.15). Dante changes "sheep" to "shepherd" in order to denounce the false leaders of the church. Florence's money perverts the sheep and the lamb, "and turns the shepherd into a wolf"; through all the pastures "rapacious wolves are seen in shepherds' clothing" (*Paradiso* 9.132, 27.55). Milton decries those who "for their bellies' sake, / Creep and intrude and climb into the fold" (*Lycidas* 114–15); Michael foretells that after the Apostles "Wolves shall succeed for teachers, grievous wolves" (*PL* 12.508). (*See* **Sheep**.)

The wolf is one of three beasts of battle that frequently appear together in Old English poetry (*see* **Raven**); it is the companion of the Germanic battle-god Odin/Wotan as it is of Roman Mars. The giant wolf Fenrir looms large in Norse myth.

The she-wolf (Latin *lupa*) is a symbol of Rome because of the legend that she suckled Romulus and Remus. But *lupa* also came to mean "prostitute" (Plautus, *Epidicus* 403, Martial 1.34.8). (Chaucer makes a she-wolf an exemplar of lust in *Manciple's Tale* 183–86.) Both these associations may lie behind Dante's choice of the *lupa* as the third and most dismaying of the beasts he encounters at the opening of the *Inferno* (1.49–60). As the emblem of voracity it may stand for the category of "incontinent" sins (such as lust, greed, and wrath), those that Dante may have committed. (*See* **Leopard, Lion**.)

As an emblem of noble suffering, Byron asserts that "the wolf dies in silence" (*Childe Harold* 4.185). That line inspired Alfred de Vigny's poem "The Death of the Wolf."

Wood   *see* **Forest**

Woodpecker   Though some of its Greek names are as descriptive as its name in English (*drykolaptes*, "oak-chisel"; *pelekas*, "ax"), the woodpecker has little symbolic meaning in Greek literature. In Latin, however, the *picus* is the bird of Mars and an actor in the founding of Rome: Ovid tells that the *Martia picus* helped defend the infants Romulus and Remus and brought food to them (*Fasti* 3.37, 3.54). Ovid also tells at length the story of King Picus, son of Saturn; happily married to Canens ("Singing"), he refuses Circe's amorous advances and is transformed into a woodpecker who furiously attacks oaks (*Met*. 14.320–96). Virgil alludes to the story in the *Aeneid* (7.189–91).

Worm   From the Bible onward the worm is the lowest of creatures, as far removed as possible from God. Compared to God, however, man is also a worm. If even the stars are not pure in God's sight, Bildad tells Job, "How much less man, that is a worm? and the son of man, which is a worm?" (25.6). The Psalm that begins, "My God, my God, why hast thou forsaken me?" which Christ repeats on the cross, goes on, "But I am a worm, and no man" (22.6). Sidney's version of Psalm 6 begins "Lord, let not me a worme by thee be shent [disgraced]." "Worm" has long been a term of abuse among humans, of course; Shakespeare's Pistol tells Falstaff, "Vile worm, thou wast o'erlooked [bewitched] even in thy birth" (MWW 5.5.83). Coleridge calls man "Vain sister of the worm" who should "Ignore thyself, and strive to know thy God!" ("Self-Knowledge"). The Earth Spirit, whom Goethe's Faust conjures up, disdainfully asks him, "Is this you?... | A fearful shrinking worm?" (496–98). A similar spirit calls Byron's Manfred "Thou worm! whom I obey and scorn" (1.125). In a mood like Coleridge's, a character of Tennyson's calls God "The guess of a worm in the dust and the shadow of its desire – | Of a worm as it writhes in a world of the weak trodden down by the strong, | Of a dying worm in a world, all massacre, murder, and wrong" ("Despair" 30–32).

Yet God cares for worms, even real worms. Blake's Thel expresses wonder at this discovery: "That God would love a Worm I knew, and punish the evil foot | That wilful, bruis'd its helpless form: but that he cherish'd it | With milk and oil. I never knew" (Book of Thel 5.9–11). After all, Blake says elsewhere, God "is become a worm that he may nourish the weak" (Annotations to Lavater), and man may become either one, depending on his mental power: "Let the Human Organs be kept in their perfect Integrity | At will Contracting into Worms, or Expanding into Gods" (Jerusalem 55.36–37). In much the same spirit Shelley writes, "I know | That Love makes all things equal: I have heard | By mine own heart this joyous truth averred: | The spirit of the worm beneath the sod | In love and worship, blends itself with God" (Epipsychidion 125–29). Wondering if God has anything at all to do with the world, Tennyson tries to believe that "somehow good | Will be the final goal of ill" and "That not a worm is cloven in vain" (In Memoriam 54.1–2, 9).

Humble though it may be, the worm may resent an injury and strike back: as the proverb puts it, "the worm will turn." Greene, in A Groatsworth of Wit, has "Tread on a worm and it will turne" (sec 12); Shakespeare: "The smallest worm will turn, being trodden upon" (3H6 2.2.17). The madman in Shelley's Julian and Maddalo claims, "Even the instinctive worm on which we tread | Turns, though it wound not" (412–13).

If mortals are like worms in their mortality, worms are symbols of mortality itself. Homer's only mention of an earthworm (Greek skolex) comes in a simile for a fallen warrior extended on the ground (Iliad 13.654). Mainly, however, worms devour the dead. Shakespeare's Rosalind recites the commonplace, "Men have died from time to time, and worms have eaten them," though she adds, "but not for love" (AYLI 4.1.106–08). We go to a "wormy grave" (Shelley, Laon and Cythna 3751) where we meet the "coffin-worm" (Keats, Eve of St. Agnes 374). Blake makes the most of this inevitable fate. Thel complains that she will only have lived "to be at death the food of worms," but one of her comforters replies, "Then if thou art the food of worms... | How great thy use. how great thy blessing; every thing that lives | Lives not alone, nor for itself" (3.23–27). A more frequent way to cope is through gallows humor. So Hamlet tells the king that Polonius is at supper, "Not where he eats, but where a is eaten. A certain convocation of politic worms are e'en at

him. Your worm is your only emperor for diet: we fat all creatures else to fat
us, and we fat ourselves for maggots" (4.3.19–23). This is in a way Blake's point,
though it stresses that the worm occupies the top link of the food chain. So in
the graveyard Hamlet says that a dead courtier is "now my Lady Worm's"
(5.1.87). Byron's Sardanapalus dismisses the notion that some men are gods:
"the worms are gods; / At least they banqueted upon your gods, / And died for
lack of further nutriment" (1.2.269–71). As death is the great leveller (*see*
Death), worms are revolutionaries; Byron says every monarch is called Your
Highness "till they are consign'd / To those sad hungry Jacobins the worms, /
Who on the very loftiest kings have dined" (*Don Juan* 6.99–101). Stevens
imagines "The Worms at Heaven's Gate," who sing "Out of the tomb, we bring
Badroulbadour, / Within our bellies," piece by piece.

Sometimes "worm" is used for "caterpillar." Jonson can exploit two senses
of "worm" in his "Epigram 15: On Court-Worm": "All men are worms: but this
no man. In silk / 'Twas brought to court first wrapped, and white as milk; /
Where, afterwards, it grew a butterfly; / Which was a caterpillar. So 'twill die."
(*See* **Butterfly, Caterpillar**.)

"Worm" can also mean "canker-worm," the worm that kills the rose (Milton,
Lycidas 45). Blake's "Sick Rose" is destroyed by "The invisible worm, / That flies
in the night / In the howling storm."

In *Beowulf* a "worm" (Old English *wyrm*) is a dragon (886, 891, etc.): "Then
the worm woke; cause of strife was renewed: for then he moved over the
stones, hard-hearted beheld his foe's footprints – with secret stealth he had
stepped forth too near the dragon's head" (2287–90, trans. Donaldson). In
biblical translations it was used for the serpent, or Satan, and it survived into
modern poetry. Adam laments, "O Eve, in evil hour thou didst give ear / To
that false worm" (Milton, *PL* 9.1067–68). Pope refers to "That ancient Worm,
the Devil" ("To Moore" 12). Something of this sense lingers in Blake's "invisible
worm" that destroys the virgin rose.

The book of Isaiah ends with God's foretelling the grim end of "the men
that have transgressed against me: for their worm shall not die, neither shall
their fire be quenched" (66.24). Christ echoes the phrase three times in his
description of hell (Mark 9.44–48). Milton's Messiah promises to drive the rebel
angels down "To chains of darkness, and the undying worm" (6.739).

Another important worm is the worm of conscience. No one knows,
Chaucer writes, how "The worm of conscience may agryse [shudder] / Of
wikked lyf" (*Physician's Tale* 280–81). Shakespeare's Queen Margaret cries at
Richard, "The worm of conscience still begnaw thy soul!" (*R3* 1.3.221). More
cheerfully, Benedick announces "it is most expedient for the wise, if Don
Worm (his conscience) find no impediment to the contrary, to be the
trumpet of his own virtues" (*MAAN* 5.2.83–86). Some writers combine this
worm with the undying worm of the Bible; so Byron: "The worm that will not
sleep – and never dies" torments one's mind with remorse (*Abydos* 2.646).
Indeed our word "remorse" comes from Latin *remordere*, from *mordere*, "bite";
we say our conscience gnaws or eats away at our life or peace of mind. It is a
frequent image in Baudelaire: "How can we kill the old, the long Remorse, /
Who lives, wriggles, and twists itself / And feeds off us as the worm off the
dead" ("L'Irréparable"); see "Remords posthume" and "Spleen (II)." (*See*
Serpent.)

Akin to a worm in the mind is a maggot in the brain, but its meaning is closer to a bee in the bonnet. In seventeenth- to eighteenth-century British usage such a maggot usually meant a mad or perverse desire or "craze." "Are you not mad, my friend?...Have you not maggots in your braines?" (Fletcher, *Women Pleased* 3.4). The latest fashion might be called a maggot. Pope, with an implicit pun on the "grub" of Grub Street, where hack writers lived, notes how "Maggots half-form'd in rhyme exactly meet, / And learned to crawl upon poetic feet" (*Dunciad* 1.61–62). Samuel Wesley chose a self-disparaging title for a volume of his verse: *Maggots; or Poems on Several Subjects*.

Wormwood   Wormwood, or absinthe, is a plant of the *Artemisia* family, known for its bitter taste, especially *Artemisia Absinthium*.

In the Old Testament, wormwood (Hebrew *laana*) is only used metaphorically as a source of bitterness, often paired with the term (*rosh*) that the Authorized Version renders "gall" (Deut. 29.18). God will feed those who follow the false Baalim "with wormwood, and give them water of gall to drink" (Jer. 9.15; cf. 23.15, Deut. 29.18). In the New Testament it appears once, as the name of the star (Greek *apsinthos*) that falls when the third angel blows his trumpet; it turns a third of the water to wormwood and many men die of poisoning (Rev. 8.11).

A soul in Dante's *Purgatorio* says he has been guided "to drink the sweet wormwood [*assenzo*] of the torments" (23.86). After a particularly apt line in the play he demanded, Hamlet comments, "That's wormwood" (3.2.176). Jonson fears that a book called *Epigrams* will be taken to be "bold, licentious, full of gall, / Wormwood, and sulphur, sharp, and toothed withal" (2.3–4). Byron's Childe Harold quaffed life's enchanted cup too quickly, "and he found / The dregs were wormwood" (*Childe Harold* 3.73–74). Hugo enjoins his daughter to pray for her mother, who "always drank the wormwood [*l'absinthe*] and left you the honey" ("La prière pour tous," part 2).

Hugo is not referring here to the alcoholic drink called absinthe, which indeed became popular in his day. The word "vermouth" is also derived from the source of "wormwood."

Y

Yellow   Various terms for yellowish hues in Greek and Latin literature are applied to hair, grain, sand, dawn, the sun, and gold. In modern literature it is frequently the distinctive color of autumn or the harvest. Spenser's personification of Autumn is "all in yellow clad" (*FQ* 7.7.30). Shakespeare has "yellow autumn" (*Sonnets* 104), Thomson "Autumn's yellow lustre" ("Autumn" 1322); the grove is yellow in Pope's "Autumn" (75). Related to this use is "the yellow leaf" of age that Macbeth has fallen into (5.3.23); time will also affect "my papers, yellowed with their age" (*Sonnets* 17).

Yellow may be a sign of disease as well as age, particularly jaundice (from French *jaune*, "yellow"), a disease affecting the yellow bile. Metaphorically when one is jaundiced one is jealous, envious, or bilious (irascible) (*see*

Humor); speaking of fault-finding critics, Pope declares, "all looks yellow to the Jaundic'd Eye" (*Essay on Criticism* 559). At the climax of the *Romance of the Rose* Jean plucks the rose despite "Jealousy with all its garland of marigolds" (21741–42); Chaucer imitates this with "Jalousye, / That wered of yelewe goldes a garland" (*Knight's Tale* 1928–29). In his comic version of *Oedipus*, Shelley has the usually saffron-robed Hymen "clothed in yellow jealousy" (1.283). Browning speaks of "making Envy yellow" ("At the 'Mermaid'" 143).

In some countries during the Middle Ages traitors and heretics were made to wear yellow; Jews wore a yellow star, a practice reimposed by the Nazi regime. Paintings of Judas often had him in yellow clothing.

See **Gold, Marigold**.

Yew   A "Cheerless, unsocial plant" (Blair, *The Grave* 22), the "dismal yew" (Shakespeare, *Titus* 2.3.107) is frequently found, like the cypress, in graveyards. Gray puts one in his famous churchyard (*Elegy* 13); Verlaine sees "The little yews of the cemetary / Tremble in the winter wind" ("Sub Urbe"); while Eliot's meditation on the grave in Part IV of "Burnt Norton" wonders if "Chill / Fingers of yew be curled / Down on us?"

It is presumably because yew berries and leaves are poisonous that the tree acquired its deathly associations, and perhaps also because of its dark foliage. It is not mentioned in the Bible, and it is not prominent in Greek literature; words for it (*milax, smilax, milos,* etc.) often refer to other plants as well, such as bryony. It was Latin writers who gave the yew (*taxus*) its distinctive meanings and locations. A path sloping down to the underworld, according to Ovid, is shaded by deadly yew trees (*Metamorphoses* 4.432); Seneca puts one by Cocytus (*Hercules* 694); Lucan's Erichtho in the underworld passes through a wood shaded by "yews impervious to Phoebus" (6.654). Virgil calls the yew "harmful" (*taxique nocentes, Georgics* 2.257), Seneca "death-dealing" (*mortifera . . . taxus, Oedipus* 555).

Another reason for its deadliness is its sturdy and flexible branches: as Virgil notes, they make good bows (*Georgics* 2.448). In Chaucer's catalog of trees his epithet for the yew is "shetere" (shooter) (*PF* 180), while in Spenser's similar catalog he lists "The Eugh, obedient to the benders will" (*FQ* 1.1.9). Hence the conceit in the report to King Richard that "Thy very beadsmen learn to bend their bows / Of double-fatal yew against thy state" (*R2* 3.2.116–17).

Yoke   A yoke is a burden or a bond or both. The burdensome aspect of being under a yoke is the more frequently found, especially in the Old Testament, where "yoke" (Hebrew *'ol*) usually refers to social or political subservience, though it might sometimes refer to any law or government. Isaac tells Esau, "thou . . . shalt serve thy brother [Jacob]; and it shall come to pass when thou shalt have the dominion, that thou shalt break his yoke from off thy neck" (Gen. 27.40). "Because thou servedst not the Lord thy God," Moses warns his people, "Therefore shalt thou serve thine enemies," and the Lord "shall put a yoke of iron upon thy neck, until he have destroyed thee" (Deut. 28.47–48). The Lord tells Ezekiel, I shall break there the yokes of Egypt" (Ezek. 30.18). The phrase "to break the yoke" occurs over a dozen times.

In the New Testament, Jesus says that to follow him is to assume a new and lighter yoke. "Take my yoke upon you, and learn of me: for I am meek and lowly of heart: and ye shall find rest unto your souls. / For my yoke is easy, and my burden is light" (Matt. 11.29–30).

A "yoke" of oxen or other beasts meant a pair, as in 1 Samuel 11.7 and Luke 14.19; Job had "five hundred yoke of oxen" (1.3). Hence it meant (once in the New Testament) a bond between two people or groups. Paul addresses his friend or friends as "true yokefellow" (*suzuge*) among his "fellowlabourers" at Philippi (Phil. 4.3). The original Greek of Jesus' famous saying "What therefore God hath joined together, let not man put asunder" (Matt. 19.6) uses *sunezeuxen*, "yoked together"; in fact English "join" derives through French from Latin *iungere*, "to yoke."

Classical Greek often uses "yoke" (*zeugos*) as a pair of anything. So Aeschylus has the "yoke of the Atridae" in *Agamemnon* 44, the pair of brothers Agamemnon and Menelaus. "To pull the same yoke" is the Greek equivalent of "to be in the same boat." Odysseus, says Agamemnon, was my "zealous yoke-fellow" at Troy (842).

To be "yoked in marriage" is commonplace, particularly in Sophocles and Euripides, e.g., *Oedipus Tyrannus* 826, *Bacchae* 468. It is common in Latin, too, as we read in Virgil's *Aeneid* 4.28, where Dido still feels "joined" (*iunxit*) to her dead husband. Horace reminds an impatient husband of a young girl that she is not yet ready to submit to the yoke (*Odes* 2.5.1); here, surely, the sense of "burden" is also present, the duties of marriage. But "yoke" could mean simply "mate" or "unite in sex," as in Lucretius 5.962 and Ovid, *Met.* 14.762.

Sappho uses "yokemate" (*syndugos*) to mean "spouse" (frag. 213). Euripides often uses "unyoked" (*azux*) to mean "unmarried" or "virgin," as in *Bacchae* 694, "maidens still unyoked." The chorus of the *Hippolytus* speaks of the "foal [daughter] of Oechalia formerly unyoked (*azuga*) to a marriage bed" now "yoked" (*zeuxas'*) to Heracles by Aphrodite (545–48). Venus likes to place incompatible bodies and minds, Horace writes, under her "yoke of bronze" (1.33.10–11). In Latin, *coniunx* is common for "spouse" (or "concubine"). Catullus' wedding hymn, for example, concludes by blessing the "good wedded couple" (*boni coniuges*) (61.225–26). The verb *coniugo* meant "unite in marriage"; from the adjective *coniugalis* comes English "conjugal," meaning "marital." Among the epithets of Juno, goddess of marriage, are *Iuga* and *Iugalis*.

The Greeks were fond of the "yoke of necessity" image. Prometheus feels such a yoke on the rock in Aeschylus, *Prometheus* 108, where it is almost literal; Hermes later calls him a colt newly yoked (1009); Io asks Zeus why she too is yoked in her sufferings (578). Sometimes "yoke" might be translated "harness," as in the passage about the colt; in the *Choephorae* the colt (Orestes) is yoked or harnessed to a chariot of distress (if the text is correct at 795). Sometimes "harness" or "strap" serves the same meaning, as when Agamemnon "donned the harness of necessity" (Aeschylus, *Agamemnon* 218). In that play Cassandra has taken on the "yoke of slavery" (953) and then is told again by the chorus to yield to necessity and "take on this new yoke" (1071). Men are "yoked to fate" in Pindar, *Nem.* 7.6.

The "yoke of slavery" is found in Sophocles, *Ajax* 944, and several other places in Greek and Latin. The herald in the *Agamemnon* reports that his king has "cast a yoke on the neck of Troy" (529). "To send under the yoke" (*sub iugum mittere*) was a standard phrase in Latin for formally defeating an enemy, and indeed there was a ceremony, described in Livy 9.6.1ff., in which an army was made to pass under a yoke, which may have been an arrangement of three spears. Latin *subiungo* (or *subiugo*) is the origin of English "subjugate"; see Virgil, *Aeneid* 8.502.

In deploying the "yoke of marriage" image Chaucer explicitly wards off the suggestion of subservience, where he has one of the subjects of a lord advise him: "Boweth your nekke under that blisful yok / Of soveraynetee, noght of servyse, / Which that men clepe spousaille or wedlok" (*Clerk's Tale* 113–15). Spenser, on the other hand, gives a brief catalog of "Proud wemen, vaine, forgetfull of their yoke" (*FQ* 1.5.50); he also has "*Cupids* yoke" (*Colin Clout* 566). When Shakespeare's Hermia refuses to wed the man her father chooses, she says she would rather live as a nun than "yield my virgin patent up / Unto his lordship whose unwished yoke / My soul consents not to give sovereignty" (*MND* 1.1.80–82). Though it is not yet a question of marriage, Racine's Aricie says her pride "has never bent under the amorous yoke" until now (*Phèdre* 2.1.444).

The yoke of political subjugation is often used by Shakespeare in his historical plays. Northumberland is ready to "shake off our slavish yoke" under Richard II (*R2* 2.1.291), Richmond rallies his friends "Bruised underneath the yoke of tyranny" of Richard III (*R3* 5.2.2), and Malcolm tells Macduff, "I think our country sinks beneath the yoke" of Macbeth (*Macbeth* 4.3.39).

To Milton's Satan God's government is a yoke to be cast off (*PL* 4.975, 5.786); and Mammon unwittingly evokes the yoke of Christ when he declares he prefers "Hard liberty before the easy yoke / Of servile pomp" (2.256–57). But after the fall Adam acknowledges the sin of rebellion "against God and his just yoke / Laid on our necks" (10.1045–46).

Part of the ideology of English political reformers in the seventeenth century and afterward was the notion of the "Norman Yoke" forced upon England by William the Conqueror in 1066. Similar phrases turn up in the literature of many countries with a history of foreign subjugation. As the Swiss contemplate revolting against Austrian rule, one of them, according to Schiller, draws a parallel: "The docile and domesticated ox, / That friend of man, who bends his burdened neck / So patiently beneath the yoke, will leap / When he is angered, whet his mighty horns, / And throw his enemy up toward the clouds" (*Wilhelm Tell* 1.651–55, trans. Jordan).

Z

Zephyr   *see* **West wind**

Zodiac   *see* **Star, Sun**

Authors cited

Name	Dates	Language or nation
Achilles Tatius	fl. AD *c.* 150	Greek
Aelian (Claudius Aelianus)	AD *c.* 170–235	Greek
Aeschylus	525–456 BC	Greek
Aesop	6C BC	Greek
Akenside, Mark	1721–70	English
Alanus de Insulis (Alain de Lille)	*c.* 1128–1202	Latin
Alcaeus	7C BC	Greek
Alcman	7C BC	Greek
Alcott, Bronson	1799–1888	American
Alfieri, Vittorio	1749–1803	Italian
Ambrose	d. AD 397	Latin
Amos	8C BC	Hebrew
Anacreon	6C BC	Greek
Antipater of Sidon	1C BC	Greek
ap Gwilym, Dafydd	14C AD	Welsh
Apollonius of Rhodes	*c.* 295–215 BC	Greek
Apuleius, Lucius(?)	AD *c.* 125–160+	Latin
Archilochus	7C BC	Greek
Argentarius, Marcus	1C AD?	Greek
Arion	p7C BC	Greek
Ariosto, Ludovico	1474–1533	Italian
Aristophanes	*c.* 445–*c.* 385 BC	Greek
Aristotle	384–322 BC	Greek
Arnim, Achim von	1781–1831	German
Arnold, Matthew	1822–88	English
Athanasius	AD 293?–373	Greek
Athenaeus	fl. AD *c.* 200	Greek
Atta, Titus Quintus	d. 77 BC	Latin
Augustine (Aurelius Augustinus)	354–430	Latin
Ausonius (Decimus Magnus Ausonius)	*c.* 310–*c.* 393	Latin
Austen, Jane	1775–1817	English
Bacchylides	5C BC	Greek
Bacon, Francis	1561–1626	English
Baïf, Jean Antoine de	1532–89	French
Baratynsky, Evgeny	1800–44	Russian

Barbauld, Anna Laetitia	1743–1825	English
Barlow, Joel	1754–1812	American
Bates, Katharine Lee	1859–1929	American
Baudelaire, Charles	1821–67	French
Beattie, James	1735–1803	English
Beddoes, Thomas Lovell	1803–49	English
Berkeley, George	1685–1753	English (Irish)
Bernard Silvestris	fl. *c.* 1150	Latin
Bion (of Smyrna)	2C BC	Greek
Blair, Robert	1699–1746	English (Scottish)
Blake, William	1757–1827	English
Blok, Alexander	1880–1921	Russian
Boccaccio, Giovanni	1313–75	Italian
Boethius, Anicius Manlius Severinus	AD *c.* 476–*c.* 524	Latin
Borges, Jorge Luis	1899–1986	Spanish (Argentine)
Boswell, James	1740–95	English (Scottish)
Bowles, William Lisle	1762–1850	English
Bradstreet, Anne	*c.* 1610–72	English/American
Brentano, Clemens	1778–1842	German
Bridges, Robert	1844–1930	English
Brontë, Charlotte	1816–55	English
Brontë, Emily	1818–48	English
Brooks, Gwendolyn	1917–	American
Browne, Thomas	1605–82	English
Browning, Elizabeth Barrett	1806–61	English
Browning, Robert	1812–89	English
Brun, Friederike	1765–1835	German
Bryant, William Cullen	1794–1878	American
Bunyan, John	1628–88	English
Burnett, Frances Hodgson	1849–1924	English/American
Burns, Robert	1759–96	English (Scottish)
Burton, Robert	1577–1640	English
Byron, George Gordon, Lord	1788–1824	English
Calderón de la Barca, Pedro	1600–1681	Spanish
Callimachus	*c.* 310–*c.* 240 BC	Greek
Camoens, Luis Vaz de	*c.* 1524–80	Portuguese
Campbell, Thomas	1777–1844	English
Carew, Thomas	1595–1640	English
Carroll, Lewis (Charles Dodgson)	1832–98	English
Castro, Rosalia de	1837–85	Spanish/Galician
Catullus, Gaius Valerius	*c.* 84–*c.* 54 BC	Latin

Cazotte, Jacques	1719–92	French
Celan, Paul	1920–70	German (Romanian)
Cervantes Saavedra, Miguel de	1547–1616	Spanish
Césaire, Aimé	1913–	French (Martinican)
Chapman, George	1559?–1634	English
Chateaubriand, François-René de	1768–1848	French
Chaucer, Geoffrey	c. 1343–1400	English
Chekhov, Anton Pavlovich	1860–1904	Russian
Chénier, André	1762–1794	French
Choerilus	6C BC	Greek
Cicero (Marcus Tullius Cicero)	106–43 BC	Latin
Clanvowe, Thomas	fl. 1390	English
Clare, John	1793–1864	English
Claudian (Claudius Claudianus) late	4C AD	Latin
Clement of Alexandria	AD c. 200	Greek
Coleridge, Samuel Taylor	1772–1834	English
Collins, William	1721–59	English
Conrad, Joseph	1857–1924	English (b. Polish)
Corneille, Pierre	1606–84	French
Coronado, Carolina	1823–1911	Spanish
Cowley, Abraham	1618–67	English
Cowper, William	1731–1800	English
Crabbe, George	1754–1832	English
Daniel	2C BC	Hebrew
Dante Alighieri	1265–1321	Italian
Darío, Rubén	1867–1916	Spanish (Nicaraguan)
Darwin, Erasmus	1731–1802	English
Davies, John	1569–1626	English
Denham, John	1615–69	English
Deschamps, Eustache	c. 1345–1406	French
Desportes, Philippe	1546–1606	French
Dickens, Charles	1812–70	English
Dickinson, Emily	1830–86	American
Diderot, Denis	1713–84	French
Donne, John	1572–1631	English
Dostoyevsky, Fyodor	1821–81	Russian
Drayton, Michael	1563–1631	English
Dryden, John	1631–1700	English
Du Bellay, Joachim	1522–60	French
Dunbar, Paul Laurence	1872–1906	American
Dwight, Timothy	1752–1817	American

Eco, Umberto	1932–	Italian
Eichendorff, Joseph von	1788–1857	German
Eliot, T. S.	1888–1965	American
Emerson, Ralph Waldo	1803–82	American
Ennius, Quintus	239–169 BC	Latin
Erasmus, Desiderius	c. 1469–1536	Dutch
Euripides	c. 485–406 BC	Greek
Ezekiel	6C BC	Hebrew
Faulkner, William	1897–1961	American
Fielding, Henry	1707–54	English
Finch, Anne (Lady Winchelsea)	d. 1720	English
Fisher, Dorothy Canfield	1879–1958	American
Fitzgerald, Edward	1809–83	English
Flaubert, Gustave	1821–80	French
Fletcher, John	1579–1625	English
Forster, E. M.	1879–1970	English
Foscolo, Ugo	1778–1827	Italian (Greek)
France, Anatole	1844–1924	French
Froissart, Jean	1337–post-1414	French
Frost, Robert	1875–1963	American
Galen (Galenus)	AD 129–99	Greek
Garcia Lorca, Federico	1898–1936	Spanish
Garcia Marquez, Gabriel	1928–	Spanish (Colombian)
Garcilaso de la Vega	1503–36	Spanish
Garnier, Robert	c. 1544–90	French
Gascoigne, George	1539?–77	English
Gay, John	1685–1732	English
Gellius, Aulus	AD c. 130–c. 180	Latin
Gibbon, Edward	1737–94	English
Goethe, Johann Wolfgang von	1749–1832	German
Golding, William	1911–93	English
Góngora, Luis de	1561–1625	Spanish
Gosse, Edmund	1849–1928	English
Gottfried von Strassburg	13C	Old High German
Gower, John	1330?–1408	English
Gray, Thomas	1716–71	English
Green, Matthew	1696–1737	English
Greene, Robert	1558–92	English
Grimm, Jakob	1785–1863	German
Grimm, Wilhelm	1786–1859	German
Guthlac	c. 700	Old English
Hardy, Thomas	1840–1928	English
Hawthorne, Nathaniel	1804–64	American

Hazlitt, William	1778–1830	English
Heine, Heinrich	1797–1856	German
Hellman, Lillian	1906–84	American
Hemingway, Ernest	1899–1961	American
Henley, William Ernest	1849–1903	English
Heraclitus of Ephesus	c. 540–c. 480 BC	Greek
Heraclitus of Halicarnassus	3C BC	Greek
Herbert, George	1593–1633	English
Herder, Johann Gottfried von	1744–1803	German
Herodotus	c. 490–c. 425 BC	Greek
Herrera, Fernando de	1534–97	Spanish
Herrick, Robert	1591–1674	English
Hesiod	c. 700 BC	Greek
Hippocrates	c. 460–c. 370 BC	Greek
Hoffmann, E. T. A.	1776–1822	German
Hölderlin, Friedrich	1770–1843	German
Homer	8C BC	Greek
Hood, Thomas	1799–1845	English
Horace (Quintus Horatius Flaccus)	65–68 BC	Latin
Hosea	8C BC	Hebrew
Howe, Julia Ward	1819–1910	American
Hunt, Leigh	1784–1859	English
Ibsen, Henrik	1828–1906	Norwegian
Ibycus	6C BC	Greek
Irving, Washington	1783–1859	American
Isaiah	8C BC	Hebrew
Isidore of Seville	fl. AD 602–36	Latin
James the Apostle	1C AD	Greek
James, Henry	1843–1916	American
Jammes, Francis	1868–1938	French
Jeffers, Robinson	1887–1962	American
Jeremiah	6C BC	Hebrew
Jewett, Sarah Orne	1849–1909	American
Joel	5C BC?	Hebrew
John the Evangelist	1C AD	Greek
John of Patmos	1C AD	Greek
Jonson, Ben	1572–1637	English
Joyce, James	1882–1941	English (Irish)
Juvenal (Decimus Iunius Iuvenalis)	2C AD	Latin
Kafka, Franz	1883–1924	German (Czech)
Keats, John	1795–1821	English
Kerouac, Jack	1922–69	Canadian/American

Khayam, Omar	1050?–1123?	Persian
King, Henry	1592–1669	English
King, Martin Luther, Jr.	1929–68	American
Kipling, Rudyard	1865–1936	English
La Cruz, Sor Juana Inés de	1651–95	Spanish
Lactantius	AD *c.* 240–*c.* 320	Latin
Lamartine, Alphonse de	1790–1869	French
Landon, Letitia Elizabeth	1802–38	English
Landor, Walter Savage	1775–1864	English
Langland, William	*c.* 1332–?	English
Lawrence, D. H. (David Herbert)	1885–1930	English
Lebrun-Pindare, Ponce D. E.	1729–1807	French
Leopardi, Giacomo	1798–1837	Italian
Lessing, Gotthold Ephraim	1729–81	German
London, Jack	1876–1916	American
Longfellow, Henry Wadsworth	1807–82	American
Lorca, Federico García	1898–1936	Spanish
Lorris, Guillaume de	?–*c.* 1235	French
Lovelace, Richard	1618–57	English
Lowry, Malcolm	1909–57	English
Lucan (Marcus Annaeus Lucanus)	AD 39–65	Latin
Lucian	AD 115–*c.* 180	Greek
Lucretius (Titus Lucretius Carus)	98–*c.* 55 BC	Latin
Luke the Evangelist	1C AD	Greek
Lyly, John	1554–1606	English
Machaut, Guillaume de	*c.* 1300–77	French
Machiavelli, Niccolo	1469–1527	Italian
Malachi	5C BC	Hebrew
Mallarmé, Stéphane	1842–98	French
Mandelstam, Osip	1891–1938	Russian
Mangan, James Clarence	1803–49	English (Irish)
Mann, Thomas	1875–1955	German
Marino, Giovan Battista	1569–1625	Italian
Mark the Evangelist	1C AD	Greek
Marlowe, Christopher	1564–93	English
Martial (Marcus Valerius Martialis)	AD 40–103	Latin
Marvell, Andrew	1621–78	English
Masefield, John	1878–1967	English

Matthew the Evangelist	1C AD	Greek
McCrae, John	1872–1918	Canadian
Meleager	c. 140–70 BC	Greek
Melville, Herman	1819–91	American
Meredith, George	1828–1909	English
Meun, Jean de	?–c. 1305	French
Micah	6C BC?	Hebrew
Middleton, Thomas	1580–1627	English
Milton, John	1608–74	English
Mimnermus	7C BC	Greek
Mitchell, Margaret	1900–49	American
Montagu, Mary Wortley	1689–1762	English
Montale, Eugenio	1896–1981	Italian
Moore, Thomas	1779–1852	English
Mörike, Eduard	1804–75	German
Morrison, Toni	1931–	American
Morton, Thomas	1575–1646	American
Moschus	c. 150 BC	Greek
Müller, Wilhelm	1794–1827	German
Musset, Alfred de	1810–57	French
Nabokov, Vladimir	1899–1977	Russian/American
Nashe, Thomas	1567–1601	English
Nietzsche, Friedrich	1844–1900	German
Nonnus	5C AD	Greek
Novalis (Friedrich von Hardenberg)	1772–1801	German
O'Casey, Sean	1880–1964	English (Irish)
Opie, Amelia	1769–1853	English
Orwell, George (Eric Blair)	1903–50	English
Ovid (Publius Ovidius Naso)	43 BC – AD 17	Latin
Paine, Thomas	1737–1809	English/American
Parmenides	c. 515–c. 450 BC	Greek
Pascoli, Giovanni	1855–1912	Italian
Paul the Apostle	d. AD 64	Greek
Peacock, Thomas Love	1785–1666	English
Persius (Aulus Persius Flaccus)	AD 34–62	Latin
Peter the Apostle	1C AD	Greek
Petrarch (Petrarca), Francesco	1304–74	Italian
Philostratus	fl. AD c. 200	Greek
Phrynichus	fl. c. 510–475 BC	Greek
Pindar	518–438 BC	Greek

Platen-Hallermünde, August, Graf von	1796–1835	German
Plato	427–347 BC	Greek
Plautus (Titus Maccius Plautus)	c. 250–184 BC	Latin
Pliny the Elder (G. Plinius Secundus)	AD 23/4–79	Latin
Plutarch	AD 46–c. 120	Greek
Poe, Edgar Allan	1809–49	American
Polidori, John William	1795–1821	English
Pope, Alexander	1688–1744	English
Pound, Ezra	1885–1972	American
Propertius, Sextus	c. 48–c. 16 BC	Latin
Pushkin, Alexander Sergeyevich	1799–1837	Russian
Quevedo y Villegas, Francisco de	1580–1645	Spanish
Quintilian (Marcus Fabius Quintilianus)	AD c. 35–c. 95	Latin
Quintus Smyrnaeus	4C AD	Greek
Rabelais, François	1494?–1553	French
Racine, Jean	1639–99	French
Radcliffe, Ann	1764–1823	English
Ralegh, Sir Walter	1552–1618	English
Randolph, Thomas	1605–35	English
Richard of St. Victor	d. 1173	Latin (b. Scotland)
Richardson, Samuel	1689–1761	English
Rilke, Rainer Maria	1875–1926	German
Rimbaud, Arthur	1854–91	French
Robinson, Mary	1758–1800	English
Ronsard, Pierre de	1524–85	French
Rosenberg, Isaac	1890–1917	English
Rossetti, Christina	1830–94	English
Rossetti, Dante Gabriel	1828–82	English
Saint-Amant, Antoine-Girard de	1594–1661	French
Sainte-Beuve, Charles-Augustin	1804–69	French
Saint-Pierre, Bernardin de	1737–1814	French
Sappho	7C BC	Greek
Sartre, Jean-Paul	1905–80	French
Scève, Maurice	1501?–63?	French
Schelling, Friedrich W. J. von	1775–1854	German

Schiller, J. C. Friedrich von	1759–1805	German
Schlegel, Friedrich	1772–1829	German
Scott, Walter	1771–1832	English (Scottish)
Seneca, Lucius Annaeus (the Younger)	c. 4 BC–AD 65	Latin
Sepheris, George	1900–71	Greek
Servius (Marius Servius Honoratus)	5C AD	Latin
Sewell, Anna	1820–78	English
Shakespeare, William	1564–1616	English
Shelley, Percy Bysshe	1792–1822	English
Shenstone, William	1714–63	English
Shirley, James	1596–1666	English
Sidney, Phillip	1554–1586	English
Silone, Ignazio	1900–78	Italian
Simonides	556–468 BC	Greek
Skelton, John	c. 1460–1529	English
Socrates	469–399 BC	Greek
Solomon	10C BC	Hebrew
Solon	c. 640–c. 560 BC	Greek
Sophocles	c. 496–406/5 BC	Greek
Southey, Robert	1774–1843	English
Spenser, Edmund	1552–99	English
Sponde, Jean de	1557–95	French
Staël, Germaine de	1766–1817	French (Swiss)
Statius (Publius Papinius Statius)	AD 45–c. 96	Latin
Steinbeck, John	1902–68	American
Stendhal (Marie Henri Beyle)	1783–1842	French
Stevens, Wallace	1879–1955	American
Stevenson, Robert Louis	1850–94	English (Scottish)
Stoker, Bram	1847–1912	English
Strindberg, August	1849–1912	Swedish
Sturluson, Snorri	c. 1220	Icelandic
Sue, Eugène	1804–57	French
Suetonius (Gaius Suetonius Tranquillus)	AD c. 70–?	Latin
Swift, Jonathan	1667–1745	English (Irish)
Swinburne, Algernon Charles	1837–1909	English
Tacitus, Publius Cornelius	AD 56/57–c. 117	Latin
Tasso, Torquato	1544–95	Italian
Tennyson, Alfred, Lord	1809–92	English

Terence (Publius Terentius Afer)	193/183–159 BC	Latin
Tertullian	AD c. 160–c. 225	Latin
Theocritus	3C BC	Greek
Theognis	6C BC	Greek
Thomas, Dylan	1914–53	English (Welsh)
Thompson, Francis	1859–1907	English
Thomson, James	1700–48	English (Scottish)
Tieck, Ludwig	1773–1853	German
Tolkien, J. R. R.	1892–1973	English
Tolstoy, Leo	1828–1910	Russian
Turgenev, Ivan S.	1818–83	Russian
Twain, Mark (Samuel Clemens)	1835–1910	American
Tyrtaeus	7C BC	Greek
Tyutchev, Fyodor I.	1803–73	Russian
Valerius Flaccus, Gaius	AD c. 40–c. 90	Latin
Valéry, Paul	1871–1945	French
Varro, Marcus Terentius	116–27 BC	Latin
Vaughan, Henry	1621–95	English
Vega Carpio, Lope de	1562–1613	Spanish
Verlaine, Paul	1844–96	French
Verne, Jules	1828–1905	French
Vigny, Alfred de	1797–1863	French
Villiers de l'Isle-Adam, Philippe	1838–89	French
Villon, François	1431–?	French
Virgil (Publius Virgilius Maro)	70–19 BC	Latin
Wagner, Richard	1813–83	German
Walker, Alice	1944–	American
Waller, Edmund	1606–87	English
Walther von der Vogelweide	c. 1170–1230	Old High German
Wesley, Samuel	1662–1735	English
West, Nathanael	1903–40	American
Wheatley, Phillis	c. 1753–84	American
Whitman, Walt	1819–92	American
Wilde, Oscar	1854–1900	English (Irish)
Wilson, Harriet E.	1808–c. 1870	American
Wollstonecraft, Mary	1759–97	English
Wordsworth, William	1770–1850	English
Wroth, Lady Mary	1587?–1651?	English
Xenophon	c. 428–c. 354 BC	Greek
Yeats, William Butler	1865–1939	English (Irish)
Young, Edward	1683–1765	English

Bibliography

General

Biedermann, Hans. *Dictionary of Symbolism: Cultural Icons and the Meanings Behind Them*. Trans. James Hulbert. New York: Facts on File, 1992.

Chevalier, Jean and Alain Gheerbrant. *The Penguin Dictionary of Symbols*. Trans. John Buchanan-Brown. London: Penguin, 1996. (French edn. 1969.)

Curtius, Ernst Robert. *European Literature and the Latin Middle Ages*. Trans. Willard Trask. New York: Pantheon (Bollingen), 1953.

Daemmrich, Horst S. and Ingrid G. Daemmrich. *Themes and Motifs in Western Literature: a Handbook*. Tübingen: Francke Verlag, 1987.

Daemmrich, Horst S. and Ingrid G. Daemmrich. *Themen und Motive in der Literatur: ein Handbuch*. Second, enlarged edition. Tübingen: Francke Verlag, 1995.

Ferguson, George. *Signs and Symbols in Christian Art*. New York: Oxford University Press, 1954.

Frye, Northrop. *Anatomy of Criticism*. Princeton University Press, 1957.

The Great Code: the Bible and Literature. New York: Harcourt Brace, 1981.

Hamilton, A. C., ed. *The Spenser Encyclopedia*. University of Toronto Press, 1990.

Lakoff, George and Mark Turner. *More than Cool Reason: a Field Guide to Poetic Metaphor*. University of Chicago Press, 1989.

Onians, R. B. *The Origins of European Thought*. Cambridge University Press, 1951.

Otto, A. *Die Sprichwörter und sprichwörtlichen Redensarten der Römer*. Leipzig, 1890; rpt. Hildesheim: Olms, 1965.

Pöschl, Viktor, ed. *Bibliographie zur Antiken Bildersprache*. Heidelberg: C. Winter, 1964.

Roberts, Helene E., ed. *Encyclopedia of Comparative Iconography*. Chicago and London: Fitzroy Dearborn, 1998.

Seigneuret, Jean-Charles, ed. *Dictionary of Literary Themes and Motifs*. 2 vols. New York: Greenwood Press, 1988.

Smith, Eric. *Dictionary of Classical Reference in English Poetry*. Cambridge: D. S. Brewer, 1984.

Stevenson, Burton. *The Home Book of Proverbs, Maxims and Familiar Phrases*. New York: Macmillan, 1948.

Whittick, Arnold. *Symbols, Signs, and Their Meanings*. London: Leonard Hill, 1960.

Ziolkowski, Theodore. *Varieties of Literary Thematics*. Princeton University Press, 1983. See the appendix called "A Practical Guide to Literary Thematics."

Animals

Allen, Mary. *Animals in American Literature*. Urbana: University of Illinois Press, 1983.

Edinger, Harry G. "Episodes in the History of the Literary Bear." *Mosaic* 4:1 (1970): 1-12.

Gilman, Sander L. "The Uncontrollable Steed: a Study of the Metamorphosis of a Literary Image." *Euphorion* 66 (1972): 32–54.

Loetscher, Hugo. *Der Predigende Hahn: Das literarisch-moralische Nutztier.* Zurich: Diogenes, 1992.

Perry, Ben Edwin, ed. *Babrius and Phaedrus* (Loeb Classical Library). Cambridge, Mass.: Harvard and London: Heinemann, 1965. See "Appendix: an Analytical Survey of Greek and Latin Fables in the Aesopic Tradition."

Robbins, Mary. "The Truculent Toad in the Middle Ages." In Nona C. Flores, ed. *Animals in the Middle Ages.* New York: Garland, 1996.

Stebbins, Eunice Burr. *The Dolphin in the Literature and Art of Greece and Rome.* Menasha, Wis.: Banta, 1929.

Thomas, Keith. *Man and the Natural World: Changing Attitudes in England 1500–1800.* London: Penguin, 1983.

Birds

Armstrong, Edward A. *The Folklore of Birds.* London: Collins, 1958.

Baird, J. L. and John R. Kane. *Rossignol: an Edition and Translation. With Introductory Essay on the Nightingale Tradition* by J. L. Baird. Kent, Ohio: Kent State University Press, 1978.

Broek, R. van den. *The Myth of the Phoenix, According to Classical and Early Christian Traditions.* Leiden: E. J. Brill, 1972.

Graham, Victor E. "The Pelican as Image and Symbol." *Revue de littérature comparée* 36:2 (1962): 235–43.

Harrison, Thomas P. *They Tell of Birds: Chaucer, Spenser, Milton, Drayton.* 1956; rpt. Westport, Conn.: Greenwood Press, 1969.

Harting, James E. *The Birds of Shakespeare.* 1871; rpt. Chicago: Argonaut, 1965.

Level, Brigitte. *Le Poète et l'oiseau: Vers une ornithomythie poétique.* Paris: Klincksieck, 1975.

Lévi-Strauss, Claude. *The Savage Mind.* Trans. of *La Pensée sauvage.* University of Chicago Press, 1966.

Lutwack, Leonard. *Birds in Literature.* Gainesville: University Press of Florida, 1994.

Martin, Ernest Whitney. *The Birds of the Latin Poets.* Palo Alto, Calif.: Stanford University Press, 1914.

Pfeffer, W. *The Change of Philomel: the Nightingale in Medieval Literature* (American University Studies Series III, Comparative Literature, vol. xiv). New York/Berne/Frankfurt a. M., 1985.

Rowland, Beryl. *Birds with Human Souls: A Guide to Bird Symbolism.* Knoxville: University of Tennessee Press, 1978.

Thompson, D'Arcy W. *A Glossary of Greek Birds.* London: Oxford University Press, 1936.

Young, Arthur M. "Of the Nightingale's Song." *Classical Journal* 46.4 (January 1951): 181–84.

Colors

André, J.*Étude sur les termes de couleur dans la langue latine*. Paris: Klincksieck, 1949.

Irwin. E. *Colour Terms in Greek Poetry*. Toronto: Hakkert, 1974.

Gardens and forests

Giamatti, A. Bartlett. *The Earthly Paradise and the Renaissance Epic*. Princeton University Press, 1966.

Harrison, Robert Pogue. *Forests: the Shadow of Civilization*. University of Chicago Press, 1992.

Stewart, Stanley. *The Enclosed Garden: the Tradition and the Image in Seventeenth-Century Poetry*. Madison: University of Wisconsin Press, 1966.

Hunting

Allen, Michael. "The Chase: Development of a Renaissance Theme." *Comparative Literature* 20.4 (Fall 1968): 301–12.

Thiébaux, Marcelle. *The Stag of Love: the Chase in Medieval Literature*. Ithaca: Cornell University Press, 1974.

Mirror

Abrams, M. H. *The Mirror and the Lamp: Romantic Theory and the Critical Tradition*. New York: Oxford University Press, 1953.

Grabes, Herbert. *The Mutable Glass: Mirror-Imagery in Titles and Texts of the Middle Ages and English Renaissance*. Trans. Gordon Collier. Cambridge University Press, 1982.

La Belle, Jennijoy. *Herself Beheld: The Literature of the Looking Glass*. Ithaca: Cornell University Press, 1988.

Musical instruments

Abrams, M. H. "The Correspondent Breeze: a Romantic Metaphor." *Kenyon Review* 19 (1957): 113–30. Rev. rpt. in M. H. Abrams, ed., *English Romantic Poets*, 2nd edn. London: Oxford University Press, 1974.

Bidney, Martin. "The Aeolian Harp Reconsidered: Music of Unfulfilled Longing in Tjutchev, Mörike, Thoreau, and Others." *Comparative Literature Studies* 22.3 (1985): 329–43.

Grigson, Geoffrey. *The Harp of Aeolus and other Essays*. London: Routledge, 1947.

O'Malley, Glenn. "Shelley's 'Air-Prism': the Synesthetic Scheme of *Alastor*." *Modern Philology* 55 (1958): 178–87.

West, M. L. *Ancient Greek Music*. Oxford: Clarendon Press, 1992.

Numbers

Fowler, Alastair. *Spenser and the Numbers of Time*. New York: Barnes & Noble, 1964.

Hieatt, A. Kent. *Short Time's Endless Monument: The Symbolism of the Numbers in Edmund Spenser's "Epithalamion."* New York: Columbia University Press, 1960.

Schimmel, Annemarie. *The Mystery of Numbers*. Oxford University Press. 1993

Plants

Baker, Carlos. "The Traditional Background of Shelley's Ivy-Symbol." *Modern Language Quarterly* 4.2 (June 1943): 205–08.

Berges, Ruth. "The Linden Tree in German Legend, Poetry, and Song." *Forum* 6:2 (1968): 33–39.

Demetz, Peter. "The Elm and the Vine: Notes Toward the History of a Marriage Topos." *PMLA* 73 (1958): 521–32.

Draper, John W. "Notes on the Symbolic Use of the Willow." Appendix A of *The Funeral Elegy and the Rise of English Romanticism*. New York: NYU Press, 1929.

Forster, Edward S. "Trees and Plants in the Greek Tragic Writers." *Greece and Rome* 21 (January 1952): 57–63.

Fussell, Paul. *The Great War and Modern Memory*. Oxford University Press, 1975. (On the poppy: pp. 246–54.)

Goody, Jack. *The Culture of Flowers*. Cambridge University Press, 1993.

Knight, Philip. *Flower Poetics in Nineteenth-Century France*. Oxford: Clarendon Press, 1986.

McCartney, Eugene Stock. "How the Apple Became the Token of Love." *Transactions and Proceedings of the American Philological Association* 56 (1925): 70–81.

Seward, Barbara. *The Symbolic Rose*. New York: Columbia University Press, 1960.

Trapp, J. B. "The Owl's Ivy and the Poet's Bays: an Inquiry into Poetic Garlands." *Journal of the Warburg and Courtauld Institutes* 21 (1958): 227–55.

Sea, ship

Auden, W. H. *The Enchafèd Flood, or The Romantic Iconography of the Sea*. Charlottesville: University Press of Virginia, 1950.

Seasons and time

Enkvist, Nils Erik. *The Seasons of the Year: Chapters on a Motif from Beowulf to the Shepherd's Calendar*. Denmark: Helsingfors, 1957.

Gironce-Evrard, Marie-Anne. *La symbolique des saisons dans la poésie lyrique en Italie, en Espagne et en France (1465-1645)*. Villeneuve d'Ascq: Presses Universitaires du Septentrion, 2000.

Panofsky, Erwin. *Studies in Iconology*. Oxford University Press, 1939.

Preston, Keith. "Aspects of Autumn in Roman Poetry." *Classical Philology* 13 (1918): 272–82.

Tuve, Rosemond. *Seasons and Months: Studies in a Tradition of Middle English Poetry*. 1933; rpt. Cambridge: D. S. Brewer, 1974.

"Spring in Chaucer and before Him." *MLN* 52 (1937): 9–16.

Wilhelm, James J. *The Cruelest Month: Spring, Nature, and Love in Classical and Medieval Lyrics*. New Haven: Yale University Press, 1965.

Spinning and weaving

Scheid, John and Jesper Svenbro. *The Craft of Zeus: Myths of Weaving and Fabric*. Trans. Carol Volk. Cambridge, Mass.: Harvard University Press, 1996.

Snyder, Jane McIntosh. "The Web of Song." *Classical Journal* 76 (1981): 193–96.

Stars and other heavenly bodies

Eade, J. C. *The Forgotten Sky: A Guide to Astrology in English Literature*. Oxford: Clarendon Press, 1984.

Kay, Richard. *Dante's Christian Astrology*. Philadelphia: University of Pensylvania Press, 1994.

Meadows, A. J. *The High Firmament: A Survey of Astronomy in English Literature*. Leicester: University of Leicester Press, 1969.

Miscellaneous

Barney, Stephen A. "The Plowshare of the Tongue: the Progress of a Symbol from the Bible to *Piers Plowman*." *Mediaeval Studies* 35 (1973): 261–93.

Boedeker, Deborah. *Descent from Heaven: Images of Dew in Greek Poetry and Religion*. Chico, Calif.: Scholars Press, 1984.

Bosquet, Marie-Françoise and Françoise Sylvos, eds. *L'imaginaire du volcan*. Rennes: Presses Universitaires de Rennes, 2005.

Cline, Ruth H. "Heart and Eyes." *Romance Philology* 25.3 (1972): 263–97.

Doob, Penelope Reed. *The Idea of the Labyrinth from Classical Antiquity through the Middle Ages*. Ithaca: Cornell University Press, 1990.

Gellrich, Jesse M. *The Idea of the Book in the Middle Ages*. Ithaca: Cornell University Press, 1985.

Kermode, Frank. *Romantic Image*. London: Routledge & Kegan Paul, 1957. ("dancer" and "tree")

Korfmacher, W. C. "Nightfall in the Greek Lyric Poets." *Classical Journal* 46.4 (January 1951): 177–80.

Lawler, Lilian B. "The Dance in Metaphor." *Classical Journal* 46.8 (May 1951): 383–91.

Nicolson, Marjorie Hope. *Mountain Gloom and Mountain Glory: the Development of the Aesthetics of the Infinite*. Ithaca: Cornell University Press, 1959.

Thacker, Christopher. "'Wish'd, Wint'ry, Horrors': the Storm in the Eighteenth Century." *Comparative Literature* 19.1 (1967): 36–57.

Weidhorn, Manfred. *Dreams in Seventeenth-Century English Literature*. The Hague: Mouton, 1970.